CASENOTE® Legal Briefs

# CONTRACTS

Keyed to Courses Using

### Ayres and Klass's
### Studies in Contract Law
### Ninth Edition

Authored by: Publisher's Editorial Staff

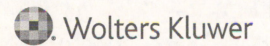
Wolters Kluwer

Copyright © 2017 CCH Incorporated. All Rights Reserved.

Published by Wolters Kluwer in New York.

Wolters Kluwer Legal & Regulatory U.S. serves customers worldwide with
CCH, Aspen Publishers, and Kluwer Law International products.
(www.WKLegaledu.com)

To contact Customer Service, e-mail customer.service@wolterskluwer.com,
call 1-800-234-1660, fax 1-800-901-9075, or mail correspondence to:

Wolters Kluwer
Attn: Order Department
P.O. Box 990
Frederick, MD 21705

Printed in the United States of America.

1 2 3 4 5 6 7 8 9 0

ISBN 978-1-4548-9364-6

## About Wolters Kluwer Legal & Regulatory U.S.

Wolters Kluwer Legal & Regulatory U.S. delivers expert content and solutions in the areas of law, corporate compliance, health compliance, reimbursement, and legal education. Its practical solutions help customers successfully navigate the demands of a changing environment to drive their daily activities, enhance decision quality and inspire confident outcomes.

Serving customers worldwide, its legal and regulatory portfolio includes products under the Aspen Publishers, CCH Incorporated, Kluwer Law International, ftwilliam.com and MediRegs names. They are regarded as exceptional and trusted resources for general legal and practice-specific knowledge, compliance and risk management, dynamic workflow solutions, and expert commentary.

# Format for the Casenote® Legal Brief

**Nature of Case:** This section identifies the form of action (e.g., breach of contract, negligence, battery), the type of proceeding (e.g., demurrer, appeal from trial court's jury instructions), or the relief sought (e.g., damages, injunction, criminal sanctions).

**Fact Summary:** This is included to refresh your memory and can be used as a quick reminder of the facts.

**Rule of Law:** Summarizes the general principle of law that the case illustrates. It may be used for instant recall of the court's holding and for classroom discussion or home review.

**Facts:** This section contains all relevant facts of the case, including the contentions of the parties and the lower court holdings. It is written in a logical order to give the student a clear understanding of the case. The plaintiff and defendant are identified by their proper names throughout and are always labeled with a (P) or (D).

## Palsgraf v. Long Island R.R. Co.

Injured bystander (P) v. Railroad company (D)

N.Y. Ct. App., 248 N.Y. 339, 162 N.E. 99 (1928).

**Party ID:** Quick identification of the relationship between the parties.

**NATURE OF CASE:** Appeal from judgment affirming verdict for plaintiff seeking damages for personal injury.

**FACT SUMMARY:** Helen Palsgraf (P) was injured on R.R.'s (D) train platform when R.R.'s (D) guard helped a passenger aboard a moving train, causing his package to fall on the tracks. The package contained fireworks which exploded, creating a shock that tipped a scale onto Palsgraf (P).

### 🏛 RULE OF LAW
The risk reasonably to be perceived defines the duty to be obeyed.

**FACTS:** Helen Palsgraf (P) purchased a ticket to Rockaway Beach from R.R. (D) and was waiting on the train platform. As she waited, two men ran to catch a train that was pulling out from the platform. The first man jumped aboard, but the second man, who appeared as if he might fall, was helped aboard by the guard on the train who had kept the door open so they could jump aboard. A guard on the platform also helped by pushing him onto the train. The man was carrying a package wrapped in newspaper. In the process, the man dropped his package, which fell on the tracks. The package contained fireworks and exploded. The shock of the explosion was apparently of great enough strength to tip over some scales at the other end of the platform, which fell on Palsgraf (P) and injured her. A jury awarded her damages, and R.R. (D) appealed.

**ISSUE:** Does the risk reasonably to be perceived define the duty to be obeyed?

**HOLDING AND DECISION:** (Cardozo, C.J.) Yes. The risk reasonably to be perceived defines the duty to be obeyed. If there is no foreseeable hazard to the injured party as the result of a seemingly innocent act, the act does not become a tort because it happened to be a wrong as to another. If the wrong was not willful, the plaintiff must show that the act as to her had such great and apparent possibilities of danger as to entitle her to protection. Negligence in the abstract is not enough upon which to base liability. Negligence is a relative concept, evolving out of the common law doctrine of trespass on the case. To establish liability, the defendant must owe a legal duty of reasonable care to the injured party. A cause of action in tort will lie where harm,

though unintended, could have been averted or avoided by observance of such a duty. The scope of the duty is limited by the range of danger that a reasonable person could foresee. In this case, there was nothing to suggest from the appearance of the parcel or otherwise that the parcel contained fireworks. The guard could not reasonably have had any warning of a threat to Palsgraf (P), and R.R. (D) therefore cannot be held liable. Judgment is reversed in favor of R.R. (D).

**DISSENT:** (Andrews, J.) The concept that there is no negligence unless R.R. (D) owes a legal duty to take care as to Palsgraf (P) herself is too narrow. Everyone owes to the world at large the duty of refraining from those acts that may unreasonably threaten the safety of others. If the guard's action was negligent as to those nearby, it was also negligent as to those outside what might be termed the "danger zone." For Palsgraf (P) to recover, R.R.'s (D) negligence must have been the proximate cause of her injury, a question of fact for the jury.

**Concurrence/Dissent:** All concurrences and dissents are briefed whenever they are included by the casebook editor.

### ▶ ANALYSIS
The majority defined the limit of the defendant's liability in terms of the danger that a reasonable person in defendant's situation would have perceived. The dissent argued that the limitation should not be placed on liability, but rather on damages. Judge Andrews suggested that only injuries that would not have happened but for R.R.'s (D) negligence should be compensable. Both the majority and dissent recognized the policy-driven need to limit liability for negligent acts, seeking, in the words of Judge Andrews, to define a framework "that will be practical and in keeping with the general understanding of mankind." The Restatement (Second) of Torts has accepted Judge Cardozo's view.

**Analysis:** This last paragraph gives you a broad understanding of where the case "fits in" with other cases in the section of the book and with the entire course. It is a hornbook-style discussion indicating whether the case is a majority or minority opinion and comparing the principal case with other cases in the casebook. It may also provide analysis from restatements, uniform codes, and law review articles. The analysis will prove to be invaluable to classroom discussion.

### Quicknotes

**FORESEEABILITY** A reasonable expectation that change is the probable result of certain acts or omissions.

**NEGLIGENCE** Conduct falling below the standard of care that a reasonable person would demonstrate under similar conditions.

**PROXIMATE CAUSE** The natural sequence of events without which an injury would not have been sustained.

**Issue:** The issue is a concise question that brings out the essence of the opinion as it relates to the section of the casebook in which the case appears. Both substantive and procedural issues are included if relevant to the decision.

**Holding and Decision:** This section offers a clear and in-depth discussion of the rule of the case and the court's rationale. It is written in easy-to-understand language and answers the issue presented by applying the law to the facts of the case. When relevant, it includes a thorough discussion of the exceptions to the case as listed by the court, any major cites to the other cases on point, and the names of the judges who wrote the decisions.

**Quicknotes:** Conveniently defines legal terms found in the case and summarizes the nature of any statutes, codes, or rules referred to in the text.

Wolters Kluwer Legal & Regulatory U.S. is proud to offer *Casenote® Legal Briefs*—continuing thirty years of publishing America's best-selling legal briefs.

*Casenote® Legal Briefs* are designed to help you save time when briefing assigned cases. Organized under convenient headings, they show you how to abstract the basic facts and holdings from the text of the actual opinions handed down by the courts. Used as part of a rigorous study regimen, they can help you spend more time analyzing and critiquing points of law than on copying bits and pieces of judicial opinions into your notebook or outline.

*Casenote® Legal Briefs* should never be used as a substitute for assigned casebook readings. They work best when read as a follow-up to reviewing the underlying opinions themselves. Students who try to avoid reading and digesting the judicial opinions in their casebooks or online sources will end up shortchanging themselves in the long run. The ability to absorb, critique, and restate the dynamic and complex elements of case law decisions is crucial to your success in law school and beyond. It cannot be developed vicariously.

*Casenote® Legal Briefs* represents but one of the many offerings in Legal Education's Study Aid Timeline, which includes:

- *Casenote® Legal Briefs*
- *Emanuel® Law Outlines*
- Emanuel® *Law in a Flash* Flash Cards
- Emanuel® *CrunchTime®* Series

Each of these series is designed to provide you with easy-to-understand explanations of complex points of law. Each volume offers guidance on the principles of legal analysis and, consulted regularly, will hone your ability to spot relevant issues. We have titles that will help you prepare for class, prepare for your exams, and enhance your general comprehension of the law along the way.

To find out more about our law school tools for success, visit us at *www.WKLegaledu.com* or email us at *legaledu@wolterskluwer.com*. We'll be happy to assist you.

# How to Brief a Case

## A. Decide on a Format and Stick to It

Structure is essential to a good brief. It enables you to arrange systematically the related parts that are scattered throughout most cases, thus making manageable and understandable what might otherwise seem to be an endless and unfathomable sea of information. There are, of course, an unlimited number of formats that can be utilized. However, it is best to find one that suits your needs and stick to it. Consistency breeds both efficiency and the security that when called upon you will know where to look in your brief for the information you are asked to give.

Any format, as long as it presents the essential elements of a case in an organized fashion, can be used. Experience, however, has led *Casenote*® *Legal Briefs* to develop and utilize the following format because of its logical flow and universal applicability.

**NATURE OF CASE:** This is a brief statement of the legal character and procedural status of the case (e.g., "Appeal of a burglary conviction").

There are many different alternatives open to a litigant dissatisfied with a court ruling. The key to determining which one has been used is to discover *who is asking this court for what*.

This first entry in the brief should be kept as *short as possible*. Use the court's terminology if you understand it. But since jurisdictions vary as to the titles of pleadings, the best entry is the one that addresses who wants what in this proceeding, not the one that sounds most like the court's language.

**RULE OF LAW:** A statement of the general principle of law that the case illustrates (e.g., "An acceptance that varies any term of the offer is considered a rejection and counteroffer").

Determining the rule of law of a case is a procedure similar to determining the issue of the case. Avoid being fooled by red herrings; there may be a few rules of law mentioned in the case excerpt, but usually only one is *the* rule with which the casebook editor is concerned. The techniques used to locate the issue, described below, may also be utilized to find the rule of law. Generally, your best guide is simply the chapter heading. It is a clue to the point the casebook editor seeks to make and should be kept in mind when reading every case in the respective section.

**FACTS:** A synopsis of only the essential facts of the case, i.e., those bearing upon or leading up to the issue.

The facts entry should be a short statement of the events and transactions that led one party to initiate legal proceedings against another in the first place. While some cases conveniently state the salient facts at the beginning of the decision, in other instances they will have to be culled from hiding places throughout the text, even from concurring and dissenting opinions. Some of the "facts" will often be in dispute and should be so noted. Conflicting evidence may be briefly pointed up. "Hard" facts must be included. Both must be *relevant* in order to be listed in the facts entry. It is impossible to tell what is relevant until the entire case is read, as the ultimate determination of the rights and liabilities of the parties may turn on something buried deep in the opinion.

Generally, the facts entry should not be longer than three to five *short* sentences.

It is often helpful to identify the role played by a party in a given context. For example, in a construction contract case the identification of a party as the "contractor" or "builder" alleviates the need to tell that that party was the one who was supposed to have built the house.

It is always helpful, and a good general practice, to identify the "plaintiff" and the "defendant." This may seem elementary and uncomplicated, but, especially in view of the creative editing practiced by some casebook editors, it is sometimes a difficult or even impossible task. Bear in mind that the *party presently* seeking something from this court may not be the plaintiff, and that sometimes only the cross-claim of a defendant is treated in the excerpt. Confusing or misaligning the parties can ruin your analysis and understanding of the case.

**ISSUE:** A statement of the general legal question answered by or illustrated in the case. For clarity, the issue is best put in the form of a question capable of a "yes" or "no" answer. In reality, the issue is simply the Rule of Law put in the form of a question (e.g., "May an offer be accepted by performance?").

The major problem presented in discerning what is *the* issue in the case is that an opinion usually purports to raise and answer several questions. However, except for rare cases, only one such question is really the issue in the case. Collateral issues not necessary to the resolution of the matter in controversy are handled by the court by language known as *"obiter dictum"* or merely *"dictum."* While dicta may be included later in the brief, they have no place under the issue heading.

To find the issue, ask *who wants what* and then go on to ask *why did that party succeed or fail in getting it*. Once this is determined, the "why" should be turned into a question.

The complexity of the issues in the cases will vary, but in all cases a single-sentence question should sum up the issue. *In a few cases,* there will be two, or even more rarely, three issues of equal importance to the resolution of the case. Each should be expressed in a single-sentence question.

Since many issues are resolved by a court in coming to a final disposition of a case, the casebook editor will reproduce the portion of the opinion containing the issue or issues most relevant to the area of law under scrutiny. A noted law professor gave this advice: "Close the book; look at the title on the cover." Chances are, if it is Property, you need not concern yourself with whether, for example, the federal government's treatment of the plaintiff's land really raises a federal question sufficient to support jurisdiction on this ground in federal court.

The same rule applies to chapter headings designating sub-areas within the subjects. They tip you off as to what the text is designed to teach. The cases are arranged in a casebook to show a progression or development of the law, so that the preceding cases may also help.

It is also most important to remember to *read the notes and questions* at the end of a case to determine what the editors wanted you to have gleaned from it.

**HOLDING AND DECISION:** This section should succinctly explain the rationale of the court in arriving at its decision. In capsulizing the "reasoning" of the court, it should always include an application of the general rule or rules of law to the specific facts of the case. Hidden justifications come to light in this entry: the reasons for the state of the law, the public policies, the biases and prejudices, those considerations that influence the justices' thinking and, ultimately, the outcome of the case. At the end, there should be a short indication of the disposition or procedural resolution of the case (e.g., "Decision of the trial court for Mr. Smith (P) reversed").

The foregoing format is designed to help you "digest" the reams of case material with which you will be faced in your law school career. Once mastered by practice, it will place at your fingertips the information the authors of your casebooks have sought to impart to you in case-by-case illustration and analysis.

## B. Be as Economical as Possible in Briefing Cases

Once armed with a format that encourages succinctness, it is as important to be economical with regard to the time spent on the actual reading of the case as it is to be economical in the writing of the brief itself. This does not mean "skimming" a case. Rather, it means reading the case with an "eye" trained to recognize into which "section" of your brief a particular passage or line fits and having a system for quickly and precisely marking the case so that the passages fitting any one particular part of the brief can be easily identified and brought together in a concise and accurate manner when the brief is actually written.

It is of no use to simply repeat everything in the opinion of the court; record only enough information to trigger your recollection of what the court said. Nevertheless, an accurate statement of the "law of the case," i.e., the legal principle applied to the facts, is absolutely essential to class preparation and to learning the law under the case method.

To that end, it is important to develop a "shorthand" that you can use to make marginal notations. These notations will tell you at a glance in which section of the brief you will be placing that particular passage or portion of the opinion.

Some students prefer to underline all the salient portions of the opinion (with a pencil or colored underliner marker), making marginal notations as they go along. Others prefer the color-coded method of underlining, utilizing different colors of markers to underline the salient portions of the case, each separate color being used to represent a different section of the brief. For example, blue underlining could be used for passages relating to the rule of law, yellow for those relating to the issue, and green for those relating to the holding and decision, etc. While it has its advocates, the color-coded method can be confusing and time-consuming (all that time spent on changing colored markers). Furthermore, it can interfere with the continuity and concentration many students deem essential to the reading of a case for maximum comprehension. In the end, however, it is a matter of personal preference and style. Just remember, whatever method you use, underlining must be used sparingly or its value is lost.

If you take the marginal notation route, an efficient and easy method is to go along underlining the key portions of the case and placing in the margin alongside them the following "markers" to indicate where a particular passage or line "belongs" in the brief you will write:

N    (NATURE OF CASE)
RL   (RULE OF LAW)
I    (ISSUE)
HL   (HOLDING AND DECISION, relates to the RULE OF LAW behind the decision)
HR   (HOLDING AND DECISION, gives the RATIONALE or reasoning behind the decision)
HA   (HOLDING AND DECISION, applies the general principle(s) of law to the facts of the case to arrive at the decision)

Remember that a particular passage may well contain information necessary to more than one part of your brief, in which case you simply note that in the margin. If you are using the color-coded underlining method instead of marginal notation, simply make asterisks or checks in the margin next to the passage in question in the colors that indicate the additional sections of the brief where it might be utilized.

The economy of utilizing "shorthand" in marking cases for briefing can be maintained in the actual brief writing process itself by utilizing "law student shorthand" within the brief. There are many commonly used words and phrases for which abbreviations can be substituted in your briefs (and in your class notes also). You can develop abbreviations that are personal to you and which will save you a lot of time. A reference list of briefing abbreviations can be found on page x of this book.

## C. Use Both the Briefing Process and the Brief as a Learning Tool

Now that you have a format and the tools for briefing cases efficiently, the most important thing is to make the time spent in briefing profitable to you and to make the most advantageous use of the briefs you create. Of course, the briefs are invaluable for classroom reference when you are called upon to explain or analyze a particular

case. However, they are also useful in reviewing for exams. A quick glance at the fact summary should bring the case to mind, and a rereading of the rule of law should enable you to go over the underlying legal concept in your mind, how it was applied in that particular case, and how it might apply in other factual settings.

As to the value to be derived from engaging in the briefing process itself, there is an immediate benefit that arises from being forced to sift through the essential facts and reasoning from the court's opinion and to succinctly express them in your own words in your brief. The process ensures that you understand the case and the point that it illustrates, and that means you will be ready to absorb further analysis and information brought forth in class. It also ensures you will have something to say when called upon in class. The briefing process helps develop a mental agility for getting to the *gist* of a case and for identifying, expounding on, and applying the legal concepts and issues found there. The briefing process is the mental process on which you must rely in taking law school examinations; it is also the mental process upon which a lawyer relies in serving his clients and in making his living.

# Abbreviations for Briefs

| | | | |
|---|---|---|---|
| acceptance | acp | offer | O |
| affirmed | aff | offeree | OE |
| answer | ans | offeror | OR |
| assumption of risk | a/r | ordinance | ord |
| attorney | atty | pain and suffering | p/s |
| beyond a reasonable doubt | b/r/d | parol evidence | p/e |
| bona fide purchaser | BFP | plaintiff | P |
| breach of contract | br/k | prima facie | p/f |
| cause of action | c/a | probable cause | p/c |
| common law | c/l | proximate cause | px/c |
| Constitution | Con | real property | r/p |
| constitutional | con | reasonable doubt | r/d |
| contract | K | reasonable man | r/m |
| contributory negligence | c/n | rebuttable presumption | rb/p |
| cross | x | remanded | rem |
| cross-complaint | x/c | res ipsa loquitur | RIL |
| cross-examination | x/ex | respondeat superior | r/s |
| cruel and unusual punishment | c/u/p | Restatement | RS |
| defendant | D | reversed | rev |
| dismissed | dis | Rule Against Perpetuities | RAP |
| double jeopardy | d/j | search and seizure | s/s |
| due process | d/p | search warrant | s/w |
| equal protection | e/p | self-defense | s/d |
| equity | eq | specific performance | s/p |
| evidence | ev | statute | S |
| exclude | exc | statute of frauds | S/F |
| exclusionary rule | exc/r | statute of limitations | S/L |
| felony | f/n | summary judgment | s/j |
| freedom of speech | f/s | tenancy at will | t/w |
| good faith | g/f | tenancy in common | t/c |
| habeas corpus | h/c | tenant | t |
| hearsay | hr | third party | TP |
| husband | H | third party beneficiary | TPB |
| injunction | inj | transferred intent | TI |
| in loco parentis | ILP | unconscionable | uncon |
| inter vivos | I/v | unconstitutional | unconst |
| joint tenancy | j/t | undue influence | u/e |
| judgment | judgt | Uniform Commercial Code | UCC |
| jurisdiction | jur | unilateral | uni |
| last clear chance | LCC | vendee | VE |
| long-arm statute | LAS | vendor | VR |
| majority view | maj | versus | v |
| meeting of minds | MOM | void for vagueness | VFV |
| minority view | min | weight of authority | w/a |
| Miranda rule | Mir/r | weight of the evidence | w/e |
| Miranda warnings | Mir/w | wife | W |
| negligence | neg | with | w/ |
| notice | ntc | within | w/i |
| nuisance | nus | without | w/o |
| obligation | ob | without prejudice | w/o/p |
| obscene | obs | wrongful death | wr/d |

# Table of Cases

# CHAPTER 1

# Introduction to Contract Law

## *Quick Reference Rules of Law*

# Bailey v. West

Volunteer (P) v. Racehorse purchaser (D)

R.I. Sup. Ct., 105 R.I. 61, 249 A.2d 414 (1969).

**NATURE OF CASE:** Cross-appeals from judgment for plaintiff in action for value of services.

**FACT SUMMARY:** West (D) purchased Bascom's Folly, a racehorse. The horse arrived lame and West (D) had him shipped back to the original owner, who refused to take the horse back. The horse was then taken to Bailey's (P) farm, where Bailey (P) took care of the horse.

## 🏛 RULE OF LAW
(1) An "implied in fact" contract may not be found where intent to contract is lacking.
(2) A mere volunteer may not recover under a theory of quasi-contract for the value of services gratuitously rendered.

**FACTS:** West (D) purchased a racehorse from Strauss. When the horse arrived, it was lame. West (D) sent the horse back, but Strauss refused it. The driver telephoned West's (D) trainer for instructions. The trainer said the horse was not West's (D) and West (D) would not pay anything for its care. The driver delivered the horse to Bailey (P). He informed Bailey (P) that there was a dispute over ownership. Bailey (P) cared for the horse for a number of months, sending bills to both Strauss and West (D). After Strauss prevailed against West (D) in a suit for the purchase price, Bailey (P) brought suit against West (D) for the reasonable value of the services rendered to the horse. The trial court found that there was a contract "implied in fact" between the parties and that West (D) was liable for the services. West (D) appealed on the basis that the parties had never intended a contract be formed, so there was no "implied in fact" contract, and also contended that Bailey (P) could not recover in quasi-contract since he was a mere volunteer. The state's highest court granted review.

**ISSUE:**
(1) May an "implied in fact" contract be found where intent to contract is lacking?
(2) May a mere volunteer recover under a theory of quasi-contract for the value of services gratuitously rendered?

**HOLDING AND DECISION:** (Paolino, J.)
(1) No. An "implied in fact" contract may not be found where intent to contract is lacking. With respect to the trial court's finding of a contract "implied in fact," the court apparently ignored the requirement that it must have appeared that the parties intended to enter into a contractual relationship. There was no mutual agreement or misleading conduct between the parties. Indeed, Bailey (P) never even spoke to West (D) or one of his agents. Since the intent of the parties is an essen-

tial element to recovery in an "implied in fact" contract, Bailey (P) cannot recover. Reversed as to this issue.
(2) No. A mere volunteer may not recover under a theory of quasi-contract for the value of services gratuitously rendered. A quasi-contract is imposed by law generally to avoid unjust enrichment. Where a benefit is conferred that aids the defendant, courts hold that it is inequitable for him not to pay for it. However, where the service was gratuitously rendered without being requested, the plaintiff is a mere volunteer and will normally be denied restitution for the reasonable value of the services. Here, Bailey (P) was never authorized to perform a service for West (D). They had had no prior dealings. Bailey (P) knew of the disputed ownership claims. Further, Bailey (P) knew from the bill of lading that the horse was being returned by West (D). Under these circumstances, Bailey (P) could not reasonably believe that West (D) would either authorize or pay for his services. West (D) is not liable in quasi-contract. Reversed as to this issue. Reversed and remanded.

## ⊳ ANALYSIS

A mere volunteer may recover when the benefits are conferred by mistake and the defendant accepted them knowing of plaintiff's error. For example, if plaintiff paints defendant's house by mistake, thinking it belongs to another, and the defendant, realizing a mistake has been made, allows plaintiff to complete the work, he will be estopped from denying the existence of a contract and will be liable for the reasonable value of the services.

■━■

## Quicknotes

**"IMPLIED-IN-FACT" CONTRACT** Refers to conditions which arise by physical or moral inference: (a) prerequisites or circumstances which a reasonable person would assume necessary to render or receive performance; and (b) the good-faith cooperation of the promisee in receiving the performance of the promisor.

**QUASI-CONTRACT** An implied contract created by law to prevent unjust enrichment.

**RESTITUTION** The return or restoration to rightful owner to prevent unjust enrichment.

■━■

# Bolin Farms v. American Cotton Shippers Association

Cotton farmers (P) v. Cotton purchaser (D)

370 F. Supp. 1353 (W.D. La. 1974).

**NATURE OF CASE:** Motion for summary judgment in suit to have contracts declared null and void.

**FACT SUMMARY:** Bolin Farms (P), cotton farmers, sought nullification of a "forward" sales contract on the grounds that the price of cotton had skyrocketed subsequent to formation of the contract of sale.

## 🏛 RULE OF LAW
A subsequent change in the price of goods does not relieve the seller of contract obligations.

**FACTS:** Bolin Farms (P), cotton farmers, brought a diversity suit in federal district court to test the contracts by which they concededly obligated themselves to sell and deliver their cotton. American Cotton Shippers Association (D) agreed to purchase the cotton planted by Bolin Farms (P) on specific acreage at a price agreed upon between January and March of 1973, irrespective of what the market price might be at harvest time. Meanwhile, the price of cotton unexpectedly jumped to double the price agreed upon. Bolin Farms (P) thereupon sought a declaration to have the contracts declared null and void to enable Bolin Farms (P) to achieve a better price than they bargained for. American Cotton Shippers Association (D) moved for a summary judgment.

**ISSUE:** Does a subsequent change in the price of goods relieve the seller of contract obligations?

**HOLDING AND DECISION:** (Hunter, C.J.) No. A subsequent change in the price of goods does not relieve the seller of contract obligations. Here, the actual cotton produced was physically to be delivered to the buyers to be physically received and paid for on delivery. The contracts negotiated by Bolin Farms (P) prior to planting were known as "forward" sales contracts. Each cotton farmer was experienced, having been a cotton producer for several years. Each was familiar with the forward sale contract procedure. The sales were for a fair market price at the time they were made, hence, as a matter of law, the price and circumstances prevailing at the time are determinative. Whatever causes the market to go up and down after the date of a contract has no relevancy to its validity. The motion for summary judgment of American Cotton Shippers Association (D) is granted.

## ▶ ANALYSIS

In *Bolin Farms*, the court, noting that there were many causes for the upward spiral in the price of the cotton from the time of the contract formation to the time of the actual sale, makes clear that the cause of a subsequent

price fluctuation has no relevancy to the validity of a contract.

■■■

## Quicknotes

**SUMMARY JUDGMENT** Judgment rendered by a court in response to a motion made by one of the parties, claiming that the lack of a question of material fact in respect to an issue warrants disposition of the issue without consideration by the jury.

■■■

# Williams v. Walker-Thomas Furniture Co.

Unsophisticated consumer (D) v. Retailer (P)

121 U.S. App. D.C. 315, 350 F.2d 445 (D.C. Cir. 1965).

**NATURE OF CASE:** Appeal from affirmance of decision upholding a contract in replevin action.

**FACT SUMMARY:** Williams (D) made a series of purchases, on credit, from Walker-Thomas Furniture Co. (P) but defaulted on her payments.

🏛 **RULE OF LAW**
Where, in light of the general commercial background of a particular case, it appears that gross inequality of bargaining power between the parties has led to the formation of a contract on terms to which one party has had no meaningful choice, a court may refuse to enforce such a contract on the grounds it is unconscionable.

**FACTS:** Beginning about 1957, Walker-Thomas Furniture Co. (Walker-Thomas) (P), a retail furniture company, began using a standard form contract for all credit transactions which contained, inter alia, a clause by which the company (P) reserved the right, upon default by a purchaser, to repossess all items contemporaneously being purchased by the buyer at the time of the repossession. This clause was accompanied by one which stated that all credit purchases made from Walker-Thomas (P) were to be handled through one account, with each installment payment spread pro rata over all items purchased (even where purchased separately and at different times) until all items were paid for. Williams (D) began purchasing items from Walker-Thomas (P) in 1957. In 1962, she bought a stereo set there. When she defaulted on a payment soon thereafter, Walker-Thomas (P) filed this action to replevy (i.e., repossess) all items she had purchased (and was still paying for) since 1957. From judgment for Walker-Thomas (P), this appeal followed.

**ISSUE:** Where, in light of the general commercial background of a particular case, it appears that gross inequality of bargaining power between the parties has led to the formation of a contract on terms to which one party has had no meaningful choice, may a court refuse to enforce such a contract on the grounds it is unconscionable?

**HOLDING AND DECISION:** (Wright, J.) Yes. Where, in light of the general commercial background of a particular case, it appears that gross inequality of bargaining power between the parties has led to the formation of a contract on terms to which one party has had no meaningful choice, a court may refuse to enforce such a contract on the grounds it is unconscionable. It is true that the common law, operating by the caveat emptor rationale, refused to look into the essential fairness of a contract absent

evidence of out-and-out fraud. The Uniform Commercial Code (U.C.C.), however, notably § 2-302, as adopted in this jurisdiction, has accepted the rule that courts should seek to prevent overreaching in contracts of adhesion such as the one at bar. Williams (D), and others, comes from a socioeconomic class for which credit is difficult to obtain. To permit Walker-Thomas (P) to exploit this condition with provisions such as those pointed out above is clearly unconscionable. Remanded.

**DISSENT:** (Danaher, J.) The court ignores many policy considerations in its decision today. For one, the high risk of granting credit to the poor for companies like Walker-Thomas (P) is not even addressed. A more cautious approach is warranted.

▶ **ANALYSIS**

This case reflects the major application that the U.C.C. § 2-302 concept of unconscionability has had to date: adhesion (i.e., form) contracts. Note that the general common-law rule regarding such contracts remains the general rule today. That rule is that a person who signs a contract will be held responsible for any clauses or conditions which a reasonable man making a reasonable inspection would have discovered. The U.C.C. rule merely qualifies this to say that where one party to a form contract has no real choice over whether to accept the terms because of his relative economic position, then the fact he knows of the terms will not be enough to constitute a "meeting of the minds" on his part necessary to form a valid contract.

◼━◼

**Quicknotes**

**CAVEAT EMPTOR** Let the buyer beware; doctrine that a buyer purchases at his own risk.

**REPLEVIN** An action to recover personal property wrongfully taken.

**UNCONSCIONABILITY** A situation in which a contract, or a particular contract term, is unenforceable if the court determines that such terms are unduly oppressive or unfair to one party to the contract.

◼━◼

# Sullivan v. O'Connor

Patient (P) v. Plastic surgeon (D)

Mass. Sup. Jud. Ct., 363 Mass. 579, 296 N.E.2d 183 (1973).

**NATURE OF CASE:** Appeal from verdict for plaintiff in action for medical malpractice and breach of contract.

**FACT SUMMARY:** O'Connor (D), a doctor, promised to improve Sullivan's (P) appearance by cosmetic surgery. In fact, O'Connor's (D) efforts left Sullivan (P) with more of a disfigurement than previously.

## 🏛 RULE OF LAW
A physician who breaches his contractual obligation to effect a particular result is liable to his patient for the cost of any measures or treatment necessitated by the physician's breach and for any pain and suffering resulting therefrom.

**FACTS:** Dr. O'Connor (D) expressly promised to enhance and improve the appearance of Sullivan (P), an entertainer, by performing cosmetic surgery on her nose. However, after two operations, Sullivan's (P) nose looked worse than it had previously. As a result of the surgery, the nose was disfigured, apparently permanently. Sullivan (P) sued to recover damages from O'Connor (D), alleging both breach of contract and medical malpractice, the latter theory of recovery being based on negligence. A jury trial resulted in a verdict for Sullivan (P) on the contract count and for O'Connor (D) on the count alleging malpractice. On appeal, O'Connor (D) took exception to the trial judge's instruction that Sullivan (P) could recover all out-of-pocket expenses occasioned by O'Connor's (D) breach of his promise, plus any pain and suffering caused by her condition or by a third operation which Sullivan (P) endured in a vain attempt to restore her nose to its previous shape. The state's highest court granted review.

**ISSUE:** Is a physician who breaches his contractual obligation to effect a particular result liable to his patient for the cost of any measures or treatment necessitated by the physician's breach and for any pain and suffering resulting therefrom?

**HOLDING AND DECISION:** (Kaplan, J.) Yes. A physician who breaches his contractual obligation to effect a particular result is liable to his patient for the cost of any measures or treatment necessitated by the physician's breach and for any pain and suffering resulting therefrom. Because contracts involving promises by physicians are necessarily predicated on matters which can be no more certain than medical science itself, it does not seem fair to award a patient the difference in value between the actual condition of his bodily part after treatment and the condition which the physician promised to bring about. But the patient should be entitled to recover more than just the money he expended on the doctor's treatment. It is a reasonable compromise which permits the patient to recover all his out-of-pocket expenses, including additional costs incurred in trying to remedy the doctor's failure to perform his promise, plus an amount which compensates him for any pain and suffering, physical or mental, occasioned by the physician's breach. Plaintiff's exceptions waived and Defendant's exceptions overruled.

## ▶ ANALYSIS
Ordinarily, a nonbreaching party is entitled to recover such compensatory damages as will place him in the same situation as he would have enjoyed had the contract never been breached. Under some circumstances, the nonbreaching party will be awarded restitution only of whatever he has given in performance of the contract, i.e., he will be restored to the position he occupied prior to execution.

## Quicknotes

**BREACH OF CONTRACT** Unlawful failure by a party to perform its obligations pursuant to contract.

**CONTRACTUAL OBLIGATION** A duty that someone agrees to perform pursuant to a contract.

**EXPRESS PROMISE** The expression of an intention to act, or to forbear from acting, granting a right to the promisee to expect and enforce its performance.

**MEDICAL MALPRACTICE** Conduct on the part of a doctor falling below that demonstrated by other doctors of ordinary skill and competency under the circumstances, resulting in damages.

**NEGLIGENCE** Conduct falling below the standard of care that a reasonable person would demonstrate under similar conditions.

# Hadley v. Baxendale

Shipper (P) v. Shipping company (D)

Ct. of Exchequer, 9 Exch. 341, 156 Eng. Rep. 145 (1854).

**NATURE OF CASE:** Appeal from verdict for plaintiff in action for breach of a carrier contract.

**FACT SUMMARY:** Hadley (P), a mill operator in Gloucester, arranged to have Baxendale's (D) company, a carrier, ship his broken mill shaft to the engineer in Greenwich for a copy to be made. Hadley (P) suffered a £300 loss when Baxendale (D) unreasonably delayed shipping the mill shaft, causing the mill to be shut down longer than anticipated.

## 🏛 RULE OF LAW
An injured party may recover damages for a breach of contract that reasonably may be considered as arising naturally from the breach as well as those damages for breach that it may reasonably be supposed the parties contemplated at the time they made the contract.

**FACTS:** Hadley (P), a mill operator in Gloucester, arranged to have Baxendale's (D) shipping company return his broken mill shaft to the engineer in Greenwich, who was to make a duplicate. Hadley (P) delivered the broken shaft to Baxendale (D), who, in consideration for his fee, promised to deliver the shaft to Greenwich in a reasonable time. Baxendale (D) did not know that the mill was shut down while awaiting the new shaft. Baxendale (D) was negligent in delivering the shaft within a reasonable time. Reopening of the mill was delayed five days, costing Hadley (P) lost profits and paid-out wages of £300. Hadley (P) had paid Baxendale (D) £24 to ship the mill shaft. Baxendale (D) paid into court £25 in satisfaction of Hadley's (P) claim. The jury awarded an additional £25 for a total £50 award, and the Court of Exchequer granted review.

**ISSUE:** May an injured party recover damages for a breach of contract that reasonably may be considered as arising naturally from the breach as well as those damages for breach that it may reasonably be supposed the parties contemplated at the time they made the contract?

**HOLDING AND DECISION:** (Alderson, B.) Yes. An injured party may recover damages for a breach of contract that reasonably may be considered as arising naturally from the breach as well as those damages for breach that it may reasonably be supposed the parties contemplated at the time they made the contract. The jury requires a rule for its guidance in awarding damages justly. When a party breaches his contract, the damages he pays ought to be those arising naturally from the breach itself and, in addition, those as may reasonably be supposed to have been in contemplation of the parties, at the time they

made the contract, as the probable result of the breach of it. Therefore, if the special circumstances under which the contract was made were known to both parties, the resulting damages upon breach would be those reasonably contemplated as arising under those communicated and known circumstances. But if the special circumstances were unknown, then damages can only be those expected to arise generally from the breach. Hadley's (P) telling Baxendale (D) that he ran a mill and that his mill shaft which he wanted shipped was broken did not notify Baxendale (D) that the mill was shut down. Baxendale (D) could have believed reasonably that Hadley (P) had a spare shaft or that the shaft to be shipped was not the only defective machinery at the mill. Here, it does not follow that a loss of profits could fairly or reasonably have been contemplated by both parties in case of breach. Such a loss would not have flowed naturally from the breach without the special circumstances having been communicated to Baxendale (D). The jury should have been so instructed. Reversed and new trial ordered.

## ▶ ANALYSIS

This case lays down two rules guiding damages. First, only those damages as may fairly and reasonably be considered arising from the breach itself may be awarded. Second, those damages which may reasonably be supposed to have been in contemplation of the parties at the time they made the contract as the probable result of a breach of it may be awarded. The second is distinguished from the first because with the latter, both parties are aware of the special circumstances under which the contract is made. Usually, those special circumstances are communicated by the plaintiff to the defendant before the making of the contract. But that is not an absolute condition. If the consequences of the breach are foreseeable, the party which breaches will be liable for the lost profits or expectation damages. Foreseeability and assumption of the risk are ways of describing the bargain. If there is an assumption of the risk, the seller or carrier must necessarily be aware of the consequences. A later English case held that there would be a lesser foreseeability for a common carrier than a seller, as a seller would tend to know the purpose and use of the item sold while the common carrier probably would not know the use of all items it carried. If all loss went on to the seller, this would obviously be an incentive not to enter into contracts. Courts balance what has become a "seller beware" attitude by placing limitations on full recovery. The loss must be foreseeable when the

*Continued on next page.*

contract is entered into. It cannot be overly speculative. The seller's breach must be judged by willingness, negligence, bad faith, and availability of replacement items. Restatement (First) § 331(2) would allow recovery in the situation in this case under an alternative theory. If the breach were one preventing the use and operation of property from which profits would have been made, damages can be measured by the rental value of the property or by interest on the value of the property. Uniform Commercial Code § 2-715(2) allows the buyer consequential damages for any loss which results from general or particular needs of which the seller had reason to know.

■■■■

## *Quicknotes*

**BREACH OF CONTRACT** Unlawful failure by a party to perform its obligations pursuant to contract.

**DAMAGES** Monetary compensation that may be awarded by the court to a party who has sustained injury or loss to his person, property or rights due to another party's unlawful act, omission or negligence.

**NEGLIGENCE** Conduct falling below the standard of care that a reasonable person would demonstrate under similar conditions.

■■■■

# The Bases of Contract Liability

## Quick Reference Rules of Law

# Kirksey v. Kirksey

Sister-in-law (P) v. Brother-in-law (D)

Ala. Sup. Ct., 8 Ala. 131 (1845).

**NATURE OF CASE:** Appeal from verdict for plaintiff in action to recover damages for breach of a promise.

**FACT SUMMARY:** Kirksey (D) promised "Sister Antillico" (P) a place to raise her family "if you come down and see me."

## 🏛 RULE OF LAW
To be legally enforceable, an executory promise must be supported by sufficient, bargained-for consideration.

**FACTS:** Kirksey (D) wrote to "Sister Antillico" (P) a letter containing the following clause: "If you will come down and see me, I will let you have a place to raise your family." "Sister Antillico" (P) moved 60 miles to Kirksey's (D) residence, where she remained for over two years. Kirksey (D) then required her to leave, although her family was not yet "raised." "Sister Antillico" (P) contended that the loss which she sustained in moving was sufficient consideration to support Kirksey's (D) promise to furnish her with "a place" until she could raise her family. Verdict was rendered for "Sister Antillico" (P), and the state's highest court granted review.

**ISSUE:** To be legally enforceable, must an executory promise be supported by sufficient, bargained-for consideration?

**HOLDING AND DECISION:** (Ormond, J.) Yes. To be legally enforceable, an executory promise must be supported by sufficient, bargained-for consideration. Otherwise, the promise is a promise to make a gift. Any expenses incurred by the promisee in "coming down and seeing" are merely conditions necessary to acceptance of the gift. In this case, Kirksey (D) did not appear to be bargaining either for "Sister Antillico's" (P) presence or for her 60-mile move. Instead, Kirksey (D) merely wished to assist her out of what he perceived as a grievous and difficult situation. Reversed.

## ▶ ANALYSIS

This well-known case demonstrates the court's insistence on finding a bargained-for exchange before it will enforce an executory promise. A promise to make a gift is generally not legally binding until it is executed. Compare Williston's famous hypothetical in which a benevolent man says to a tramp: "If you go around the corner to the clothing shop there, you may purchase an overcoat on my credit." This hypo highlights the conceptual problem of the present case in that it is unreasonable to construe the walk around

the corner as the price of the promise, yet it is a legal detriment to the tramp to make the walk. Perhaps a reasonable (though not conclusive) guideline is the extent to which the happening of the condition will benefit the promisor. The present case might be decided differently today under the doctrine of promissory estoppel which had not yet been developed in 1845.

━━━

## Quicknotes

**BARGAINED FOR EXCHANGE** A requirement for adequate consideration; the promise made by the offeror induces the return promise or performance on the part of the offeree and that the promise or performance on the part of the offeree induces the promise made by the offeror.

**BREACH** The violation of an obligation imposed pursuant to contract or law, by acting or failing to act.

**CONSIDERATION** Value given by one party in exchange for performance, or a promise to perform, by another party.

**EXECUTORY PROMISE** A promise to perform an action that has not yet been performed.

**PROMISE** The expression of an intention to act, or to forbear from acting, granting a right to the promisee to expect and enforce its performance.

**PROMISEE** Party to whom a promise is made.

**PROMISSORY ESTOPPEL** A promise that is enforceable if the promisor should reasonably expect that it will induce action or forbearance on the part of the promisee, and does in fact cause such action or forbearance, and it is the only means of avoiding injustice.

━━━

# Hamer v. Sidway

## Assignee of nephew's interest (P) v. Executor of uncle's estate (D)

N.Y. Ct. App., 124 N.Y. 538, 27 N.E. 256 (1891).

**NATURE OF CASE:** Appeal from reversal of judgment for plaintiff in action to recover upon a contract.

**FACT SUMMARY:** William Story (D) promised to pay $5,000 to William Story 2d (P) if he would forbear in the use of liquor, tobacco, swearing, or playing cards or billiards for money until he became 21 years of age.

> 🏛 **RULE OF LAW**
> Forbearance on the part of a promisee is suffi-
> cient consideration to support a contract.

**FACTS:** William Story (D) agreed with his nephew William Story 2d (P) that if W. Story 2d (P) would refrain from drinking liquor, using tobacco, swearing, and playing cards or billiards for money until he became 21 years of age, W. Story (D) would pay him $5,000. Upon becoming 21 years of age, W. Story 2d (P) received a letter from W. Story (D) stating he had earned the $5,000, and it would be kept at interest for him. Twelve years later, W. Story (D) died, and this action was brought by the assignee of W. Story 2d (P) against the executor (D) of the estate of W. Story (D). Judgment was entered in favor of W. Story 2d (P) at the trial at special term and was reversed at general term of the supreme court. The assignee of W. Story 2d (P) appealed, and the state's highest court granted review.

**ISSUE:** Is forbearance on the part of a promisee suffi-cient consideration to support a contract?

**HOLDING AND DECISION:** (Parker, J.) Yes. Forbearance on the part of a promisee is sufficient consid-eration to support a contract. Valuable consideration may consist either of some right, interest, profit, or benefit accruing to the one party or some forbearance, detriment, loss, or responsibility given, suffered, or undertaken by the other. Therefore, there was adequate consideration to sup-port the promise made in the instant case. Reversed.

## ▌ *ANALYSIS*

The surrendering or forgoing of a legal right constitutes a sufficient consideration for a contract if the minds of the parties meet on the relinquishing of the right as a consid-eration. Consideration may be forbearance to sue on a claim, extension of time, or any other giving up of a legal right in consideration of a promise.

---

## *Quicknotes*

**CONSIDERATION** Value given by one party in exchange for performance, or a promise to perform, by another party.

**FORBEARANCE** Refraining from doing something that one has the legal right to do.

**PROMISEE** Party to whom a promise is made.

# Langer v. Superior Steel Corp.

### Retired employee (P) v. Former employer (D)

Pa. Super. Ct., 105 Pa. Super. 579, 161 A. 571 (1932).

**NATURE OF CASE:** Appeal from judgment for defendant in action of assumpsit to recover damages for breach of contract.

**FACT SUMMARY:** Superior Steel Corp. (D) promised Langer (P), who was retiring from its employ, a lifetime pension if Langer (P) would refrain from seeking competitive employment.

> ## RULE OF LAW
> Sufficient consideration exists if one refrains from doing anything that he has a right to do, whether or not there is any actual loss or detriment to him or actual benefit to the promisor.

**FACTS:** Superior Steel Corp. (Superior) (D) promised Langer (P), upon his retirement as a superintendent with the company, that he "will receive a pension of $100 per month as long as you live and preserve your present attitude of loyalty to the company and its officers and are not employed in any competitive position." Superior (D) paid the sum of $100 a month for four years when it discontinued payments. Langer (P) brought an action in assumpsit for an alleged breach of contract, and in defense, Superior (D) argued that the offer of a pension was merely gratuitous. The state's intermediate appellate court granted review.

**ISSUE:** Does sufficient consideration exist if one refrains from doing anything that he has a right to do, whether or not there is any actual loss or detriment to him or actual benefit to the promisor?

**HOLDING AND DECISION:** (Baldrige, J.) Yes. Sufficient consideration exists if one refrains from doing anything that he has a right to do, whether or not there is any actual loss or detriment to him or actual benefit to the promisor. Such forbearance involves a detriment to the performing party. While it is helpful to determine whether the promisor will also be benefited, in doubtful cases, a showing that the promisee has, as a result of the promise, incurred a detriment is usually sufficient to prevent the promise from being interpreted as a mere gratuity. In the present case, by receiving the monthly payments, Langer (P) also impliedly accepted the conditions imposed and thus was prevented from securing other employment. Unlike in *Kirksey v. Kirksey*, here there was a benefit to be derived by the promisor. An alternative basis for regarding this case as involving an enforceable contract, rather than a mere gratuity, is promissory estoppel. A promise which the promisor should reasonably expect to induce action or forbearance of a definite and substantial character on the part of the promisee and which does induce same is binding if injustice can be avoided only by enforcement of the promise. Under either theory, Langer (P) is entitled to enforce Superior's (D) promise. Reversed.

## ▶ ANALYSIS

A majority of courts have embraced the "legal detriment" rule for determining the sufficiency of consideration. Under the approach, proof that one party's act or performance results in a legal benefit being conferred on the other is not, by itself, sufficient to establish consideration. Restatement 384(a) adopts the minority view in positing in the alternative that either legal detriment or legal benefit is sufficient.

---

## Quicknotes

**ACTION IN ASSUMPSIT** Action to recover damages for breach of an oral or written promise to perform or pay pursuant to a contract.

**BREACH OF CONTRACT** Unlawful failure by a party to perform its obligations pursuant to contract.

**FORBEARANCE** Refraining from doing something that one has the legal right to do.

**LEGAL DETRIMENT** The relinquishment of a right to do or not to do something that the person had a privilege or right to do or not to do, and which is sufficient consideration for the formation of a contract.

**PROMISE** The expression of an intention to act, or to forbear from acting, granting a right to the promisee to expect and enforce its performance.

**PROMISEE** Party to whom a promise is made.

**PROMISSORY ESTOPPEL** A promise that is enforceable if the promisor should reasonably expect that it will induce action or forbearance on the part of the promisee, and does in fact cause such action or forbearance, and it is the only means of avoiding injustice.

# Pennsy Supply, Inc. v. American Ash Recycling Corp.

Paving subcontractor (P) v. Paving material supplier (D)

Pa. Super. Ct., 895 A.2d 595 (2006).

**NATURE OF CASE:** Appeal from dismissal of action for breach of contract and breach of express and implied warranties.

**FACT SUMMARY:** Pennsy Supply, Inc. (Pennsy) (P), a paving subcontractor, contended that even though it obtained a material called AggRite from American Ash Recycling Corp. (American Ash) (D) free of charge, there was sufficient consideration to support breach of contract and breach of warranty claims based on Pennsy's (P) relieving American Ash (D) of its legal obligation to dispose of the AggRite, a material classified as hazardous waste.

## RULE OF LAW

Notwithstanding a lack of actual bargaining between parties, there can be consideration where the promise induces the detriment and the detriment induces the promise.

**FACTS:** Pennsy Supply, Inc. (Pennsy) (P), a paving subcontractor, was permitted by its construction contract to obtain, free of charge, from American Ash Recycling Corp. (American Ash) (D) a material called AggRite and use the AggRite in the construction project. The AggRite was classified as a hazardous waste. Pennsy (P) obtained 11,000 tons of AggRite. When the paving developed extensive cracking, remedial work cost Pennsy (P) $251,940, and Pennsy (P) incurred an additional $133,777 to dispose of the AggRite it removed. Pennsy (P) brought suit against American Ash (D) for breach of contract and breach of express and implied warranties. Pennsy (P) claimed that American Ash (D) promoted the use of its AggRite material to avoid the high cost of disposing of the material itself; that American Ash (D) incurred a benefit from Pennsy's (P) use of the material in the form of avoidance of the costs of disposal sufficient to ground contract and warranty claims; and that Pennsy's (P) relief of American Ash's (D) legal obligation to dispose of a material classified as hazardous waste, such that American Ash (D) avoided the costs of disposal thereof at a hazardous waste site, constituted sufficient consideration to ground contract and warranty claims. The trial court ruled that, at best, American Ash (D) had made a conditional gift of the AggRite, and that there was insufficient consideration to support a contract or warranties between the parties. Accordingly, the trial court dismissed the action. The state's intermediate appellate court granted review.

**ISSUE:** Notwithstanding a lack of actual bargaining between parties, can there be consideration where the promise induces the detriment and the detriment induces the promise?

**HOLDING AND DECISION:** (Melvin, J.) Yes. Notwithstanding a lack of actual bargaining between parties, there can be consideration where the promise induces the detriment and the detriment induces the promise. It is fundamental that consideration is an essential element of an enforceable contract and that consideration must actually be bargained for as the exchange for the promise. Here, accepting Pennsy's (P) allegations as true, American Ash's (D) promise to supply the AggRite free of charge induced Pennsy (P) to assume the detriment of collecting and taking title to the material, and this detriment induced American Ash (D) to make the promise to provide free AggRite. Thus, American Ash (D) did not make a conditional gift of the AggRite, because the allegations show that it indeed did expect something in return for providing the AggRite at no cost. The fact that there was no actual bargaining process between the parties, or even that Pennsy (P) did not know or understand at the time it requested the AggRite that its use of the AggRite would enable American Ash (D) to avoid disposal costs, does not alter this conclusion. Under the bargain theory of consideration all that is required that the promise and consideration be in "the relation of reciprocal conventional inducement, each for the other." Here, the promise induced the detriment, and the detriment induced the promise; that is consideration. Reversed.

## ANALYSIS

The consideration formula used by the court in this case is known as the Holmesian formula for consideration, because it was stated by Justice Oliver Wendell Holmes, Jr., who stated that "the promise must induce the detriment and the detriment must induce the promise." Under this classic formulation of consideration, if the promisor makes the promise for the purpose of inducing the detriment, the detriment induces the promise. If, however, the promisor does not make the promise with any particular interest in the detriment that the promisee will suffer to take advantage of the promised benefit, the detriment is incidental or conditional to the promisee's receipt of the benefit, and what's at issue is a conditional gift. Thus, even though the promisee suffers a detriment induced by the promise, the purpose of the promisor was not to have the promisee suffer the detriment because the promisor did not seek that detriment in exchange for the promise. In other words,

*Continued on next page.*

if the detriment incurred by the promisee is of no benefit to the promisor but occurs merely to enable the promisee to receive a gift, the occurrence of the detriment brought about by the promisee in reliance on the promise is not properly construed as consideration but as a condition to a gift.

## Quicknotes

**BREACH OF CONTRACT**  Unlawful failure by a party to perform its obligations pursuant to contract.

**BREACH OF EXPRESS WARRANTY**  The breach of an express promise made by one party to a contract on which the other party may rely, relieving that party from the obligation of determining whether the fact is true and indemnifying the other party from liability if that fact is shown to be false.

**CONSIDERATION**  Value given by one party in exchange for performance, or a promise to perform, by another party.

**PROMISE**  The expression of an intention to act, or to forbear from acting, granting a right to the promisee to expect and enforce its performance.

# In re Greene

[Parties not identified.]

45 F.2d 428 (S.D.N.Y. 1930).

**NATURE OF CASE:** Appeal from order of referee permitting claim against bankrupt's estate.

**FACT SUMMARY:** The preamble to an instrument signed by Greene (D), in which he promised to pay his former mistress (P) hundreds of thousands of dollars, recited that the consideration was $1.

> ### 🏛 RULE OF LAW
> A consideration given by one party that is only token or nominal does not constitute sufficient consideration.

**FACTS:** Prior to 1926, Greene (D) had lived in adultery with claimant (P). Greene (D) gave her substantial sums of money and a $70,000 house. In 1926, their relationship ended, and they executed a written, sealed agreement in which Greene (D) promised to pay the claimant (P) $1,000 a month, to assign to her a $100,000 life insurance policy and to maintain the premiums on it, and to pay the rent for four years on an apartment she had leased. The agreement recited that Greene (D) would no longer be liable for mortgage interest, taxes, or other charges on the house he had given the claimant (P). The preamble to the instrument stated that consideration was $1 by the claimant (P) to Greene (D) "and other good and valuable considerations." Greene (D) made payments only up to 1928, and when he went bankrupt, the claimant (P) sought to enforce the agreement against his bankrupt estate. The bankruptcy referee held that the claim was valid. The district court granted review.

**ISSUE:** Does a consideration given by one party that is only token or nominal constitute sufficient consideration?

**HOLDING AND DECISION:** (Woolsey, J.) No. A consideration given by one party that is only token or nominal does not constitute sufficient consideration. A $1 consideration, being nominal, will not support an executory promise to pay, in the present case, hundreds of thousands of dollars. The promise is unenforceable since there appears no other sufficient consideration in the written agreement. Past illicit intercourse is not consideration. "Other good and valuable considerations" is plausible, but there is no proof that in fact anything good or valuable had been given at the time the contract was made. Greene's (D) purported immunity from having to pay taxes and other charges on the claimant's (P) house is not enough since he was never chargeable with these expenses; his previous payments were gratuitous. Finally, although the parties here may have intended to make a valid agreement, the most solemn and formal document possible cannot dis-guise what is in reality a gift. A seal is only presumptive evidence of consideration on an executory instrument. The agreement is unenforceable. Order of the referee reversed.

## ▶ ANALYSIS

Although, in a standard contract, a recital of a token or nominal consideration indicates that a gift, rather than a bargain, was intended, a $1 sum, or less, may be adequate to sustain certain types of agreements. In option and guaranty contracts, the party giving the nominal or token consideration is bargaining for something of a speculative nature or value. Thus, in one case, a consideration of $0.25 for a 4-month option to purchase land for $100,000 was held sufficient to render the contract enforceable.

■■■■

## Quicknotes

**CONSIDERATION** Value given by one party in exchange for performance, or a promise to perform, by another party.

**EXECUTORY PROMISE** A promise to perform an action that has not yet been performed.

■■■■

# Cohen v. Cowles Media Co.

### News source (P) v. Newspaper publisher (D)

Minn. Sup. Ct., 479 N.W.2d 387 (1992).

**NATURE OF CASE:** Remand from appeal of an award of damages for breach of contract and fraudulent misrepresentation.

**FACT SUMMARY:** Editors of two newspapers (D) broke their promises to Cohen (P), the source for a story, to keep his identity confidential.

## 🏛 RULE OF LAW
Under the doctrine of promissory estoppel, a court should consider all aspects of a transaction's substance in determining whether enforcement is necessary to prevent an injustice.

**FACTS:** Cohen (P) supplied the Minneapolis Star Tribune (Tribune), published by Cowles Media Co. (D), and the St. Paul Pioneer Press Dispatch (Dispatch) with disparaging information regarding a candidate for public office. The reporter for the Tribune and the Dispatch promised Cohen (P) that he would not be revealed as the source for the information. However, editors at the Tribune and the Dispatch later decided that it was important to reveal Cohen (P) as the source for the information because he was allied with an opposing candidate. After the story was published, Cohen (P) was fired from his job. Cohen (P) filed suit against Cowles (D) and the Dispatch's publisher (D) for breach of contract and fraudulent misrepresentation. The jury awarded Cohen (P) $200,000 in compensatory damages and $250,000 in punitive damages. On appeal, the court set aside recovery on the basis of fraudulent misrepresentation but affirmed recovery of the compensatory damages on the basis of breach of contract. The Minnesota Supreme Court found that promissory estoppel could form the basis for recovery but held that First Amendment concerns precluded recovery of damages. The United States Supreme Court, concluding that the First Amendment was not implicated, overruled this decision and remanded the case to determine whether a retrial would be necessary.

**ISSUE:** Under the doctrine of promissory estoppel, should a court consider all aspects of a transaction's substance in determining whether enforcement is necessary to prevent an injustice?

**HOLDING AND DECISION:** (Simonett, J.) Yes. Under the doctrine of promissory estoppel, a court should consider all aspects of a transaction's substance in determining whether enforcement is necessary to prevent an injustice. A promise that is expected to, and does, induce definite action by the promisee is binding if injustice can be avoided only by enforcing the promise. The promise must be definite, clear, and intended to induce reliance. In the instant case, the record is clear that the Dispatch's and the Tribune's reporters made unambiguous promises to treat Cohen (P) as an anonymous source, and Cohen (P) provided the information based on these promises. Thus, the only remaining issue is whether this promise must be enforced to prevent an injustice. Neither side in this case clearly holds the higher moral ground. However, even the Tribune's witnesses acknowledged the importance of protecting the confidentiality of information sources. Additionally, it does not appear that there was a compelling need to break the promises in the present case. Therefore, it would be unjust to Cohen (P) unless the promises were enforced. Accordingly, the award of compensatory damages is affirmed but under a theory of promissory estoppel.

## ▶ ANALYSIS

The court ruled that the damages instruction the trial court provided for breach of contract was also valid for promissory estoppel recovery. A study examining the effect of this decision on publishers revealed that there was no substantial change in policies regarding confidential sources. In fact, most publishers thought the result was just and proper.

---

## Quicknotes

**BREACH OF CONTRACT** Unlawful failure by a party to perform its obligations pursuant to contract.

**COMPENSATORY DAMAGES** Measure of damages necessary to compensate victim for actual injuries suffered.

**FRAUDULENT MISREPRESENTATION** A statement or conduct by one party to another that constitutes a false representation of fact.

**PROMISSORY ESTOPPEL** A promise that is enforceable if the promisor should reasonably expect that it will induce action or forbearance on the part of the promisee, and does in fact cause such action or forbearance, and it is the only means of avoiding injustice.

**PUNITIVE DAMAGES** Damages exceeding the actual injury suffered for the purposes of punishment of the defendant, deterrence of the wrongful behavior or comfort to the plaintiff.

---

# First Hawaiian Bank v. Zukerkorn

Creditor (P) v. Debtor (D)

Hawaii Ct. App., 2 Haw. App. 383 (1981).

**NATURE OF CASE:** Appeal from summary judgment for plaintiff in action to collect payment on various debts.

**FACT SUMMARY:** Zukerkorn (D) contended that he did not, as a matter of law, make a new promise to pay two stale debts he owed to First Hawaiian Bank (P), collection of which was otherwise barred by the applicable statute of limitations, since he disputed: having expressly agreed to pay the stale debts; having acknowledged the debts; or having paid a part of the debts.

## RULE OF LAW
Even if a debtor has expressly acknowledged and/or made part payment on a stale debt, the collection of which is otherwise barred by the applicable statute of limitations, the debtor has not renewed the debt as a matter of law where it is disputed whether the debtor made an express promise to pay the debt.

**FACTS:** Zukerkorn (D) executed in favor of First Hawaiian Bank ("the Bank") (P) a $6,394 demand note dated November 22, 1965, and a $2,500 two-year note dated September 23, 1966. He made no payments on either note. On August 6, 1973, he obtained an automobile purchase loan from the Bank (P), and he paid it off on April 6, 1976. Around December 11, 1975, Zukerkorn (D) applied to the Bank (P) for a credit card. Zukerkorn (D) admitted the Bank (P) told him that he owed "a small amount of money on an old account"; that issuance of the card was conditioned on his agreement to pay $100 per month on the old account; that he agreed to the condition; and that he received a credit card. He denied the Bank's (P) assertion that the November 22, 1965, and the September 23, 1966, notes were specifically identified and that his agreement specifically related to them. He also denied the Bank's (P) assertion that he paid $200 in cash at or about the time he made the agreement. Both parties agreed that after the agreement, Zukerkorn (D) made payments on the automobile loan, on the credit card account, and that pursuant to his agreement (the terms of which were in dispute), he made small payments on several occasions over a period of a little over three months in 1976. On March 3, 1978, the Bank (P) sued Zukerkorn (D) on the November 22, 1965, note; the September 23, 1966, note; and on the balance due on the credit card account. The trial court entered summary judgment for the Bank (P) on all its claims. The state's intermediate appellate court granted review.

**ISSUE:** Even if a debtor has expressly acknowledged and/or made part payment on a stale debt, the collection of which is otherwise barred by the applicable statute of limitations, has the debtor renewed the debt as a matter of law where it is disputed whether the debtor made an express promise to pay the debt?

**HOLDING AND DECISION:** (Burns, J.) No. Even if a debtor has expressly acknowledged and/or made part payment on a stale debt, the collection of which is otherwise barred by the applicable statute of limitations, the debtor has not renewed the debt as a matter of law where it is disputed whether the debtor made an express promise to pay the debt. First, summary judgment on the credit card debt is affirmed. As to the stale debts, Zukerkorn (D) has created a genuine issue of material fact as to whether he did something to start the statute of limitations running anew on those. The applicable law is that a new promise by a debtor to pay a debt, whether then barred by the applicable statute of limitations or not, binds the debtor for a new limitations period. The promise may be express or implied. If it is express, it may be unconditional or conditional, but if conditional, it is not effective until the condition is performed. The promise may be implied from an express acknowledgment of the debt or from part payment of the debt. However, an express acknowledgment of the debt or part payment thereof is only prima facie evidence of a new promise. Such prima facie evidence may be rebutted by other evidence and by the circumstances under which it is made. Zukerkorn (D) denies having taken any of these actions. He asserts that he agreed to pay, and did pay, "a small amount on an old account," but denies having acknowledged the existence of the two stale debts, or that he agreed to pay them, or that he did pay them. Even if Zukerkorn (D) admitted acknowledging the debts or making partial payment on them, such evidence would only create a rebuttable presumption that he made a new promise to pay the debts, and Zukerkorn (D) must be permitted to rebut the presumption such evidence creates. Therefore, the trial court erred in implying a new promise, as a matter of law, from this evidence. That determination must be left to the trier of fact at trial. Therefore, the trial court erred in granting summary judgment as to the Bank's (P) claims relating to the stale debts. Affirmed in part, reversed in part, and remanded.

## ▶ ANALYSIS

The approach taken by the court in this case is similar to that adopted by the Restatement (Second) of Contracts, § 82, which provides: A promise to pay all or part of an antecedent contractual or quasi-contractual indebtedness

*Continued on next page.*

owed by the promisor is binding if the indebtedness is still enforceable or would be except for the effect of a statute of limitations. The following facts operate as such a promise unless other facts indicate a different intention: (1) A voluntary acknowledgment to the obligee, admitting the present existence of the antecedent indebtedness; or (2) A voluntary transfer of money, a negotiable instrument, or other thing by the obligor to the obligee, made as interest on or part payment of or collateral security for the antecedent indebtedness; or (3) A statement to the obligee that the statute of limitations will not be pleaded as a defense. As with the court's decision in this case, the Restatement leaves room for a showing that, notwithstanding these facts, other facts may indicate a different intention.

═■══■═

## Quicknotes

**EXPRESS PROMISE** The expression of an intention to act, or to forbear from acting, granting a right to the promisee to expect and enforce its performance.

**OBLIGEE** Promisee; a party who is the recipient of a promise or obligation to perform.

**OBLIGOR** Promisor; a party who has promised or is obligated to perform.

**PROMISE** The expression of an intention to act, or to forbear from acting, granting a right to the promisee to expect and enforce its performance.

**PROMISOR** Party who promises to render an obligation to another in the future.

**STATUTE OF LIMITATIONS** A law prescribing the period in which a legal action may be commenced.

■══■

# Mills v. Wyman

Caretaker (P) v. Father of ill child (D)

Mass. Sup. Jud. Ct., 20. Mass. (3 Pick.) 207 (1825).

**NATURE OF CASE:** Appeal from dismissal of action to recover upon an alleged promise.

**FACT SUMMARY:** Mills (P) took care of Wyman's (D) son without being requested to do so, and for so doing Wyman (D) promised compensation for expenses arising out of the rendered care. Wyman (D) later refused to compensate Mills (P).

 **RULE OF LAW**
A moral obligation is insufficient consideration for a promise.

**FACTS:** Mills (P) nursed and cared for Levi Wyman, the son of Wyman (D). Upon learning of Mills's (P) acts of kindness toward his son, Wyman (D) promised to repay Mills (P) his expenses incurred in caring for Levi Wyman. Later, Wyman (D) refused to compensate Mills (P) for his expenses. Mills (P) filed an action in the Court of Common Pleas, where Wyman (D) was successful in obtaining a nonsuit against Mills (P). Mills (P) appealed, and the state's highest court granted review.

**ISSUE:** Is a moral obligation sufficient consideration for a promise?

**HOLDING AND DECISION:** (Parker, C.J.) No. A moral obligation is insufficient consideration for a promise. It is said a moral obligation is sufficient consideration to support an express promise. However, the universality of the rule cannot be supported. Therefore, there must be some other preexisting obligation that will suffice as consideration. Affirmed.

**▶ ANALYSIS**

In cases such as this one, the nearly universal holding is that the existing moral obligation is not sufficient basis for the enforcement of an express promise to render the performance that it requires. The general statement is that it is not sufficient consideration for the express promise. The difficulties and differences of opinion involved in the determination of what is a moral obligation are probably much greater than those involved in determining the existence of a legal obligation. This tends to explain the attitude of the majority of courts on the subject and justifies the generally stated rule.

## Quicknotes

**CONSIDERATION** Value given by one party in exchange for performance, or a promise to perform, by another party.

**EXPRESS PROMISE** The expression of an intention to act, or to forbear from acting, granting a right to the promisee to expect and enforce its performance.

**MORAL OBLIGATION** A duty that is not enforceable at law, but is consistent with ethical notions of justice.

**NONSUIT** Judgment against a party who fails to make out a case.

**PROMISE** The expression of an intention to act, or to forbear from acting, granting a right to the promisee to expect and enforce its performance.

# Webb v. McGowin

## Crippled savior (P) v. Estate of saved individual (D)

Ala. Ct. App., 27 Ala. App. 82, 168 So. 196 (1935).

**NATURE OF CASE:** Appeal from dismissal of action to collect on a promise.

**FACT SUMMARY:** Webb (P) saved the now-deceased J. McGowin from grave bodily injury or death by placing himself in grave danger and subsequently suffering grave bodily harm. J. McGowin, in return, promised Webb (P) compensation. McGowin's executors (D) refused to pay the promised compensation.

## RULE OF LAW

A moral obligation is sufficient consideration to support a subsequent promise to pay where the promisor has received a material benefit.

**FACTS:** Webb (P), while in the scope of his duties for the W. T. Smith Lumber Co., was clearing the floor, which required him to drop a 75-lb. pine block from the upper floor of the mill to the ground. Just as Webb (P) was releasing the block, he noticed J. McGowin below and directly under where the block would have fallen. In order to divert the fall of the block, Webb (P) fell with it, breaking an arm and leg and ripping his heel off. The fall left Webb (P) a cripple and incapable of either mental or physical labor. In return for Webb's (P) act, J. McGowin promised to pay Webb (P) $15 every two weeks for the rest of Webb's (P) life. J. McGowin paid the promised payments until his death eight years later. Shortly after J. McGowin's death, the payments were stopped, and Webb (P) brought an action against N. McGowin (D) and J. F. McGowin (D) as executors of J. McGowin's estate for payments due him. The executors (D) of the estate were successful in obtaining a nonsuit against Webb (P) in the lower court. Webb (P) appealed, and the state's intermediate appellate court granted review.

**ISSUE:** Is a moral obligation sufficient consideration to support a subsequent promise to pay where the promisor has received a material benefit?

**HOLDING AND DECISION:** (Bricken, J.) Yes. A moral obligation is sufficient consideration to support a subsequent promise to pay where the promisor has received a material benefit. It is well settled that a moral obligation is a sufficient consideration to support a subsequent promise to pay where the promisor has received a material benefit, although there was no original duty or liability resting on the promisor. Reversed and remanded.

**CONCURRENCE:** (Samford, J.) Although the questions in this case are not free from doubt, and the strict letter of the rule would bar plaintiff's recovery, the law ought not to be separated from justice, at least not where there is such doubt.

## ANALYSIS

In most cases where the moral obligation is asserted, the court feels that the promise should not be enforced; instead of going into the uncertain field of morality, the court chooses to rely upon the rule that moral obligation is not a sufficient consideration. On the other hand, in cases where the promise is one that would have been kept by most citizens and the court feels that enforcement is just, a few courts will enforce the promise using the *Webb v. McGowin* rule. In general, the *Webb v. McGowin* rule is the minority rule and *Mills v. Wyman*, Mass. Sup. Jud. Ct., 20. Mass. (3 Pick.) 207 (1825), is the majority rule.

---

## Quicknotes

**DUTY** An obligation owed by one individual to another.

**LIABILITY** Any obligation or responsibility.

**MATERIAL BENEFIT** An advantage gained by entering into a contract that is essential to the performance of the agreement and without which the contract would not have been entered into.

**MORAL OBLIGATION** A duty that is not enforceable at law, but is consistent with ethical notions of justice.

**PROMISE** The expression of an intention to act, or to forbear from acting, granting a right to the promisee to expect and enforce its performance.

**PROMISOR** Party who promises to render an obligation to another in the future.

# Thomas v. Thomas

Sister-in-law (P) v. Brother-in-law's executor (D)

Q.B., 2 Q.B. 851, 114 Eng. Rep. 330 (1842).

**NATURE OF CASE:** Appeal from judgment for plaintiff in suit for enforcement of a contract.

**FACT SUMMARY:** Contract beneficiary (P) brought suit against contractor's executor (D) for enforcement of contract.

 **RULE OF LAW**
A promise to perform an act may constitute a valuable consideration.

**FACTS:** John Thomas, the deceased husband of Eleanor (P), owned dwelling houses. John told his brother Samuel that he wanted Eleanor (P) to have one of the houses or a certain amount of money. This was incorporated into a written instrument subsequent to John's death in which John agreed to pay to Samuel, as landlord, one dollar annually for Eleanor (P) to be able to remain in the dwelling house. Eleanor (P) did take possession of the dwelling house for a period of time. However, after Samuel's death, Samuel's executors (D) refused to execute a conveyance to Eleanor (P) pursuant to the agreement with John and instead brought an ejectment suit to oust Eleanor (P) from her premises. Eleanor (P) brought suit in trial court for enforcement of John's agreement with his brother to enable her to remain in the dwelling. The court found in her favor, and Samuel's executors (D) appealed.

**ISSUE:** May a promise to perform an act constitute a valuable consideration?

**HOLDING AND DECISION:** (Lord Denman, C.J.) Yes. A promise to perform an act may constitute a valuable consideration. Here, there is nothing whatever to show that the ground rent was payable to a superior landlord. The stipulation for its payment was not a mere proviso, but an express agreement. The agreement showed a sufficient legal consideration quite independent of the moral feeling that disposed the executors to enter into such a contract. Affirmed for the wife Eleanor Thomas (P).

**CONCURRENCE:** (Lord Patterson, J.) Motive is not the same thing with consideration. Consideration means something that is of some value in the eye of the law, moving from the plaintiff.

**CONCURRENCE:** (Lord Coleridge, J.) Here, it is conceded that mere motive need not be stated.

▶ **ANALYSIS**

The *Thomas* case expresses the viewpoint that a court is not obligated to look for legal consideration in any particular part of the contract merely because the consideration is usually stated in some particular part.

■—■

**Quicknotes**

**CONSIDERATION** Value given by one party in exchange for performance, or a promise to perform, by another party.

**CONVEYANCE** The transfer of property, or title to property, from one party to another party.

**EJECTMENT** An action to oust someone in unlawful possession of real property and to restore possession to the party lawfully entitled to it.

**EXECUTOR** – A person designated by an individual to effectuate the disposition of the individual's property pursuant to a testamentary instrument after the individual's death.

**PROMISE** The expression of an intention to act, or to forbear from acting, granting a right to the promisee to expect and enforce its performance.

■—■

# Browning v. Johnson

## Osteopath-seller (P) v. Osteopath-purchaser (D)

Wash. Sup. Ct., 70 Wash. 2d 145, 422 P.2d 314 (1967).

**NATURE OF CASE:** Appeal from judgment for defendant in action for declaratory judgment and restitution.

**FACT SUMMARY:** Browning (P) contended that a contract he made with Johnson (D) to cancel a prior sale contract was unsupported by consideration and was a product of mutual mistake.

## ⛫ RULE OF LAW
A promise that has induced detriment as part of a unilateral contract is supported by sufficient consideration such that the contract must be enforced, regardless of whether the consideration is "adequate."

**FACTS:** Browning (P) and Johnson (D) were both osteopathic doctors and entered into a contract of sale whereby Browning (P) agreed to sell his practice and equipment to Johnson (D). Browning (P) changed his mind about selling and sought to be released from the contract. The parties then entered into a contract canceling the sale contract, whereby Browning (P) promised to pay Johnson (D) $40,000 if Johnson (D) would give up the sale contract. Browning (P) later regretted this bargain, too, and filed an action for declaratory judgment and restitution. The trial court held that the sale contract lacked mutuality and was unenforceable, but that the contract canceling the sale contract was supported by "adequate" consideration and was enforceable. The state's highest court granted review.

**ISSUE:** Is a promise that has induced detriment as part of a unilateral contract supported by sufficient consideration such that the contract must be enforced, regardless of whether the consideration is "adequate"?

**HOLDING AND DECISION:** (Langenbach, J.) Yes. A promise that has induced detriment as part of a unilateral contract is supported by sufficient consideration such that the contract must be enforced, regardless of whether the consideration is "adequate." First, as a terminological matter, "adequate" consideration must be distinguished from "sufficient" consideration. The former is concerned with comparative value, whereas the latter is concerned with that which will support a promise. Also, the former does not necessarily affect the latter. Here, Browning (P) bargained for Johnson's (D) act of giving up the sale contract. Thus, the issue is whether the law regards Johnson's (D) act of giving up that contract as legally "sufficient" consideration to support Browning's (P) promise to pay him for such an act. Regardless of whether the trial court in its holding meant that there was sufficient consideration to support the promise, or that there was not such inadequate consideration as to constitute fraud, the facts show, without having to consider the relative value of that which was exchanged, that there was sufficient consideration to support Browning's (P) promise to pay. The contract at issue is a unilateral contract, which means that a promise has been given in exchange for an act or forbearance. Consideration sufficient to support a promise made as part of a unilateral contract is satisfied where the promisee [Johnson (D)] has incurred a detriment, or the promisor [Browning (P)] has received a benefit at the promisor's request. A detriment is something given up to which the promisee had a right to not give up, or doing or not doing something that the promisee had a right not to do, or not to refrain from doing. Here, both parties were equally informed, had equal bargaining power, and were equally represented by counsel. The bargain was freely entered and made, with each party agreeing on an exchange that each felt would benefit him. Even though Browning (P) may have come to regret the bargain he so made, that alone is insufficient justification for avoiding the contract; Johnson's (D) detriment, induced by Browning (P)—giving up the sale contract—was sufficient consideration for Browning's (P) promise to pay $40,000. Accordingly, the contract will be enforced, and it is not necessary to reach the issue of whether there was mutual mistake. Affirmed.

## ▌ ANALYSIS

The Restatement (Second) of Contracts has done away with the distinction between "sufficient" and "adequate" consideration, instead noting that if a performance is bargained for, there is consideration, and if the consideration requirement is met, there is no additional requirement that there be equivalence in the values exchanged. Determining equivalency of values may be difficult, since subjective considerations may provide value to the parties of which only they are aware. Nonetheless, consideration must have some value.

━■━

## Quicknotes

**CONSIDERATION** Value given by one party in exchange for performance, or a promise to perform, by another party.

*Continued on next page.*

**DECLARATORY JUDGMENT** A judgment of the court establishing the rights of the parties.

**MUTUAL MISTAKE** A mistake by both parties to a contract, who are in agreement as to what the contract terms should be, but the agreement as written fails to reflect that common intent; such contracts are voidable or subject to reformation.

**PROMISE** The expression of an intention to act, or to forbear from acting, granting a right to the promisee to expect and enforce its performance.

**PROMISEE** Party to whom a promise is made.

**RESTITUTION** The return or restoration to rightful owner to prevent unjust enrichment.

**SALE CONTRACT** Contract pursuant to which one party agrees to sell, and the other to purchase, specified goods.

**UNILATERAL CONTRACT** An agreement pursuant to which a party agrees to act without an express exchange for performance on the part of the other party.

# Apfel v. Prudential-Bache Securities, Inc.

Originator of securities issuing system (P) v. Investment bank (D)

N.Y. Ct. App., 81 N.Y.2d 470, 616 N.E.2d 1095 (1993).

**NATURE OF CASE:** Appeal from modification of judgment permitting breach of contract.

**FACT SUMMARY:** Apfel (P) sold a method for computerized securities transactions to Prudential-Bache Securities, Inc. (D), which paid on the agreement for a few years before reneging.

🏛 **RULE OF LAW**
An idea does not have to be novel to serve as consideration in a contract selling the idea to another where the idea has value to the buyer.

**FACTS:** Apfel (P) approached Prudential-Bache Securities, Inc. (Prudential-Bache) (D) with a proposal for issuing municipal securities through a computerized system. After negotiating, Apfel (P) conveyed his idea for a stipulated rate based on use for a term from October 1982 to January 1988. Prudential-Bache (D) was to pay even if the idea became public knowledge. For the first year, Prudential-Bache (D) was the only underwriter using such a system. In 1985, Prudential-Bache (D) refused to make further payments. Apfel (P) filed suit. On motions for summary judgment, the trial court dismissed all causes of action except a claim for breach of contract. The ruling was immediately appealed. The appellate division modified the ruling and held that novelty was required for consideration based on an idea, but the issue was factual. Prudential-Bache (D) appealed, seeking certification of the question of whether novelty was required for consideration based upon an idea.

**ISSUE:** Does an idea have to be novel to serve as consideration in a contract selling the idea to another where the idea has value to the buyer?

**HOLDING AND DECISION:** (Simons, J.) No. An idea does not have to be novel to serve as consideration in a contract selling the idea to another where the idea has value to the buyer. Contract law has long held that consideration exchanged may be grossly unequal and still suffice. Ideas, however, pose a special problem. Since they lack tangibility, it is often difficult to prove the source of an idea. Where the idea is novel, the seller can conclusively show that there was no other source for the idea. In this case, Prudential-Bache (D) does not deny that Apfel (P) conveyed the idea. Instead, Prudential-Bache (D) cites cases where novelty was required to find an idea was conveyed in a contract. However, these cases have been misconstrued. Novelty was only required to prove the source of the idea. Here, the source is admitted. And Prudential-Bache (D) clearly received something of value

since for one year it was the only underwriter using the method. The answer to the certified question is that novelty is not required for an idea to suffice as consideration. Affirmed as modified.

▶ **ANALYSIS**

The intangible nature of ideas makes their sale a difficult proposition. To negotiate a contract, the idea must be expressed to the other party; however, that party then also knows the idea. The idea may have tremendous value, more than sufficient to serve as the basis for a contract. Proving that the idea belonged to the seller can be quite a different matter altogether.

━━━

## Quicknotes

**BREACH OF CONTRACT** Unlawful failure by a party to perform its obligations pursuant to contract.

**CONSIDERATION** Value given by one party in exchange for performance, or a promise to perform, by another party.

**NOVELTY** Requirement for patentability that an invention possess some element that is not found in any prior invention.

**SUMMARY JUDGMENT** Judgment rendered by a court in response to a motion made by one of the parties, claiming that the lack of a question of material fact in respect to an issue warrants disposition of the issue without consideration by the jury.

━━━

# Levine v. Blumenthal

Landlord (P) v. Tenant (D)

N.J. Sup. Ct., 117 N.J.L. 23, 186 A. 457 (1936).

**NATURE OF CASE:** Appeal from judgment for plaintiff in action to recover rent.

**FACT SUMMARY:** Blumenthal (D) told Levine (P) that he could not afford to pay the higher rent called for by the lease for the second year of occupancy. Levine (P) accepted a lower rent for one year and then sued for the deficiency.

## RULE OF LAW
Neither economic disasters nor acceptance of partial payments are adequate consideration for the modification of contractual obligations.

**FACTS:** Blumenthal (D) rented a store from Levine (P) for two years. The lease required Blumenthal (D) to pay $175 per month the first year, $200 per month the second year. At the end of the first year, Blumenthal (D) told Levine (P) that economic conditions were so bad he couldn't afford to pay the higher rent and would have to leave or maybe go out of business. Levine (P) agreed to allow Blumenthal (D) to remain if he continued to pay $175 per month. Blumenthal (D) left at the end of the second year, having paid $175 the entire second year, except for the last month's rent, which was never paid. Levine (P) sued for the last month's rent plus $25 per month for the last 11 months of the contract. Blumenthal (D) argued accord and satisfaction as to the $175 payments paid under the oral modification. He also argued that his remaining as a tenant during the economic crisis was adequate consideration to support the modification. The trial judge held that there was no consideration for the modification and found for Levine (P). The state's highest court granted review.

**ISSUE:** Are either economic disasters or acceptance of partial payments adequate consideration for the modification of contractual obligations?

**HOLDING AND DECISION:** (Heher, J.) No. Neither economic disasters nor acceptance of partial payments are adequate consideration for the modification of contractual obligations. The payment of part of an obligation is not consideration for excusing repayment of the whole debt. Some additional type of consideration is required. General economic adversity will never supply the needed consideration nor will Blumenthal's (D) claim of accord and satisfaction. The debt is totally liquidated. There was no dispute as to amount owed. Blumenthal (D) did no more than he was legally obligated to do. There was no consideration for a reduced rental. Since there was no dispute as to the amount due, there was no accord and satisfaction. Judgment affirmed.

## ► ANALYSIS

In *Watkins & Son v. Carrig*, 91 N.H. 459 (1941), the court came to the opposite conclusion. There, it held that a promise in adjustment of a contractual promise already outstanding (i.e., a modification) may be enforceable. If the parties are acting to meet changed conditions and circumstances, the court should enforce the agreement if it is a reasonable practice or understanding in business and commerce.

---

## Quicknotes

**ACCORD AND SATISFACTION** The performance of an agreement between two parties, one of whom has a valid claim against the other, to settle the controversy.

**CONSIDERATION** Value given by one party in exchange for performance, or a promise to perform, by another party.

**CONTRACTUAL OBLIGATION** A duty that someone agrees to perform pursuant to a contract.

**DEBT** An obligation incurred by a person who promises to render payment or compensation to another.

**LIQUIDATE** To pay or settle by other means an obligation or debt.

# Alaska Packers' Association v. Domenico

Cannery operator (D) v. Seaman (P)

117 F. 99 (9th Cir. 1902).

**NATURE OF CASE:** Appeal from judgment for plaintiffs in action for breach of contract.

**FACT SUMMARY:** A group of seamen (P), who had agreed to ship from San Francisco to Alaska at a fixed pay, refused to continue working once they reached Alaska and demanded a new contract with more compensation.

## 🏛 RULE OF LAW
A promise to pay a man for doing that which he is already under contract to do is without consideration.

**FACTS:** A group of seamen (P) entered into a written contract with Alaska Packers' Association (Packers) (D) to go from San Francisco to Alaska on the Packers' (D) ships and to work as sailors and fishermen. Compensation was fixed at $60 for the season and $0.02 for each salmon caught. Once they had reached port in Alaska, the seamen (P) refused to continue work and demanded that compensation be increased to $100. A superintendent for Packers (D), unable to hire a new crew, drew up a new contract, substituted in the sum of $100, and signed it, although he expressed doubt at the time that he had the authority to do so. The seamen (P) resumed work, but upon the ship's return to San Francisco, Packers (D) refused to honor the new contract. The seamen (P) filed suit for breach of contract, and the district court entered judgment for them. The court of appeals granted review.

**ISSUE:** Is a promise to pay a man for doing that which he is already under contract to do without consideration?

**HOLDING AND DECISION:** (Ross, J.) Yes. A promise to pay a man for doing that which he is already under contract to do is without consideration. The performance of a preexisting legal duty guaranteed by contract is not sufficient consideration to support a promise. No astute reasoning can change the plain fact that the party who refuses to perform and thereby coerces a promise from the other party to pay him an increased compensation for doing that which he is legally bound to do takes an unjustifiable advantage of the necessities of the other party. The parties in the present case have not voluntarily rescinded or modified their contract. The Packers (D) second contract with the seamen (P) is unenforceable, although the seamen (P) completed their performance in reliance on it. Reversed and remanded.

## ▶ ANALYSIS

A few cases have held that the promise to pay additional compensation is enforceable. Consideration is found in the

promisee's giving up his power to breach the first contract. In other words, by refusing to continue work, the promisee has invoked the option to pay money damages rather than to invest his labor in further performance. This view has been questioned on the ground that a promisee may have the power to breach a contract but certainly not the legal right, and in any event, he should not be encouraged to do so.

▬▬

## Quicknotes

**BREACH OF CONTRACT** Unlawful failure by a party to perform its obligations pursuant to contract.

**COMPENSATION** Payment given in exchange for a service rendered or injury incurred, intended to satisfy the receiving party as an equivalent transfer of value.

**CONSIDERATION** Value given by one party in exchange for performance, or a promise to perform, by another party.

**PROMISE** The expression of an intention to act, or to forbear from acting, granting a right to the promisee to expect and enforce its performance.

**PROMISEE** Party to whom a promise is made.

▬▬

# Angel v. Murray

Citizen (P) v. City official (D)

R.I. Sup. Ct., 113 R.I. 482, 322 A.2d 630 (1974).

**NATURE OF CASE:** Appeal from judgment for plaintiff in suit seeking repayment of money allegedly paid improperly.

**FACT SUMMARY:** Angel (P) objected when the City of Newport (D) paid Maher (D) $10,000 per year more than the original contract price for collecting refuse in the City (D).

> **RULE OF LAW**
> An agreement by which a party is promised additional compensation for performing a duty which he is already contractually obligated to undertake may be enforced if the new agreement was voluntarily entered into and was prompted by the occurrence of events which were not anticipated when the original contract was executed.

**FACTS:** Maher (D) entered into a series of contracts to collect refuse for the City of Newport (D). One of these contracts, executed in 1964, obligated Maher (D) to pick up all refuse generated within the City (D). The contract entitled Maher (D) to receive $137,000 per year for five years. On two occasions, however, Maher (D) appeared before the city council and was awarded an additional $10,000 per year. In each instance, Maher (D) cited the fact that the city's dwelling units had increased by 400 instead of by the 10 to 25 new units that had been anticipated. After the additional payments had been made, Angel (P) and others (P) sued Maher (D), the City (D), and Murray (D), who was the Director of Finance for the City (D). The suit sought repayment of the $20,000 that had been paid over and above the original contract price. The trial judge, reasoning that Maher (D) had had a preexisting duty to collect the City's (D) refuse and therefore was not entitled to additional compensation for performing that service, granted the relief sought. Maher (D) appealed, and the state's highest court granted review.

**ISSUE:** May an agreement by which a party is promised additional compensation for performing a duty which he is already contractually obligated to undertake be enforced if the new agreement was voluntarily entered into and was prompted by the occurrence of events which were not anticipated when the original contract was executed?

**HOLDING AND DECISION:** (Roberts, C.J.) Yes. An agreement by which a party is promised additional compensation for performing a duty which he is already contractually obligated to undertake may be enforced if the new agreement was voluntarily entered into and was prompted by the occurrence of events that were not

anticipated when the original contract was executed. The trial court erred in concluding that the $20,000 could not be allocated without the approval of the city manager. But it was also error to apply the preexisting duty rule to this case. Recently, courts have come to realize that rule should be applied cautiously. It is true that Maher (D) was already obligated to collect the City's (D) refuse and thus gave no new consideration in exchange for the City's (D) promises to pay him additional amounts totaling $20,000. But, those promises were made before the parties had fully performed the original refuse collection contract, and the new agreement was entered into voluntarily. Moreover, the modification was fair and equitable and was motivated by events that were not anticipated at the time of the original contract. Under these circumstances, § 89D(a) of the Restatement (Second) of Contracts clearly entitles Maher (D) to retain the $20,000 paid pursuant to the City's (D) promises. Reversed and remanded.

**ANALYSIS**

Countless cases have recognized and applied the preexisting duty rule. However, the rule has, over the years, become riddled with exceptions. Perhaps the most important of these exceptions is that which renders a modification enforceable if it appends any additional condition, no matter how insignificant, to the preexisting duty of the party seeking to enforce the new agreement. Thus, a requirement changing the time or place of delivery or the mode of payment may make the preexisting duty rule inapplicable. In fact, the present viability of the rule is questionable in light of § 2-209 of the Uniform Commercial Code, which provides "[a]n agreement modifying a contract within this Article needs no consideration to be binding."

---

## Quicknotes

**COMPENSATION** Payment given in exchange for a service rendered or injury incurred, intended to satisfy the receiving party as an equivalent transfer of value.

**CONSIDERATION** Value given by one party in exchange for performance, or a promise to perform, by another party.

**DUTY** An obligation owed by one individual to another.

**JUDGMENT** A determination of the rights among the parties by a court having jurisdiction over the matter.

*Continued on next page.*

**PREEXISTING DUTY** A common-law doctrine that renders unenforceable a promise to perform a duty, which the promisor is already legally obligated to perform.

**PROMISE** The expression of an intention to act, or to forbear from acting, granting a right to the promisee to expect and enforce its performance.

**PROMISEE** Party to whom a promise is made.

# Rehm-Zeiher Co. v. F.G. Walker Co.

Whiskey merchant (P) v. Distiller (D)

Ky. Ct. App., 156 Ky. 6, 160 S.W. 777 (1913).

**NATURE OF CASE:** Appeal from judgment for defendant in action to recover damages for breach of contract.

**FACT SUMMARY:** Buyer (P) agreed to purchase from Seller (D) a given number of whiskey cases a year for five years but reserved the right to refuse acceptance at any time for "any unforeseen reason."

**RULE OF LAW**
A reservation in a purchase agreement by the buyer under which the buyer may, at buyer's own discretion, refuse to make any purchase voids the contract for lack of mutuality.

**FACTS:** Rehm-Zeiher Co. (P), a seller of whiskey, agreed to purchase from F.G. Walker (D), a distiller, 2,000 cases of whiskey in 1909, 3,000 in 1910, 4,000 in 1911, and 5,000 in 1912. The contract recited that "If for any unforeseen reason [Rehm-Zeiher (P)] find that they cannot use the full amount . . . [F.G. Walker (D)] agrees to release them from the contract for the amount desired by [Rehm-Zeiher (P)]." In 1909, Rehm-Zeiher (P) only ordered and received 786 cases of the 2,000 called for by the contract, and in 1910 it only ordered and received 1,200 cases of the 3,000 called for by the contract. In 1911, with whiskey having advanced in price, F.G. Walker (D) refused to make any further deliveries. Rehm-Zeiher (P) thereupon brought a suit for breach of contract. The trial court ruled for F.G. Walker (D), and the state's intermediate appellate court granted review.

**ISSUE:** Does a reservation in a purchase agreement by the buyer under which the buyer may, at buyer's own discretion, refuse to make any purchase void the contract for lack of mutuality?

**HOLDING AND DECISION:** (Carroll, J.) Yes. A reservation in a purchase agreement by the buyer under which the buyer may, at buyer's own discretion, refuse to make any purchase voids the contract for lack of mutuality. Where a buyer in a purchase contract has reserved unto himself the right to evade his obligation for any "unforeseen reason" and left the meaning of these words to his own discretion, the contract is void for lack of mutuality. Any reason Rehm-Zeiher (P) might assign for not taking the whiskey would relieve it of any obligation to do so; the reason need not be a good one or reasonable. Thus, the fact that Rehm-Zeiher (P) accepted a part of the whiskey in 1909 and 1910 did not oblige them to take any of it in the subsequent years. Mutuality being lacking, the contract may be distinguished from one in which A has agreed to furnish B all the goods that B will require in the operation of his business. This form of an output contract is not lacking in mutuality. Courts, in recognition of the fluctuating needs of business, have upheld such contracts despite their indefiniteness. While the quantity under contract is incapable of exact measurements, it is capable of an approximately accurate forecast ascertainable by the vendor. Affirmed.

**ANALYSIS**

A promise to buy "all that I want" is termed illusory and is unenforceable by either party for want of mutuality. However, a promise to buy "all that I need" encumbers the promisor with a legal detriment since he must purchase from the promisee-supplier or not at all. Similarly, a promise to sell "all that I produce" is enforceable because the promisor, in being restricted to sell his goods to only one purchaser, has suffered a legal detriment.

---

**Quicknotes**

**BREACH OF CONTRACT** Unlawful failure by a party to perform its obligations pursuant to contract.

**DAMAGES** Monetary compensation that may be awarded by the court to a party who has sustained injury or loss to his person, property or rights due to another party's unlawful act, omission or negligence.

**JUDGMENT** A determination of the rights among the parties by a court having jurisdiction over the matter.

**MUTUALITY** Reciprocal actions of two parties; in a contract context, refers to a mutual promise between two parties to perform an action in exchange for performance on the part of the other party.

**PROMISE** The expression of an intention to act, or to forbear from acting, granting a right to the promisee to expect and enforce its performance.

**PROMISOR** Party who promises to render an obligation to another in the future.

# McMichael v. Price

## Seller of sand (D) v. Purchaser of sand (P)

Okla. Sup. Ct., 177 Okla. 186, 58 P.2d 549 (1936).

**NATURE OF CASE:** Appeal from verdict for plaintiff in action for damages for breach of a requirements contract.

**FACT SUMMARY:** Price (P), a salesman of sand doing business as Sooner Sand Company, agreed to purchase all the sand he could sell for out-of-city shipment from McMichael (D), who agreed to furnish all the sand Price (P) could sell for out-of-city shipment at 60 percent of the current market price of sand at place of destination of shipment.

> ### 🏛 RULE OF LAW
> Where one party promises to sell to another all that the latter can use, the obligation of the parties to sell and buy must be mutual to render the contract binding.

**FACTS:** Price (P), doing business as Sooner Sand Company, made the following agreement with McMichael (D): Price (P) agreed to purchase and accept from McMichael (D) all the sand of various grades and quality that Price (P) could sell for shipment outside the city of Tulsa provided McMichael (D) furnished and loaded sand at least equal in quality to the sand sold by other companies in the Tulsa area for a sum per ton representing 60 percent of the current market price per ton at the place of destination of shipment. McMichael (D) agreed to furnish all sand of various grades and quality that Price (P) could sell for shipment outside of Tulsa and load all sand in suitable railway cars within a reasonable time after receiving a verbal or written order from Price (P). McMichael (D) failed to deliver, alleging Price (P) was not bound to any promise. A jury rendered a judgment for Price (P), and the state's highest court granted review.

**ISSUE:** Where one party promises to sell to another all that the latter can use, must the obligation of the parties to sell and buy be mutual to render the contract binding?

**HOLDING AND DECISION:** (Osborn, V.C.J.) Yes. Where one party promises to sell to another all that the latter can use, the obligation of the parties to sell and buy must be mutual to render the contract binding. The contract is specific in requiring Price (P) to buy all sand he can sell from McMichael (D), and McMichael (D) is to furnish all sand Price (P) can sell to Price (P). While McMichael (D) claims that Price (P) had no established business at the time, the contract states Price (P) is engaged in the business of selling and shipping sand. Even so, Price (P) was an experienced sand salesman, which McMichael (D) knew. The parties anticipated that on account of

Price's (P) experience, acquaintances, and connections, he would be able to sell a substantial amount to their mutual profit. Affirmed.

## ▶ ANALYSIS

This was a "requirement" contract, that is, McMichael (D) was to provide according to Price's (P) needs. An "output" contract is one where buyer agrees to take all the goods seller produces. The court looks to see if buyer has "a free way out" of the contract. The modern view is to find the requirement of mutuality satisfied without a commitment by the buyer to take a fixed quantity of goods. Uniform Commercial Code § 2-306 states the essential test to be whether the buyer is acting in good faith. Some courts will not find a contract where the buyer is a middleman or does not have an established business. There are cases on both sides, but those courts which would determine this case oppositely would find the lack of an established business to make the requirements of the buyer indefinite and, hence, his promise illusory.

## Quicknotes

**BREACH OF CONTRACT** Unlawful failure by a party to perform its obligations pursuant to contract.

**DAMAGES** Monetary compensation that may be awarded by the court to a party who has sustained injury or loss to his person, property or rights due to another party's unlawful act, omission or negligence.

**ILLUSORY PROMISE** A promise that is not legally enforceable because performance of the obligation by the promisor is completely within his discretion.

**MUTUALITY** Reciprocal actions of two parties; in a contract context, refers to mutual promises between two parties to perform an action in exchange for performance on the part of the other party.

**PROMISE** The expression of an intention to act, or to forbear from acting, granting a right to the promisee to expect and enforce its performance.

**PROMISEE** Party to whom a promise is made.

# Wood v. Lucy, Lady Duff-Gordon

Fashion promoter (P) v. Fashion designer (D)

N.Y. Ct. App., 222 N.Y. 88, 118 N.E. 214 (1917).

**NATURE OF CASE:** Appeal from reversal of judgment for plaintiff in action for damages for breach of a contract for an exclusive right.

**FACT SUMMARY:** Wood (P), in a complicated agreement, received the exclusive right for one year, renewable on a year-to-year basis if not terminated by 90-day notice, to endorse designs with Lucy's (D) name and to market all her fashion designs, for which she would receive one-half the profits derived. Lucy (D) broke the contract by placing her endorsement on designs without Wood's (P) knowledge.

---

**RULE OF LAW**
If a promise may be implied from the writing even though it is imperfectly expressed, there is a valid contract.

---

**FACTS:** Lucy (D), a famous-name fashion designer, contracted with Wood (P) that for her granting to him an exclusive right to endorse designs with her name and to market and license all of her designs, they were to split the profits derived by Wood (P) in half. The exclusive right was for a period of one year, renewable on a year-to-year basis and terminable upon 90 days' notice. Lucy (D) placed her endorsement on fabrics, dresses, and millinery without Wood's (P) knowledge and in violation of the contract. Lucy (D) claimed that the agreement lacked the elements of a contract, as Wood (P) allegedly was not bound to do anything. The trial court held for Wood (P), the state's intermediate appellate court reversed, and the state's highest court granted review.

**ISSUE:** If a promise may be implied from the writing even though it is imperfectly expressed, is there a valid contract?

**HOLDING AND DECISION:** (Cardozo, J.) Yes. If a promise may be implied from the writing even though it is imperfectly expressed, there is a valid contract. While the contract did not precisely state that Wood (P) had promised to use reasonable efforts to place Lucy's (D) endorsement and market her designs, such a promise can be implied. The implication arises from the circumstances. Lucy (D) gave an exclusive privilege, and the acceptance of the exclusive agency was an acceptance of its duties. Lucy's (D) sole compensation was to be one-half the profits resulting from Wood's (P) efforts. Unless he gave his efforts, she could never receive anything. Without an implied promise, the transaction could not have had such business efficacy as they must have intended it to have. Wood's (P) promise to make monthly accountings and to

acquire patents and copyrights as necessary showed the intention of the parties that the promise has value by showing that Wood (P) had some duties. The promise to pay Lucy (D) half the profits and make monthly accountings was a promise to use reasonable efforts to bring profits and revenues into existence. Reversed.

---

▶ **ANALYSIS**

A bilateral contract can be express, implied in fact, or a little of each. The finding of an implied promise for the purpose of finding sufficient consideration to support an express promise is an important technique of the courts in order to uphold agreements that seem to be illusory and to avoid problems of mutuality of obligation. This case is the leading case on the subject. It is codified in Uniform Commercial Code § 2-306(2), where an agreement for exclusive dealing in goods imposes, unless otherwise agreed, an obligation to use best efforts by both parties.

---

## Quicknotes

**BILATERAL CONTRACT** An agreement pursuant to which each party promises to undertake an obligation, or to forbear from acting.

**BREACH OF CONTRACT** Unlawful failure by a party to perform its obligations pursuant to contract.

**EXPRESS CONTRACT** A contract the terms of which are specifically stated; may be oral or written.

**IMPLIED CONTRACT** An agreement between parties that may be inferred from their general course of conduct.

**IMPLIED PROMISE** A promise inferred by law from a document as a whole and the circumstances surrounding its implementation.

**MUTUALITY OF OBLIGATION** Requires that both parties to a contract be bound or else neither is bound.

**PROMISE** The expression of an intention to act, or to forbear from acting, granting a right to the promisee to expect and enforce its performance.

**PROMISEE** Party to whom a promise is made.

# Omni Group, Inc. v. Seattle-First National Bank

Real estate developer (P) v. Property owner (D)

Wash. Ct. App., 32 Wash. App. 22, 645 P.2d 727 (1982).

**NATURE OF CASE:** Appeal from the denial of enforcement of a contract for the sale of realty.

**FACT SUMMARY:** The Clarks (D) contended that by making their contractual obligations subject to a satisfactory engineer's and architect's feasibility report, Omni Group, Inc. (P) rendered its promise to purchase the Clarks' (D) land illusory and the contract unenforceable.

## RULE OF LAW

A contract condition calling for a party's satisfaction with the performance of an act does not render that party's promise to perform illusory and the contract unenforceable.

**FACTS:** Omni Group, Inc. (Omni) (P) signed an earnest money agreement to purchase the Clarks' (D) land. The agreement provided that Omni's (P) performance was subject to its receiving a satisfactory engineer's and architect's feasibility report concerning the land's development potential. Subsequently, Omni (P) notified the Clarks (D) it would forgo the study. After further negotiations, the Clarks (D) refused to go through with the transaction, and Omni (P) sued for breach of contract. The Clarks (D) defended on the basis that by making its performance conditional upon receipt of a satisfactory feasibility report, Omni (P) rendered its promise illusory, and, therefore, the contract lacked consideration and was unenforceable. The trial court entered judgment for the Clarks (D), and Omni (P) appealed.

**ISSUE:** Does a contract condition calling for a party's satisfaction with the performance of an act render that party's promise to perform illusory and the contract unenforceable?

**HOLDING AND DECISION:** (James, J.) No. A contract condition calling for a party's satisfaction with the performance of an act does not render that party's promise to perform illusory and the contract unenforceable. A contract condition which requires a party's satisfaction with the performance of an act imposes on that party the duty to exercise his judgment, concerning whether the performance is satisfactory, in good faith. In this case, Omni's (P) acceptance of the feasibility report was not left to its unfettered discretion. It was bound to act in good faith in either accepting it or rejecting it. Therefore, the promise was not illusory; it supplied sufficient consideration for the Clarks' (D) promise to sell, and a valid contract was formed. Reversed and remanded.

## ANALYSIS

This case illustrates the requirement of good faith in contracts calling for the satisfaction of a party as a condition precedent to his obligations under the contract. This requirement exists where the performance must meet the subjective satisfaction of the party. In such a case, some courts allow evidence of the unreasonableness of the rejection of performance to show a lack of good faith. The good faith rule is codified in Restatement (Second) of Contracts, § 254, and is derived from the *Case of Devoine Co. v. International Co.*, 136 A. 37 (Md. 1927).

## Quicknotes

**BREACH OF CONTRACT** Unlawful failure by a party to perform its obligations pursuant to contract.

**CONSIDERATION** Value given by one party in exchange for performance, or a promise to perform, by another party.

**GOOD FAITH** An honest intention to abstain from taking advantage of another.

**ILLUSORY PROMISE** A promise that is not legally enforceable because performance of the obligation by the promisor is completely within his discretion.

**PROMISE** The expression of an intention to act, or to forbear from acting, granting a right to the promisee to expect and enforce its performance.

**PROMISEE** Party to whom a promise is made.

# Ricketts v. Scothorn

Executor of promisor's estate (D) v. Promisee (P)

Neb. Sup. Ct., 57 Neb. 51, 77 N.W. 365 (1898).

**NATURE OF CASE:** Appeal from judgment for plaintiff in action to compel payment on a promissory note given without consideration.

**FACT SUMMARY:** In reliance on her grandfather's promise to pay money, Scothorn (P) quit her employment.

## RULE OF LAW
Equitable estoppel may make binding a promise unsupported by consideration if the promise reasonably induced action or forbearance and if injustice will be avoided by its enforcement.

**FACTS:** J.C. Ricketts gave his granddaughter, Scothorn (P), a promissory note for $2,000 on demand. Ricketts indicated that the note was for the purpose of freeing Scothorn (P) from the necessity of working. Scothorn (P) immediately quit her employment. J.C. Ricketts thereafter died, and Scothorn (P) sued A.D. Ricketts (D), executor of the estate, for the amount due on the note. The trial court rendered judgment for Scothorn (P), and the state's highest court granted review.

**ISSUE:** May equitable estoppel make binding a promise unsupported by consideration if the promise reasonably induced action or forbearance and if injustice will be avoided by its enforcement?

**HOLDING AND DECISION:** (Sullivan, J.) Yes. Equitable estoppel may make binding a promise unsupported by consideration if the promise reasonably induced action or forbearance and if injustice will be avoided by its enforcement. When a promisee is induced by a promise to change his position in accordance with the real or apparent intention of the promisor, the doctrine of estoppel precludes the promisor from later claiming that the promise was not supported by consideration. This remedy is equitable in nature and is designed to prevent the gross injustice which would otherwise result. Affirmed.

## ANALYSIS

In this leading case, the court recognizes that Scothorn's (P) abandoning her job was not consideration for the note. Rather, the note was a pure gift and, thus, absent reliance, would ordinarily not be enforced because of lack of a bargained-for consideration. Traditionally, the estoppel doctrine had been limited to cases where one party had represented a fact to another party who then relied on the fact as represented. In the present case, the court for the first time extended the estoppel doctrine to promissory expressions (hence, "promissory estoppel") (Cf. Rest. (2d)

§ 90, states the most recent version of the doctrine.) Caveat: Courts have often confused and blended the doctrine of estoppel with the doctrine of consideration, resulting in such statements as: "The reliance on the promise serves as the consideration for that promise." This is conceptually misleading since the promissory estoppel doctrine is basically a twentieth-century exception to the general rule which requires every enforceable promise to be supported by a bargained-for consideration.

## Quicknotes

**CONSIDERATION** Value given by one party in exchange for performance, or a promise to perform, by another party.

**EQUITABLE ESTOPPEL** A doctrine that precludes a person from asserting a right to which he or she was entitled due to his or her action, conduct or failing to act, causing another party to justifiably rely on such conduct to his or her detriment.

**ESTOPPEL** An equitable doctrine precluding a party from asserting a right to the detriment of another, who justifiably relied on the conduct.

**GIFT** A transfer of property to another person that is voluntary and without consideration.

**PROMISSORY NOTE A** written promise to tender a stated amount of money at a designated time and to a designated person.

# Allegheny College v. National Chautauqua County Bank of Jamestown

## College (P) v. Executor of donor's estate (D)

N.Y. Ct. App., 246 N.Y. 369, 159 N.E. 173 (1927).

**NATURE OF CASE:** Appeal from affirmance of judgment for defendant in action to enforce pledge of charitable contribution.

**FACT SUMMARY:** Johnston pledged $5,000 after her death to Allegheny College (P) if it would set up a memorial fund in her name.

## 🏛 RULE OF LAW
When a donee complies with conditions imposed on a charitable gift promised by a donor, there is sufficient consideration to support the promised gift.

**FACTS:** Johnston promised Allegheny College ("the College") (P) $5,000 30 days after her death if sufficient funds remained after the payment of her specific bequests. She stated that the money should be used to fund a scholarship in her name. She gave the College (P) $1,000 as a down payment. She later attempted to revoke the bequest. After her death, the College (P) submitted a $4,000 claim to her executor, National Chautauqua County Bank of Jamestown ("the Bank") (D). The Bank (D) refused to honor the request. At trial, the court found for the Bank (D) on the basis that no consideration for the promise was present, and the state's intermediate appellate court affirmed. The College (P) appealed on the basis that their efforts to comply with Johnston's scholarship requests were adequate consideration to enforce the gift. The state's highest court granted review.

**ISSUE:** When a donee complies with conditions imposed on a charitable gift promised by a donor, is there sufficient consideration to support the promised gift?

**HOLDING AND DECISION:** (Cardozo, C.J.) Yes. When a donee complies with conditions imposed on a charitable gift promised by a donor, there is sufficient consideration to support the promised gift. Consideration does not have to be measured in terms of its economic worth. Even a slight legal detriment or the performance of some condition may be adequate consideration. This is especially true with respect to charitable pledges. Courts are very liberal in attempting to find consideration to support the pledge. Therefore, when, as here, the contributor has imposed conditions that the donee has attempted to honor, there is sufficient consideration to support the pledge. By accepting the $1,000 down payment, the College (P) impliedly agreed to comply with Johnston's scholarship request. It is not necessary to determine whether promissory estoppel was present. The College's (P) attempt to perform its obligation under the pledge is sufficient consideration. Judgment reversed.

**DISSENT:** (Kellogg, J.) The pledge was a gift, not an exchange of promises. Since the College (P) has not performed the "condition," under the majority's rationale, the contract has not been accepted. The College (P), in order to accept the pledge, would have to perform. The act is the bargained-for consideration, and until it has been performed, the promise need not be kept. Here, however, there is no showing that the pledge was a unilateral contract. It was a gift not supported by consideration.

## ▎ ANALYSIS

Most cases enforcing gifts are based on a theory of detrimental reliance and equitable estoppel on the gift. For example, where an uncle tells his nephew to purchase a set of skis and the uncle will pay him later for them, it would be unfair to refuse enforcement if the nephew's reliance was reasonable, e.g., uncle was rich or uncle was penniless.

━━━

## Quicknotes

**CHARITABLE CONTRIBUTION** A gift of property or value given for charitable uses to a qualified organization or entity, and deductible by the grantor against his or her current tax liability.

**CONSIDERATION** Value given by one party in exchange for performance, or a promise to perform, by another party.

**DONEE** A person to whom a gift is made.

**DONOR** A person who gives real or personal property or value.

**PROMISSORY ESTOPPEL** A promise that is enforceable if the promisor should reasonably expect that it will induce action or forbearance on the part of the promisee, and does in fact cause such action or forbearance, and it is the only means of avoiding injustice.

━━━

# Congregation Kadimah Toras-Moshe v. DeLeo

Temple (P) v. Estate administrator (D)

Mass. Sup. Jud. Ct., 405 Mass. 365, 540 N.E.2d 691 (1989).

**NATURE OF CASE:** Appeal from summary dismissal of action for damages for breach of contract.

**FACT SUMMARY:** Congregation Kadimah Toras-Moshe (P) sought to enforce a decedent's oral promise to donate money to it.

## RULE OF LAW
An oral promise to donate money is unenforceable where there has been no reliance on or detriment from the promise.

**FACTS:** During the course of a terminal illness, in the presence of witnesses, a decedent orally promised to donate $25,000 to Congregation Kadimah Toras-Moshe ("the Congregation") (P). The decedent did not complete the gift before his death. When DeLeo (D), the estate's administrator, refused to give over the money, the Congregation (P) sued, having already incorporated the sum into its budget. The trial court dismissed, and the state's highest court granted review.

**ISSUE:** Is an oral promise to donate money enforceable where there has been no reliance on or detriment from the promise?

**HOLDING AND DECISION:** (Liacos, C.J.) No. An oral promise to donate money is unenforceable where there has been no reliance on or detriment from the promise. A gratuitous promise to do or give something to another, without any benefit accruing to the promisor, lacks the element of consideration, and therefore no contract has been entered. Justifiable detrimental reliance may constitute consideration. Here, however, the mere incorporation of the $25,000 into the Congregation's (P) budget was insufficient to create an estoppel. While the Congregation's (P) incorporation of the promised funds into its budget reflected its hope or expectation of receiving the funds, a hope or expectation, even if well founded, is not equivalent of either legal detriment or reliance. As there was no consideration or basis for an estoppel here, the promise was unenforceable. Affirmed.

## ANALYSIS

In a sense, an attempt to enforce an oral promise after the promisor's death would be very much like attempting to enforce an oral will, a situation wide open to fraudulent claims. This approach is rejected in almost all jurisdictions.

Due to serious proof problems with oral wills, virtually all states require wills to be written and witnessed.

## Quicknotes

**BREACH OF CONTRACT** Unlawful failure by a party to perform its obligations pursuant to contract.

**CONSIDERATION** Value given by one party in exchange for performance, or a promise to perform, by another party.

**ORAL PROMISE** An oral declaration of a person's intention to do or refrain from doing an act which by itself, is not legally binding.

# Agreement

## Quick Reference Rules of Law

# Embry v. Hargadine, McKittrick Dry Goods Co.

## Employee (P) v. Employer (D)

Mo. Ct. App., 127 Mo. App. 383, 105 S.W. 777 (1907).

**NATURE OF CASE:** Appeal from jury verdict in action to enforce renewal of employment contract.

**FACT SUMMARY:** Embry (P) was allegedly rehired by Hargadine, McKittrick Dry Goods Co. (McKittrick) (D) after his employment contract had expired. Hargadine, McKittrick (D) denied the rehiring.

## 🏛 RULE OF LAW
The secret feelings, intentions, or beliefs of a party will not affect the formation of a contract if the party's words and acts indicate that the party intended to enter into a binding agreement.

**FACTS:** Embry (P) was working for Hargadine, McKittrick Dry Goods Co. (McKittrick) (D) under a written employment contract. After its expiration, Embry (P) approached McKittrick (D) and demanded a new contract or he would immediately quit. According to Embry (P), McKittrick (D) agreed to rehire him. Embry (P) was terminated in February of the next year. He brought suit to recover the amount due him under the contract. McKittrick (D) swore that the conversation never took place and that Embry (P) had not been rehired. The judge instructed the jury that even if the conversation occurred as related by Embry (P), to form a contract both parties must have intended to enter into a binding agreement. The jury found against Embry (P). He appealed on the basis that the judge's instruction was incorrect, that if McKittrick (D) conveyed by word and deed his intent to rehire Embry (P), a binding contract was formed regardless of McKittrick's (D) secret intention.

**ISSUE:** Will the secret feelings, intentions, or beliefs of a party affect the formation of a contract if the party's words and acts indicate that the party intended to enter into a binding agreement?

**HOLDING AND DECISION:** (Goode, J.) No. The secret feelings, intentions, or beliefs of a party will not affect the formation of a contract if the party's words and acts indicate that the party intended to enter into a binding agreement. If the other party reasonably relies on the promise, an undisclosed intention will not affect the formation of a binding contract. Therefore, the trial judge's instructions were erroneous. If the jury reasonably believed that McKittrick (D) had promised to rehire Embry (P), it is immaterial whether McKittrick (D) meant his promise or not. It is obvious that Embry (P) believed a valid contract had been formed because he remained on the job. His reliance was reasonable since McKittrick (D) was the president of the company and had the authority to rehire him.

Therefore, the case must be remanded for a new trial since it cannot be determined on what basis the jury found for McKittrick (D). The same holding applies where a reasonable person would interpret the meaning of a conversation as the formation of a binding contract. The fact that McKittrick (D) did not intend to rehire Embry (P) is immaterial if the natural interpretation of the conversation is that he was being rehired. Again, McKittrick's (D) undisclosed intent is immaterial. Reversed and remanded.

## ▶ ANALYSIS

In order to analyze the manifest intentions of the parties, there are several standards of interpretation that may be applied to their words. First, there is the general accepted meaning of the terms used. Then, there is the meaning of the term according to trade or custom. Finally, there is the meaning the parties may have assigned to the term in the course of past dealings. By utilizing these methods, a court attempts to determine what the parties thought they were doing and to give effect to their legitimate expectations.

---

## Quicknotes

**PROMISE** The expression of an intention to act, or to forbear from acting, granting a right to the promisee to expect and enforce its performance.

**PROMISEE** Party to whom a promise is made.

# Lucy v. Zehmer

Real property purchaser (P) v. Unintended real property seller (D)

Va. Sup. Ct. App., 196 Va. 493, 84 S.E.2d 516 (1954).

**NATURE OF CASE:** Appeal from judgment for defendants in action for specific performance of a land sale contract.

**FACT SUMMARY:** Zehmer (D) claimed his offer to sell his farm to Lucy (P) was made in jest.

## RULE OF LAW
The assent necessary to form a contract will be imputed to a person based on the reasonable meaning given to his words and acts, rather than depending on his unexpressed intentions.

**FACTS:** Zehmer (D) and his wife (D) contracted to sell their 471-acre farm to Lucy (P) for $50,000. Zehmer (D) contended that his offer was made in jest while the three of them were drinking and that Zehmer (D) only desired to bluff Lucy (P) into admitting he did not have $50,000. Lucy (P) appeared to have taken the offer seriously by discussing its terms with Zehmer (D), rewriting it to enable Mrs. Zehmer (D) to sign also, by providing for title examination, and by taking possession of the agreement. Lucy (P) offered $5 to bind the deal and the next day sold a one-half interest to his brother (P) in order to raise money. When the Zehmers (D) refused to sell the land, Lucy (P) brought suit for specific performance, which the trial court denied. The state's highest court granted review.

**ISSUE:** Will the assent necessary to form a contract be imputed to a person based on the reasonable meaning given to his words and acts, rather than depending on his unexpressed intentions?

**HOLDING AND DECISION:** (Buchanan, J.) Yes. The assent necessary to form a contract will be imputed to a person based on the reasonable meaning given to his words and acts, rather than depending on his unexpressed intentions. The existence of an offer depends upon the reasonable meaning to be given the offeror's acts and words. For the formation of a contract, the mental assent of the parties is not required. If the words and acts of one of the parties have but one reasonable meaning, his undisclosed intention is immaterial except when an unreasonable meaning that he attaches to his manifestations is known to the other party. Accordingly, one cannot say he was merely jesting when his conduct and words would warrant reasonable belief that a real agreement was intended. Reversed and remanded.

▶ **ANALYSIS**

Note that it is not what is said but how it is heard and reasonably understood. Mutual assent of the parties is

required for the formation of a contract, but mental assent is not. Where one party can reasonably believe from the other party's acts and words that a real agreement is intended, the other party's real but unexpressed intention is immaterial. Mutual assent is an objective determination based upon what a reasonable man would believe. An offer is an expression of will or intention creating a power of acceptance upon the offeree. If the offer to sell the farm had been for a price of $50, the court could judge the ridiculousness of the offer in determining whether a reasonable man would believe it to be serious.

■■■

## Quicknotes

**MUTUAL ASSENT** A requirement of a valid contract that the parties possess a mutuality of assent as manifested by the terms of the agreement and not by a hidden intent.

**POSSESSION** The holding of property with the right of disposition.

**SPECIFIC PERFORMANCE** An equitable remedy whereby the court requires the parties to perform their obligations pursuant to a contract.

■■■

# Raffles v. Wichelhaus

Cotton seller (P) v. Cotton purchaser (D)

Ct. of Exchequer, 2 H. & C. 906, 159 Eng. Rep. 375 (1864).

**NATURE OF CASE:** Action for damages for breach of a contract for the sale of goods.

**FACT SUMMARY:** Raffles (P) contracted to sell cotton to Wichelhaus (D) to be delivered from Bombay at Liverpool on the ship "Peerless." Unknown to the parties was the existence of two different ships carrying cotton, each named "Peerless" arriving at Liverpool from Bombay, but at different times.

## 🏛 RULE OF LAW
There is no manifestation of mutual assent to an exchange if the parties attach materially different meanings to their manifestations and neither knows or has reason to know the meaning attached by the other.

**FACTS:** Raffles (P) contracted to sell Wichelhaus (D) 125 bales of Surrat cotton to arrive from Bombay at Liverpool on the ship "Peerless." Wichelhaus (D) was to pay 17 percent pence per pound of cotton within an agreed-upon time after the arrival of the goods in England. Unknown to the parties, there were two ships called "Peerless," each of which was carrying cotton from Bombay to Liverpool. One ship was to sail in October by Wichelhaus (D) for delivery of the goods while Raffles (P) had expected the cotton to be shipped on the "Peerless" set to sail in December. As Wichelhaus (D) could not have the delivery he expected, he refused to accept the later delivery.

**ISSUE:** Is there a manifestation of mutual assent to an exchange if the parties attach materially different meanings to their manifestations and neither knows or has reason to know the meaning attached by the other?

**HOLDING AND DECISION:** (Per curiam) No. There is no manifestation of mutual assent to an exchange if the parties attach materially different meanings to their manifestations and neither knows or has reason to know the meaning attached by the other. While the contract did not show which particular "Peerless" was intended, the moment it appeared two ships called "Peerless" were sailing from Bombay to Liverpool with a load of cotton, a latent ambiguity arose, and parol evidence was admissible for the purpose of determining that both parties had intended a different "Peerless" to be subject in the contract. When there is an ambiguity, it is given the meaning that each party intended it to have. However, if different meanings were intended there is no contract if the ambiguity relates to a material term. Consequently, there was no meeting of the minds and no binding contract. Judgment for the defendants.

## ▶ ANALYSIS

When there is no integration of the contract, the standard for its interpretation is the meaning that the party making the manifestation should reasonably expect the other party to give it, i.e., a standard of reasonable expectation. This case illustrates an exception to this rule. Where there is an ambiguity, if both parties give the same meaning to it, there is a contract. If the parties each give a different meaning to the ambiguity, then there is no contract, as occurred here. The ambiguity struck at a material term, as payment was to be made within an agreed upon time after delivery. The parties could not even agree on the time of delivery. The other exception occurs when one party has reason to know of the ambiguity and the other does not, so it will bear the meaning given to it by the latter, that is the party who is without fault. Note that under Uniform Commercial Code § 2-322, delivery ex ship, it would make no difference which ship would be carrier of the goods and the case would have gone the other way. However, Restatement (First) § 71 would appear to follow the general rule of the present case.

---

## Quicknotes

**BREACH OF CONTRACT** Unlawful failure by a party to perform its obligations pursuant to contract.

**DAMAGES** Monetary compensation that may be awarded by the court to a party who has sustained injury or loss to his person, property or rights due to another party's unlawful act, omission or negligence.

**MUTUAL ASSENT** A requirement of a valid contract that the parties possess a mutuality of assent as manifested by the terms of the agreement and not by a hidden intent.

---

# Wrench, LLC v. Taco Bell Corp.

Cartoon character developer (P) v. Fast food chain (D)

51 F. Supp. 2d 840 (W.D. Mich. 1999), *rev'd on other grounds*, 256 F.3d 446 (6th Cir. 2001).

**NATURE OF CASE:** Motion for summary judgment in action for breach of implied-in-fact contract, misappropriation, conversion, and unfair competition.

**FACT SUMMARY:** Wrench, LLC (P), which created and developed the cartoon character Psycho Chihuahua, contended that Taco Bell Corp. (D) breached an implied-in-fact contract by using a Chihuahua in its advertising without compensating Wrench (P) for such use.

## RULE OF LAW
An implied-in-fact contract is created where the plaintiff discloses an idea to the defendant at the defendant's request and the defendant understands that the plaintiff expects compensation for the use of the idea.

**FACTS:** Wrench, LLC (P) created and promoted a cartoon character called Psycho Chihuahua, a "feisty, edgy, confident Chihuahua with a big dog attitude." Taco Bell Corp. (D) is a national fast food chain. At a trade show, some of Taco Bell's (D) creative services employees saw Psycho Chihuahua and thought the character might be a good fit for Taco Bell's (D) retail licensing program. These employees were not part of Taco Bell's (D) marketing department. They discussed with Wrench (P) the possibility of using the character, and promoted the character at Taco Bell (D). A few months later, Wrench (P) hired a licensing agent, who became involved in communications with the Taco Bell (D) employees interested in using Psycho Chihuahua. The discussions expanded the potential use from retail licensing to advertising. A couple of months later, the licensing agent sent Taco Bell (D) a proposal for the use of the Psycho Chihuahua character. The proposal provided that Taco Bell (D) would pay Wrench (P) a percentage based upon the amount of money spent on advertising, a percentage of Taco Bell's (D) retail licensing sales, and a percentage based on the cost of premiums, such as toys sold in Taco Bell (D) restaurants. Taco Bell (D) neither accepted nor rejected the proposal. Discussions continued, and, a few months later, Taco Bell (D) asked Wrench (P) to prepare a presentation for Taco Bell's (D) marketing department, which Wrench (P) did, but the presentation was never made to the marketing department. The creative services department, however, was impressed with the presentation and accompanying materials. Around this time, Taco Bell (D) hired a new advertising agency. This agency, which had previously prepared a commercial for an automobile company involving a Chihuahua that could drive, eventually came up with a commercial that

involved a male Chihuahua passing up a female Chihuahua for Taco Bell (D) food. This happened to be an idea that Wrench (P) had previously presented. At around the same time—about a year after first seeing Psycho Chihuahua—the creative services employees continued discussions with Wrench's (P) licensing agent about the use of the Psycho Chihuahua character, and continued to hope that they could persuade the company's marketing department to use it. The materials for a campaign using the character were passed on to the marketing department, which forwarded them to the advertising agency. A few months later, Taco Bell (D) started airing commercials using a feisty Chihuahua that said, "Yo Quiero Taco Bell!" The commercials were very successful, and Taco Bell (D) continues to use its Chihuahua character. Wrench (P) sued Taco Bell (D) for breach of implied-in-fact contract, misappropriation, conversion, and unfair competition. Taco Bell (D) moved for summary judgment on all claims, contending that no implied-in-fact contract was proved, that even if it was, it was preempted by federal copyright law, that the idea to use a Chihuahua in its commercials was independently created by its advertising agency, and that Wrench's (P) ideas were not novel.

**ISSUE:** Is an implied-in-fact contract created where the plaintiff discloses an idea to the defendant at the defendant's request and the defendant understands that the plaintiff expects compensation for the use of the idea?

**HOLDING AND DECISION:** (Quist, J.) Yes. An implied-in-fact contract is created where the plaintiff discloses an idea to the defendant at the defendant's request and the defendant understands that the plaintiff expects compensation for the use of the idea. A contract may be implied-in-fact from the parties' conduct, language, and other relevant circumstances. If a contract is to be implied, there must be mutual assent and consideration, and the essential elements of an express contract must be present. An implied-in-fact contract often arises where one party accepts a benefit from another party for which compensation is normally expected. Where evidence shows that the parties understood that compensation would be paid for services rendered, a promise to pay fair value may be implied, even if no agreement was reached as to price, duration, or other terms of the contract. Taco Bell (D) concedes that the parties had a basic understanding that if Taco Bell (D) used the Psycho Chihuahua idea, concept, or image, Taco Bell (D) would compensate Wrench (P) for the fair value of such use. However, it argues that there was

*Continued on next page.*

no agreement on essential terms of a licensing agreement, such as price, duration, scope of use, and exclusivity, and that, therefore, there can be no implied-in-fact contract. Wrench (P) counters that agreement on such terms is not necessary to support an implied-in-fact contract, but that the mere understanding that Taco Bell (D) would pay for the use of the Psycho Chihuahua idea, concept, or image is sufficient to support such a contract. Courts in several jurisdictions agree with Wrench's (P) position. The reasoning of those courts is persuasive. Therefore, Wrench (P) has presented sufficient evidence to create a genuine issue of material fact as to whether an implied-in-fact contract existed between it and Taco Bell (D). [The district court ruled that although Wrench (P) made out a claim for an implied-in-fact contract, such a claim was preempted by the federal Copyright Act. Accordingly, the court granted summary judgment to Taco Bell (D).]

## ▶ ANALYSIS

On appeal, the Sixth Circuit reversed and remanded, holding that the state contract claim was not preempted by federal copyright law, and, in 2003, a jury awarded Wrench (P) over $30 million in damages.

## Quicknotes

**BREACH OF CONTRACT** Unlawful failure by a party to perform its obligations pursuant to contract.

**CONVERSION** The act of depriving an owner of his property without permission or justification.

**IMPLIED-IN-FACT CONTRACT** Refers to conditions which arise by physical or moral inference: (a) prerequisites or circumstances which a reasonable person would assume necessary to render or receive performance; and (b) the good-faith cooperation of the promisee in receiving the performance of the promisor.

**MISAPPROPRIATION** The unlawful use of another's property or funds.

**MOTION FOR SUMMARY JUDGMENT** Judgment rendered by a court in response to a motion by one of the parties, claiming that the lack of a question of material fact in respect to an issue warrants disposition of the issue without consideration by the jury.

**SUMMARY JUDGMENT** Judgment rendered by a court in response to a motion made by one of the parties, claiming that the lack of a question of material fact in respect to an issue warrants disposition of the issue without consideration by the jury.

**UNFAIR COMPETITION** Any dishonest or fraudulent rivalry in trade and commerce, particularly imitation and counterfeiting.

# Lonergan v. Scolnick

Potential real property buyer (P) v. Real property seller (D)

Cal. Ct. App., 129 Cal. App. 2d 179, 276 P.2d 8 (1954).

**NATURE OF CASE:** Appeal from judgment for defendant in action for specific performance or damages.

**FACT SUMMARY:** Lonergan (P) made inquiries concerning property which Scolnick (D) had advertised in a newspaper. He received a form letter describing the land and a second letter which responded to questions he had asked. Scolnick (D) sold the property to someone else.

## 🏛 RULE OF LAW
There can be no contract unless the minds of the parties have met and mutually agreed upon some specific thing.

**FACTS:** Lonergan (P) made inquiries concerning property which Scolnick (D) had advertised in a newspaper. Scolnick (D) sent him a form letter describing the property. On April 7, 1952, Lonergan (P) wrote Scolnick (D), asking him for a legal description of the property and whether a certain bank would be a satisfactory escrow agent. Scolnick (D) wrote back on April 8, stating that Lonergan (P) would have to act fast, inasmuch as Scolnick (D) expected to have a buyer in the next week. Lonergan (P) responded on April 14 that he would proceed immediately to have escrow opened. On April 12, Scolnick (D) sold the property to someone else. The trial court determined, based on this evidence, that no contract had been formed, and ruled for Scolnick (D). The state's intermediate appellate court granted review.

**ISSUE:** Can there be a contract where the minds of the parties have not met and mutually agreed upon some specific thing?

**HOLDING AND DECISION:** (Barnard, J.) No. There can be no contract unless the minds of the parties have met and mutually agreed upon some specific thing. This agreement is usually evidenced by one party making an offer that is accepted by the other. However, if from a promise or manifestation of intention or from existing circumstances the person to whom the promise or manifestation is addressed knows or has reason to know that the person making it does not intend it to constitute an expression of fixed purpose until he has given a further expression of assent, no offer has been made. Such was the case here. The newspaper ad was merely a request for an offer. The form letter sent by Scolnick (D) contained no definitive offer, and his letter of April 8 added nothing that caused previous communications to ripen into an offer. In fact, it stated that he expected a buyer within the week, indicating that he intended to sell to the first comer. Lonergan's (P) letter of April 15, stating that he was opening escrow, therefore could not have created a contract between the parties since there had been no offer. Affirmed.

## ▶ ANALYSIS

In *Fairmount Glass Works v. Grunden-Martin Woodenware Co.*, 51 S.W. 196 (Ky. 1899), the plaintiff inquired as to the defendant's lowest price on 10 loads of Mason jars. The reply was "$4.50 and $5.00 for immediate acceptance." The defendant refused to fill plaintiff's subsequent order. The court held that defendant's reply "was not a quotation of prices but a definite offer to sell." In *Harvey v. Facey*, A.C. 552 (1893), plaintiff telegraphed defendant, "Will you sell us Bumper Hall Pen? Telegraph lowest price." The defendant replied, "Lowest price for Bumper Hall Pen £900." Plaintiff responded, "We agree to buy Bumper Hall Pen for £900." The court held that there was no contract.

## Quicknotes

**ESCROW** A written contract held by a third party until the conditions therein are satisfied, at which time it is delivered to the obligee.

**OBLIGEE** Promisee; a party who is the recipient of a promise or obligation to perform.

**OFFER** A proposed promise to undertake performance of an action, or to refrain from acting, that is to become binding upon acceptance by the offeree.

**OFFEREE** A person or party to whom an offer to enter into a contractual agreement is made.

**SPECIFIC PERFORMANCE** An equitable remedy whereby the court requires the parties to perform their obligations pursuant to a contract.

# Southworth v. Oliver

Offeree of real property (P) v. Offeror of real property (D)

Or. Sup. Ct., 284 Or. 361, 587 P.2d 994 (1978).

**NATURE OF CASE:** Action for a declaratory judgment.

**FACT SUMMARY:** Southworth (P) claimed that a certain "writing" mailed by Oliver (D) constituted an "offer" to sell 2,933 acres of ranch land and that his acceptance thereof resulted in a specifically enforceable contract.

## RULE OF LAW
An "offer" has been made if, under all of the facts and circumstances existing at the time, a reasonable person in the position of the alleged offeree would have been led to believe that an offer was being made.

**FACTS:** Southworth (P) obtained a decree of specific performance that required Oliver (D) to proceed with the sale of ranch lands that Southworth (P) claimed had been the subject of an "offer" to sell by Oliver (D). Having decided to sell some of his property, Oliver (D) had inquired if Southworth (P) would be interested in buying it. According to Southworth (P), Oliver (D) agreed to determine the value and price of the land, and Southworth (P) would look into obtaining the money to purchase it. Later, Oliver (D) sent letters to Southworth (P) and three other neighbors setting forth the terms of sale and price of the land and stating that he was also selling allotment permits at a specified price per head. Southworth (P) treated this as an offer and sent a letter back indicating his acceptance. When Oliver (D) refused to go through with the sale, saying his own letter had not been an offer, Southworth (P) brought this action suit in equity for a declaratory judgment.

**ISSUE:** Does an "offer" exist if, under the facts and circumstances existing at the time, a reasonable person would have been led to believe that an offer was being made?

**HOLDING AND DECISION:** [Judge not stated in casebook excerpt.] Yes. In attempting to determine if an offer has been made, the question is whether, under all the facts and circumstances existing at the time, a reasonable person would have understood that an offer was being made or would have been led to believe such. A price quotation, standing alone, is not an offer. However, there may be circumstances under which a price quotation, when considered together with facts and circumstances, may constitute an offer which, if accepted, will result in a binding contract. Furthermore, such an offer may be made to more than one person. This proposal was definite.

It was addressed to particular persons, and a reasonable person would have been led to believe an offer to sell was being made. Affirmed.

## ANALYSIS

Restatement of Contracts, § 25, Comment (a) (1932), notes the difficulty in drawing an exact line between offers and negotiations preliminary thereto. It suggests that particular attention must be given to whether or not there was any direct language indicating intent to defer formation of a contract, to the usages of business, and to all accompanying circumstances.

## Quicknotes

**DECLARATORY JUDGMENT** A judgment of the court establishing the rights of the parties.

**OFFER** A proposed promise to undertake performance of an action, or to refrain from acting, that is to become binding upon acceptance by the offeree.

**OFFEREE** A person or party to whom an offer to enter into a contractual agreement is made.

**SPECIFIC PERFORMANCE** An equitable remedy whereby the court requires the parties to perform their obligations pursuant to a contract.

# Lefkowitz v. Great Minneapolis Surplus Store

## Customer (P) v. Advertiser (D)

Minn. Sup. Ct., 251 Minn. 188, 86 N.W.2d 689 (1957).

**NATURE OF CASE:** Action to recover damages for breach of contract.

**FACT SUMMARY:** Great Minneapolis Surplus Store (D) advertised one fur stole on a "first come first served" basis but would not sell the stole to Lefkowitz (P), who accepted the alleged offer.

## 🏛 RULE OF LAW
A newspaper advertisement that is clear, definite, and explicit, and leaves nothing to negotiation is an offer, acceptance of which creates a binding contract.

**FACTS:** Great Minneapolis Surplus Store (Surplus Store) (D) published the following advertisement in a Minneapolis newspaper: "SATURDAY 9 A.M. 2 BRAND NEW PASTEL MINK 3-SKIN SCARFS Selling for $89.50 Out they go Saturday. Each . . . $1.00 BLACK LAPIN STOLE Beautiful, worth $139.50 . . . $1.00. FIRST COME FIRST SERVED." Lefkowitz (P) was the first to present himself on Saturday and demanded the Lapin Stole for one dollar. Surplus Store (D) refused to sell to him because of a "house rule" that the offer was intended for women only. Lefkowitz (P) sued Surplus Store (D) and was awarded $138.50 as damages. Surplus Store (D) appealed.

**ISSUE:** Is a newspaper advertisement that is clear, definite, and explicit, and leaves nothing to negotiation an offer, acceptance of which creates a binding contract?

**HOLDING AND DECISION:** (Murphy, J.) Yes. A newspaper advertisement that is clear, definite, and explicit, and leaves nothing to negotiation is an offer, acceptance of which creates a binding contract. The test of whether a binding obligation may originate in advertisements addressed to the public is "whether the facts show that some performance was promised in positive terms in return for something requested." Whether an advertisement is an offer or merely an invitation for offers depends on the legal intention of the parties and the surrounding circumstances. Where an offer is clear, definite, and explicit, and leaves nothing open for negotiation, it constitutes an offer such that acceptance of it will create a contract. With respect to the Lapin fur, Surplus Store's (D) advertisement was such an offer. As to Surplus Store's (D) alleged "house rule," while an advertiser has the right at any time before acceptance to modify his offer, he does not have the right, after acceptance, to impose new or arbitrary conditions not contained in the published offer. Affirmed.

## ▸ ANALYSIS

Although most advertisements for goods at a certain price are held not to be offers, the present case presents an interesting exception to that rule. Restatement (Second), § 25 (Illustration No. 1), indicates that the basis of the court's decision is that the words "first come first served" create language of promise which is ordinarily lacking in advertisement for the sale of goods. Probably it was this factor in conjunction with the statement of a quantity (to wit, one) that motivated the court. Caveat: The Uniform Commercial Code has dealt a blow to the present court's insistence that nothing be left open for negotiation [see Uniform Commercial Code § 2-204(3)].

---

## Quicknotes

**ACCEPTANCE** Assent to the specified terms of an offer resulting in the formation of a binding agreement.

**BREACH OF CONTRACT** Unlawful failure by a party to perform its obligations pursuant to contract.

**DAMAGES** Monetary compensation that may be awarded by the court to a party who has sustained injury or loss to his person, property or rights due to another party's unlawful act, omission or negligence.

**OFFER** A proposed promise to undertake performance of an action, or to refrain from acting, that is to become binding upon acceptance by the offeree.

**OFFEREE** A person or party to whom an offer to enter into a contractual agreement is made.

# Leonard v. Pepsico, Inc.

Customer (P) v. Advertiser (D)

88 F. Supp. 2d 116 (S.D.N.Y. 1999), *aff'd*, 210 F.3d 88 (2d Cir. 2000).

**NATURE OF CASE:** Defense motion for summary judgment.

**FACT SUMMARY:** Leonard (P) brought suit against Pepsico, Inc. (D) for refusing to comply with terms of an alleged contract.

## 🏛 RULE OF LAW
An advertisement is not necessarily an enforceable offer simply because it may appear to be a so-called public offer of a reward for performance of a public act.

**FACTS:** Leonard (P), after viewing a television commercial from Pepsico, Inc. (D) offering a Harrier Jet Fighter for 7,000,000 "Pepsi points," raised $700,000 (the equivalent of such points) which he proffered to Pepsico (D) as an "acceptance" of its "offer," demanding the Harrier. Pepsico (D) refused to supply the Harrier, arguing that its commercial was obviously done in jest and that no reasonable person could possibly have considered it a real offer. Leonard (P) brought suit on the alleged contract, and Pepsico (D) moved for summary judgment.

**ISSUE:** Is an advertisement an offer simply because it may appear to be a so-called public offer of a reward for performance of a public act?

**HOLDING AND DECISION:** (Wood, J.) No. An advertisement is not an offer simply because it may appear to be a so-called public offer of a reward for performance of a public act. The Harrier Jet commercial did not direct that anyone who appeared at Pepsi (D) headquarters with 7,000,000 Pepsi Points on the Fourth of July would receive a Harrier Jet. Instead, the commercial urged consumers to accumulate Pepsi Points and refer to the Pepsi catalog to determine how they could redeem their Pepsi Points. The commercial sought a reciprocal promise, expressed through acceptance of, and compliance with, the terms of the order form. It was not a unilateral offer. The catalog contains no mention of the Harrier Jet. No reasonable person would expect a soft drink company to give away a fighter jet. Furthermore, there was no writing between the parties to satisfy the statute of frauds. Defense motion for summary judgment granted.

## ▶ ANALYSIS

The *Leonard* case notes that because the alleged offer by Pepsico (D) in this case was, at most, "an advertisement to receive offers rather than an offer of reward," Leonard (P) cannot show that there was an offer made in the circumstances of this case.

## Quicknotes

**ACCEPTANCE** Assent to the specified terms of an offer resulting in the formation of a binding agreement.

**OFFER** A proposed promise to undertake performance of an action, or to refrain from acting, that is to become binding upon acceptance by the offeree.

**OFFEREE** A person or party to whom an offer to enter into a contractual agreement is made.

**SUMMARY JUDGMENT** Judgment rendered by a court in response to a motion made by one of the parties, claiming that the lack of a question of material fact in respect to an issue warrants disposition of the issue without consideration by the jury.

# La Salle National Bank v. Vega

Trustee (P) v. Offeror of property (D)

Ill. App. Ct., 167 Ill. App. 3d 154, 520 N.E.2d 1129 (1988).

**NATURE OF CASE:** Appeal from partial summary judgment denying existence of a contract.

**FACT SUMMARY:** After Vega's (D) offer to sell his property to La Salle National Bank (La Salle) (P) was not accepted in the manner specified, he later contracted with a subsequent purchaser, and La Salle (P) sought to enforce the specific performance of the contract.

### 🏛 RULE OF LAW
An offer may be accepted only by a person in whom the offeror intended to create a power of acceptance and in the manner specified by the offeror.

**FACTS:** Vega (D) agreed to sell his property to the beneficiaries of a trust held by La Salle National Bank (P), as trustee. The agreement specifically required the contract be presented to the trust for execution. The contract was signed by Vega (D) and the purchasing agent but not by the trustee. When the contract was not presented to the trust, Vega (D) later entered into a contract with Borg for the sale of the property. The trial court, in an action to determine the validity of the contracts, granted partial summary judgment on the ground that the first contract was void for lack of proper acceptance, and La Salle (P) appealed.

**ISSUE:** Can an offer be accepted by someone other than the person to whom it was made?

**HOLDING AND DECISION:** (Lindberg, J.) No. An offer may be accepted only by a person in whom the offeror intended to create a power of acceptance. Thus, the offer is considered personal to the offeree, and the power to accept it cannot be transferred to a third party. Furthermore, no contract is formed when the acceptance does not satisfy the mode indicated in the offer. Here, the agreement specified that the contract would not be effective until it was presented to and executed by the trust. Since the trust never executed the sale contract, there was no acceptance, and, thus, there was no contract between La Salle (P) and Vega (D). Affirmed.

---

### ▶ ANALYSIS

When an offer does not specify the mode of acceptance, the acceptance may be given in any manner and medium reasonable under the circumstances. It is no longer required for the acceptance to match the offer. Uniform Commercial Code § 2-207 provides that a document may contain additional or different terms from the offer and still constitute an acceptance.

### Quicknotes

**ACCEPTANCE** Assent to the specified terms of an offer resulting in the formation of a binding agreement.

**OFFER** A proposed promise to undertake performance of an action, or to refrain from acting, that is to become binding upon acceptance by the offeree.

**OFFEREE** A person or party to whom an offer to enter into a contractual agreement is made.

**OFFEROR** Party who makes an offer.

**PARTIAL SUMMARY JUDGMENT** Judgment rendered by a court in response to a motion by one of the parties, claiming that the lack of a question of material fact in respect to one of the issues warrants disposition of that issue without going to the jury.

**SPECIFIC PERFORMANCE** An equitable remedy whereby the court requires the parties to perform their obligations pursuant to a contract.

**SUMMARY JUDGMENT** Judgment rendered by a court in response to a motion made by one of the parties, claiming that the lack of a question of material fact in respect to an issue warrants disposition of the issue without consideration by the jury.

# Hendricks v. Behee

## Escrowee (P) v. Offeror (D)

Mo. Ct. App., 786 S.W.2d 610 (1990).

**NATURE OF CASE:** Appeal from denial of specific performance and/or damages in interpleader action.

**FACT SUMMARY:** Hendricks (P), escrowee, instituted an interpleader action to have the court decide whether a contract was formed between the seller and the buyer of real estate and to whom the deposit money, held by Hendricks (P) in escrow, was to be paid.

> ## 🏛 RULE OF LAW
> No contract is formed when the offer is revoked before the acceptance is communicated to the offeror.

**FACTS:** Behee (D) engaged in negotiations with Mr. and Mrs. Smith for the purchase of their property. On March 2, Behee (D) made a written offer that was mailed to the Smiths the next day by their agents. Unbeknownst to Behee (D), the offer was accepted and signed. Shortly after, Behee (D) notified the agents that he was withdrawing his offer of purchase. Believing the offer to have been revoked, Behee (D) demanded the refund of the escrow money held by Hendricks (P). On the other hand, the Smiths, believing that a contract was formed when they signed the mailed offer, requested the escrow money to be paid to them. Hendricks (P) instituted an interpleader action asking the court to resolve the dispute over the escrow money. Hendricks (P) was awarded $997 out of the deposit for his services, and the remainder was returned to Behee (D). The Smiths appealed.

**ISSUE:** Is a contract formed when the offer is revoked before the acceptance is communicated to the offeror?

**HOLDING AND DECISION:** (Flanigan, J.) No. No contract is formed when the offer is revoked before the acceptance is communicated to the offeror. An offer can be revoked at any time prior to the receipt or notification of acceptance, unless it is supported by an adequate consideration. Behee (D) notified the Smiths' agents of his withdrawal of the offer before the acceptance was communicated to him. Thus, the offer was properly revoked since the agents' notification and knowledge of the withdrawal was imputed to the Smiths. Therefore, no contract was formed, and the escrow money was properly returned to Behee (D). Affirmed.

## ▶ ANALYSIS

Generally, in a unilateral contract, where acceptance is by performance, the offer is considered temporarily irrevocable when the offeree partially performs. However, when the offer requests the shipment of the goods, the Uniform Commercial Code allows the offeree to accept either by shipping or by promising to ship. See §§ 1-102, 1-201, 2-102, 2-105, 2-204, 2-205, 2-206, and 2-207 for further discussion of the words "offer" and "agreement."

■■■■

## Quicknotes

**ACCEPTANCE** Assent to the specified terms of an offer resulting in the formation of a binding agreement.

**ESCROW** A written contract held by a third party until the conditions therein are satisfied, at which time it is delivered to the obligee.

**INTERPLEADER** An equitable proceeding whereby a person holding property which is subject to the claims of multiple parties may require such parties to resolve the matter through litigation.

**SPECIFIC PERFORMANCE** An equitable remedy whereby the court requires the parties to perform their obligations pursuant to a contract.

**UNILATERAL CONTRACT** An agreement pursuant to which a party agrees to act without an express exchange for performance on the part of the other party.

■■■■

# Carlill v. Carbolic Smoke Ball Co.

Reward claimant (P) v. Reward advertiser (D)

Q.B., Ct. of App., 1 Q.B. 256 (1893).

**NATURE OF CASE:** Appeal from damages award in action for breach of contract.

**FACT SUMMARY:** The Carbolic Smoke Ball Co. (D) advertised a reward to any person contracting influenza after using the Smoke Ball but refused to pay such reward to Carlill (P) when she caught influenza after using the ball.

## RULE OF LAW
An advertised reward to anyone who performs certain conditions specified in the advertisement is an offer, and the performance of such conditions is an acceptance that creates a valid contract.

**FACTS:** Carbolic Smoke Ball Co. ("the Smoke Ball Co.") (D) advertised a reward to any person who caught the influenza after having used the Carbolic Smoke Ball three times daily for two weeks. Carlill (P) used the Ball as directed and still caught the influenza. Thereafter, Carlill (P) brought an action against the Smoke Ball Co. (D) to recover damages for breach of contract. After Carlill (P) was awarded damages in the amount of the advertised reward, the Smoke Ball Co. (D) appealed.

**ISSUE:** Is an advertised reward to anyone who performs certain conditions specified in the advertisement an offer, and is the performance of such conditions an acceptance that creates a valid contract?

**HOLDING AND DECISION:** (Lord Lindley, J.) Yes. An advertised reward to anyone who performs certain conditions specified in the advertisement is an offer, and the performance of such conditions is an acceptance which creates a valid contract. Here, the Smoke Ball Co. (D) advertised a reward to anyone who caught the influenza after using the Smoke Ball for three weeks. The Smoke Ball Co. (D), though, contends that such advertisement was too "vague" to create an enforceable offer since it did not specify any time limit to the guarantee. Such contention, however, is without merit. The advertisement could be reasonably construed as offering a reward only to those persons who caught the influenza within a "reasonable time" after having used the Smoke Ball. Therefore, the advertisement was a valid offer which Carlill (P) accepted by performance of the specified conditions. Affirmed.

**CONCURRENCE:** (Lord Bowen, J.) Here, the advertised offer requested deeds, not words, and, therefore, Carlill (P) did not need to give notice that she was going to perform such deeds to accept it. Furthermore, the contract so formed was supported by ample consideration since it operated to the Smoke Ball Co.'s (D) benefit by stimulating sales and to Carlill's (P) detriment by causing her to use the ball.

**CONCURRENCE:** (Lord Smith, J.) Here, the Smoke Ball Co.'s (D) offer was supported by valid consideration, and it was accepted by Carlill's (P) deeds.

## ANALYSIS

This case illustrates a situation in which an advertisement is considered an offer (i.e., when there is no problem as to quantity because the ad specifies a reward to anyone who uses the product). The ordinary advertisement, though, which states that an item has been reduced in price, is not considered an offer because no quantity of the item is specified. Instead, such advertisements are generally held to represent only an intention to sell or a preliminary proposal inviting offers.

## Quicknotes

**ACCEPTANCE** Assent to the specified terms of an offer resulting in the formation of a binding agreement.

**BREACH OF CONTRACT** Unlawful failure by a party to perform its obligations pursuant to contract.

**CONSIDERATION** Value given by one party in exchange for performance, or a promise to perform, by another party.

**OFFER** A proposed promise to undertake performance of an action, or to refrain from acting, that is to become binding upon acceptance by the offeree.

**OFFEREE** A person or party to whom an offer to enter into a contractual agreement is made.

# Corinthian Pharmaceutical Systems, Inc. v. Lederle Laboratories
## Drug distributor (P) v. Drug manufacturer (D)
### 724 F. Supp. 605 (S.D. Ind. 1989).

**NATURE OF CASE:** Motion for summary judgment in action for specific performance of sales contract.

**FACT SUMMARY:** Corinthian Pharmaceutical Systems, Inc. (Corinthian) (P), distributor of DTP vaccine, placed an order with Lederle Laboratories (D), manufacturer, for 1,000 vials of vaccine, but when only part of the order was delivered and the remainder was to be shipped later at a higher price, Corinthian (P) brought an action for breach of contract.

> 🏛 **RULE OF LAW**
> A seller's price quote and a partial shipment of the buyer's order are not a valid offer and acceptance to form an enforceable contract.

**FACTS:** Corinthian Pharmaceutical Systems, Inc. (Corinthian) (P) distributed DTP vaccines, which were purchased from Lederle Laboratories (D) on a regular basis. As a routine business practice, Lederle (D) issued price lists to its customers. The list stated that the prices were subject to change without notice and that any changes take effect at the time of shipment. In an internal memo to its representatives, Lederle (D) indicated that the price for the vaccine would be increased to $171 per vial due to the high cost of insurance and product liability lawsuits. The content of the memo was leaked to Corinthian (P) before the price increase was to be announced to the other customers. Corinthian (P) immediately placed an order for 1,000 vials through Lederle's (D) computer ordering system. The order stated that $64.32 would be the payable price for each vial. Lederle (D) made a partial shipment of 50 vials at the price indicated in Corinthian's (P) order, which was accepted. At the same time, Lederle (D) sent a letter to Corinthian (P) indicating that the partial shipment was to accommodate it and the remainder would be shipped for the price of $171 per vial. Subsequently, Corinthian (P) brought an action for breach of contract, seeking specific performance of the order. Lederle (D) moved for summary judgment.

**ISSUE:** Are a seller's price quote and a partial shipment of the buyer's order a valid offer and acceptance to form an enforceable contract?

**HOLDING AND DECISION:** (McKinney, J.) No. A seller's price quote and a partial shipment of the buyer's order are not a valid offer and acceptance to form an enforceable contract. A contract is formed when the offer is properly accepted and supported by consideration. An offer is a manifestation of one's willingness to enter into a bargain. Thus, price quotations are not offers but only invitations for the recipient to make an offer. As a result, Lederle's (D) price lists sent to Corinthian (P) did not constitute an offer. The offer was actually made by Corinthian (P) when it placed an order via the computer ordering system. Since the parties were merchants and the offer was for a sale of goods, Uniform Commercial Code (U.C.C.) § 2-206 governed the mode of acceptance. The Code allows for acceptance to be in any reasonable form and manner. In addition, it provides that shipment of non-conforming goods by the seller who gives notice that the shipment is merely an accommodation is not an acceptance but a counteroffer. Here, Lederle's (D) partial shipment, although non-conforming, was a counteroffer, since it was followed by a notification that the shipment is only an accommodation. Thus, there was no contract formed between the parties. Motion for summary judgment granted.

▶ **ANALYSIS**

This case involved the manner by which the offeree must indicate his commitment or promise. U.C.C. § 2-206 no longer requires that an acceptance be the mirror image of the offer, which was required by common law. Furthermore, the commitment may either be demonstrated by promissory language or a promissory act.

---

## Quicknotes

**ACCEPTANCE** Assent to the specified terms of an offer resulting in the formation of a binding agreement.

**BREACH OF CONTRACT** Unlawful failure by a party to perform its obligations pursuant to contract.

**OFFER** A proposed promise to undertake performance of an action, or to refrain from acting, that is to become binding upon acceptance by the offeree.

**OFFEREE** A person or party to whom an offer to enter into a contractual agreement is made.

**NON-CONFORMING GOODS** Goods tendered pursuant to a contract for sale that do not conform with the contract's requirements or which are otherwise defective in some way.

**SPECIFIC PERFORMANCE** An equitable remedy whereby the court requires the parties to perform their obligations pursuant to a contract.

*Continued on next page.*

**SUMMARY JUDGMENT** Judgment rendered by a court in response to a motion made by one of the parties, claiming that the lack of a question of material fact in respect to an issue warrants disposition of the issue without consideration by the jury.

## Industrial America, Inc. v.

# Industrial America, Inc. v. Fulton Industries, Inc.

Business broker (P) v. Business acquirer (D)

Del. Sup. Ct., 285 A.2d 412 (1971).

**NATURE OF CASE:** Cross-appeals from judgment in suit to recover a brokerage commission.

**FACT SUMMARY:** Industrial America, Inc. (P), a business brokerage firm, responded on behalf of one of its clients to an advertisement in which Fulton Industries, Inc. (D) had expressed a desire to acquire other businesses.

## 🏛 RULE OF LAW
If an offer invites acceptance by performance, an offeree's performance will be deemed an acceptance unless a contrary intention on his part is shown.

**FACTS:** Industrial America, Inc. (P) was a brokerage firm, headed by Deutsch, which specialized in sales and mergers of businesses. The company (P) was contacted by Bush Hog, Inc., a farm machinery company that sought a merger with another corporation. Deutsch made several unsuccessful efforts to negotiate a merger agreement on behalf of Bush Hog but engaged in no discussions after early 1965. In the fall of that year, Deutsch was informed by a friend that Fulton Industries, Inc. (Fulton) (D) was seeking other companies to acquire, either by sale or by merger. Deutsch then located a Wall Street Journal advertisement in which Fulton (D) had expressed its desire to acquire other companies. The advertisement concluded with the words "Brokers fully protected." Deutsch immediately responded to the advertisement, and Fulton (D) eventually asked Deutsch to arrange a meeting between representatives of Bush Hog and Fulton (D). Deutsch then contacted Bush Hog, but the two companies ultimately arranged their meeting without using Deutsch as an intermediary. Neither company made further use of Deutsch's services, although a merger between the companies eventually occurred. Deutsch later sued to recover his brokerage commission, and Bush Hog was ordered to pay $125,000 to Industrial America (P). However, an action against Fulton (D) resulted in no recovery because the trial jury found that Deutsch had never accepted Fulton's (D) newspaper "offer." Both sides appealed, and the state's highest court granted review.

**ISSUE:** If an offer invites acceptance by performance, will an offeree's performance be deemed an acceptance unless a contrary intention on his part is shown?

**HOLDING AND DECISION:** (Herrmann, J.) Yes. If an offer invites acceptance by performance, an offeree's performance will be deemed an acceptance unless a contrary intention on his part is shown. It is the manifestation of assent, and not the subjective intent or the motivations of the parties, that is relevant to the formation of a contract. In effect, a rebuttable presumption is created that the offeree's performance was to operate as an acceptance. Thus, Deutsch must be deemed to have accepted Fulton's (D) offer, and his letter to Fulton (D) served as notice of his acceptance, to the extent that such notice was necessary. It follows that Industrial America (P) is entitled to a judgment against Fulton (D) and its successor, Allied Products Corporation (D). Remanded to enter judgment for the plaintiff.

## ▶ ANALYSIS

Some contracts may be accepted only by performance. Others may be accepted only by a promise. Still others may be accepted by either performance or by promise. It has traditionally been assumed that a bilateral contract invites promissory acceptance, while a unilateral contract is to be accepted by performance. However, § 2-206(1) of the Uniform Commercial Code, without distinguishing between bilateral and unilateral contracts, provides that an offer ordinarily "shall be construed as inviting acceptance, in any manner and by any medium reasonable in the circumstances." Section 2-206 is consistent with a developing trend toward permitting any offer to be accepted either by a promise or by performance, unless the offeror has specified the mode of acceptance that will be recognized.

---

## Quicknotes

**ACCEPTANCE** Assent to the specified terms of an offer resulting in the formation of a binding agreement.

**BILATERAL CONTRACT** An agreement pursuant to which each party promises to undertake an obligation, or to forbear from acting.

**MERGER** The acquisition of one company by another, after which the acquired company ceases to exist as an independent entity.

**OFFER** A proposed promise to undertake performance of an action, or to refrain from acting, that is to become binding upon acceptance by the offeree.

**OFFEREE** A person or party to whom an offer to enter into a contractual agreement is made.

**UNILATERAL CONTRACT** An agreement pursuant to which a party agrees to act without an express exchange for performance on the part of the other party.

---

# Glover v. Jewish War Veterans of United States

Reward claimant (P) v. Nongovernmental organization (D)

D.C. Ct. App., 68 A.2d 233 (1949).

**NATURE OF CASE:** Appeal from directed verdict for defendant in action to recover an award.

**FACT SUMMARY:** Glover (P) gave information leading to the arrest of a murderer without any knowledge that a reward had been offered for such information by the Jewish War Veterans (D), a nongovernmental group.

### 🏛 RULE OF LAW
A person who complies with the conditions of a reward offered by a private party but who has no knowledge of the reward is not entitled to collect the reward.

**FACTS:** In response to questioning by police officers, Glover (P) gave information leading to the arrest of a murderer. At the time she did so, she had no knowledge that a reward had been offered for such information by the Jewish War Veterans (D), a nongovernmental organization. She found out about the reward a few days later and brought suit claiming the reward. The trial court directed the jury to enter a verdict for the Jewish War Veterans (D). The state's intermediate appellate court granted review.

**ISSUE:** Is a person, who complies with the conditions of a reward offered by a private party but who has no knowledge of the reward, entitled to collect the reward?

**HOLDING AND DECISION:** (Clagett, J.) No. A person who complies with the conditions of a reward offered by a private party but who has no knowledge of the reward is not entitled to collect the reward. Questions regarding rewards offered by private individuals and groups are to be decided according to contract law. There can be no contract in such cases unless the person claiming the reward knew about it when she gave the desired information and acted with the intention of accepting it. An offeree cannot accept an offer unless she knows of its existence. Hence, Glover (P) cannot recover since she did not know of the reward when she gave the information to the police. Affirmed.

### ▶ ANALYSIS

There are cases in which the courts have enforced a promise even though the person rendering the required service did so in ignorance of the promise. Most, but not all, of these have been cases in which the promise was made by some public corporation, such as a state or a city. These cases are usually based on the theory that the government has benefited equally whether or not the claimant knew of the reward when she gave the information or upon the theory that the published promise of a reward was a public grant and not within the field of contract.

### Quicknotes

**OFFEREE** A person or party to whom an offer to enter into a contractual agreement is made.

**PROMISE** The expression of an intention to act, or to forbear from acting, granting a right to the promisee to expect and enforce its performance.

▬▬▬

# Ever–Tite Roofing Corp. v. Green
Roofing contractor (P) v. House owner (D)

La. Ct. App., 83 So. 2d 449 (1955).

**NATURE OF CASE:** Appeal from dismissal of action for damages for breach of contract.

**FACT SUMMARY:** The Greens (D) attempted to withdraw from a roofing contract after the Ever-Tite Roofing Corp. (P) workmen had arrived to perform the work.

## RULE OF LAW
Where a contract does not specify a time within which it may be accepted, a "reasonable time" will be implied.

**FACTS:** The Greens (D) signed a document setting out work to be done and price to be paid to Ever-Tite Roofing Corp. (Ever-Tite) (P) for reroofing their residence. A provision in the agreement stated that it would become binding upon either written acceptance or commencement of performance by Ever-Tite (P), after credit approval was obtained. Nine days later, Ever-Tite (P) loaded its trucks and sent its workmen and material to the Greens' (D) residence, where they were not permitted to work, as other roofers had been retained in their stead. The Greens (D) contend they had given Ever-Tite (P) timely notice of their withdrawal from the contract, before Ever-Tite (P) commenced actual performance of the work. Ever-Tite (P) sued the Greens (D) for breach of contract.

**ISSUES:** Where a contract does not specify a time within which it may be accepted, will a "reasonable time" be implied?

**HOLDING AND DECISION:** (Ayres, J.) Yes. Where a contract does not specify a time within which it may be accepted, a "reasonable time" will be implied. Contrary to the lower court's ruling, Ever-Tite (P) commenced performance by the loading of its trucks and transporting of its materials and workmen to the Greens' (D) residence. Thus, Ever-Tite (P) did accept the offer before withdrawal of the Greens' (D) acceptance, even though actual work was not begun. Since the contract specified no time period within which it was to be accepted, "a reasonable time must be allowed therefor in accordance with the facts and circumstances and the evident intention of the parties." Since the Greens (D) knew a delay was necessary for credit approval, and since Ever-Tite (P) proceeded with due diligence, Ever-Tite (P) accepted by commencing performance within a reasonable time. Reversed and rendered.

## ANALYSIS

The problem here is somewhat different from that of *White v. Corlies and Tift*, 46 N.Y. 467 (1871), where the manner of acceptance was simply omitted from the contract. The court there held with the original Restatement in its assumption that the offer looked toward a bilateral contract. The modern view, however, as stated in Uniform Commercial Code § 2-206, is that the offeree may choose either manner of acceptance when not explicitly restricted to a certain type of acceptance. Where an acceptance is contingent upon credit approval, as in this case, it is especially important that the manner of acceptance be clearly set out in the offer so that the parties will know exactly when the contract is formed. The provision of the offer requiring "written acceptance" or "commencing performance of the work" as alternate terms of acceptance could have been made more explicit by stating: (1) a specific time period allowed for acceptance and (2) what acts would constitute commencement of performance.

## Quicknotes

**ACCEPTANCE** Assent to the specified terms of an offer resulting in the formation of a binding agreement.

**BILATERAL CONTRACT** An agreement pursuant to which each party promises to undertake an obligation, or to forbear from acting.

**BREACH OF CONTRACT** Unlawful failure by a party to perform its obligations pursuant to contract.

**DUE DILIGENCE** The standard of care as would be taken by a reasonable person in accordance with the attendant facts and circumstances.

**OFFEREE** A person or party to whom an offer to enter into a contractual agreement is made.

# Russell v. Texas Co.

## Surface owner of land (P) v. Oil and gas lessee (D)

238 F.2d 636 (9th Cir. 1956).

**NATURE OF CASE:** Cross-appeals from judgment for plaintiff in an action seeking damages under a revocable license and for use of real property.

**FACT SUMMARY:** Russell (P), the surface owner of certain land, sent an offer of a revocable license to use the surface to Texas Co. (D), the occupier of the land. The offer stated that Texas's (D) continued use would constitute an acceptance. Texas (D) did continue to use the land.

## RULE OF LAW
Where the offeree exercises dominion over things that are offered to him, such exercise of dominion, in the absence of other circumstances showing a contrary intention, is an acceptance.

**FACTS:** Russell (P) was the surface owner of certain property. Texas Co. (D) had a mineral right lease on the land but was operating in excess of the rights granted to it by its lease. Russell (P) sent Texas (D) an offer of a revocable license for use of surface rights at a daily rental. The offer stated that Texas's (D) continued use would constitute an acceptance of the offer. Texas (D) continued to use the land but claimed that there was no contract because it did not intend to accept Russell's (P) offer. The district court awarded damages for amounts due under the license as well as for use of the land. Both parties appealed, with Texas Co. (D) claiming Russell's (P) offer had not been accepted, and the court of appeals granted review.

**ISSUE:** Where the offeree exercises dominion over things which are offered to him, is such exercise of dominion, in the absence of other circumstances showing a contrary intention, an acceptance?

**HOLDING AND DECISION:** (Halbert, J.) Yes. Where the offeree exercises dominion over things which are offered to him, such exercise of dominion, in the absence of other circumstances showing a contrary intention, is an acceptance. Here, Russell's (P) offer stated that continued use would constitute an acceptance. Texas (D) did continue its use of the land and, hence, came unequivocally within the terms specified for acceptance. The true test is whether or not the offeror was reasonably led to believe that the offeree's act was an acceptance. This test is met by the facts here. Affirmed.

## ANALYSIS

There is a legal acceptance where silence is accompanied by acts of the offeree that warrant an inference of assent.

Such acts may include the offeree's exercise of dominion over things offered to him or his taking the benefit of the offered services under circumstances that would indicate to a reasonable person that they were offered with the expectation of compensation. The duty imposed on the offeree by this rule is not a quasi-contractual duty to pay a fair value but a duty to pay or perform according to the terms of the offer.

---

## Quicknotes

**ACCEPTANCE** Assent to the specified terms of an offer resulting in the formation of a binding agreement.

**DAMAGES** Monetary compensation that may be awarded by the court to a party who has sustained injury or loss to his person, property or rights due to another party's unlawful act, omission or negligence.

**OFFER** A proposed promise to undertake performance of an action, or to refrain from acting, that is to become binding upon acceptance by the offeree.

**OFFEREE** A person or party to whom an offer to enter into a contractual agreement is made.

# Ammons v. Wilson & Co.

## Wholesale grocer (P) v. Meat packer (D)

Miss. Sup. Ct., 176 Miss. 645, 170 So. 227 (1936).

**NATURE OF CASE:** Appeal from judgment for defendant in action to recover damages for breach of contract.

**FACT SUMMARY:** Ammons (P) gave Wilson & Co.'s (D) traveling salesperson an order. In previous dealings between them, Wilson (D) had always shipped Ammons's (P) orders within a week, but this time he was silent for 12 days before rejecting Ammons's (P) offer.

> ## RULE OF LAW
> Where an offeree fails to reply to an offer, his silence or inaction operates as an acceptance where, because of previous dealings or otherwise, the offeree has given the offeror reason to understand that the silence or inaction is intended as a manifestation of assent and the offeror does so understand.

**FACTS:** Ammons (P) gave Wilson & Co.'s (Wilson) (D) traveling salesperson an order. Ammons (P) heard nothing from Wilson (D) until 12 days later when he was advised by Wilson (D), in response to his inquiry as to when the shipment would be made, that the orders had been declined. Ammons (P) had previously placed several orders with Wilson (D) through its traveling salesperson. All of these orders had been accepted and shipped within a week.

**ISSUE:** Where an offeree fails to reply to an offer, does his silence or inaction operate as an acceptance where, because of previous dealings or otherwise, the offeree has given the offeror reason to understand that the silence or inaction is intended as a manifestation of assent and the offeror does so understand?

**HOLDING AND DECISION:** (Anderson, J.) Yes. Where an offeree fails to reply to an offer, his silence or inaction operates as an acceptance where, because of previous dealings or otherwise, the offeree has given the offeror reason to understand that the silence or inaction is intended as a manifestation of assent and the offeror does so understand. Here, it was a question for the jury whether or not Wilson's (D) delay of 12 days before rejecting the order, in view of the past history of such transactions between the parties, constituted an implied acceptance. However, because the evidence as to damages was uncertain, the case is remanded. Reversed and remanded.

## ▶ ANALYSIS

There are many cases in which, because of the past relations of the parties or of accompanying circumstances, the silence of the offeree after receipt of an offer has been held to constitute acceptance and create a contract. These are all cases in which the conduct of the party denying a contract has been such as to lead the other reasonably to believe that silence, without communication, constituted an acceptance. However, circumstances which will impose a contractual obligation by mere silence (not coupled with additional circumstances) are rare.

## Quicknotes

**ACCEPTANCE** Assent to the specified terms of an offer resulting in the formation of a binding agreement.

**BREACH OF CONTRACT** Unlawful failure by a party to perform its obligations pursuant to contract.

**DAMAGES** Monetary compensation that may be awarded by the court to a party who has sustained injury or loss to his person, property or rights due to another party's unlawful act, omission or negligence.

**OFFER** A proposed promise to undertake performance of an action, or to refrain from acting, that is to become binding upon acceptance by the offeree.

**OFFEREE** A person or party to whom an offer to enter into a contractual agreement is made.

**OFFEROR** Party who makes an offer.

# Schreiber v. Olan Mills

Telemarketing calls recipient (P) v. Company engaged in telemarketing (D)

Pa. Super. Ct., 627 A.2d 806 (1993).

**NATURE OF CASE:** Appeal from dismissal of action for breach of a purported contract.

**FACT SUMMARY:** Schreiber (P), who received telemarketing calls from Olan Mills (D), contended that a letter he wrote to Olan Mills (D), in which he warned Olan Mills (D) that if he received any additional Olan Mills (D) telemarketing calls, he would bill Olan Mills (D) for his "listening services," became an enforceable contract when Olan Mills (D) made further phone contacts with Schreiber (P).

## 🏛 RULE OF LAW
An enforceable contract cannot be created where none of the elements necessary for the creation of a contract—offer, acceptance, consideration, and meeting of the minds—is present.

**FACTS:** Olan Mills (D) engaged in telemarketing to generate business. When Schreiber (P) received a telemarketing call from Olan Mills (D), he sent a detailed letter to Olan Mills (D) asserting that if Olan Mills' (D) telemarketers contacted him again, the letter would serve as a contract for his "listening services," for which he would charge $100 per hour. The letter also indicated that Schreiber (P) would assess a late payment penalty if his bills were not paid, along with collection and attorney's fees. Olan Mills (D) called Schreiber (P) two more times, which prompted him to bill Olan Mills (D) $479. When his bill was not paid, Schreiber (P) brought suit to collect the fees. Olan Mills (D) argued that no contract had been formed, and sought dismissal of the action. The trial court agreed that the requirements for the formation of a contract were absent, finding that there was no meeting of the minds, and no ordinary course of dealing or common understanding showing a mutual intent to contract for Schreiber's (P) "listening services." Accordingly, the trial court ruled that, as a matter of law, no contract had been formed. It dismissed the action, and Schreiber (P) appealed. The state's intermediate appellate court granted review.

**ISSUE:** Can an enforceable contract be created where none of the elements necessary for the creation of a contract—offer, acceptance, consideration, and meeting of the minds—is present?

**HOLDING AND DECISION:** (Popovich, J.) No. An enforceable contract cannot be created where none of the elements necessary for the creation of a contract—offer, acceptance, consideration, and meeting of the minds—is present. Although the conduct of parties may indicate that one of the parties has accepted the other party's offer for services, here it is evident that Schreiber's (P) letter did not constitute an offer for his "listening services," but rather was in the nature of a cease and desist demand. The sole purpose of the letter was to encourage Olan Mills (D) to remove Schreiber (P) from its calling lists—and not to solicit a purchaser for "listening services." The sole purpose of any additional calls that Olan Mills (D) made to Schreiber (P) was to solicit orders—and not to obtain "listening services." There can be no bargained-for-exchange (consideration) if one of the parties acts without any intention of binding itself to a purported contract for services, and, here, there was no "unconditional" manifestation on the part of Olan Mills (D) or its representative that a contract was acknowledged by Olan Mills' (D) behavior. Therefore, in this case there was no offer, acceptance, consideration or mutual meeting of the minds to effectuate the elemental aspects of a contract. Affirmed.

## ▌ ANALYSIS

An offeree may not be bound by the terms of the offer where those terms are manifestly unreasonable, so that even if, arguendo, Schreiber's (P) letter constituted an offer for his listening services, Olan Mills (D) could argue that Schreiber's (P) conditioning acceptance on conduct it would have engaged in regardless of the offer, i.e., making telemarketing calls, was unreasonable.

## *Quicknotes*

**ACCEPTANCE** Assent to the specified terms of an offer resulting in the formation of a binding agreement.

**BARGAINED FOR EXCHANGE** A requirement for adequate consideration; the promise made by the offeror induces the return promise or performance on the part of the offeree and that the promise or performance on the part of the offeree induces the promise made by the offeror.

**CONSIDERATION** Value given by one party in exchange for performance, or a promise to perform, by another party.

**OFFER** A proposed promise to undertake performance of an action, or to refrain from acting, that is to become binding upon acceptance by the offeree.

# Beneficial National Bank, U.S.A. v. Payton

Credit card issuer (P) v. Credit cardholder (D)

214 F. Supp. 2d 679 (S.D. Miss. 2001).

**NATURE OF CASE:** Cross-motion by defendant to dismiss for lack of subject-matter jurisdiction, and cross-motion by plaintiff to compel arbitration, in action to compel arbitration under a credit cardholder agreement.

**FACT SUMMARY:** A year after Payton (D) obtained a credit card from Beneficial National Bank, U.S.A. (Beneficial) (P), Beneficial (P) sent a notice to all its cardholders advising that a mandatory arbitration provision would become part of the cardholder agreement unless the cardholder rejected the change, which Payton (D) did not do. The account was assigned to Household Bank (SB), N.A. (Household) (P), which had a similar arbitration provision in its agreement, and Payton (D) continued to use the card. Subsequently, Payton (D) sought to litigate a dispute he had with Beneficial (P) and Household (P). Beneficial (P) and Household (P), in turn, brought suit seeking to compel arbitration, contending mandatory arbitration of disputes had become part of Payton's (D) cardholder agreement; Payton (D) sought to dismiss the action to compel, contending that the court lacked subject-matter jurisdiction because the mandatory arbitration provision had not become part of the agreement.

## 🏛 RULE OF LAW

A mandatory arbitration provision becomes part of a credit cardholder agreement where the cardholder has agreed that the credit card issuer may change the terms of the cardholder agreement; the credit card issuer apprises the cardholder of the arbitration provision and provides the cardholder the option of opting out of the arbitration agreement, but the cardholder fails to do so; and the cardholder continues to use the card.

**FACTS:** Payton (D) obtained a credit card from Beneficial (P) and signed a cardholder agreement. The agreement permitted Beneficial (P) to change the terms of the agreement with respect to both existing balances and future purchases. A year later, Beneficial (P) sent a notice to all its cardholders advising that a mandatory arbitration provision would become part of the cardholder agreement unless the cardholder rejected the change by giving timely notice of rejection, which Payton (D) did not do. Around a-year-and-a-half after that, Payton's (D) account was assigned to Household Bank (SB), N.A. (Household) (P). As part of the transfer, cardholders were notified of the change in an insert that contained a mandatory arbitration provision like the one Beneficial (P) had previously sent. Payton (D) continued to use the card notwithstanding this

notice. A couple of years later, Payton (D) filed suit in state court against Beneficial (P) and Household (P), claiming Household (P) had induced him by fraudulent misrepresentations and other wrongful conduct to enter into a consumer transaction. Household (P) and Beneficial (P) then brought suit in federal district court to compel arbitration under § 4 of the Federal Arbitration Act (FAA), contending that Payton's (D) state-court claims were governed by the arbitration provisions that were, according to them, part of Payton's (D) cardholder agreement. Payton (D) argued that, as a matter of law, the arbitration provisions had not become part of his cardholder agreement, and moved to dismiss for lack of subject-matter jurisdiction. Beneficial (P) and Household (P) moved to compel arbitration, arguing that the arbitration provision added to Payton's (D) cardholder agreement was valid and enforceable, since Payton (D) had initially agreed that Beneficial (P) could change the terms of the agreement, subject to certain notification requirements which Beneficial (P) had fulfilled, and that because Payton (D) continued to use his card after it was transferred to Household (P) after he was apprised of Household's (P) arbitration terms, he was bound thereby.

**ISSUE:** Does a mandatory arbitration provision become part of a credit cardholder agreement where the cardholder has agreed that the credit card issuer may change the terms of the cardholder agreement; the credit card issuer apprises the cardholder of the arbitration provision and provides the cardholder the option of opting out of the arbitration agreement, but the cardholder fails to do so; and the cardholder continues to use the card?

**HOLDING AND DECISION:** (Lee, C.J.) Yes. A mandatory arbitration provision becomes part of a credit cardholder agreement where the cardholder has agreed that the credit card issuer may change the terms of the cardholder agreement; the credit card issuer apprises the cardholder of the arbitration provision and provides the cardholder the option of opting out of the arbitration agreement, but the cardholder fails to do so; and the cardholder continues to use the card. Payton (D) first argues he never affirmatively agreed to arbitrate any disputes with Beneficial (P) or Household (P), and that the original cardholder agreement did not grant Beneficial (P) the right to add altogether new terms to the existing agreement. This argument must be rejected because the agreement permitted Beneficial (P) to "change" the terms of the agreement, and Payton (D) could anticipate that

*Continued on next page.*

such "change" would encompass an arbitration provision. Payton (D) next argues that notwithstanding his failure to affirmatively opt out of the arbitration provision was immaterial since a valid and binding arbitration agreement may not be predicated on nothing more than a failure to reject the arbitration agreement. The precedent on which Payton (D) relies for this argument, however, has been rejected in this jurisdiction. Payton (D) further argues that even if the arbitration provision became part of his cardholder agreement, his state-court claims did not fall within the scope of the arbitration provision since they related to allegedly wrongful acts that were committed prior to the purported effective date of the arbitration agreement. He argues, in other words, that the arbitration provision may not be applied retroactively to events which predated the alleged arbitration agreement. This argument is also unconvincing. It has been held that if an arbitration clause contains retroactive time-specific language, then the arbitration provision may be applied retroactively to events relating to past events. Although the provision at bar did not contain retroactive time-specific language, it was sufficiently broad to cover Payton's (D) state-court claims, especially given that any ambiguity as to the availability of arbitration is to be resolved in favor of arbitration. Finally, Payton's (D) argument that the provision is substantively unconscionable must also be rejected since it has not been shown that arbitral forum specified by the arbitration provision is fraught with bias that would affect the decisions of arbitrators. Motion to compel is granted to Beneficial (P) and Household (P).

## ▶ ANALYSIS

This decision renders consumer silence effective as acceptance, which is contrary to the long-standing contract default rule that there can be no acceptance by silence. Ostensibly, this principle would enable companies to unilaterally change numerous substantive terms of their consumer contracts, including price or other key terms, not just those related to arbitration. Other courts, however, have rejected the approach taken by the court in this case. For example, in *Long v. Fidelity Water Systems, Inc.,* 2000 U.S. Dist. LEXIS 7827 (N.D. Cal. 2000), the district court ruled in favor of the card holder, ruling that the card issuer never obtained any affirmative consent from card holder regarding incorporation of the arbitration clause as part of the existing contract, and suggesting that acceptance of an arbitration agreement may not be found merely on a party's silence in failing to reject the agreement.

## Quicknotes

**ACCEPTANCE** Assent to the specified terms of an offer resulting in the formation of a binding agreement.

**ARBITRATION CLAUSE** Provision contained in a contract pursuant to which both parties agree that any disputes arising thereunder will be resolved through arbitration.

**SUBJECT-MATTER JURISDICTION** The authority of the court to hear and decide actions involving a particular type of issue or subject.

# Dickinson v. Dodds

Offeree of real property (P) v. Offeror of real property (D)

Ct. App., Ch. Div., 2 Ch.D. 463 (1876).

**NATURE OF CASE:** Action for specific performance of a contract for the sale of real property.

**FACT SUMMARY:** On June 10, 1874, Dodds (D) gave writing to Dickinson (P) giving the latter until 9 a.m., June 12, 1874, to accept Dodds's (D) offer to purchase his land and buildings upon it for £800. On the afternoon of June 11, 1874, Dodds (D) sold the same property to Allan (D) for £800 and accepted a £40 deposit.

## RULE OF LAW
An offer may be withdrawn by an indirect revocation where the offeree receives reliable information from a third party that the offeror has engaged in conduct indicative to a reasonable person that the offer was withdrawn.

**FACTS:** On June 10, 1874, Dodds (D) gave Dickinson (P) a writing that stated that the former agreed to sell his land and buildings upon it to the latter for £800, the offer to be left open until June 12, 1874, 9 a.m. Dickinson (P) decided to accept on the morning of June 11, 1874, but did not immediately convey his acceptance, believing he had until next morning. That afternoon, one Berry informed Dickinson (P) that Dodds (D) had decided to sell the property to Allan (D). Dickinson (P) went to Dodds's (D) mother-in-law's home, where he was staying, and left his acceptance there, but it never got to Dodds (D). The next morning at 7 a.m., Berry, as Dickinson's (P) agent, attempted to give a copy of the acceptance to Dodds (D), who said it was too late. On June 11, 1874, the day before, Dodds (D) had sold the property to Allan (D) for £800 and had accepted a £40 deposit.

**ISSUE:** May an offer be withdrawn by an indirect revocation where the offeree receives reliable information from a third party that the offeror has engaged in conduct indicative to a reasonable person that the offer was withdrawn?

**HOLDING AND DECISION:** (Lord James, J.) Yes. An offer may be withdrawn by an indirect revocation where the offeree receives reliable information from a third party that the offeror has engaged in conduct indicative to a reasonable person that the offer was withdrawn. The writing was not an agreement to sell but an offer. Both parties had not yet agreed to go through with the deal. There was no consideration given for the promise. The promise was not binding, so Dodds (D) was free to do whatever he wanted before receiving acceptance from Dickinson (P). There did not have to be an express and actual withdrawal of the offer. From the circumstances,

Dickinson (P) knew that Dodds (D) had changed his mind. It was clear from his statements and actions. Accordingly, there was no meeting of the minds between the two parties and no contract.

**CONCURRENCE:** (Lord Mellish, J.) The mere offer to sell property can be revoked at any time, so it would be absurd to hold an offeror liable to an offeree who has knowledge that an offer has been revoked. That the offer was in writing makes no difference.

## ANALYSIS

As seen, an indirect revocation may arise through a third party or by the circumstances. The first Restatement stated that the doctrine of indirect revocation should be limited to the sale of land and chattels, but Restatement (Second), § 42, now holds oppositely. There is always a concern as to what information is reliable. The information must be true and put a reasonable man acting in good faith to inquiry. But what if the offeree hears reliably that the offeror has made the same offer to a second person? Professor Grismore believes that a reasonable man would conclude that since he was given no notice of revocation, the offeror is willing to run the risk of two open offers.

---

## Quicknotes

**GOOD FAITH** An honest intention to abstain from taking advantage of another.

**OFFER** A proposed promise to undertake performance of an action, or to refrain from acting, that is to become binding upon acceptance by the offeree.

**OFFEREE** A person or party to whom an offer to enter into a contractual agreement is made.

**OFFEROR** Party who makes an offer.

**SPECIFIC PERFORMANCE** An equitable remedy whereby the court requires the parties to perform their obligations pursuant to a contract.

# Humble Oil & Refining Co. v. Westside Investment Corp.

Option holder (P) v. Option grantor (D)

Tex. Sup. Ct., 428 S.W.2d 92 (1968).

**NATURE OF CASE:** Appeal from affirmance of summary judgment for defendant in action for specific performance.

**FACT SUMMARY:** Westside Investment Corp. (Westside) (D) granted Humble Oil & Refining Co. (Humble) (P) an irrevocable option to purchase certain property. Humble (P) requested that Westside (D) agree to an additional term and then communicated its unqualified exercise of the option.

> 🏛 **RULE OF LAW**
> If an original offer is irrevocable and creates in the offeree a "binding option," the rule that a counteroffer terminates the power of acceptance does not apply.

**FACTS:** Humble Oil & Refining Co. (Humble) (P) paid Westside Investment Corp. (Westside) (D) $50 for an irrevocable option to purchase certain property. Humble (P) then wrote Westside (D) that it sought to amend the sales contract to provide that Westside (D) would extend all utility lines to the property prior to the closing date. Before the option expired, Humble (P) wrote a second letter to Westside (D), in which it stated that it was exercising its option, that this exercise was not qualified in any way, and that Westside (D) could disregard the proposed amendment in the previous letter. Westside (D) considered the proposed amendment to be a rejection of the option contract. Humble (P) brought suit for specific performance. The trial court granted summary judgment for Westside (D), and the state's intermediate appellate court affirmed. The state's highest court granted review.

**ISSUE:** If an original offer is irrevocable and creates in the offeree a "binding option," does the rule that a counteroffer terminates the power of acceptance apply?

**HOLDING AND DECISION:** (Smith, J.) No. If an original offer is irrevocable and creates in the offeree a "binding option," the rule that a counteroffer terminates the power of acceptance does not apply. In such a case, neither a counteroffer by the offeree nor the conduct of further negotiations not resulting in a contract will terminate the power of acceptance. Hence, Humble's (P) first letter did not terminate the option contract. It did not surrender or reject the option. Considered as an independent agreement, the option gave Humble (P) the right to purchase within the specified time and bound Westside (D) to keep the option open during that time. The offer of an option was still binding when Humble (P) exercised the option. Hence, Humble (P) is entitled to specific performance and the case is remanded for trial.

▌**ANALYSIS**

One view is that an option consists of two separate elements: one, the offer to perform a certain act (such as to sell property), which is an incomplete contract until it is accepted, and the other, the agreement to give the optionee a certain time within which to exercise his option of accepting. A second view is that an option is a unilateral writing which lacks the mutual elements of a contract but which, upon acceptance by the optionee, ripens into an executory contract that is binding upon both parties. Other authorities hold that a binding option is a contract and also an offer which, when accepted, will create another contract. The Restatement (Second) provides that the power to accept an option is not terminated by revocation, counteroffer, or the death of the offeror.

## Quicknotes

**ACCEPTANCE** Assent to the specified terms of an offer resulting in the formation of a binding agreement.

**COUNTEROFFER** An offer made by the offeree which has the effect of rejecting the offer deemed unsatisfactory and of proposing a different offer.

**OFFER** A proposed promise to undertake performance of an action, or to refrain from acting, that is to become binding upon acceptance by the offeree.

**OFFEREE** A person or party to whom an offer to enter into a contractual agreement is made.

**OFFEROR** Party who makes an offer.

**REVOCATION** The cancellation or withdrawal of some authority conferred, or of destruction or making void an instrument drafted.

**SPECIFIC PERFORMANCE** An equitable remedy whereby the court requires the parties to perform their obligations pursuant to a contract.

**SUMMARY JUDGMENT** Judgment rendered by a court in response to a motion made by one of the parties, claiming that the lack of a question of material fact in respect to an issue warrants disposition of the issue without consideration by the jury.

# Marchiondo v. Scheck

Real estate broker (P) v. Real estate seller (D)

N.M. Sup. Ct., 78 N.M. 440, 432 P.2d 405 (1967).

**NATURE OF CASE:** Appeal from dismissal of action to recover real estate commission.

**FACT SUMMARY:** Scheck (D) offered to sell realty to a specified prospective buyer and agreed to pay Marchiondo (P) a broker's commission. Later Scheck (D) revoked the offer. Shortly after the revocation and within the time limit set by the offer, Marchiondo (P) obtained the offeree's acceptance.

> # RULE OF LAW
> Where an offer invites an offeree to accept by rendering a performance, a unilateral contract with a condition is created when the offeree partially performs, so that the offeror is fully liable on the contract when the offeree completes performance.

**FACTS:** Scheck (D) offered to sell real estate to a specified prospective buyer and agreed to pay Marchiondo (P) a percentage of the sales price as a commission. The offer set a six-day time limit for acceptance, and Marchiondo (P) received Scheck's (D) revocation of the offer on the sixth day. Later that day, Marchiondo (P) obtained the offeree's acceptance. Marchiondo (P) brought suit to recover his broker's commission. The trial court dismissed the action, and the state's highest court granted review.

**ISSUE:** Where an offer invites an offeree to accept by rendering a performance, is a unilateral contract with a condition created when the offeree partially performs, so that the offeror is fully liable on the contract when the offeree completes performance?

**HOLDING AND DECISION:** (Wood, J.) Yes. Where an offer invites an offeree to accept by rendering a performance, a unilateral contract with a condition is created when the offeree partially performs, so that the offeror is fully liable on the contract when the offeree completes performance. The offeror's duty of performance under an option contract so created is conditional on the offeree's completion of performance in accordance with the terms of the offer. In such a case, the offeree's part performance furnishes the acceptance and consideration for a binding contract conditional upon the offeree's full performance. Hence, here Scheck's (D) right to revoke his offer depends upon whether Marchiondo (P) had partially performed before he received Scheck's (D) revocation. What constitutes part performance will vary from case to case since what can be done toward performance is determined by what is authorized to be done. Hence, it is a question of fact to be determined at the trial. This case is remanded to the trial court so that it can make a finding on the issue of

Marchiondo's (P) part performance prior to the revocation. Reversed and remanded.

▶ **ANALYSIS**

In many cases involving real estate brokers, it has been held that the owner is no longer privileged to revoke after the broker has taken substantial steps toward rendering performance by advertising the property, soliciting prospective sellers, showing the property, or otherwise. Where notice of revocation is given when the broker's services have proceeded to the point where success is probable, the court may be convinced it was given for the purpose of avoiding payment of the commission while at the same time enjoying the benefit of the services. Such a revocation is in bad faith, and the broker may be held entitled to the commission on the ground that the owner has wrongfully prevented fulfillment of the condition precedent to the right to payment.

---

## Quicknotes

**ACCEPTANCE** Assent to the specified terms of an offer resulting in the formation of a binding agreement.

**BAD FAITH** Conduct that is intentionally misleading or deceptive.

**CONDITION PRECEDENT** The happening of an uncertain occurrence that is necessary before a particular right or interest may be obtained or an action performed.

**PART PERFORMANCE** Partial performance of a contract, promise or obligation.

**REVOCATION** The cancellation or withdrawal of some authority conferred, or of destruction or making void an instrument drafted.

**UNILATERAL CONTRACT** An agreement pursuant to which a party agrees to act without an express exchange for performance on the part of the other party.

# James Baird Co. v. Gimbel Brothers, Inc.

Contractor (P) v. Supplier (D)

64 F.2d 344 (2d Cir. 1933).

**NATURE OF CASE:** Appeal from judgment for defendant in action for breach of a contract for the sale of goods.

**FACT SUMMARY:** Gimbel Brothers, Inc. (Gimbel) (D) offered to supply linoleum to various contractors who were bidding on a public construction contract. James Baird Co. (Baird) (P), relying on Gimbel's (D) quoted prices, submitted a bid and later the same day received a telegraphed message from Gimbel (D) that its quoted prices were in error. Baird's (P) bid was accepted.

## RULE OF LAW
The doctrine of promissory estoppel is inapplicable to cases where there is an offer for exchange where the offer is not intended to become a promise until consideration is received.

**FACTS:** Gimbel (D), having heard that bids were being taken for a public building, had an employee obtain the specifications for linoleum required for the building and submitted offers to various possible contractors, including Baird (P), of two prices for linoleum depending upon the quality used. The offer was made in ignorance of a mistake as to the actual amount of linoleum needed, causing Gimbel's (D) prices to be about half the actual cost. The offer concluded as follows: "If successful in being awarded this contract, it will be absolutely guaranteed . . . and . . . we are offering these prices for reasonable (sic) prompt acceptance after the general contract has been awarded." Baird (P) received this on the 28th, the same day on which Gimbel (D) discovered its mistake, and telegraphed all contractors of the error, but the communication was received by Baird (P) just after Baird (P) submitted its lump-sum bid relying on Gimbel's (D) erroneous prices. Baird's (P) bid was accepted on the 30th. Baird (P) received Gimbel's (D) written confirmation of the error on the 31st but sent an acceptance despite this two days later. Gimbel (D) refused to recognize a contract.

**ISSUE:** Is the doctrine of promissory estoppel applicable to cases where there is an offer for exchange where the offer is not intended to become a promise until consideration is received?

**HOLDING AND DECISION:** (Hand, J.) No. The doctrine of promissory estoppel is inapplicable to cases where there is an offer for exchange where the offer is not intended to become a promise until consideration is received. First, looking at the language of Gimbel's (D) offer, Gimbel's (D) use of the phrase "if successful in being awarded this contract" clearly shows Gimbel's (D) intent of not being bound simply by a contractor relying or acting upon the quoted prices. This is reinforced by the phrase "prompt acceptance after the general contract has been awarded." No award had been made at the time, and reliance on the prices cannot be said to be an award of the contract. Had a relying contractor been awarded the contract and then repudiated it, Gimbel (D) would not have had any right to sue for breach, nor could Gimbel (D) have gone against his estate had the relying contractor gone bankrupt. The contractors could have protected themselves by insisting on a contract guaranteeing the prices before relying upon them. The court will not strain to find a contract in aid of one who fails to protect himself. The theory of promissory estoppel is not available, as it is appropriate in donative or charitable cases where harsh results to the promisee arising from the promisor's breaking his relied-upon promise are to be protected against. However, an offer for an exchange, either being an act or another promise, is not meant to become a promise until consideration is received. Here, the linoleum was to be delivered for the contractor's acceptance, not his bid. An option contract has not arisen, as it is clear from the language of the offer that Gimbel (D) had no intention of assuming a one-sided obligation. Affirmed.

## ANALYSIS

Later cases have held the doctrine of promissory estoppel not to be as narrow. The majority of courts that have considered the issue hold that justifiable detrimental reliance on an offer renders it irrevocable. Naturally, the contractor must have something upon which to justifiably rely. The court in its decision notes that Restatement (Second) § 90 follows its view. However, Restatement (Second) § 90 has expanded the section so as to enlarge its scope according to the more modern viewpoint. It must be shown that the offeror foresaw that his promise would reasonably induce forbearance or action. The first inkling of this doctrine probably arose in the well-known *Hamer v. Sidway*, 27 N.E. 256 (1891), where an uncle promised to pay his nephew $5,000 for refraining from the use of liquor, swearing, and other activities until his 21st birthday and reached full maturity in Justice Traynor's decision in *Drennan v. Star Paving Company*, 51 Cal. 2d 409, 333 P.2d 757 (1958). Generally, this case is a good example of the manner in which the court will examine the words and actions of the parties in order to determine their intent and, hence, the

*Continued on next page.*

existence of a contract. It appears that Gimbel (D) could have used the defense of unilateral mistake based upon a clerical error, as seen in *M. F. Kemper Construction Co. v. City of Los Angeles,* 235 P.2d 7 (1951).

━ ▬ ━

## Quicknotes

**ACCEPTANCE** Assent to the specified terms of an offer resulting in the formation of a binding agreement.

**BREACH OF CONTRACT** Unlawful failure by a party to perform its obligations pursuant to contract.

**PROMISE** The expression of an intention to act, or to forbear from acting, granting a right to the promisee to expect and enforce its performance.

**PROMISEE** Party to whom a promise is made.

**PROMISOR** Party who promises to render an obligation to another in the future.

**PROMISSORY ESTOPPEL** A promise that is enforceable if the promisor should reasonably expect that it will induce action or forbearance on the part of the promisee, and does in fact cause such action or forbearance, and it is the only means of avoiding injustice.

━ ▬ ━

Contractor (P) v.

# Drennan v. Star Paving Co.

## Contractor (P) v. Subcontractor (D)

Cal. Sup. Ct., 51 Cal. 2d 409, 333 P.2d 757 (1958).

**NATURE OF CASE:** Appeal from grant of damages for failure to perform according to a bid.

**FACT SUMMARY:** Drennan (P), a contractor, in preparing his bid on a public construction project, used the bid for paving work by subcontractor Star Paving Co. (Star) (D), but after Drennan (P) was awarded the contract, Star (D) informed Drennan (P) that its paving bid was in error.

### 🏛 RULE OF LAW
A promise which the promisor should reasonably expect to induce action or forbearance of a definite and substantial character on the part of a promisee and which does induce such action or forbearance is binding if injustice can be avoided only by enforcement of the promise.

**FACTS:** Drennan (P) was preparing a bid on a public school construction project. On the day the bid was to be submitted, Star Paving Co. (Star) (D) phoned in its bid of $7,131.60 for paving. That bid was recorded and posted on a master sheet by Drennan (P). It was customary in the area for bids to be phoned in on the day set for bidding and for general contractors to rely on them in computing their own bids. Star's (D) bid for paving was low and used by Drennan (P) in preparing his bid, which was low. The contract was awarded to Drennan (P) that same evening. The next day, Star (D) informed Drennan (P) of an error in its paving bid and refused to do the paving for less than $15,000. Drennan (P), after several months of searching, engaged another company to do the paving for $10,948.66 and sued for the cost difference. From adverse judgment in the lower courts, Star (D) appealed.

**ISSUE:** Is a promise which the promisor should reasonably expect to induce action or forbearance of a definite and substantial character on the part of a promisee and which does induce such action or forbearance binding if injustice can only be avoided by enforcement of the promise?

**HOLDING AND DECISION:** (Traynor, J.) Yes. A promise which the promisor should reasonably expect to induce action or forbearance of a definite and substantial character on the part of a promisee and which does induce such action or forbearance is binding if injustice can be avoided only by enforcement of the promise. Star (D) had reason to expect that if its bid was low it would be used by Drennan (P) and so induced "action . . . of a definite and substantial character on the part of the promisee." Star's

(D) bid did not state nor clearly imply revocability at any time before acceptance. Where there is an offer for a unilateral contract, the theory that the offer is revocable at any time before complete performance is obsolete. When any part of the consideration requested in the offer is given or tendered by the offeree, the offeror is bound. That is, the main offer includes a subsidiary promise, which is implied, that if part of the requested performance is given, the offeror will not revoke his offer, and if tender is made, it will be accepted. Restatement § 45. In more extreme cases, merely acting in justifiable reliance of an offer may serve as sufficient reason to make the promise binding. Restatement § 90. Section 90's purpose is to make a promise binding even though consideration is lacking; its absence is not fatal to the enforcement of the subsidiary promise. Reasonable reliance acts in lieu of ordinary consideration. Star (D) had a stake in Drennan's (P) reliance on its bid. This interest plus Drennan's (P) being bound by his own bid make it only fair that Drennan (P) should have the chance to accept Star's (D) bid after the general contract was awarded Drennan (P). While Star's (D) bid was the result of mistake, it was not such a mistake that Drennan (P) knew or should have known was in error. A 160 percent variance in paving bids was not unusual in the area. Because the mistake misled Drennan (P) as to the paving cost under the circumstances, Star's (D) bid should be enforced. Affirmed.

### ▶ ANALYSIS

The case greatly broadened the view of promissory estoppel, Restatement § 90, as interpreted by Judge Hand in *James Baird Co. v. Gimbel Bros.*, 64 F. 2d 344 (1933), goes beyond the area of charitable or donative promises to general business use. This view was adopted in Restatement (Second) § 90 written after this case. Note a subcontractor's bid must be more than a mere estimate, and of course, if it reasonably appears to be based upon a mistake, reliance cannot be justified. The cases that apply promissory estoppel show the subcontractor to be bound by his bid, but the general contractor is not bound to accept the bid. Note that Judge Traynor works into Restatement § 90 through § 45 (the Brooklyn Bridge hypothetical), expanding the view that giving or tendering consideration will bind the promise to include justifiable reliance to have the same effect. In the *Drennan* case, circumstances and business practices peculiar to the area were important. Telephoned bids were a common

*Continued on next page.*

practice. Wide variances in paving costs were expected, thereby adding strength to Drennan's (P) position, as an error in a paving bid would not be reasonably noticed. Also see Restatement (Second) § 89B(2) for this viewpoint as extended to option contracts.

━━■■■━━

## Quicknotes

**DAMAGES** Monetary compensation that may be awarded by the court to a party who has sustained injury or loss to his person, property or rights due to another party's unlawful act, omission or negligence.

**FORBEARANCE** Refraining from doing something that one has the legal right to do.

**PROMISE** The expression of an intention to act, or to forbear from acting, granting a right to the promisee to expect and enforce its performance.

**PROMISEE** Party to whom a promise is made.

**PROMISOR** Party who promises to render an obligation to another in the future.

**PROMISSORY ESTOPPEL** A promise that is enforceable if the promisor should reasonably expect that it will induce action or forbearance on the part of the promisee, and does in fact cause such action or forbearance, and it is the only means of avoiding injustice.

# Adams v. Lindsell

## Wool purchaser (P) v. Wool merchant (D)

K.B., 106 Eng. Rep. 250 (1818).

**NATURE OF CASE:** Action for breach of contract.

**FACT SUMMARY:** One day after Adams (P) had mailed his acceptance of Lindsell's (D) offer to sell wool, Lindsell (D) sold the wool to another.

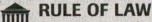

## RULE OF LAW
An acceptance of an offer is effective upon dispatch.

**FACTS:** On September 2, 1817, Lindsell (D), a wool dealer, mailed a letter to Adams (P) in which he offered to sell Adams (P) some wool. Because Lindsell (D) had misaddressed the letter, Adams (P) did not receive it until September 5. On that same day, Adams (P) mailed his acceptance of Lindsell's (D) offer, which did not reach Lindsell (D) until September 9. On September 8, Lindsell (D), unaware that Adams (P) had accepted his offer, sold the wool to another person. In an action by Adams (P) for nondelivery of the wool, Lindsell (D) claimed that, in the usual course of the mails, the acceptance should have reached him on September 7.

**ISSUE:** Is an acceptance of an offer effective upon dispatch?

**HOLDING AND DECISION:** [Judge not stated in casebook excerpt.] Yes. An acceptance of an offer is effective upon dispatch. An acceptance is immediately effective upon its being put out of the offeree's possession. If an offeror is not to be considered bound by his offer until he has received notice of the offeror's acceptance, then the offeree likewise should not be bound until he has received notification that the offeror has received his answer and agreed to it. There is no end to this line of reasoning. If an acceptance is only effective upon receipt, no contract could ever be completed by the mails. To give some stability and sense of finality to bargaining, an offeror must be considered in law as making, during every instant of the time his letter is en route, the same identical offer: a contract is formed by the offeree's acceptance, which is communicated upon dispatch. In the present case, the delay was caused by Lindsell's (D) neglect in properly addressing his offer. Hence, he is liable for any loss that has been sustained. Rule discharged.

## ▶ ANALYSIS

Although *Adams v. Lindsell* states the generally adopted rule, it has met with substantial criticism. Langdell has summarized the opposing view in terms of allocating the hardship between the offeror or offeree: "the hardship consists in making one liable on a contract which he is ignorant of having made; adopting the other view, it consists in depriving one of the benefit of a contract which he supposes he has made. Between these two evils, the latter must be favored since it leaves everything in status quo." *Summary of the Law of Contracts*, 2d ed., 1880, pp. 20-21.

━━▬━━

## Quicknotes

**ACCEPTANCE** Assent to the specified terms of an offer resulting in the formation of a binding agreement.

**BREACH OF CONTRACT** Unlawful failure by a party to perform its obligations pursuant to contract.

**OFFER** A proposed promise to undertake performance of an action, or to refrain from acting, that is to become binding upon acceptance by the offeree.

**OFFEREE** A person or party to whom an offer to enter into a contractual agreement is made.

**OFFEROR** Party who makes an offer.

━━▬━━

# Minneapolis & St. Louis Railway Co. v. Columbus Rolling-Mill Co.

Railroad company (P) v. Manufacturer (D)

119 U.S. 149 (1886).

**NATURE OF CASE:** Appeal from verdict for defendant in action for specific performance of a contract for the sale of goods.

**FACT SUMMARY:** Columbus Rolling-Mill Co. (Columbus) (D) offered to sell between 2,000 to 5,000 tons of 50 lb. rails for $54 per gross ton. Minneapolis & St. Louis Railway Co. (Minneapolis) (P) placed an order for 1,200 tons, which Columbus (D) refused to fill. Minneapolis (P) then placed a second order for 2,000 tons, which Columbus (D) also refused to fill.

## RULE OF LAW
An "acceptance" of an offer that does not assent to the offer as made is a rejection by the offeree and a counteroffer to the offeror, who then acquires the right to accept or reject the counteroffer.

**FACTS:** On December 5, 1879, Minneapolis & St. Louis Railway Co. (Minneapolis) (P) inquired as to prices of 500 to 3,000 tons of 50 lb. steel rails and 2,000 to 5,000 tons of iron rails, for a March 1880 delivery. On December 8, 1879, Columbus Rolling-Mill Co. (Columbus) (D) replied by letter, stating that it did not produce steel rails but would sell 2,000 to 5,000 50 lb. iron rails for $54 per gross ton. Columbus (D) would permit notification by Minneapolis (P) of its acceptance to Columbus's (D) offer until December 20, 1879. On December 16, 1879, Minneapolis (P) telegraphed Columbus (D) of its acceptance and placed an order for 1,200 tons of 50 lb. iron rails at $54 per gross ton and sent a letter the same day confirming the telegraphed acceptance and terms and requested a contract. On December 18, 1879, Columbus (D) telegraphed its refusal to book this order. On December 19, 1879, Minneapolis (P) telegraphed an order for 2,000 tons of 50 lb. iron rails and requested a contract for this. Columbus (D) refused and denied the existence of a contract.

**ISSUE:** Is an "acceptance" of an offer that does not assent to the offer as made a rejection by the offeree and a counteroffer to the offeror, who then acquires the right to accept or reject the counteroffer?

**HOLDING AND DECISION:** (Gray, J.) Yes. An "acceptance" of an offer that does not assent to the offer as made is a rejection by the offeree and a counteroffer to the offeror, who then acquires the right to accept or reject the counteroffer. Minneapolis's (P) failure to place an order within the terms of the offer is a rejection of the offer. By so doing, Minneapolis (P) put an end to negotiations, unless the party making the original offer, Columbus (D), offered to renew negotiations or assented to the offeree's modifica-

tion. Columbus (D) never assented to Minneapolis's (P) modification of 1,200 tons to Columbus's (D) offer of a minimum 2,000 tons to a maximum 5,000 tons. Neither did Columbus (D) reopen negotiations. Accordingly, Minneapolis's (P) second acceptance within the terms, and referral back to the date of the original offer, was ineffectual in creating any rights in Minneapolis (P) against Columbus (D). Affirmed.

## ANALYSIS

Under Restatement of Contracts, § 38, while a counteroffer is a rejection as it manifests the offeree's unwillingness to assent to the offer as made, there are two exceptions. A counteroffer will not have the effect of a rejection where (1) the offeror expressly invites a counteroffer or (2) the offeree in making the counteroffer states he still has the original offer under consideration. Neither exception has effect in this case. Minneapolis's (P) referral in its second acceptance to the original offer is not enough to meet the second exception above, as Minneapolis (P) never stated its continued consideration of the original offer in its first acceptance.

---

## Quicknotes

**ACCEPTANCE** Assent to the specified terms of an offer resulting in the formation of a binding agreement.

**COUNTEROFFER** An offer made by the offeree which has the effect of rejecting the offer deemed unsatisfactory and of proposing a different offer.

**OFFER** A proposed promise to undertake performance of an action, or to refrain from acting, that is to become binding upon acceptance by the offeree.

**OFFEREE** A person or party to whom an offer to enter into a contractual agreement is made.

**OFFEROR** Party who makes an offer.

**SPECIFIC PERFORMANCE** An equitable remedy whereby the court requires the parties to perform their obligations pursuant to a contract.

---

# DTE Energy Technologies, Inc. v. Briggs Electric, Inc.

Electric generator seller (P) v. Electrical subcontractor (D)

2007 WL 674321 (E.D. Mich. 2007).

**NATURE OF CASE:** Motion to dismiss in action for breach of contract and for declaratory judgment.

**FACT SUMMARY:** DTE Energy Technologies, Inc. (P) contended that a forum-selection clause that was sent to Briggs Electric, Inc. (Briggs) (D) as part of an Order Acknowledgment, in response to Briggs's (D) Purchase Order, was enforceable.

## RULE OF LAW

Under the Uniform Commercial Code (U.C.C.), a forum-selection clause in a contract between merchants will not be enforced where it is contained in fine print, is considered an additional term, and materially alters the parties' contract.

**FACTS:** DTE Energy Technologies, Inc. (DTE) (P), a Michigan corporation, sold electric generators to Briggs Electric, Inc. (Briggs) (D), an electrical subcontractor on a project in California. Briggs (D) had sent a Purchase Order to DTE (P), which was seemingly confirmed by DTE (P) in an email around 20 days later. A little less than a month later, DTE (P) sent an Order Acknowledgment to Briggs (D), which had attached to it DTE's (P) Standard Terms and Conditions of Sale. This document contained a forum-selection clause that required that any disputes be adjudicated in a Michigan court applying Michigan law. Each party eventually had claims against the other (DTE (P) claimed breach of contract and nonpayment; Briggs (D) claimed damages from delay) and Briggs (D) sought mediation in California to determine the parties' contractual rights. In response, DTE (P) brought suit in Michigan federal district court for breach of contract and for a declaration that it did not have to mediate its dispute in California. Briggs (D) contended that its Purchase Order constituted an offer that DTE (P) accepted by its conduct, whereas DTE (P) contended that its Order Acknowledgment and the Standard Terms and Conditions of Sale attached thereto should be construed as the offer, which Briggs (D) accepted when it sent payment without objection to the terms contained therein. Briggs (D) contended that it had not agreed to the forum-selection clause, and moved to dismiss for lack of jurisdiction.

**ISSUE:** Under the U.C.C., will a forum-selection clause in a contract between merchants be enforced where it is contained in fine print, is considered an additional term, and materially alters the parties' contract?

**HOLDING AND DECISION:** (Duggan, J.) No. Under the U.C.C., a forum-selection clause in a contract

between merchants will not be enforced where it is contained in fine print, is considered an additional term, and materially alters the parties' contract. Contrary to DTE's (P) argument, the Purchase Order was sufficiently definite to constitute an offer since it contained price, quantity, and delivery terms. It was also irrelevant that Briggs (D) was not yet the subcontractor on the project when it sent the Purchase Order. Moreover, the Order Acknowledgment referenced, and reflected the terms of, the Purchase Order. Accordingly, the Purchase Order constituted the offer in the transaction, as asserted by Briggs (D). Accordingly, the task is to determine that effect the forum-selection clause had, i.e., whether it was a part of the contract. U.C.C. § 2-207 provides that a written confirmation operates as an acceptance even though its terms are not identical to those contained in the offer. One exception to this general rule is that a party can state "acceptance is expressly made conditional on assent to the additional or different terms." This has been interpreted as meaning that an acceptance must be expressly conditional on the offeror's assent to those terms. DTE (P) argues that even if the Purchase Order constituted an offer, it expressly rejected the offer in its Order Acknowledgment because the terms attached thereto indicated that they constituted the parties' entire understanding and agreement. This argument is rejected because this "entire agreement" provision did not contemplate Briggs's (D) assent to the additional or different terms, but instead made any additional or different terms binding with or without Briggs's (D) assent. Therefore, the additional terms are construed as proposals for addition to the contract. When two merchants are involved, as here, the additional terms become part of the contract unless there is an applicable exception. One exception is where the additional term "materially alters" the contract. Briggs (D) claims that an exception applies— namely, that the forum-selection clause is an additional term and that it "materially alters" the terms of the parties' contract. Determinative of this issue is that the state's highest court would rule that a unilateral addition of a forum-selection clause to a contract governed by the U.C.C. constitutes a material alteration of that contract. Therefore, Briggs (D) is not bound by the forum-selection clause since it was contained in the fine print of the additional terms and materially altered the contract. Motion to dismiss granted.

*Continued on next page.*

# ▶ ANALYSIS

The rule contained in U.C.C. § 2-207 altered the common law's "mirror image" rule, which requires that the terms of an acceptance must be identical to those made in the offer for there to be a binding contract. If the acceptance is not identical, assent is not manifested. Under the common law, any modifications made by the offeree in the acceptance constituted an absolute rejection of the offer and a counteroffer. The rule in § 2-207 attempts to temper the absolutist approach of the common law to facilitate commerce between merchants who rely on standard forms.

■—■—■

# Quicknotes

**ACCEPTANCE** Assent to the specified terms of an offer resulting in the formation of a binding agreement.

**BREACH OF CONTRACT** Unlawful failure by a party to perform its obligations pursuant to contract.

**DECLARATORY JUDGMENT** A judgment of the court establishing the rights of the parties.

**FORUM SELECTION CLAUSE** Provision contained in a contract setting forth the particular forum in which the parties would resolve a matter if a dispute were to arise.

**JURISDICTION** The authority of a court to hear and declare judgment in respect to a particular matter.

**MIRROR-IMAGE RULE** The common-law rule that for acceptance to be effective the offeree must accept each and every term of the offer.

**MOTION TO DISMISS** Motion to terminate an action based on the adequacy of the pleadings, improper service or venue, etc.

**OFFER** A proposed promise to undertake performance of an action, or to refrain from acting, that is to become binding upon acceptance by the offeree.

**OFFEREE** A person or party to whom an offer to enter into a contractual agreement is made.

**OFFEROR** Party who makes an offer.

■—■—■

# Textile Unlimited, Inc. v. A..BMH and Company, Inc.

Yarn purchaser (D) v. Yarn seller (P)

240 F.3d 781 (9th Cir. 2001).

**NATURE OF CASE:** Appeal from district court's order staying an arbitration proceeding.

**FACT SUMMARY:** When A..BMH and Company, Inc. (P) claimed that Textile Unlimited, Inc. (Textile) (D) had contractually submitted to arbitration, Textile (D) argued that the Federal Arbitration Act did not require venue in the contractually designated arbitration locale.

## 🏛 RULE OF LAW
The Federal Arbitration Act does not require venue in the contractually designated arbitration locale.

**FACTS:** During a ten-month period, Textile Unlimited, Inc. (Textile) (D) bought yarn from A..BMH and Company, Inc. (A..BMH) (P) in 38 transactions. Each transaction followed the pattern that Textile (D) would send a purchase order, and A..BMH (P) would respond with an invoice and an order acknowledgement. Both the invoice and acknowledgment contained additional terms tucked onto the back, specifically that the sale would be subject to an arbitration clause requiring arbitration in Atlanta, Georgia. Textile (D) did not request any alterations in these invoices. After receiving a shipment in September 1998, Textile (D) refused to pay, alleging that the yarn was defective. A..BMH (P) submitted the matter to arbitration in Atlanta. Textile (D) protested, arguing that the arbitration clause had not been properly woven into the contract and filed suit in the U.S. District Court for the Central District of California to enjoin the arbitration. The arbitrator, nevertheless, found the case was arbitrable. Textile (D) moved to stay the arbitration. The district court granted the request, determining that venue was proper in the Central District of California, notwithstanding the Atlanta venue requirement set forth in the alleged arbitration agreement. A..BMH (P) appealed.

**ISSUE:** Does the Federal Arbitration Act require venue in the contractually designated arbitration locale?

**HOLDING AND DECISION:** (Thomas, J.) No. The Federal Arbitration Act does not require venue in the contractually designated arbitration locale. This result is consistent with the underpinnings of arbitration theory. One of the threads running through federal arbitration jurisprudence is the notion that arbitration is a matter of contract and a party cannot be required to submit to arbitration any dispute which he or she has not agreed to submit. Requiring a party to contest the very existence of an arbitration agreement in a forum dictated by the disputed arbitration clause would run counter to that fundamental principle. Affirmed.

## ▶ ANALYSIS
Nothing in the Federal Arbitration Act requires that an action to enjoin arbitration be brought in the district where the contract designated the arbitration to occur.

## Quicknotes
**ARBITRATION** An alternative resolution process where a dispute is heard and decided by a neutral third party, rather than through legal proceedings.

**ENJOIN** The ordering of a party to cease the conduct of a specific activity.

**VENUE** The specific geographic location over which a court has jurisdiction to hear a suit.

# Hill v. Gateway 2000

Computer purchaser (P) v. Computer vendor (D)

105 F.3d 1147 (7th Cir.), *cert. denied*, 522 U.S. 808 (1997).

**NATURE OF CASE:** Appeal of denial of a motion to compel arbitration.

**FACT SUMMARY:** Hill (P) brought a RICO suit against Gateway 2000 (Gateway) (D) after purchasing a mail order computer. Gateway (D) moved to compel arbitration. The motion was denied, and Gateway (D) appealed.

## 🏛 RULE OF LAW
Terms sent in the box with a product that state that they govern the sale unless the product is returned within 30 days are binding on a buyer who does not return the product.

**FACTS:** Hill (P) purchased a computer from Gateway 2000 (Gateway) (D) through a telephone order and subsequently brought suit against Gateway (D), in which a civil Racketeer Influence and Corrupt Organizations Act (RICO) claim and other claims were asserted. Gateway (D) thereupon sought enforcement of an arbitration clause which had been included in the terms sent to Hill (P) in the box in which the computer was shipped. The federal district court denied the arbitration request, and Gateway (D) appealed.

**ISSUE:** Are terms sent in the box with a product that state that they govern the sale unless the product is returned within 30 days binding on a buyer who does not return the product?

**HOLDING AND DECISION:** (Easterbrook, J.) Yes. Terms sent in the box with a product that state that they govern the sale unless the product is returned within 30 days are binding on a buyer who does not return the product. The Hills (P) conceded noticing the statement of terms but denied reading it closely enough to discover the agreement to arbitrate. An agreement to arbitrate must be enforced except upon such grounds as exist at law or in equity for the revocation of any contract. A contract need not be read to be effective. People who accept products take the risk that the unread terms may in retrospect prove unwelcome. Terms inside Gateway's (D) box stand or fall together. If they constitute the parties' contract because the Hills (P) had an opportunity to return the computer after reading them, then all must be enforced. The court rejects the Hills' (P) argument that the provision in the box should be limited to executory contracts and to licenses in particular. Both parties' performance of this contract was complete when the box arrived at their home. The case does not depend on the fact that the seller characterized the transaction as a license rather than as a contract,

but rather treated it as a contract for the sale of goods and reserved the question whether for other purposes a "license" characterization might be preferable. All debates about characterization to one side, the transaction here was not executory. Vacated and remanded for arbitration.

## ▶ ANALYSIS

While observing that the federal Magnuson-Moss Warranty Act requires firms to distribute their warranty terms on request, the court noted that the Hills (P) did not contend that Gateway (D) would have refused to enclose the remaining terms also. Concealment would be bad for business, scaring some customers away and leading to excessive returns from others. Second, said the court, shoppers can consult public sources (computer magazines, the web sites of vendors) that may contain this information. Third, they may inspect the documents after the product's delivery. In this case, the Hills (P) took the third option. By keeping the computer beyond 30 days, the Hills (P) accepted Gateway's (D) offer, including the arbitration clause.

## Quicknotes

**ARBITRATION** An alternative resolution process where a dispute is heard and decided by a neutral third party, rather than through legal proceedings.

**RICO** Racketeer Influenced and Corrupt Organization laws; federal and state statutes enacted for the purpose of prosecuting organized crime.

# Klocek v. Gateway

## Computer purchaser (P) v. Computer vendor (D)

104 F. Supp. 2d 1332 *vacated*, 2000 WL 1372886, (D. Kan. 2000), *aff'd*, 2001 WL 1568346 (D. Kan. 2001).

**NATURE OF CASE:** Motion to dismiss on the ground that claims brought by the purchaser of a computer must be arbitrated pursuant to the vendor's standard agreement included with the computer.

**FACT SUMMARY:** [Facts not stated in casebook excerpt.]

## ■ RULE OF LAW

Terms shipped with a computer do not become part of the sales contract where the vendor does not expressly make its acceptance conditional on the buyer's assent to the additional, shipped terms and where the buyer does not expressly agree to the terms.

**FACTS:** [Facts not stated in casebook excerpt.]

**ISSUE:** Do terms shipped with a computer become part of the sales contract where the vendor does not expressly make its acceptance conditional on the buyer's assent to the additional, shipped terms, and where the buyer does not expressly agree to the terms?

**HOLDING AND DECISION:** (Vratil, J.) No. Terms shipped with a computer do not become part of the sales contract where the vendor does not expressly make its acceptance conditional on the buyer's assent to the additional, shipped terms and where the buyer does not expressly agree to the terms. Gateway (D) bears an initial burden of showing that it is entitled to arbitration. To do so, it must demonstrate that an enforceable agreement to arbitrate exists. When deciding if such an agreement exists, the court applies state law contract formation principles. Here, the Uniform Commercial Code (U.C.C.) governs the parties' transaction under both Kansas and Missouri law. The fact that Klocek (P) paid for and received a computer is evidence of a contract for the sale of a computer. Here, the issue is whether terms received with a product become part of the parties' agreement—an issue not decided by either Kansas or Missouri state courts. Authority from other courts is split, and seems to depend on whether the court finds that the parties formed their contract before or after the vendor communicated its terms to the purchaser. Gateway (D) urges following the approach taken by the Seventh Circuit, which enforced an arbitration clause in a situation similar to the one in this case. The Seventh Circuit reasoned that by including the license with the software, the vendor proposed a contract that the buyer could accept by using the software after having an opportunity to read the license. The Seventh Circuit, however, concluded, without support, that U.C.C. § 2-207 was irrelevant because the case involved only one written form, and

that the vendor was the master of the offer. The Missouri or Kansas courts would not follow this reasoning because nothing in the language of § 2-207 precludes its application in a case that involves only one form. By its terms, § 2-207 applies to an acceptance or written confirmation. Therefore, the state courts would apply § 2-207 to the facts of this case. In addition, in typical consumer transactions, it is the purchaser who is the offeror, and the vendor who is the offeree. Here, Gateway (D) has provided no evidence that would support a finding that it was the offeror—and therefore could propose limitations on the kind of conduct that constituted acceptance. Instead, the court assumes that plaintiff offered to purchase the computer and that Gateway (D) accepted plaintiff's offer. Under § 2-207, the Standard Terms are either an expression of acceptance or written confirmation. As an expression of acceptance, they would constitute a counteroffer only if Gateway (D) expressly made its acceptance conditional on Klocek's (P) assent to the additional or different terms, but here, Gateway (D) has not shown that its mere shipment of the Standard Terms with the computer communicated to the plaintiff that the sale was conditioned on his acceptance of the Standard Terms. Because Klocek (P) was not a merchant, any additional or different terms contained in the Standard Terms did not become part of the parties' agreement unless Klocek (P) expressly agreed to them. Gateway (D) has not shown that Klocek (P) expressly agreed to the Standard Terms. It provided no evidence that it informed Klocek (P) of the five-day review-and-return period as a condition of the sales transaction, or that the parties contemplated additional terms to the agreement. The fact that Klocek (P) kept the computer past five days was insufficient to demonstrate that he expressly agreed to the Standard Terms. Therefore, Gateway (D) has not shown that Klocek (P) agreed to the arbitration provision, and its motion to dismiss is overruled.

## ▌ ANALYSIS

The decision in this case would find support from legal commentators who have found that software shrinkwrap agreements are a form of adhesion contracts and who have criticized the line of cases that support such agreements, such as those in the Seventh Circuit, on the ground that they ignore the issue of informed consumer consent. Nonetheless, several courts have followed the Seventh Circuit line of cases.

*Continued on next page.*

## *Quicknotes*

**MOTION TO DISMISS**   Motion to terminate an action based on the adequacy of the pleadings, improper service or venue, etc.

**SHRINKWRAP LICENSE**   Terms of restriction packaged inside a product.

# Specht v. Netscape Communications Corporation

Software user (P) v. Software provider (D)

306 F.3d 17 (2d Cir. 2002).

**NATURE OF CASE:** Appeal from denial of a defense motion to compel arbitration.

**FACT SUMMARY:** When Specht (P), a user of Netscape Communication Corporation's (Netscape's) (D) free software program, discovered that the program permitted Netscape (D) to track Specht's (P) Internet activity, Specht (P) sued Netscape (D) for violation of federal electronic privacy legislation.

## 🏛 RULE OF LAW
The mere act of downloading software does not unambiguously manifest assent to an arbitration provision contained in the terms of its license.

**FACTS:** Specht (P) and other electronic consumers downloaded from Netscape Communications Corporation (Netscape) (D) free software programs. Upon discovering that these programs transmitted to Netscape (D) private information about Specht's (P) downloading of files from the Internet, Specht (P) and other class members brought suit against Netscape (D) for violation of the federal Electronic Communications Privacy Act and the Computer Fraud and Abuse Act. Netscape (D) moved to compel arbitration, arguing that Specht (P), by downloading the program, agreed to an arbitration clause contained in the download license. Specht (P) was unaware of the license, which could have been viewed only by clicking to a hyperlink. The motion to compel arbitration was denied, and Netscape (D) appealed.

**ISSUE:** Does the mere act of downloading software unambiguously manifest assent to an arbitration provision contained in the terms of its license?

**HOLDING AND DECISION:** (Sotomayor, J.) No. The mere act of downloading software does not unambiguously manifest assent to an arbitration provision contained in the terms of its license. Here, Specht (P), by acting on Netscape's (D) invitation to download free software made available on Netscape's (D) webpage, did not agree to be bound by the software's license terms (which included the arbitration clause at issue); Specht (P) could not have learned the existence of those terms unless, prior to executing the download, he had scrolled down the webpage to a screen located below the download button. Since a reasonably prudent Internet user in circumstances such as these would not have known or learned of the existence of the license terms before responding to the invitation to download the free software and Netscape (D) therefore did not provide "reasonable notice" of the license terms, Specht's (P) bare act of downloading did not manifest assent to the license's arbitration provision. Having selected the SmartDownload program, Specht (P) was required neither to express unambiguous assent to that program's license agreement nor even to view the license terms or become aware of their existence, before proceeding with the invited download of the free plug-in program. Moreover, once Specht (P) had initiated the download, the existence of SmartDownload's license terms was not mentioned while the software was running or at any later point in Specht's (P) experience of the product. An offeree, regardless of apparent manifestation of his consent, is not bound by inconspicuous contractual provisions of which he is unaware, contained in a document whose contractual nature is not obvious. Reasonably conspicuous notice of the existence of contract terms and unambiguous manifestation of assent to those terms by consumers are essential if "electronic bargaining" is to have integrity and credibility. Affirmed.

## ▶ ANALYSIS

In the *Specht* case, the court noted that even for a user who, unlike Specht (P), did happen to scroll down past the download button, SmartDownload's license terms would not have been immediately displayed. Instead, if such a user had seen the notice of SmartDownload's terms and then clicked on the underlined invitation to review and agree to the terms, a hypertext link would have taken the user to a separate webpage entitled "License & Support Agreements." This webpage, in turn, required a jump to still another webpage for the actual terms of the license. The totality of these procedures, from the viewpoint of the *Specht* court, ran afoul of a clear manifestation of assent. Whether governed by the common law or by Article 2 of the Uniform Commercial Code, a transaction, in order to be a contract, requires a manifestation of agreement between the parties.

▬▬■ ▬■

## Quicknotes

**ARBITRATION** An alternative resolution process where a dispute is heard and decided by a neutral third party, rather than through legal proceedings.

**OFFEREE** A person or party to whom an offer to enter into a contractual agreement is made.

▬▬■ ▬■

# Cairo, Inc. v. Crossmedia Services, Inc.

Online business (P) v. Online business (D)

2005 WL 756610 (N.D. Cal. 2005).

**NATURE OF CASE:** Motion to dismiss for improper forum in declaratory judgment action for claims involving, inter alia, intellectual property violations and breach of contract.

**FACT SUMMARY:** Cairo, Inc. (P), which repeatedly and automatically accessed and copied Crossmedia Services, Inc.'s (CMS's) (D) web pages via computer program "robots," contended that it was not bound by CMS's (D) Terms of Use and the forum selection clause contained therein, since it had no actual knowledge of those terms (initially) and never expressly assented to the terms.

## RULE OF LAW
Knowledge of a website's terms of use may be imputed to a user that repeatedly and automatically accesses the site via a computer search program "robot," so that the user will be bound by the terms of use notwithstanding the user does not have actual knowledge of the terms.

**FACTS:** Crossmedia Services, Inc. (CMS) (D) created web pages for various retailers that showed shoppers the retailers' circulars and specials. CMS (D) also provided shoppers with access to the interactive promotional materials that CMS (D) has created for the retailers. When a shopper visited the website of one of CMS's (D) retail customers seeking the type of information hosted by CMS (D), the shopper was directed to a CMS (D) web page that, after the shopper entered certain information, displayed the retailer's interactive promotional material. Every web page hosted by CMS (D) displayed the CMS (D) name and logo and the following notice: "By continuing past this page and/or using this site, you agree to abide by the Terms of Use for this site, which prohibit commercial use of any information on this site." The Terms of Use purported to be a binding legal contract, and the user was warned that if she did not want to be bound by the agreement's terms, she should not use the website. The Terms of Use contained a forum selection clause, which provided that jurisdiction for any claims arising under the agreement would lie exclusively with the state or federal courts in Chicago, Illinois. Cairo, Inc. (Cairo) (P) went into a similar line of online business as CMS (D), with its website allowing a user to search its database of in-store sales information. Cairo (P) compiled information from retailers' weekly circular web pages, some of which were enabled by CMS (D). Cairo (P) collected sale information from retailers' web sites by means of computer programs variously referred to as "robots," "spiders," or "crawlers,"

which automatically visited retailers' web sites, recorded the relevant sales information from the retailers' weekly circular web pages, and then returned that information to a database maintained by Cairo (P). Cairo's (P) "robot" programs could not read the Terms of Use posted on a website. Within days after Cairo (P) launched its website, CMS (D) discovered that Cairo (P) was copying promotional materials from CMS's (D) web pages and posting a version of those materials on the Cairo (P) site. Accordingly, CMS (D) sent to Cairo (P) a cease and desist demand informing Cairo (P) that its conduct constituted a breach of the Terms of Use. Cairo (P) ignored the demand and continued to take materials from CMS (D) web pages. Around two weeks later, Cairo (P) filed a declaratory relief action against CMS (D) in district court for the Northern District of California, seeking a declaration that its activities did not violate any of CMS's (D) rights, including, inter alia, copyright, trademark, contract and property rights. CMS (P) moved to dismiss for improper venue, alleging that the forum selection clause in its Terms of Use required Cairo (P) to file lawsuits against CMS (D) in the state and federal courts in Chicago, Illinois. In response, Cairo (P) argued that it was not aware until the litigation of the forum selection clause, and that, in any event, no agreement existed between the parties at all, and that Cairo (P) had not assented to CMS's (D) Terms of Use or the forum selection clause therein.

**ISSUE:** May knowledge of a website's terms of use be imputed to a user that repeatedly and automatically accesses the site via a computer search program "robot," so that the user will be bound by the terms of use notwithstanding the user does not have actual knowledge of the terms?

**HOLDING AND DECISION:** (Ware, J.) Yes. Knowledge of a website's terms of use may be imputed to a user that repeatedly and automatically accesses the site via a computer search program "robot," so that the user will be bound by the terms of use notwithstanding the user does not have actual knowledge of the terms. The issue for purposes of the motion to dismiss is whether a contract exists to bind Cairo (P) to CMS's (D) terms. First, Cairo (P) visited CMS's (D) web pages even after it received notice from CMS (D) that Cairo (P) was violating the Terms of Use, so it had actual knowledge of those terms, and, under contract principles, when a benefit is offered subject to stated conditions, and the offeree (here, Cairo (P)) makes a decision to take the benefit with knowledge of

*Continued on next page.*

the terms of the offer, the taking constitutes acceptance of the terms, which accordingly become binding on the offeree. Moreover, Cairo's (P) repeated and automated use of CMS's (D) web pages can form the basis of imputing knowledge to Cairo (P) of the terms on which CMS's (D) services were offered even before Cairo's (P) notice of CMS's (D) cease and desist letter. Thus, even accepting Cairo's (P) allegation that it did not explicitly agree to CMS's (D) Terms of Use, Cairo's (P) use of CMS's (D) website under circumstances in which Cairo (P) had actual or imputed knowledge of CMS's (D) terms effectively bound Cairo (P) to CMS's (D) Terms of Use and the forum selection clause therein. Finally, even if the forum selection clause is ambiguous as to whether claims have to be arbitrated or may be litigated, it is clear that the claims may not be heard in this jurisdiction. Motion to dismiss for improper venue is granted to CMS (D).

## ANALYSIS

In reaching its conclusion, the court in this case distinguished *Specht v. Netscape Comm. Corp.*, 306 F.3d 17 (2d Cir. 2002). In *Specht*, the Second Circuit ruled that users who downloaded Netscape's software from Netscape's website were not bound by an agreement to arbitrate disputes with Netscape because users would not have seen Netscape's terms without scrolling down their computer screens, and there was no reason for them to do so. Here, not only did Cairo (P) admit having knowledge of the Terms of Use (after it was notified of them by the cease and desist letter), but the court also found that Cairo's (P) "repeated and automated" access of CMS's (D) web pages could impute the requisite knowledge to Cairo (P). If the *Cairo* case is widely followed, it could potentially have a large impact on online transactions, since agreement to a site's terms of use could be manifested by robot software without express assent, as by clicking on a "button" or checking a box, as previously required for the formation of a contract between the user and site host.

## Quicknotes

**FORUM SELECTION CLAUSE** Provision contained in a contract setting forth the particular forum in which the parties would resolve a matter if a dispute were to arise.

**KNOWLEDGE** Having information or understanding of a fact.

# Varney v. Ditmars

## Employee (P) v. Employer (D)

N.Y. Ct. App., 217 N.Y. 223, 111 N.E. 822 (1916).

**NATURE OF CASE:** Appeal from dismissal of action for wrongful discharge of an employee.

**FACT SUMMARY:** Ditmars (D) told Varney (P) that if the latter would continue working for him until the first of the year, he would close his books and give Varney (P) a fair share of his profits.

## 🏛 RULE OF LAW
For a contract to be enforceable, the promise or the agreement of the parties must be sufficiently certain and explicit so that their full intention may be ascertained to a reasonable degree of certainty.

**FACTS:** Ditmars (D) told Varney (P) that if the latter would continue working for him until the first of the year, he would close his books and give Varney (P) a fair share of his profits. Varney (P) told Ditmars (D) that he intended to stay home on Election Day, which was November 6. That day, Varney (P) became ill and was unable to return to work until December 1. Ditmars (D) informed Varney (P) that because Varney (P) did not come to work on Election Day, he was being discharged. Varney (P), claiming he had a contract to work until the end of the year, and to share in the profits, sought to recover his wages for November 7 through December 31, and to recover a fair and reasonable percentage of the profits. The trial court dismissed the action, and the state's highest court granted review.

**ISSUE:** For a contract to be enforceable, must the promise or the agreement of the parties be sufficiently certain and explicit so that their full intention may be ascertained to a reasonable degree of certainty?

**HOLDING AND DECISION:** (Chase, J.) Yes. For a contract to be enforceable, the promise or the agreement of the parties must be sufficiently certain and explicit so that their full intention may be ascertained to a reasonable degree of certainty. In the case of a contract for the sale of goods or for hire without a fixed price or consideration being named, it will be presumed that a reasonable price or consideration is intended. However, in order for a contract to be valid, the promise or agreement of the parties to it must be certain and explicit so that their full intention may be ascertained to a reasonable degree of certainty. The contract here, so far as it relates to a share of Ditmars's (D) profits is not only uncertain, but it is necessarily affected by so many other facts that are in themselves indefinite and uncertain that the intention of the parties is pure conjecture. Such an executory contract must rest for performance upon the honor and good faith of the parties

making it. The courts cannot aid parties when they are unable or unwilling to agree upon the terms of their own proposed contract. Affirmed.

**DISSENT:** (Cardozo, J.) It is not true that a promise to pay an employee a fair share of the profits is always and of necessity too vague to be enforced. Here, since Varney (P) failed to supply the data essential to computation, profits were properly not included in the damages. However, he was entitled to his loss of salary since he was to work until the end of the year.

## ▶ ANALYSIS

As indicated by *Varney v. Ditmars,* where an agreement makes no statement as to the price to be paid, the law invokes the standard of reasonableness, and a promise to pay the fair value of the services or property is implied. Likewise, a promise to pay a reasonable sum for goods or services is generally held valid. As to promises to pay a fair share of profits, like the one in *Varney,* agreements specifying the maximum percentage of profits to be paid have been upheld.

━━■━━

## Quicknotes

**EXECUTORY CONTRACT** A contract in which performance of an obligation has yet to be rendered.

**GOOD FAITH** An honest intention to abstain from taking advantage of another.

**WRONGFUL DISCHARGE** Unlawful termination of an individual's employment.

━━■━━

# Oglebay Norton Company v. Armco, Inc.

Iron ore shipper (P) v. Steel company (D)

Ohio Sup. Ct., 52 Ohio St. 3d 232, 556 N.E.2d 515 (1990).

**NATURE OF CASE:** Appeal from affirmance of declaratory judgment setting contract price.

**FACT SUMMARY:** After the parties' contract-pricing mechanisms failed, the trial court determined that it could set the price of shipments.

## 🏛 RULE OF LAW
The court can look to the parties' course of dealing to determine their intent to be bound.

**FACTS:** In 1957, Oglebay Norton Company (Oglebay) (P) and Armco, Inc. (D) entered into a long-term contract for the shipment of Armco's (D) iron ore by Oglebay (P). The parties had a long history of a close business relationship, including joint ventures, Armco's (D) ownership of Oglebay (P) stock, and interlocking directorates. Both parties recognized that Armco's (D) ever-increasing capacity requirements would require that Oglebay (P) invest substantial capital to maintain, upgrade, and purchase iron ore carrier vessels. The agreement provided for primary and secondary price rate mechanisms tied to those prices recognized by leading iron ore shippers in the industry. After many years and several extensions of the contract, the parties were unable to agree upon a shipping rate for the 1985 season after the pricing mechanisms had broken down. Oglebay (P) billed Armco (D) $7.66 per gross ton, and Armco (D) reduced the invoice amount to $5 per gross ton and paid the $5 per ton figure, indicating payment in full language on the check to Oglebay (P) and explaining its position in an accompanying letter. In late 1985, the parties again tried to agree on a rate, this time for the 1986 season, but failed to reach a mutually satisfactory price. On April 11, 1986, Oglebay (P) sought declaratory relief requesting the court declare a reasonable rate for the shipments. Armco (D) counterclaimed, asserting that the contract was unenforceable because the parties did not intend to be bound in the event that their agreed-upon pricing mechanisms broke down. The trial court held that the parties intended to be bound by the 1957 agreement, established $6.25 as a reasonable rate for Armco (D) to pay for Oglebay's (P) services, and ordered the parties to utilize a mediator if they were unable to agree on a shipping rate for each annual shipping season. The state's intermediate appellate court affirmed, and the state's highest court granted review.

**ISSUE:** Can the court look to the parties' course of dealing to determine their intent to be bound?

**HOLDING AND DECISION:** (Per curiam) Yes. The court can look to the parties' course of dealing to

determine their intent to be bound. The evidence demonstrated the long-standing and close business relationship, including (D) ownership of Oglebay (P) stock, and a seat for Armco (D) on Oglebay's (P) board of directors. The parties continued this business relationship despite the fact that the pricing mechanisms had failed, which further showed their intent to be bound in the face of such a failure. Oglebay's (P) dedication of bulk vessels to Armco's (D) service was a major and ongoing investment in reliance on the 1957 agreement. Affirmed.

## ▶ *ANALYSIS*

Consider a lease agreement where the lessor and lessee provide that the latter, at the end of the lease term, can extend his lease at a rental fee to be determined at the time he exercises his option. The common-law view would hold that such an "agreement to agree" prevents the exercise of the option. The modern and better view is that the parties intend to be bound, and they are merely exercising their right to agree on a rate when the reasonable value based on current market conditions can be determined.

▬▬▬

## *Quicknotes*

**DECLARATORY JUDGMENT** A judgment of the court establishing the rights of the parties.

▬▬▬

# Blinn v. Beatrice Community Hospital and Health Center, Inc.

Terminated employee (P) v. Employer (D)

Neb. Sup. Ct., 270 Neb. 809, 708 N.W.2d 235 (2006).

**NATURE OF CASE:** Appeal from reversal of grant of summary judgment to defendant in action for breach of contract and promissory estoppel.

**FACT SUMMARY:** Beatrice Community Hospital and Health Center, Inc. (Beatrice) (D) contended that its oral representations to Blinn (P), an at-will employee, were insufficiently definite to form the basis of a unilateral employment contract and that Blinn (P) was not entitled to promissory estoppel because it was not reasonable or foreseeable for him to rely on the representations and forgo another job opportunity.

## 🏛 RULE OF LAW

(1) A unilateral contract for employment other than employment at will is not created where the representations made by the employer are insufficiently definite to constitute an offer for such a contract.
(2) A claim for promissory estoppel is made out where the promisee can show that his reliance on a promise was reasonable and foreseeable even though the promise was not sufficiently definite to form a contract.

**FACTS:** Blinn (P), aged 67, was an at-will employee of Beatrice Community Hospital and Health Center, Inc. (Beatrice) (D). He received an offer from a different employer for a job with more pay and a guarantee that he could keep the job until he retired. When he showed the offer to a Beatrice (D) administrator, and asked whether for assurances that Beatrice (D) would retain him until he retired, he was told "we've got at least five more years of work to do." When he sought similar assurances from the chairman of the board, he was told "We want you to stay" and was assured he could stay at Beatrice (D) until he retired. Blinn (P) was fired around 6 months later, and he sued Beatrice (D) for breach of contract, alleging that his at-will employment status had been changed by the oral representations he had received from the administrator and board chairman, which, he asserted, constituted an oral employment contract for a term of at least "five more years." He also claimed that the representations induced him to forgo the job offer he had received and asserted a claim for promissory estoppel. The trail court granted summary judgment to Beatrice (D), and the state's intermediate appellate court reversed, finding that the theory of employment until retirement had been tried by implied consent because there was evidence that Beatrice (D) had assured Blinn (P) that he could work there until he retired; that the evidence created a genuine issue of material fact about whether Beatrice (D) made an offer to Blinn (P) to work there until he retired; and that there was a genuine issue of material fact about whether Beatrice's (D) representations gave rise to promissory estoppel. The state's highest court granted review.

**ISSUE:**
(1) Is a unilateral contract for employment other than employment at will created where the representations made by the employer are insufficiently definite to constitute an offer for such a contract?
(2) Is a claim for promissory estoppel made out where the promisee can show that his reliance on a promise was reasonable and foreseeable even though the promise was not sufficiently definite to form a contract?

**HOLDING AND DECISION:** [Judge not stated in casebook excerpt.]
(1) No. A unilateral contract for employment other than employment at will is not created where the representations made by the employer are insufficiently definite to constitute an offer for such a contract. Oral representations by an employer may form a contractual basis for modifying an employee's employment at-will status. However, the employee bears the burden of showing that the representations are sufficiently definite in form to constitute an offer for a unilateral contract of employment beyond employment at will. It must be shown that the employer manifested a clear intent to make and be bound by such a promise, thus justifying the employee's understanding that such a commitment was made. Whether such an offer has been made is determined objectively from the outward manifestations of the parties. Applying these principles here, it is clear that Beatrice's (D) representations were not sufficiently definite in form to constitute an offer of a unilateral contract. The statement that "we've got at least five more years of work to do" is not a clear offer of definite employment and does not manifest intent to create a unilateral contract—regardless of what Blinn's (P) subjective understanding was. Therefore, the appellate court erred in finding there was a genuine issue of material fact as to the breach of contract claim. Reversed as to this issue.
(2) Yes. A claim for promissory estoppel is made out where the promisee can show that his reliance on a promise was reasonable and foreseeable even though the promise was not sufficiently definite to form a contract. Under state law, the doctrine of promissory estoppel does not require that the promise giving rise to the

*Continued on next page.*

claim be as sufficiently definite as it would need to be for purposes of contract formation. All that is needed is that the promisee's reliance be reasonable and foreseeable. Here, although Beatrice's (D) representations were, as previously determined, insufficiently definite to form an oral contract for employment beyond employment at will, those same representations may have reasonably and foreseeably induced Blinn (P) to forgo his other offer of employment. Accordingly, the appellate court did not err in finding there was a genuine issue of material fact related to Blinn's (P) promissory estoppel theory. Contrary to the dissent's position, however, such a ruling does not expand prior case law that held that a cause of action for promissory estoppel can be alleged in connection with detrimental reliance on a promise of at-will employment. That is because the question in this case is not whether reliance upon a promise of at-will employment is actionable, but whether the employer [Beatrice (D)] is estopped from claiming that Blinn's (P) employment was at will, based on his reliance on Beatrice's (D) promises. This state's position on promissory estoppel differs from that of the Restatement view, which requires the same degree of definiteness of the promise for both promissory estoppel and contract formation; there is no requirement of definiteness to make out a case for promissory estoppel. Under state law, therefore, promissory estoppel requires only that the promisee's reliance on the promise be reasonable and foreseeable, even if the promisor did not intend to be bound, since a promisor need not intend a promise to be binding in order to foresee that a promisee may reasonably rely on it. For contract formation, there must be intent by the promisor to be bound. The dissent, by requiring definiteness, misconstrues the state's promissory estoppel jurisprudence. Here, there is sufficient evidence for a trier of fact to conclude that Blinn's (P) reliance was reasonable and foreseeable. Affirmed as to this issue.

## ▶ ANALYSIS

Under the Restatement view of promissory estoppel when a promise is made, but a contract is not formed because of a lack of consideration, reasonable reliance by the promisee can still render the promisor liable for breach of the promise. Thus, analysis of the promise is the same as that for a contract, except that the promisee's reliance on the promise replaces the missing consideration.

## Quicknotes

**BREACH OF CONTRACT** Unlawful failure by a party to perform its obligations pursuant to contract.

**PROMISE** The expression of an intention to act, or to forbear from acting, granting a right to the promisee to expect and enforce its performance.

**PROMISEE** Party to whom a promise is made.

**PROMISOR** Party who promises to render an obligation to another in the future.

**PROMISSORY ESTOPPEL** A promise that is enforceable if the promisor should reasonably expect that it will induce action or forbearance on the part of the promisee, and does in fact cause such action or forbearance, and it is the only means of avoiding injustice.

**SUMMARY JUDGMENT** Judgment rendered by a court in response to a motion made by one of the parties, claiming that the lack of a question of material fact in respect to an issue warrants disposition of the issue without consideration by the jury.

# Metro-Goldwyn-Mayer, Inc. v. Scheider
Television studio (P) v. Actor (D)

N.Y. Ct. App., 40 N.Y.2d 1069, 360 N.E.2d 930 (1976).

**NATURE OF CASE:** Appeal from affirmance of judgment for plaintiff in action for breach of contract.

**FACT SUMMARY:** Scheider (D), who refused to perform in a television series for Metro-Goldwyn-Mayer, Inc. (P), maintained that there had not been a complete contract between the parties, but the court found otherwise.

---

**RULE OF LAW**
If the parties thereto have completed their negotiations as to what they regard as the essential elements and performance has begun on the good-faith understanding that agreement on the unsettled matters will follow, the courts will find and enforce a contract if some objective method of determining the unsettled elements is available—such as resort to the contract itself, commercial practice, or other usage and custom.

---

**FACTS:** Metro-Goldwyn-Mayer, Inc. (MGM) (P) brought suit against Scheider (D) when he refused to perform in a television series. The court found that the parties had entered into an oral contract that called for Scheider (D) to appear in both a pilot film and the television series that might develop therefrom. Initially, the parties negotiated for a period of several weeks, reaching agreement on the broad outlines of the contract and its financial dimensions, and both having explicit expectations that further agreements were to follow. Additional important provisions were negotiated over the following weeks; the only essential term without an articulated understanding was the starting date for filming the television series. The trial court supplied this term by a finding based on proof of established custom and practice in the industry, of which both parties were found to be aware, set in the context of the other understandings reached by them. Scheider (D) appealed, challenging the court's determination that there was a complete contract between the parties. The state's intermediate appellate court remanded for a second trial on damages, and the state's highest court granted review.

**ISSUE:** If the parties thereto have completed their negotiations as to what they regard as the essential elements and performance has begun on the good-faith understanding that agreement on the unsettled matters will follow, will the courts find and enforce a contract if some objective method of determining the unsettled elements is available—such as resort to the contract itself, commercial practice, or other usage and custom?

**HOLDING AND DECISION:** (Per curiam) Yes. If the parties thereto have completed their negotiations as to what they regard as the essential elements and performance has begun on the good-faith understanding that agreement on the unsettled matters will follow, the courts will find and enforce a contract if some objective method of determining the unsettled elements is available—such as resort to the contract itself, commercial practice, or other usage and custom. In many instances, parties complete their negotiations on what they regard as the essential elements of a contract and begin performance on the good-faith understanding that agreement on the unsettled matters will follow. In such instances, the courts will find and enforce a contract if some objective method of determining the unsettled elements or terms is available. Such objective criteria may be found in the agreement itself, commercial practice, or other usage and custom. If the contract can be rendered certain and complete, by reference to something certain, the court will fill in the gaps. That is precisely what was done here. Affirmed.

---

**ANALYSIS**

Section 204 of Restatement (Second) of Contracts looked to the court to supply "a term which is reasonable in the circumstances" in those instances "when the parties to a bargain sufficiently defined to be a contract have not agreed with respect to a term which is essential to a determination of their rights and duties."

---

**Quicknotes**

**BREACH OF CONTRACT** Unlawful failure by a party to perform its obligations pursuant to contract.

**DAMAGES** Monetary compensation that may be awarded by the court to a party who has sustained injury or loss to his person, property or rights due to another party's unlawful act, omission or negligence.

**GOOD FAITH** An honest intention to abstain from taking advantage of another.

# Joseph Martin, Jr., Delicatessen, Inc. v. Schumacher

Landlord (P) v. Tenant (D)

N.Y. Ct. App., 52 N.Y.2d 105, 417 N.E.2d 541 (1981).

**NATURE OF CASE:** Appeal from denial of specific enforcement.

**FACT SUMMARY:** Schumacher (D) sought to enforce a lease provision that stated that the lease may be renewed at a rental "to be agreed upon."

## RULE OF LAW

A real estate lease provision calling for the renewal of the lease at a rental to be agreed upon is unenforceable due to its omission of a material term.

**FACTS:** Schumacher (D) leased a store from Martin (P) for a five-year term at a specified rental. A clause in the lease provided that Schumacher (D), as tenant, was entitled to renew the lease for an additional five-year term at a rental "to be agreed upon." Schumacher (D) gave timely notice of his desire to exercise his privilege of renewal, and Martin (P) responded that the price would be $900 a month, almost double the current rent. Schumacher (D) hired an appraiser, who placed the fair market value of the store at $545 a month. Schumacher (D) then filed suit for specific performance. Martin (P) brought a separate eviction action, and the trial court ruled in his favor, holding that the lease provision was only an agreement to agree and therefore unenforceable. On appeal, the court expressly overruled an established line of precedents and held that Schumacher (D) should be able to prove whether a binding agreement by the parties was intended. Martin (P) appealed.

**ISSUE:** Is a real estate lease provision calling for the renewal of the lease at a rental to be agreed upon unenforceable due to its omission of a material term?

**HOLDING AND DECISION:** (Fuchsberg, J.) Yes. A real estate lease provision calling for the renewal of the lease at a rental to be agreed upon is unenforceable due to its omission of a material term. It is a well-settled principle of law that a court may enforce a contract only where the terms of that contract are sufficiently certain and specific. Otherwise, a court would be forced to impose its own conception of what the parties should or might have agreed upon, rather than attempting to implement the bargain actually made. Accordingly, definiteness and specificity as to material matters is the essence of contract law. For that reason, a mere agreement to agree on a material term in the future without any details as to the methods of ascertaining that term cannot be enforced since the court, rather than the parties, would be creating the agreement. A real estate lease that provides for a renewal term at a rental to be agreed upon is nothing more than an agreement to

agree and, hence, cannot be enforced due to its omission of a material term. Reversed.

**CONCURRENCE:** (Meyer, J.) While the majority was correct in its decision in the instant case, it goes too far in suggesting that such a lease provision would never be enforceable.

**DISSENT IN PART:** (Jasen, J.) Although the renewal clause was unenforceable due to its uncertainty, Schumacher (D) should have been able to prove his entitlement to renewal of the lease on other grounds.

## ANALYSIS

The difficulty courts have in enforcing contracts that are left incomplete by the parties is illustrated by the case of *Ansorge v. Kane,* 244 N.Y. 395 (1927). The parties had agreed on a sale of land and had specified the price and the amount that was to be paid in cash up front. The manner of the deferred payments was "to be agreed upon." When the seller reneged, the buyer sought specific performance. In denying the remedy, the court held that an agreement to agree upon such a material term as contract payments rendered the contract unenforceable. However, the court stated that had the contract been absolutely silent regarding the payments, rather than saying they would be as agreed upon, the contract could have been enforced using reasonable and customary payment terms.

---

## Quicknotes

**FAIR MARKET VALUE** The price of particular property or goods that a buyer would offer and a seller would accept in the open market following full disclosure.

**LEASE** An agreement or contract that creates a relationship between a landlord and tenant (real property) or lessor and lessee (real or personal property).

**MATERIAL TERM** A contractual term that is an essential part of the agreement, to the extent that its omission from performance can be construed as a breach of the contract.

**SPECIFIC PERFORMANCE** An equitable remedy whereby the court requires the parties to perform their obligations pursuant to a contract.

# Hoffman v. Red Owl Stores, Inc.

Individual desiring franchise (P) v. Franchisor (D)

Wis. Sup. Ct., 26 Wis. 2d 683, 133 N.W.2d 267 (1965).

**NATURE OF CASE:** Appeal from award of damages.

**FACT SUMMARY:** Hoffman (P) was assured by an agent of the Red Owl Stores, Inc. (D) that if he took certain steps he would obtain a supermarket franchise, but after taking these steps at great expense, Hoffman (P) did not receive the franchise.

## 🏛 RULE OF LAW
When a promisor makes a promise that promisor should reasonably expect to induce action on the part of the promisee and which does induce such action, promisor can be estopped from denying the enforceability of that promise.

**FACTS:** An agent of the Red Owl Stores, Inc. (Red Owl) (D) promised Hoffman (P) that Red Owl (D) would establish him in a supermarket store for the sum of $18,000. In reliance upon this promise, and upon the recommendations of the agent, Hoffman (P) purchased a grocery store to gain experience. Thereafter, upon further recommendations of the agent, Hoffman (P) sold his grocery store fixtures and inventory to Red Owl (D), before the profitable summer months started, and paid $1,000 for an option on land for building a franchise outlet. After moving near this outlet, Hoffman (P) was told that he needed $24,100 for the promised franchise. After Hoffman (P) acquired this amount, most of it through a loan from his father-in-law, he was told that he needed an additional $2,000 for the deal to go through. Finally, after acquiring the additional $2,000, Hoffman (P) was told he would be established in his new store as soon as he sold a bakery store which he owned. After doing this, though, Red Owl (D) told Hoffman (P) that in order to enhance his credit rating he must procure from his father-in-law a statement that the funds acquired from him were an outright gift and not a loan. In response, Hoffman (P) sued for damages to recover income he lost and expenses he incurred in reliance upon the promises of Red Owl (D). After an award of damages for Hoffman (P), Red Owl (D) appealed.

**ISSUE:** When a promisor makes a promise that promisor should reasonably expect to induce action on the part of the promisee and which does induce such action, can promisor be estopped from denying the enforceability of that promise?

**HOLDING AND DECISION:** [Judge not stated in casebook excerpt.] Yes. When a promisor makes a promise that promisor should reasonably expect to induce action on the part of the promisee and which does induce

such action, promisor can be estopped from denying the enforceability of that promise. Under the doctrine of promissory estoppel, as stated in § 90 of Restatement (First) of Contracts, "a promise which the promisor should reasonably expect to induce action for forbearance of a definite and substantial character on the part of the promisee and which does induce such action or forbearance is binding if injustice can be avoided only by enforcement of the promise." Of course, such damages as are necessary to prevent injustice can be awarded under the doctrine of promissory estoppel instead of specific performance. Furthermore, an action based upon promissory estoppel is not equivalent to a breach of contract action, and therefore, the promise does not have to "embrace all essential details of a proposed transaction between promisor and promisee so as to be the equivalent of an offer that would result in a binding contract between the parties if the promisee were to accept the same." Here, therefore, it is not important that no final construction plans, etc. were ever completed. It is instead important that Hoffman (P) substantially relied to his detriment on Red Owl's (D) promise and that Red Owl (D) should have reasonably foreseen such reliance. Therefore, Hoffman (P) is entitled to those damages that are necessary to prevent injustice. He is entitled to losses resulting from selling his bakery, from purchasing the option on land for a franchise, from moving near the franchise outlet, and from selling his grocery store fixtures and inventory. Hoffman's (P) reasonable damages from selling his grocery store fixtures and inventory, though, do not include any future lost profits, since he purchased the grocery store only temporarily to gain experience (i.e., he is only entitled to any loss measured by the difference between the sales price and fair market value). Affirmed.

## ▎ANALYSIS

This case illustrates the doctrine of promissory estoppel. At common law, such doctrine afforded protection to any party threatened with "substantial economic loss" after taking "reasonable steps in foreseeable reliance upon a gratuitous promise." Restatement (Second), though, does not require that the promise be gratuitous or that the reliance be "substantial." It requires only reasonable, foreseeable reliance upon any promise. Note that an action under the doctrine of promissory estoppel is not equivalent to an action for breach of contract, and, therefore, no consideration is necessary to make the promise binding. Furthermore, the promise upon which a person reasonably

*Continued on next page.*

relies will be enforced specifically or by damages whenever the court decides that the interests of justice would be served by such enforcement.

■━━■

## Quicknotes

**BREACH OF CONTRACT** Unlawful failure by a party to perform its obligations pursuant to contract.

**DAMAGES** Monetary compensation that may be awarded by the court to a party who has sustained injury or loss to his person, property or rights due to another party's unlawful act, omission or negligence.

**DETRIMENTAL RELIANCE** Action by one party, resulting in loss, which is based on the conduct or promises of another.

**PROMISSORY ESTOPPEL** A promise that is enforceable if the promisor should reasonably expect that it will induce action or forbearance on the part of the promisee, and does in fact cause such action or forbearance, and it is the only means of avoiding injustice.

**SPECIFIC PERFORMANCE** An equitable remedy whereby the court requires the parties to perform their obligations pursuant to a contract.

# Empro Manufacturing Co., Inc. v. Ball-Co Manufacturing, Inc.

Manufacturing company (P) v. Company selling assets (D)

870 F.2d 423 (7th Cir. 1989).

**NATURE OF CASE:** Appeal of dismissal of action for breach of contract.

**FACT SUMMARY:** Empro Manufacturing Co. (P) contended that a letter of intent had the effect of binding Ball-Co Manufacturing, Inc. (D), notwithstanding that the letter itself stated that the deal was subject to a later definitive agreement.

## 🏛 RULE OF LAW
Parties who have made their preliminary agreement "subject to" a later definitive agreement have manifested an objective intent not to be bound by the preliminary agreement.

**FACTS:** Empro Manufacturing Co., Inc. (Empro) (P) and Ball-Co Manufacturing, Inc. (Ball-Co) (D) signed a letter of intent containing the general provisions of the sale of Ball-Co's (D) assets to Empro (P), which proposed to pay $2.4 million, with $650,000 to be paid on closing and a ten-year promissory note for the remainder. The letter stated, "Empro's purchase shall be subject to the satisfaction of certain conditions precedent to closing including, but not limited to" the definitive Asset Purchase Agreement and, among five other conditions, "[t]he approval of the shareholders and board of directors of Empro." Empro (P) left itself numerous "outs" in the letter of intent that would permit it to walk away from the deal. The sticking point for the deal turned out to be the security for Empro's (P) promissory note, and it was Ball-Co (D) that decided to walk. When Ball-Co (D) started negotiating with someone else, Empro (P) sued, contending that the letter of intent bound Ball-Co (D) to sell only to Empro (P). The trial court dismissed, and Empro (P) appealed. The Court of Appeals for the Seventh Circuit granted review.

**ISSUE:** Have parties who have made their preliminary agreement "subject to" a later definitive agreement manifested an objective intent not to be bound by the preliminary agreement?

**HOLDING AND DECISION:** (Easterbrook, J.) Yes. Parties who have made their preliminary agreement "subject to" a later definitive agreement have manifested an objective intent not to be bound by the preliminary agreement. Contract law gives effect to parties' wishes, but these must be expressed openly. Intent in contract law is measured objectively rather than subjectively and must be determined solely from the language used when no ambiguity in its terms exists. Parties may decide for themselves

whether the results of preliminary negotiations bind them, but they do this through their words. "Subject to a definitive agreement" appears twice in the letter. The letter also recites, twice, that it contains the "general terms and conditions," implying that each side retained the right to make additional demands. The fact that Empro (P) listed as a condition that its own shareholders and board of directors had to approve the deal showed an intent not to be bound. Letters of intent and agreements in principle often, as here, do no more than set the stage for negotiations on details that may or may not be ironed out. Approaching agreement by stages is a valuable method of doing business because it allows parties to agree on the basics without bargaining away their privilege to disagree on specifics. Ball-Co (D) did not intend to be bound by the letter of intent. Affirmed.

## ▶ ANALYSIS

Compare this situation with one where the parties have agreed that their agreement is to be reduced to writing and signed by both of them. If the agreement is sufficient to be deemed to be a contract and one party withdraws before the signing, there can be no contract if the parties have clearly stated that they do not intend to be bound until the writing is signed. In *Winston v. Mediafare Entertainment Corporation*, 777 F.2d 78, 80 (2d. Cir., 1985), the Second Circuit has set forth the following factors to determine whether the parties intend to be bound before the document is fully executed: "(1) whether there has been an express reservation of the right not to be bound in the absence of a writing; (2) whether there has been partial performance of the contract; (3) whether all of the terms of the alleged contract have been agreed upon; and (4) whether the agreement at issue is the type of contract that is usually committed to writing."

■=■

## Quicknotes

**AMBIGUITY** Language that is capable of more than one interpretation.

**LETTER OF INTENT** A written draft embodying the proposed intent of the parties and which is not enforceable or binding.

**MUTUAL ASSENT** A requirement of a valid contract that the parties possess a mutuality of assent as manifested

*Continued on next page.*

by the terms of the agreement and not by a hidden intent.

**PROMISSORY NOTE** A written promise to tender a stated amount of money at a designated time and to a designated person.

# Dixon v. Wells Fargo Bank, N.A.

Mortgagor (P) v. Mortgagee (D)

798 F. Supp. 2d 336 (D. Mass. 2011).

**NATURE OF CASE:** Motion to dismiss in action for injunction; specific performance of an oral contract; and damages arising from a mortgagee's impending foreclosure on a mortgaged property.

**FACT SUMMARY:** The Dixons (P) contended that Wells Fargo Bank, N.A. (Wells Fargo) (D) was promissorily estopped from foreclosing on their house because Wells Fargo (D) had orally agreed to enter into a mortgage loan modification, and caused them, in reliance on its representations, to default on their payments.

## 🏛 RULE OF LAW
A mortgagor states a claim for promissory estoppel where the mortgagor, in reliance on the mortgagee's oral promise to consider the mortgagor for a mortgage loan modification, has taken steps, including stopping payments on the loan, that render the mortgagor worse off by subjecting the mortgagor to foreclosure.

**FACTS:** The Dixons (P) had a mortgage with Wells Fargo Bank, N.A. (Wells Fargo) (D). The Dixons (P) orally agreed with Wells Fargo (D) to take the steps necessary to be considered for a mortgage loan modification. As part of this agreement, Wells Fargo (D) instructed the Dixons (P) to stop making payments on their loan, i.e., to default, and it was contemplated that the unpaid payments would be added to the note as modified. In addition, Wells Fargo (D) requested certain financial information, which the Dixons (P) promptly supplied. Despite the Dixons' (P) compliance with Wells Fargo's (D) demands, Wells Fargo (D) refused to abide by the oral agreement to consider the Dixons (P) for a loan modification and instead sought to foreclose on the Dixon's (P) house, the fair market value of which exceeded the mortgage loan balance and any arrearage. The Dixons (P) filed suit against Wells Fargo (D), seeking (1) an injunction prohibiting Wells Fargo (D) from foreclosing on their home; (2) specific performance of the oral agreement to enter into a loan modification; and (3) damages. They argued that Wells Fargo (D) should have anticipated their compliance with the terms of its promise to consider them for a loan modification. They contended not only was it reasonable they would rely on the promise, but also that their reliance left them considerably worse off, for by entering into default they became vulnerable to foreclosure. Wells Fargo (D), having removed the action from state court to federal district court, moved for dismissal of the Dixons' (P) complaint, arguing that the

allegations were insufficient to invoke the doctrine of promissory estoppel.

**ISSUE:** Does a mortgagor state a claim for promissory estoppel where the mortgagor, in reliance on the mortgagee's oral promise to consider the mortgagor for a mortgage loan modification, has taken steps, including stopping payments on the loan, that render the mortgagor worse off by subjecting the mortgagor to foreclosure?

**HOLDING AND DECISION:** (Young, J.) Yes. A mortgagor states a claim for promissory estoppel where the mortgagor, in reliance on the mortgagee's oral promise to consider the mortgagor for a mortgage loan modification, has taken steps, including stopping payments on the loan, that render the mortgagor worse off by subjecting the mortgagor to foreclosure. This state (Massachusetts) has not used the term "promissory estoppel," but instead has used "detrimental reliance." An action based on reliance is equivalent to a contract action, and the party bringing such an action must prove all the necessary elements of a contract other than consideration, which is supplied by the detrimental reliance. However, even where detrimental reliance acts as a substitute for consideration, the promise on which a claim for promissory estoppel is based must be interchangeable with an offer, and must demonstrate an intention to act or refrain from acting in a specified way, so as to justify a promisee in understanding that a commitment has been made. The putative promise, like any offer, must be sufficiently definite and certain in its terms to be enforceable. Where an agreement to enter into a contract leaves the terms of that contract for future negotiation, it is too indefinite to be enforced, and the courts generally will not enforce such open-ended "agreements to agree." Moreover, it is believed that parties should be able to walk away from the transaction if they are unable to reach a deal. Because the complaint alleges that the parties had an "agreement to enter into a loan modification agreement," it appears that they had an unenforceable "agreement to agree," and that, therefore, Wells Fargo (D) is correct that the complaint fails to state a claim. The Dixons (P) reply that they are not seeking specific performance of a promised loan modification, but that Wells Fargo (D) is held to its promise to consider them for a loan modification. Thus, if the court were to uphold the promissory estoppel claim, it would not be "trapping" Wells Fargo (D) into a vague, indefinite, and unintended loan modification masquerading as an agreement to agree. Furthermore, because the

*Continued on next page.*

parties had not even begun to negotiate the terms of a loan modification, Wells Fargo's (D) promise is more like an agreement to negotiate, rather than an agreement to agree, but even such agreements to negotiate tend not to be enforced, since judicial enforcement of vague agreements to negotiate would risk imposing on parties contractual obligations they had not taken on themselves. Nevertheless, Wells Fargo (D) made a specific promise to consider the Dixons' (P) eligibility for a loan modification if they defaulted on their payments and submitted certain financial information. This promise was not made in exchange for a bargained-for legal detriment, as there was no bargain between the parties; instead, the legal detriment that the Dixons (P) claim to have suffered was a direct consequence of their reliance on Wells Fargo's (D) promise. Promissory estoppel has evolved into an equitable remedy that seeks to avoid injustice worked by a negotiating party that has made a promise during negotiations on which the other party has relied to its detriment. It is no longer merely a consideration substitute. This is reflected in § 90 of the Restatement (Second) of Contracts, which Massachusetts has adopted. While the courts of Massachusetts have yet to formally embrace promissory estoppel as more than a consideration substitute, the state's continued insistence that a promise be definite is arguably in tension with its adoption of § 90. This tension is not irreconcilable, however, as the case law reveals a willingness on courts' part to enforce even an indefinite promise made during preliminary negotiations where the facts suggest that the promisor's words or conduct were designed to take advantage of the promisee, even where the promisor did not act fraudulently. Here, Wells Fargo (D) convinced the Dixons (P) that to be eligible for a loan modification they had to default on their payments, and it was only because they relied on this representation and stopped making their payments that Wells Fargo (D) was able to initiate foreclosure proceedings, thus gaining the upper hand by inducing the Dixons (P) to open themselves up to a foreclosure action. In specifically telling the Dixons (P) that stopping their payments and submitting financial information were the "steps necessary to enter into a mortgage modification," Wells Fargo (D) not only should have known that the Dixons (P) would take these steps believing their fulfillment would lead to a loan modification, but also must have intended that the Dixons (P) do so. Accordingly, as a matter of fair dealing, Wells Fargo (D) should not have attempted to foreclose on the Dixon's (P) home based on a situation created solely by Wells Fargo's (D) promise. Such conduct is what permits application of the promissory estoppel doctrine here. A remaining concern is that by imposing precontractual liability for specific promises made to induce reliance during preliminary negotiations, courts will restrict parties' freedom to negotiate by reading in a duty to bargain in good faith not recognized at common law. This concern can be minimized by limiting the promisee's recovery to reliance

expenditures. Furthermore, the foreseeability and injustice requirements of § 90 render inquiry into whether the promisor acted in bad faith unnecessary, which, in turn, obviates any need to impose a precontractual duty to negotiate in good faith. Finally, contrary to the conventional wisdom that precontractual liability unduly restricts the freedom to negotiate, a default rule allowing recovery but limiting it to reliance expenditures may in fact promote more efficient bargaining. Thus, if the Dixons (P) can prove their allegations by a preponderance of the evidence, they will be entitled to the value of their expenditures in reliance on Wells Fargo's (D) promise. In sum, foreclosure is a powerful act with significant consequences, and where a bank has obtained the opportunity to foreclose by representing an intention to do the exact opposite—i.e., to negotiate a loan modification that would give the homeowner the right to stay in his or her home—the doctrine of promissory estoppel is properly invoked to provide at least reliance-based recovery. Motion to dismiss is denied.

## ▶ *ANALYSIS*

As with this case, other cases reveal that where the promisor opportunistically has strung along the promisee, the imposition of liability despite the preliminary stage of the negotiations produces the most equitable result. This balancing of the harms is explicitly made an element of recovery under the doctrine of promissory estoppel by the last words of § 90 of the Restatement, which make the promise binding only if injustice can be avoided by its enforcement. Binding the promisor to a promise made to take advantage of the promisee is also the most efficient result, since, in cases of opportunism, the "willingness to impose a liability rule can be justified as efficient since such intervention may be the most cost-effective means of controlling opportunistic behavior, which both parties would seek to control ex ante as a means of maximizing joint gains. Because private control arrangements may be costly, the law-supplied rule may be the most effective means of controlling opportunism and maximizing joint gain." See Juliet P. Kostritsky, "The Rise and Fall of Promissory Estoppel or Is Promissory Estoppel Really as Unsuccessful as Scholars Say It Is: A New Look at the Data," 37 *Wake Forest L. Rev.* 531, 574 (2002).

---

## Quicknotes

**DETRIMENTAL RELIANCE** Action by one party, resulting in loss, which is based on the conduct or promises of another.

*Continued on next page.*

**PROMISE** The expression of an intention to act, or to forbear from acting, granting a right to the promisee to expect and enforce its performance.

**PROMISEE** Party to whom a promise is made.

**PROMISOR** Party who promises to render an obligation to another in the future.

**PROMISSORY ESTOPPEL** A promise that is enforceable if the promisor should reasonably expect that it will induce action or forbearance on the part of the promisee, and does in fact cause such action or forbearance, and it is the only means of avoiding injustice.

# Douthwright v. Northeast Corridor Foundations

## Creditor (P) v. Debtor (D)

Conn. App. Ct., 72 Conn. App. 319, 805 A.2d 157 (2002).

**NATURE OF CASE:** Appeal by a debtor from a creditor's default judgment.

**FACT SUMMARY:** When Northeast Corridor Foundations (D) sent a check to Douthwright (P) for a default judgment but failed to include the court-awarded interest amount, Northeast Corridor (D) contended that the check constituted an accord and satisfaction of the entire amount.

## RULE OF LAW

As a precondition to an accord and satisfaction, the proponent must prove a genuine "dispute" between the parties and that the amount of the claim was unliquidated.

**FACTS:** On February 12, 2001, Douthwright (P) filed a statutory motion for a default judgment in the amount of $1.5 million plus interest arising from the failure of Northeast Corridor Foundations (D) to pay their full share of an oral settlement agreement. Subsequently, Northeast Corridor (D) sent Douthwright (P) a check for $1.5 million, accompanied by a cover letter which did not, however, include any payment of interest. On May 8, 2001, the trial court rendered judgment for Douthwright (P) for $40,931.45, representing interest from the period when the payment had become due until the date when Northeast Corridor (D) made the $1.5 million payment. Northeast Corridor (D) appealed, contending that its check for $1.5 million plus cover letter constituted an accord and satisfaction of the interest claim. The state's intermediate appellate court granted review.

**ISSUE:** As a precondition to an accord and satisfaction, must the proponent prove a genuine "dispute" between the parties and that the amount of the claim was unliquidated?

**HOLDING AND DECISION:** (Peters, J.) Yes. As a precondition to an accord and satisfaction, the proponent must prove a genuine "dispute" between the parties and that the amount of the claim was unliquidated. Here, the settlement agreement entitled Douthwright (P) to immediate payment, and such payment was *not* conditioned on anything else. The evidence that a settlement agreement entitled Douthwright (P) to the payment of Northeast Corridor Foundation's (D) debt on February 2, 2001, knocked out the underpinnings of Northeast Corridor's (D) claim that its obligation to pay interest was discharged by its tender and payment of a check in the principal amount of its indebtedness. After February 2, 2001, there was no basis for a good faith dispute about Northeast Corridor's (D) indebtedness to Douthwright (P). Likewise,

there was no basis for a good faith dispute about the amount of Northeast Corridor's (D) indebtedness for interest. Legislation unequivocally required Northeast Corridor (D) to pay interest at the rate of 12 percent per year after February 2, 2001. Under these circumstances, Northeast Corridor's (D) letter stating that the check was tendered as full satisfaction of its indebtedness had no legal effect. Affirmed.

## ▌ANALYSIS

In the *Douthwright* case, the Connecticut legislation conditioned a discharge on the debtor's proof of a conspicuous statement to the effect that an instrument is tendered "as full satisfaction" of the disputed debt. Here, the court found that the debtor's letter did not communicate such intent. This failure of communication meant that the requirements of the statute were not met.

## Quicknotes

**ACCORD AND SATISFACTION** The performance of an agreement between two parties, one of whom has a valid claim against the other, to settle the controversy.

**DEFAULT JUDGMENT** A judgment entered against a defendant due to his failure to appear in a court or defend himself against the allegations of the opposing party.

**GOOD FAITH** An honest intention to abstain from taking advantage of another.

# Kossian v. American National Insurance Co.

Contractor (P) v. Deed of trust beneficiary (D)

Cal. Ct. App., 254 Cal. App. 2d 647 (1967).

**NATURE OF CASE:** Appeal from summary judgment for defendant in action for unjust enrichment.

**FACT SUMMARY:** Kossian (P), who cleaned up and removed debris from a fire-damaged building, but never got paid for his services, claimed that American National Insurance Co. (D), which held a deed of trust on the property, was unjustly enriched to the extent it received both the benefit of Kossian's (P) labor and materials as well as the proceeds from fire insurance policies covering the work performed by Kossian (P).

**RULE OF LAW**

Under the equitable doctrine of unjust enrichment, a party who furnishes labor and material is entitled to reimbursement for such labor and materials to the extent the cost of such labor and materials has been recovered through indemnity insurance proceeds by a party that in no way contracted with, or induced the work of, the party furnishing the labor and materials.

**FACTS:** Reichert owned the Bakersfield Inn, a portion of which was destroyed by fire. American National Insurance Co. (American National) (D) held a deed of trust on the property, which was insured by four fire insurance policies. After the fire, but unbeknownst to American National (D), Reichert hired Kossian (P) to clean up and remove the debris from the fire-damaged part of the property for $18,900. At the time, Kossian (P) was unaware that American National (D) held a deed of trust on the property. Sometime after Kossian (P) fully performed the cleanup, Reichert declared bankruptcy. The bankruptcy trustee abandoned the property as well as any interest in the fire insurance policies—each of which contained a provision insuring against the cost of cleaning up and removing debris caused by fire damage. Then, Reichert assigned the policies to American National (D), which submitted proofs of loss and, ultimately, obtained $135, 620. This payment included at least a part of the cost of debris removal and demolition, though it was not clear what part of the $18,900 owed Kossian (P) was included. Kossian (P) brought suit to recover the amount owed him for his labor and materials, arguing that American National (D) was unjustly enriched to the extent it recovered twice—once in labor and materials and again in money from the insurance proceeds covering the labor and materials—to the detriment of Kossian (P). The trial granted summary judgment for American National (D). The state's intermediate appellate court granted review.

**ISSUE:** Under the equitable doctrine of unjust enrichment, is a party who furnishes labor and material entitled to reimbursement for such labor and materials to the extent the cost of such labor and materials has been recovered through indemnity insurance proceeds by a party that in no way contracted with, or induced the work of, the party furnishing the labor and materials?

**HOLDING AND DECISION:** (Stone, J.) Yes. Under the equitable doctrine of unjust enrichment, a party who furnishes labor and material is entitled to reimbursement for such labor and materials to the extent the cost of such labor and materials has been recovered through indemnity insurance proceeds by a party that in no way contracted with, or induced the work of, the party furnishing the labor and materials. Here, the work was done under a contract with Reichert, as the owner in possession, without the knowledge of American National (D); Kossian (P) had no lien upon the premises and was not a party to the insurance contracts; and American National (D) had not expressly or impliedly agreed to pay for the work or apply any part of the insurance proceeds thereto, nor had it in any way induced Kossian (P) to enter into the contract with Reichert. Under such circumstances, had American National (D) merely taken the property improved by Kossian's (P) work through foreclosure of its deed of trust, there would be no unjust enrichment, even though Kossian (P) would have conferred a benefit on American National (D). However, the fact that American National (D) made an insurance claim for the value of Kossian's (P) work is what gives rise to unjust enrichment in this situation. American National (D) contends that because it had no privity with Kossian (P), and because it did not engage in fraud or deceit, it is entitled to both the value of Kossian's (P) work, as well as the insurance payments covering that work. However, this argument is unavailing here. Kossian (P) does not claim entitlement to the insurance fund. Instead, he relies on the equitable ground that American National (D) should not be allowed to have the fruits of his work in addition to the money value of the work. This is merely a restatement of the doctrine of unjust enrichment, which in certain cases can have validity absent privity of relationship in those instances where an obligation is imposed by equity regardless of the parties' intent. In such cases, the obligation is imposed because good conscience dictates that under the circumstances the person benefited should make reimbursement. As a matter of equity, one party

*Continued on next page.*

should not be indemnified twice for the same loss, once in labor and materials and again in money, to the detriment (forfeiture) of the party who furnished the labor and materials. Accordingly, under the doctrine of unjust enrichment, Kossian (P) is entitled to reimbursement out of the insurance proceeds paid American National (D) for work done by Kossian (P). The percentage of the total proof of loss attributable to Kossian's (P) work was not clear. This should be clarified at trial, and, to the extent American National (D) received insurance for debris removal performed by Kossian (P), he should recover. If American National (D) received less than the value of his work, then Kossian (P) should recover proportionately. Reversed.

## ▶ *ANALYSIS*

As this case demonstrates, whether there has been "unjust enrichment" comes down to a court's sense of justice, and there is no simple rule for when restitution is justified. The court itself notes that the authors of the Restatement of Restitution recognize that the essential nature of equity cases concerned with problems of restitution makes definitive precedent unlikely, and it is by no means obvious, as a theoretical matter, how "unjust enrichment" should be defined. Thus, instead of elements of a cause of action, the Restatement provides guiding principles that cannot be stated as rules. While the Restatement provides that "A person who is unjustly enriched at the expense of another is subject to liability in restitution," the Restatement does not specify when enrichment is unjust—that must be determined by the courts interpreting precedent and their own sense of justice.

## *Quicknotes*

**DEED OF TRUST** A legal document that acts as a mortgage, placing a security interest in the deeded property with a trustee to insure the payment of a debt.

**UNJUST ENRICHMENT** Principle that one should not be unjustly enriched at the expense of another.

# Formation Defenses

## Quick Reference Rules of Law

# Professional Bull Riders, Inc. v. AutoZone, Inc.

Event organizer (P) v. Event sponsor (D)

Colo. Sup. Ct., 113 P.3d 757, *en banc* (2005).

**NATURE OF CASE:** Certified question from federal court to state court in appeal from grant of summary judgment to defendant in action for breach of oral contract.

**FACT SUMMARY:** Professional Bull Riders, Inc. (P) claimed that an oral contract it had with AutoZone, Inc. (D) that contemplated performance over two years but that gave AutoZone (D) the option of terminating after one year was not void under the statute of frauds.

> ## 🏛 RULE OF LAW
> Under the statute of frauds, an oral agreement is not void when (1) the agreement contemplates performance for a definite period of more than one year but (2) allows the party to be charged an option to terminate the agreement by a certain date less than a year from the making of the agreement and when (3) the party to be charged has not exercised that option to terminate the agreement.

**FACTS:** Professional Bull Riders, Inc. (PBR) (P), which organized bull-riding events, prepared a written agreement to provide for AutoZone, Inc.'s (D) sponsorship. By its own terms, the sponsorship agreement was to run for two seasons, unless sooner terminated as contemplated by the agreement itself. However, the contract also gave AutoZone (D) the option of terminating its sponsorship after one year. AutoZone (D) never signed the agreement. PBR (P) brought suit for breach of an oral contract, alleging that AutoZone (D) accepted its terms—since it performed for the first year, but terminated for the second—and that, as a result, the parties entered into an oral agreement mirroring the written terms. The district court, reasoning that the purported oral contract provided for a term of two years and was thus unenforceable under the state's one-year version of the statute of frauds, granted summary judgment to AutoZone (D). The court of appeals granted review, and then certified a question of law on the dispositive issue to the state's highest court.

**ISSUE:** Under the statute of frauds, is an oral agreement void when (1) the agreement contemplates performance for a definite period of more than one year but (2) allows the party to be charged an option to terminate the agreement by a certain date less than a year from the making of the agreement and when (3) the party to be charged has not exercised that option to terminate the agreement?

**HOLDING AND DECISION:** (Coats, J.) No. Under the statute of frauds, an oral agreement is not void

when (1) the agreement contemplates performance for a definite period of more than one year but (2) allows the party to be charged an option to terminate the agreement by a certain date less than a year from the making of the agreement and when (3) the party to be charged has not exercised that option to terminate the agreement. The state's version of the statute of frauds provides that oral agreements are void where by their terms they will not be performed within one year after they are entered into. Because the Statute of Frauds was originally intended to prevent perjury, and since the effectiveness of the statute to promote this purpose is in serious doubt, courts construe the statute very narrowly to void as few oral contracts as possible. The statute is thus universally understood to apply only to agreements that, by their terms, are incapable of being performed within one year. However, there is disagreement about the effect of contingencies, such as the one in the contract at issue, which may result in termination of the agreement in less than one year. Although there is not agreement about whether an option to terminate should itself be considered an alternative performance method, it is well established that a contract that envisions two or more performances does not come within the statute if any one of the alternative performances can be fully performed within one year. Thus, it must be determined whether the contract at bar contemplates alternate performances by AutoZone (D), or whether it merely provides an excuse for nonperformance. To make such a determination, the parties' intent must be determined from the contract's purpose. Although the agreement was expressed in terms of an agreement to sponsor for two seasons, with an option to terminate after sponsoring for only one season, it cannot be reasonably understood as other than an agreement of sponsorship for either one or two seasons, at AutoZone's (D) choice. The agreement did not give AutoZone (D) an option to terminate the agreement at will or on condition of the occurrence of some event, but gave AutoZone (D) two alternative ways of performing. Although the agreement contemplated performance for two seasons, if AutoZone (D) chose that option, it also contemplated that AutoZone (D) could completely perform its obligation by sponsoring PBR (P) for one full season. Therefore, the agreement by its own terms provided that performance could have been completed in less than one year. Therefore, the agreement does not come within the statute of frauds. The certified question is answered in the negative. [Presumably, the court of appeals, on the basis of this answer, reversed.]

*Continued on next page.*

# ► *ANALYSIS*

A growing number of courts have adopted the position taken by the Colorado Supreme Court in the instant case. They, too, hold that a contract does not come within the statute of frauds if one party can terminate or perform within a year, even if the contract contemplates performance for a greater period. However, there are still many courts that take the contrary view.

━━■■■━━

# *Quicknotes*

**BREACH OF CONTRACT** Unlawful failure by a party to perform its obligations pursuant to contract.

**ORAL CONTRACT** A contract that is not reduced to written form.

**STATUTE OF FRAUDS** A statute that requires specified types of contracts to be in writing in order to be binding.

**SUMMARY JUDGMENT** Judgment rendered by a court in response to a motion made by one of the parties, claiming that the lack of a question of material fact in respect to an issue warrants disposition of the issue without consideration by the jury.

# Crabtree v. Elizabeth Arden Sales Corp.

## Employee (P) v. Employer (D)

N.Y. Ct. App., 305 N.Y. 48, 110 N.E.2d 551 (1953).

**NATURE OF CASE:** Appeal from affirmance of award of damages in action for breach of an employment contract.

**FACT SUMMARY:** Crabtree (P) was hired by Arden Sales Corp. (D) to be the latter's sales manager. No formal contract was signed, but separate writings pieced together showed Crabtree (P) to have been hired for a two-year term with pay raises after the first and second six months. When he did not receive his second pay raise, Crabtree (P) sued for damages for breach.

> ## RULE OF LAW
> To satisfy the statute of frauds, the memorandum expressing the contract may be pieced together out of separate writings, connected with one another either expressly or by the internal evidence of subject matter and occasion, rather than being contained in a single document.

**FACTS:** In September 1947, Crabtree (P) began negotiating with Arden Sales Corp. (Arden) (D) for the position of the latter's sales manager. Being unfamiliar with the cosmetics business and giving up a well-paying, secure job, Crabtree (P) insisted upon an agreement for a definite term. He asked for three years at $25,000 per year. But Arden (D) offered two years, with $20,000 per year the first six months, $25,000 per year the second six months, and $30,000 per year the second year. This was written down by Arden's (D) personal secretary with the notation "2 years to make good." A few days later, Crabtree (P) telephoned to Mr. Johns, Arden's (D) executive vice president, his acceptance. Crabtree (P) received a "welcome" wire from Miss Arden (D). When he reported for work, a "payroll change" card was made up and initialed by Mr. Johns showing the above pay arrangement with a salary increase noted "as per contractual agreement." Crabtree (P) received his first pay raise as scheduled but not his second one. Miss Arden (D) allegedly refused to approve the second increase, denying Crabtree (P) had been hired for any specific period. The trial court entered judgment for Crabtree (P), the state's intermediate appellate court affirmed, and the state's highest court granted review.

**ISSUE:** To satisfy the statute of frauds may the memorandum expressing the contract be pieced together out of separate writings, connected with one another either expressly or by the internal evidence of subject matter and occasion, rather than being contained in a single document?

**HOLDING AND DECISION:** (Fuld, J.) Yes. To satisfy the statute of frauds, the memorandum expressing the contract may be pieced together out of separate writings, connected with one another either expressly or by the internal evidence of subject matter and occasion, rather than being contained in a single document. First, as it is alleged that the contract is for a period of two years, there must be written evidence of its terms to be enforceable, as the two-year performance places it within the statute of frauds. The payroll cards, one initialed by Arden's (D) executive vice president and the other by its controller, unquestionably constituted a memorandum under the statute. It is enough that they were signed with the intent to authenticate the information contained therein and that such information evidences the terms of the contract. The cards had all essential terms except for duration. But as the memorandum can be pieced together from more than one document, all that is required between the papers is a connection established simply by reference to the same subject matter or transaction. Parol evidence is permissible in order to establish the connection. As the note prepared by Arden's (D) personal secretary shows it was made in Miss Arden's (D) presence as well as that of Johns and of Crabtree (P), the dangers of parol evidence are at a minimum. All of the terms must be set out in writing and cannot be shown by parol. That memo, the paper signed by Johns, and the paper signed by the controller all refer on their faces to the Crabtree (P) transaction. The controller's paper shows that it was prepared for the purpose of a "salary increase per contractual arrangements with Miss Arden" (D). That is a reference to more comprehensive evidence, and parol evidence can so explain. "2 years to make good" probably had no other purpose than to denote the duration of the arrangement, and parol evidence may explain its meaning. Affirmed.

## ANALYSIS

When there is more than one writing and all are signed by the party to be charged, and it is clear by their contents that they relate to the same transaction, there is little problem. When not all the documents are signed, difficulties obviously crop up. It becomes difficult to say the memorandum has been authenticated to the party to be charged. When the unsigned document is physically attached to the signed writing, the statute of frauds is satisfied. And, as illustrated by this case, this is true

*Continued on next page.*

when the signed document by its terms expressly refers to the unsigned document. The cases conflict where the papers are not attached or fail to refer to the other. The minority holds that is a failure to show sufficient authentication. The better view is that if the signed document does not expressly refer to the unsigned, it is sufficient if internal evidence refers to the same subject matter or transaction. If so, extrinsic evidence is admissible to help show the connection between the documents.

---

## Quicknotes

**BREACH OF CONTRACT** Unlawful failure by a party to perform its obligations pursuant to contract.

**PAROL EVIDENCE** Evidence given verbally; extraneous evidence.

# Sullivan v. Porter

Real property purchaser (P) v. Real property seller (D)

Me. Sup. Jud. Ct., 861 A.2d 625 (2004).

**NATURE OF CASE:** Appeal from order of specific performance in action for breach of oral contract for the sale of real estate and promissory estoppel.

**FACT SUMMARY:** Porter (D), who orally agreed to sell his property to Sullivan (P), contended that there was insufficient evidence for a jury to find that an oral contract for the sale of the real property had been created, that there was insufficient evidence of "part performance" and "reasonable reliance" to remove the contract from the statute of frauds, and that specific performance was an inappropriate remedy.

## RULE OF LAW

(1) An oral agreement for the sale of real property is removed from the statute of frauds where all the elements of a contract are present, where the party seeking to remove the agreement from the statute of frauds has partially performed, and where such partial performance has been induced by the other party's misrepresentative acts or omissions.

(2) A specific performance order to sell real property is within the bounds of a court's discretion where the terms of the contract for the sale of the property are reasonably certain, the party seeking specific performance has made a significant investment in improving the property, and the property is unique.

**FACTS:** Porter and his wife (Porter) (D) owned a 52-acre farm that had a barn, farmhouse, and a horse stable, which Sullivan and Andrews (Sullivan) (P) managed. Porter (D) offered to sell the farm to Sullivan (P) for $350,000, with a $20,000 down payment and owner-financing at between five and seven percent, for a period of between 20 and 30 years. Sullivan (P) accepted this offer, and Porter (D) told him that he would contact his attorney to start the paperwork. Sullivan (P) informed Porter (D) that he would refinance his house to obtain the down payment. Porter (D) moved out of the farmhouse and gave the keys to Sullivan (P), who took possession and began improving the property, with the goal of running a horse trail riding and lesson business on the property. The farmhouse itself also required significant rehabilitation. A couple of months later, Porter (D) told Sullivan (P) that he would honor their agreement, even though there was interest from another buyer. The next day, Sullivan (P) and Porter (D) met, and Sullivan (P) offered $10,000 in cash toward the down payment, but Porter (D) declined to accept it, stating that

he did not feel right accepting the money until the paperwork was prepared. Eventually, however, Porter (D) accepted $3,000 toward the down payment. Afterward, Sullivan (P) commenced extensive renovations of the farmhouse and started the horse riding business. Porter (D) visited the property during this time and was aware of all the renovations. When asked about the paperwork, Porter (D) would always tell Sullivan (P) that he was too busy to contact his attorney. Over half a year later, Sullivan (P) forwarded to Porter (D) an appraisal valuing the property at $250,000, but affirmed that he would pay the agreed-upon $350,000. Porter (D) responded with an offer to sell the property for $450,000 with $50,000 down. Sullivan (P) brought suit, asserting the existence of an oral contract and promissory estoppel, and requesting specific performance. A jury found for Sullivan (P) on all of these, and the trial court ordered Porter (D) to sell the property on the terms agreed to. The state's highest court granted review.

## ISSUE:

(1) Is an oral agreement for the sale of real property removed from the statute of frauds where all the elements of a contract are present, where the party seeking to remove the agreement from the statute of frauds has partially performed, and where such partial performance has been induced by the other party's misrepresentative acts or omissions?

(2) Is a specific performance order to sell real property within the bounds of a court's discretion where the terms of the contract for the sale of the property are reasonably certain, the party seeking specific performance has made a significant investment in improving the property, and the property is unique?

## HOLDING AND DECISION: (Saufley, C.J.)

(1) Yes. An oral agreement for the sale of real property is removed from the statute of frauds where all the elements of a contract are present, where the party seeking to remove the agreement from the statute of frauds has partially performed, and where such partial performance has been induced by the other party's misrepresentative acts or omissions. Ordinarily a contract for the sale of real estate must be reduced to writing, unless there is clear and convincing evidence that an oral contract exists and that an exception to the statute of frauds is applicable. One such exception is the part performance doctrine, which provides that the party seeking to enforce the contract must establish by clear and convincing evidence (1) that the parties entered into

*Continued on next page.*

a contract with all the requisite terms; (2) that the party seeking to enforce the contract partially performed the contract; and (3) that the performance was induced by the other party's misrepresentations, which may include acquiescence or silence. As to the first element, there was clear evidence that there was a meeting of the minds between the parties, since their agreement had all the terms necessary for a sale of the farm, including identification of the property and buyer and seller, purchase price, down payment amount, and type of financing, even though expressed in terms of a range. Therefore, an oral contract was formed. As to the second element, which is grounded in the principle of equitable estoppel, Sullivan (P) must demonstrate meaningful partial performance. Here, the evidence was clear and convincing that Sullivan (P), while expecting paperwork from Porter (D), made extensive improvements and renovations to the property, and offered part of the down payment, a part of which was accepted, and invested in the new business. This is sufficient evidence of partial performance. Finally, as to the third element, there is also evidence that Porter (D), who knew of the renovations and who accepted a part of the down payment, induced the partial performance through silence. Porter (D) remained silent when told that Sullivan (P) would refinance his house to obtain the down payment and throughout the renovations and improvements to the property. Porter (D) also repeatedly informed Sullivan (P) that he would have paperwork drafted by his attorney. Porter's (D) actions and silent acquiescence is tantamount to a misrepresentation that induced Sullivan (P) to partially perform his contractual obligations in faith that Porter (D) was going to perform his part of the bargain. Because all elements of the partial performance doctrine were met, the contract is removed from the statute of frauds. Affirmed on this issue.

(2) Yes. A specific performance order to sell real property is within the bounds of a court's discretion where the terms of the contract for the sale of the property are reasonably certain, the party seeking specific performance has made a significant investment in improving the property, and the property is unique. A trial court has discretion to order specific performance when a remedy at law would be inadequate or impractical. An order for the sale of real property may be appropriate, since each parcel of real estate is unique. However, to be enforced by specific performance, the terms of the contract for the sale of real property must be reasonably certain. Here, the property was unique, and the terms of the contract were sufficiently specific. Also, Sullivan (P) had invested a substantial amount of time and money into renovating and improving the property, as well as into establishing a business thereon. Accordingly, the trial court did not abuse its discretion in ordering that Porter (D) sell the property to Sullivan (P) pursuant to the contract terms. Affirmed as to this issue.

## ▶ ANALYSIS

In addition to partial performance and promissory estoppel, other exceptions to the statute of frauds include admission (where the existence of the contract is admitted by defendant under oath), the merchant confirmation rule under the Uniform Commercial Code (where one merchant sends a writing sufficient to satisfy the statute of frauds to another merchant, the merchant has reason to know of the contents of the sent confirmation and the receiver does not object to the confirmation within 10 days, the confirmation is good to satisfy the statute as to both parties), and specially manufactured goods (the goods were specially manufactured for the buyer and the seller either (1) began manufacturing them, or (2) entered into a third-party contract for their manufacture, and the manufacturer cannot without undue burden sell the goods to another person in the seller's ordinary course of business).

━━━

## Quicknotes

**BREACH OF CONTRACT** Unlawful failure by a party to perform its obligations pursuant to contract.

**EQUITABLE ESTOPPEL** A doctrine that precludes a person from asserting a right to which he or she was entitled due to his or her action, conduct or failing to act, causing another party to justifiably rely on such conduct to his or her detriment.

**PART PERFORMANCE** Partial performance of a contract, promise or obligation.

**PROMISSORY ESTOPPEL** A promise that is enforceable if the promisor should reasonably expect that it will induce action or forbearance on the part of the promisee, and does in fact cause such action or forbearance, and it is the only means of avoiding injustice.

**SPECIFIC PERFORMANCE** An equitable remedy whereby the court requires the parties to perform their obligations pursuant to a contract.

━━━

# DF Activities Corp. v. Brown

Putative purchaser (P) v. Owner of property (D)

851 F.2d 920 (7th Cir. 1988).

**NATURE OF CASE:** Appeal from dismissal of action for damages for breach of contract.

**FACT SUMMARY:** DF Activities Corp. (P), which asserted that an oral contract was made with Brown (D) to buy her valuable Frank Lloyd Wright-designed chair, sought to depose Brown (D) to get an involuntary admission of the contract's existence.

## RULE OF LAW
A party asserting the statute of frauds as a defense may not be deposed for the sole purpose of eliciting an admission that a contract was made.

**FACTS:** DF Activities Corp. (DF) (P), through its art director, negotiated to buy a chair which was designed by Frank Lloyd Wright. Brown (D), the owner of the chair, denied that she agreed in a November 26 phone conversation to sell it. DF (P) contended that on that date the parties agreed to a price of $60,000, payable in two equal installments, the first being due on December 31 and the second on March 26. On December 3, DF (P) sent a letter confirming the agreement along with a check for $30,000. Two weeks later, Brown (D) returned the letter and the check with a handwritten note that said, "Since I did not hear from you until December and I spoke with you the middle of November, I have made other arrangements for the chair. It is no longer available for sale to you." Brown (D) later sold the chair for $198,000, and DF (P) sued for the difference between the price at which the chair was sold and the contract price of $60,000. Attached to Brown's (D) motion to dismiss was her affidavit denying that any agreement was made for the sale of the chair. Also attached was a letter from Brown (D) to DF (P), dated September 20, withdrawing the offer to sell the chair, and a letter from DF (P) to Brown (D), dated October 29, withdrawing DF's (P) offer to buy the chair. DF (P) sought to depose Brown (D) in order to try to extract an involuntary admission that a contract had been made. The district court granted Brown's (D) motion to dismiss, and the court of appeals granted review.

**ISSUE:** May a party asserting the statute of frauds as a defense be deposed for the sole purpose of eliciting an admission that a contract was made?

**HOLDING AND DECISION:** (Posner, J.) No. A party asserting the statute of frauds as a defense may not be deposed for the sole purpose of eliciting an admission that a contract was made. The alleged November 26 oral contract may be within the statutory exception for sales of goods for over $500, if "the party against whom enforce-

ment is sought admits in his pleading, testimony or otherwise in court that a contract was made." Uniform Commercial Code § 2-201(3)(b). Since Brown (D) swore in her affidavit that no agreement was made for the sale of the chair, there is no reason to keep the lawsuit alive. The chance of Brown (D) changing her testimony at deposition is too remote to prolong an effort to enforce an oral contract in the teeth of the statute of frauds. Affirmed.

**DISSENT:** (Flaum, J.) District courts should have the authority to exercise their discretion to determine the limits of possible discovery in contract cases. This flexibility is particularly important where, as here, the defendant's affidavit does not contain a conclusive denial of contract formation. Here, the district court abused that discretion.

## ANALYSIS

The judge writing the dissent in this case seemed to interpret the majority's holding to mean that a sworn denial of a contract was sufficient to block further discovery. The majority is more likely recognizing that, once a party has sworn to a fact, he is not likely to change his story later in the lawsuit. If a party perjures himself by giving untruthful information in an affidavit, changing his story later would be a virtual admission that he perjured himself in the prior statement made under oath. The court can always exercise its discretion to allow further discovery in the face of a defendant's sworn denial. Here, the judge considered it a waste of time to permit further discovery.

## Quicknotes

**AFFIDAVIT** A declaration of facts written and affirmed before a witness.

**BREACH OF CONTRACT** Unlawful failure by a party to perform its obligations pursuant to contract.

**DEPOSITION** A pretrial discovery procedure whereby oral or written questions are asked by one party of the opposing party or of a witness for the opposing party under oath in preparation for litigation.

**MOTION TO DISMISS** Motion to terminate an action based on the adequacy of the pleadings, improper service or venue, etc.

**STATUTE OF FRAUDS** A statute that requires specified types of contracts to be in writing in order to be binding.

# Bowling v. Sperry

## Minor (P) v. Car dealer (D)

Ind. App. Ct., 133 Ind. App. 692, 184 N.E.2d 901 (1962).

**NATURE OF CASE:** Appeal from dismissal of action to disaffirm contract and to recover purchase price.

**FACT SUMMARY:** Bowling (P) purchased a used car from Sperry (D) and subsequently attempted to disaffirm the contract and recover the purchase price.

## RULE OF LAW
A minor may, during his minority or upon reaching his majority, disaffirm any or all of his contracts except those for necessaries, regardless of whether the other party is returned to the status quo.

**FACTS:** Bowling (P), a minor, his aunt, and grandmother went to Sperry's (D) used car lot to purchase a car. The aunt lent Bowling (P) $90 to pay partially for the car. Bowling (P) paid the balance shortly thereafter. The car burned out its bearings within a week and Bowling (P) was informed that it would cost between $45 and $95 to fix it. Bowling (P) left the car at Sperry's (D) lot and demanded a return of his money. Sperry (D) refused. Bowling (P) brought suit to disaffirm the contract and to recover the $140 purchase price. Sperry (D) defended on the ground that Bowling (P) had been accompanied by two adults and that his aunt had lent him $90. Sperry (D) also maintained that the damage to the car was caused by Bowling's (P) negligence and that the car was a "necessity" to take him to and from work. The court dismissed the action on these bases, and the state's intermediate appellate court granted review.

**ISSUE:** May a minor, during his minority or upon reaching his majority, disaffirm any or all of his contracts except those for necessaries, regardless of whether the other party is returned to the status quo?

**HOLDING AND DECISION:** (Myers, J.) Yes. A minor may, during his minority or upon reaching his majority, disaffirm any or all of his contracts except those for necessaries, regardless of whether the other party is returned to the status quo. It is not necessary for the other party to the contract to be returned to a position of status quo. The contract herein was between Bowling (P) and Sperry (D) and the presence of adults with Bowling (P) or the fact that money was lent to Bowling (P) is immaterial. As a minor he had the absolute right to disaffirm the contract. While a car is no longer a luxury, Sperry (D) did not meet his burden of showing that it was a necessity for Bowling (P). Reversed and remanded.

## ANALYSIS

The law requires that minors be protected from improvident bargains. For this reason it allows them to disaffirm their contracts. An exception is made for necessaries because vendors/renters would be hesitant to supply life necessities to needy minors if they could easily avoid paying for them. "Necessaries" have been deemed those items that are necessary to sustain life (e.g., food, housing, clothing, etc.) and those necessary to maintain the minor's social position. 27 Am. Jr., Infants, Section 17.

## Quicknotes

**NEGLIGENCE** Conduct falling below the standard of care that a reasonable person would demonstrate under similar conditions.

**STATUS QUO** The existing circumstances at a particular moment.

# Heights Realty, Ltd. v. Phillips

Realtor (P) v. Conservator of incompetent's estate (D)

N.M. Sup. Ct., 106 N.M. 692, 749 P.2d 77 (1988).

**NATURE OF CASE:** Appeal from denial of damages for breach of contract.

**FACT SUMMARY:** Heights Realty, Ltd. (P) sued to recover a broker's commission and lost when the trial court deemed Phillips's (D) conservatee incompetent.

## 🏛 RULE OF LAW
The party asserting lack of capacity must rebut the presumption of competency by clear and convincing proof.

**FACTS:** On September 26, 1984, 84-year-old Mrs. Gholson listed her home for sale with Heights Realty, Ltd. (P). The agreement included a purchase price of $250,000, with a down payment of $75,000. On October 10, 1984, Mrs. Gholson changed her mind about the down payment and signed an addendum raising it to $100,000. In November 1984, an offer was made to purchase the property for $255,000, but Mrs. Gholson did not accept it. Heights Realty (P) then sued to recover its commission for having provided a buyer, but while the action was pending, Mrs. Gholson was adjudged incompetent, and Phillips (D) was named conservator of the estate. Following a bench trial, the district court found that Mrs. Gholson lacked the capacity to have validly executed the listing agreement and entered judgment in favor of Phillips (D). Heights Realty (P) appealed, claiming that the presumption of Mrs. Gholson's competency was not overcome by clear and convincing evidence. Heights Realty (P) presented testimonial evidence that Mrs. Gholson had sufficient command of her facilities to enter into the agreement, and Phillips (D) presented contrary testimony to the issue of competency. The trial court ruled for Phillips (D), and the state's highest court granted review.

**ISSUE:** Must the party asserting lack of capacity rebut the assumption of competency by clear and convincing proof?

**HOLDING AND DECISION:** (Stowers, J.) Yes. The party asserting lack of capacity must rebut the presumption of competency by clear and convincing proof. Even though some of the evidence adduced was conflicting, this goes to the question of credibility, a question solely for resolution by the trier of fact, who after hearing testimony resolved the question in favor of Mrs. Gholson. This court will not resolve conflicts or substitute its judgment where the record as a whole substantially supports the trial court's findings of fact. That the trial court found for Phillips (D) implies that the burden of proof had been sustained. Affirmed.

## ▶ ANALYSIS

The law presumes everyone to be competent. However, had Mrs. Gholson been adjudged incompetent prior to entering into the listing agreement, the incapacity would be presumed to have continued unless Height's Realty (P) could have presented proof of a lucid moment where Mrs. Gholson was capable of understanding in a reasonable manner the nature and effect of her actions.

■■■

## Quicknotes

**BREACH OF CONTRACT** Unlawful failure by a party to perform its obligations pursuant to contract.

**BURDEN OF PROOF** The duty of a party to introduce evidence to support a fact that is in dispute in an action.

**CONSERVATEE** A person for whom a court-appointed conservator has been appointed to handle his or her personal and financial matters.

**CONSERVATOR** A court-appointed custodian of property belonging to a person found to be unable to manage his property.

**DAMAGES** Monetary compensation that may be awarded by the court to a party who has sustained injury or loss to his person, property or rights due to another party's unlawful act, omission or negligence.

■■■

# Ervin v. Hosanna Ministry, Inc.

Alcohol and drug addict (P) v. Rehabilitation facility (D)

Conn. Super. Ct., 1995 WL 681532 (Unpublished) (1995).

**NATURE OF CASE:** Motion for summary judgment in personal injury suit.

**FACT SUMMARY:** When Jacqueline Ervin (P) sued Hosanna Ministry, Inc. (Hosanna) (D) for personal injuries received while she was in their alcohol/drug rehabilitation program, Hosanna (D) argued she had signed a release of liability. Ervin (P) contended such release was void due to her lack of mental capacity.

## RULE OF LAW
A person under the influence of drugs or alcohol may lack the mental capacity to execute a release of liability.

**FACTS:** Jacqueline Ervin (P) was admitted into the care and custody of Hosanna Ministry, Inc. (Hosanna) (D) for treatment and rehabilitation with respect to her alcohol/drug addictions. While in their custody, she suffered injuries allegedly resulting from the unsafe conditions of Hosanna's (D) premises. Hosanna (D) moved for a summary judgment on the basis that Ervin (P) had waived her right to bring a negligence claim based upon her having signed a general release. Ervin (P) filed an objection to the summary judgment motion on the grounds that she had no recollection of signing the release and was in a diminished capacity because of her alcohol/drug use, if she did sign it.

**ISSUE:** May a person under the influence of drugs or alcohol lack the mental capacity to execute a release of liability?

**HOLDING AND DECISION:** (Skolnick, J.) Yes. A person under the influence of drugs or alcohol may lack the mental capacity to execute a release of liability. Here, Ervin's (P) affidavit raises a genuine issue of material fact as to whether she was able actually to assent to the general release which it is alleged she signed. A party may avoid certain contractual obligations on the ground that at the time they were entered into, he or she was mentally incapacitated. Even if the court were to conclude that she signed the release, which she does not remember doing, if she was under the influence of drugs at the time, she may have lacked the mental capacity to sign the release freely and with full comprehension due to her addictions. Compulsive alcoholism may be a form of mental illness. If drunkenness is so extreme as to prevent any manifestation of assent, there is no capacity to contract. Motion for summary judgment is denied.

## ANALYSIS

The test of mental capacity to make a contract is whether at the time of execution of the instrument the maker possessed understanding sufficient to comprehend the nature, extent, and consequences of the transaction. In this regard, evidence may be considered as to the mind of the alleged incompetent before, at, and after his or her contract, in order to ascertain their real condition at the moment of entering into an agreement.

## Quicknotes

**AFFIDAVIT** A declaration of facts written and affirmed before a witness.

**NEGLIGENCE** Conduct falling below the standard of care that a reasonable person would demonstrate under similar conditions.

**PERSONAL INJURY** Harm to an individual's person or body.

**SUMMARY JUDGMENT** Judgment rendered by a court in response to a motion made by one of the parties, claiming that the lack of a question of material fact in respect to an issue warrants disposition of the issue without consideration by the jury.

# Boise Junior College District v. Mattefs Construction Co.

Public school (P) v. Contractor-bidder (D)

Idaho Sup. Ct., 92 Idaho 757, 450 P.2d 604 (1969).

**NATURE OF CASE:** Appeal from judgment for defendant in action to recover on a bid bond.

**FACT SUMMARY:** Mattefs Construction Co. (D) erroneously omitted an item representing 14 percent of its total bid submitted to Boise Junior College District (Boise) (P). Boise (P) had expected to pay $150,000 for the work and ended up paying another contractor $149,000.

## RULE OF LAW
One who errs in preparing a bid for a public works contract is entitled to rescission if he can establish that the mistake is material, enforcement of a contract pursuant to terms of the erroneous bid would be unconscionable, the mistake did not result from violation of a positive legal duty or from culpable negligence, the party to whom the bid was submitted will not be prejudiced except by loss of the bargain matters, and prompt notice of error was given.

**FACTS:** Mattefs Construction Co. (Mattefs) (D) erroneously omitted an item representing 14 percent of its total bid submitted to Boise Junior College District (Boise) (P). Boise (P) had expected to pay $150,000 for the work. Mattefs's (D) bid was $141,000 and Boise (P) ended up paying another contractor $149,000. It was found that if Mattefs (D) were compelled to perform, it would incur a pecuniary loss of $10,000. The trial court also found that Mattefs's (D) error did not result from violation of a legal duty or from culpable negligence. Boise (P) had notice of Mattefs's (D) error prior to its attempted acceptance of Mattefs's (D) bid. The trial court ruled for Mattefs (D), and the state's highest court granted review.

**ISSUE:** Is one who errs in preparing a bid for a public works contract entitled to rescission if he can establish that the mistake is material, the enforcement of a contract pursuant to terms of the erroneous bid would be unconscionable, the mistake did not result from violation of a positive legal duty or from culpable negligence, the party to whom the bid was submitted will not be prejudiced except by loss of the bargain matters, and prompt notice of error was given?

**HOLDING AND DECISION:** (Spear, J.) Yes. One who errs in preparing a bid for a public works contract is entitled to rescission if he can establish that the mistake is material, the enforcement of a contract pursuant to terms of the erroneous bid would be unconscionable, the mistake did not result from violation of a positive legal

duty or from culpable negligence, the party to whom the bid was submitted will not be prejudiced except by loss of the bargain matters, and prompt notice of error was given. Here the item omitted represented 14 percent of Mattefs's (D) total bid, which is a substantial and material omission; to enforce Mattefs's (D) bid would be unconscionable since he would incur a $10,000 loss. Since the trial court's finding that the error did not result from violation of a legal duty or from culpable negligence is supported by competent evidence it will not be disturbed on appeal. Since Boise (P) expected to pay $150,000 for the work and will still pay less than that ($149,000) if rescission is allowed, it has not shown that it will be prejudiced except by loss of the bargain matters of paying Mattefs (D) $141,000. Finally relief from mistaken bids is consistently allowed where, as was the case here, the acceptor had actual notice of the error prior to its attempted acceptance. Affirmed.

## ANALYSIS

The offeree's actual or constructive knowledge of a mistake is often an important factor in opinions granting relief to the mistaken party. As in *Boise,* relief typically takes the form of rescission, an equitable remedy invalidating the contract. Thus, it is evidently conceded that a voidable contract of some sort has been formed. However, it has also been held that if the offeree knew or should have known of the mistake, he had no power to accept the offer at all, since a meeting of the minds did not occur.

◼◼◼

## Quicknotes

**ACCEPTANCE** Assent to the specified terms of an offer resulting in the formation of a binding agreement.

**NEGLIGENCE** Conduct falling below the standard of care that a reasonable person would demonstrate under similar conditions.

**OFFEREE** A person or party to whom an offer to enter into a contractual agreement is made.

**PECUNIARY** Consisting of, or pertaining to, money.

**RESCISSION** The canceling of an agreement and the return of the parties to their positions prior to the formation of the contract.

◼◼◼

# Beachcomber Coins, Inc. v. Boskett

Retail coin dealer (P) v. Part-time coin dealer (D)

N.J. Super. Ct., App. Div., 166 N.J. Super. 442, 400 A.2d 78 (1979).

**NATURE OF CASE:** Appeal from judgment for defendant in action for rescission of a coin purchase.

**FACT SUMMARY:** Neither party knew that the supposedly rare and valuable dime Beachcomber Coins, Inc. (P) bought from Boskett (D) for $500 had a counterfeited mintage symbol and was not rare and valuable.

## RULE OF LAW

A mutual mistake as to a basic assumption on which the contract was made provides a basis for rescission of the contract for mutual mistake of fact.

**FACTS:** Boskett (D), a part-time coin dealer, had what he thought was a rare dime minted in 1916 at Denver and therefore very valuable. Beachcomber Coins, Inc. (Beachcomber) (P), a retail dealer in coins, purchased the dime from Boskett (D) for $500 after it examined the coin closely for 15 to 45 minutes. When it then received an offer of $700 for the coin subject to certification of its genuineness by the American Numismatic Society, Beachcomber (P) sent it to the Society for verification and was told that the "D" signifying Denver mintage was counterfeited and the coin was not what all parties had thought it to be. Beachcomber (P) sued for rescission of the coin purchase. The trial judge found that the customary "coin dealing procedures" were for a dealer purchasing a coin to make his own investigation of the genuineness of the coin and to "assume the risk" of his purchase if his investigation proved faulty. So, although he conceded that the ordinary prerequisites for rescission for mutual mistake of fact existed, the judge nonetheless denied rescission and held for Boskett (D). Beachcomber (P) appealed, and the state's intermediate appellate court granted review.

**ISSUE:** Does a mutual mistake as to a basic assumption on which the contract was made provide a basis for rescission of the contract for mutual mistake of fact?

**HOLDING AND DECISION:** (Conford, J.) Yes. A mutual mistake as to a basic assumption on which the contract was made provides a basis for rescission of the contract for mutual mistake of fact. The evidence indicates that there was such a mutual mistake of fact in this case. Beachcomber (P) and Boskett (D) both labored under the same misapprehension as to a particular essential fact, i.e., that the coin was a genuine Denver-minted dime. The fact that Beachcomber (P) may have been negligent in its inspection of the coin would not bar its seeking rescission. "Negligent failure of a party to know or to discover the facts as to which both parties are under a mistake does not

preclude rescission or reformation on account thereof," according to the Restatement. As to the trial judge's conclusion that the custom of the trade is for the dealer to assume the risk if his investigation proves faulty, it is not supported by the evidence. This is, therefore, a perfect case for rescission. Reversed.

## ANALYSIS

If both parties are conscious that a pertinent fact may not be true and make their agreement at the risk of that possibility, there is no basis for a subsequent rescission. Such is the case when two parties contract for the sale of a particular item on the basis of their individual appraisals of its value, thereby assuming the risk it is actually worth more or less.

## Quicknotes

**MUTUAL MISTAKE** A mistake by both parties to a contract, who are in agreement as to what the contract terms should be, but the agreement as written fails to reflect that common intent; such contracts are voidable or subject to reformation.

**RESCISSION** The canceling of an agreement and the return of the parties to their positions prior to the formation of the contract.

# Sherwood v. Walker

Cattle purchaser (P) v. Cattle breeder (D)

Mich. Sup. Ct., 66 Mich. 568, 33 N.W. 919 (1887).

**NATURE OF CASE:** Appeal from judgment for plaintiff in action of replevin for a cow.

**FACT SUMMARY:** The Walkers (D), having sold a cow to Sherwood (P) in the mistaken belief that it was barren, refused to deliver it.

## RULE OF LAW

Where the parties to a contract for the sale of personal property are mutually mistaken as to a material fact that affects the substance of the whole consideration, the contract is unenforceable and rescindable.

**FACTS:** The Walkers (D) agreed to sell Sherwood (P) a certain cow, "Rose 2nd of Aberlone," for a price based on live weight of the cow. At the time the contract was entered into, the Walkers (D) indicated their belief that the animal was barren. To this, Sherwood (P) replied that he thought she could be made to breed but that he believed she was not with calf. The cow was not weighed at the time. When the Walkers (D) discovered that the cow was pregnant, and could have been sold for up to $1,000, they refused to deliver it, whereupon Sherwood (P) brought an action of replevin. The trial court held for Sherwood (P), ruling that the contract should have been performed at the agreed-upon price. The state's highest court granted review.

**ISSUE:** Where the parties to a contract for the sale of personal property are mutually mistaken as to a material fact which affects the substance of the whole consideration, is the contract unenforceable and rescindable?

**HOLDING AND DECISION:** (Morse, J.) Yes. Where the parties to a contract for the sale of personal property are mutually mistaken as to a material fact which affects the substance of the whole consideration, the contract is unenforceable and rescindable. However, the mutual mistake must not only be as to some material fact but must also affect the substance of the whole consideration. Here, the mistake was as to a crucial, material fact. The parties would not have made the contract if they knew that the cow was capable of breeding. A barren cow is a different creature than a breeding one. The cow was sold for beef, when in fact she had considerable value as a breeder. As a result, there was no contract formed. Reversed and new trial granted.

**DISSENT:** (Sherwood, J.) There was no "mutual" mistake here since Sherwood (P) believed the cow would breed. Regardless, no conditions were attached to the sale by either party.

## ANALYSIS

The court's interpretation of the facts in this case suggests the difficulties inherent in ascertaining all the surrounding circumstances in mistaken assumption analysis. As a result, many commentators have suggested an alternative approach. Following the cue of Uniform Commercial Code § 2-615, these commentators have urged that the nondelivery of goods should be excused where, owing to an unexpected occurrence, "the nonoccurrence of which was a basic assumption on which the contract was made," performance has been rendered commercially impracticable.

## Quicknotes

**MATERIAL FACT** A fact without the existence of which a contract would not have been entered.

**MUTUAL MISTAKE** A mistake by both parties to a contract, who are in agreement as to what the contract terms should be, but the agreement as written fails to reflect that common intent; such contracts are voidable or subject to reformation.

**REPLEVIN** An action to recover personal property wrongfully taken.

# Lenawee County Board of Health v. Messerly

County agency (P) v. Innocent purchaser (D)

Mich. Sup. Ct., 417 Mich. 17, 331 N.W.2d 203 (1982).

**NATURE OF CASE:** Appeal from reversal of denial of rescission in action for injunction and related cross-actions.

**FACT SUMMARY:** When the Lenawee County Board of Health (P) found a defective sewage system shortly after the Pickles purchased rental property from Mr. and Mrs. Messerly (D) and sought a permanent injunction proscribing human habitation, the Pickles sought rescission of their contract on grounds of mutual mistake.

## RULE OF LAW

Where there are two equally innocent parties who are mutually mistaken about a basic assumption that materially affects performance of their contract, rescission of the contract is within the equitable discretion of the court, which may base its decision on which party more likely assumed the risk of loss.

**FACTS:** When Mr. Bloom owned the property on which there was a three-unit apartment building, he installed a septic tank without a permit and in violation of the applicable health code. This was not known to the Messerlys (D) when they subsequently bought it, nor to Barnes when he purchased it on a land contract from the Messerlys (D). After Barnes defaulted on the land contract, an arrangement was made whereby the land was quit-claimed back to the Messerlys (D), and they sold it on a new land contract to the Pickles. About six days later, the Pickles discovered raw sewage seeping out of the ground. The Lenawee County Board of Health (P) condemned the property and sought an injunction against human habitation until it was brought into compliance with the sanitation code. In resulting cross-actions, the Pickles sought rescission of the contract on grounds of mutual mistake. Focusing on the "as is" clause in their land contract, the trial court denied rescission and awarded the Messerlys (D) a judgment against the Pickles on the land contract. The court of appeals reversed, and the state's highest court granted review.

**ISSUE:** Where there are two equally innocent parties who are mutually mistaken about a basic assumption that materially affects performance of their contract, is rescission of the contract within the equitable discretion of the court, which may base its decision on which party more likely assumed the risk of loss?

**HOLDING AND DECISION:** (Ryan, J.) Yes. Where there are two equally innocent parties who are mutually mistaken about a basic assumption that material-

ly affects performance of their contract, rescission of the contract is within the equitable discretion of the court, which may base its decision on which party more likely assumed the risk of loss. A mutual mistake that is the prerequisite for rescission is one that relates to a basic assumption of the parties upon which the contract was made and which materially affects the agreed-upon performance of the parties. However, rescission need not be granted in every case where there is such a mistake. It cannot be ordered to relieve a party who has assumed the risk of loss in connection with the mistake. Furthermore, where both parties are innocent, as in this case, the court exercises its equitable powers to determine which blameless party should assume the loss. Here, the "as is" clause suggests it should be the Pickles. Reversed.

## ▶ ANALYSIS

According to 1 Restatement (Second) of Contracts, § 124, a party bears the risk of mistake if it is allocated to him by agreement of the parties, or he is aware at the time of contracting of his limited knowledge of the facts to which the mistake relates but treats his limited knowledge as sufficient, or the court allocates it to him because "it is reasonable in the circumstances to do so."

---

## Quicknotes

**INJUNCTION** A court order requiring a person to do, or prohibiting that person from doing, a specific act.

**MUTUAL MISTAKE** A mistake by both parties to a contract, who are in agreement as to what the contract terms should be, but the agreement as written fails to reflect that common intent; such contracts are voidable or subject to reformation.

**RESCISSION** The canceling of an agreement and the return of the parties to their positions prior to the formation of the contract.

---

# OneBeacon America Insurance Co. v. Travelers Indemnity Co. of Illinois

Insurer (P) v. Insurer (D)

465 F.3d 38 (1st Cir. 2006).

**NATURE OF CASE:** Appeal from grant of summary judgment to defendant in action for declaratory judgment and contract reformation.

**FACT SUMMARY:** OneBeacon America Insurance Co. (OneBeacon) (P) contended that its insurance policy covering vehicles leased from Leasing Associates, Inc. and LAI Trust (collectively "LAI") should be reformed because although the boilerplate language of the policy could be interpreted as providing coverage for lessees, it was not the parties' intent to have OneBeacon (P) provide such coverage. Therefore, OneBeacon (P) claimed that Travelers Indemnity Company of Illinois (Travelers) (D) was not entitled to any reimbursement from OneBeacon (P) for monies paid by Travelers (D) on a claim arising from an accident involving LAI's lessee.

---

### 🏛 RULE OF LAW
A contract will be reformed where its written language does not reflect the true intent of the parties and where there is no public policy justification for refusing reformation.

---

**FACTS:** OneBeacon America Insurance Co. (OneBeacon) (P) provided general insurance for vehicles owned by LAI, a motor vehicle leasing agency. Its policy defined an "insured" to include LAI and "Anyone else while using with your permission a covered auto you own. . . ." However, LAI's standard lease required lessees to insure the leased vehicles at their own expense, either by applying to be added to the OneBeacon (P) policy or through another insurer. The lease set minimum coverage limits, and required that LAI be named as an additional insured and the first loss payee, and that the coverage be with insurers acceptable to LAI. The lease also addressed the option of obtaining insurance through LAI, "at Lessor's sole discretion." If insurance was so provided, the lessee would have to pay extra rent to cover the additional premium. In addition, a document entitled "Lease Supplement—Insurance," stated that LAI would obtain insurance coverage only for specifically identified vehicles and that the monthly rent payable under the lease could be increased in LAI's sole discretion to cover a premium increase. Other underwriting criteria also had to be met. A vehicle leased from LAI was, at the lessee's option, covered by Travelers Indemnity Company of Illinois (Travelers) (D). This vehicle was involved in an accident, and Travelers (D) paid out $5 million on behalf of the lessee as part of a settlement. During the settlement process, Travelers (D) became aware of the OneBeacon (P) policy, and, based on its definition of "insured" sought reimbursement from

OneBeacon (P) for $1 million, the policy limit. OneBeacon (P) refused, and brought suit for a declaration that its policy did not cover the lessee, and, in the alternative, for reformation of the insurance policy to reflect its and LAI's intent that the policy not cover lessees and that the policy therefore reflected a "mutual mistake." At trial, although OneBeacon (P) admitted that the plain language of the policy could be read as covering lessees, it presented abundant evidence that its and LAI's intent had been all along that the policy not cover lessees (to wit, LAI's detailed lease requirements that lessees obtain additional insurance). Both parties agreed that the facts were undisputed, and the district court granted summary judgment to Travelers (D). The court of appeals granted review.

**ISSUE:** Will a contract be reformed where its written language does not reflect the true intent of the parties and where there is no public policy justification for refusing reformation?

**HOLDING AND DECISION:** (Lipez, J.) Yes. A contract will be reformed where its written language does not reflect the true intent of the parties and where there is no public policy justification for refusing reformation. A written contract may be reformed if its language "does not reflect the true intent of both parties." Because in a reformation case one of the parties is requesting that the court change the contract to reflect the parties' true intent, the usual rules of contract interpretation, including the parol evidence rule, do not apply, since the court must determine the parties' true intent. The party seeking reformation has the burden of proof to show "fully, clearly, and decisively" that there was a mutual mistake, which may have arisen merely from the parties' inattention. In this case, therefore, OneBeacon (P) must show with a great degree of certainty that the contract language did not reflect the parties' intent. The mutual mistake to be corrected is the expression of intent (the writing), not any mistake about factual assumptions (the underlying agreement itself). Moreover, even if reformation is warranted because of a mistaken expression of intent, it may nevertheless be denied in the court's discretion because there might be policy justifications for denying it. Applying these principles here, OneBeacon (P) has presented ample and convincing evidence that the parties to the policy did not intend the policy to cover lessees. Both OneBeacon (P) and Travelers (D) agreed there was no factual dispute, so the issue is whether the facts as presented fully, clearly, and decisively prove mutual mistake—they do. The evidence clearly showed that LAI

*Continued on next page.*

intended to shift responsibility for liability coverage on its vehicles to the lessees, and that OneBeacon (P) did not intend to provide such coverage unless it was applied for, approved, and paid for by the lessee. The evidence, and all inferences to be drawn from it, showed that OneBeacon (P) at no time undertook to provide coverage to lessees. Since Travelers (D) agreed that the facts were undisputed, it can argue about their legal significance, but cannot challenge the asserted facts themselves. Even so, the evidence presented was reliable and consistent. In sum, LAI's lease agreement, particularly when taken together with the lease supplement specifically addressing insurance, is compelling evidence that LAI intended that its own insurance coverage for a particular vehicle would terminate once the vehicle was leased. The process put in place to ensure continuing coverage by the lessee—either through another insurer or through OneBeacon (P)—supports the inference that One-Beacon (P) also assumed the policies would cover LAI-owned vehicles after they were leased only if the requisite application steps had been completed. This is especially so given that the mistake occurred in boilerplate language. For all these reasons, OneBeacon (P) has met its legal burden of showing mistake warranting reformation of the policy, so the final issue is whether there are any equitable considerations for denying reformation. Here, Travelers' (D) strained argument that reforming the contract would leave vehicles uninsured is rejected, since LAI required lessees to obtain additional liability insurance coverage on all leased vehicles. Also, there is no detrimental reliance to be feared—after all, Travelers (D) learned about the policy only during settlement negotiations, and no other party's justifiable expectations would be defeated. Reversed and remanded for entry of judgment for OneBeacon (P).

## ▶ ANALYSIS

The Restatement (Second) of Contracts § 155 approach to reformation is as follows: "Where a writing that evidences or embodies an agreement in whole or in part fails to express the agreement because of a mistake of both parties as to the contents or effect of the writing, the court may at the request of a party reform the writing to express the agreement, except to the extent that rights of third parties such as good faith purchasers for value will be unfairly affected." Under this approach, when a party asks for reformation of a contract, it is not asking the court to interpret the contract but rather to change it to conform to the parties' intent. It does not matter that the contract unambiguously says one thing; a court still will accept extrinsic evidence in evaluating a claim that both parties to the contract intended it to say something else.

▬▬▬

## Quicknotes

**BURDEN OF PROOF** The duty of a party to introduce evidence to support a fact that is in dispute in an action.

**DECLARATORY JUDGMENT** A judgment of the court establishing the rights of the parties.

**MUTUAL MISTAKE** A mistake by both parties to a contract, who are in agreement as to what the contract terms should be, but the agreement as written fails to reflect that common intent; such contracts are voidable or subject to reformation.

**PAROL EVIDENCE** Evidence given verbally; extraneous evidence.

**SUMMARY JUDGMENT** Judgment rendered by a court in response to a motion made by one of the parties, claiming that the lack of a question of material fact in respect to an issue warrants disposition of the issue without consideration by the jury.

▬▬▬

# Ayer v. Western Union Telegraph Co.

Lumber dealer (P) v. Telegraph company (D)

Me. Sup. Jud. Ct., 79 Me. 493, 10 A. 495 (1887).

**NATURE OF CASE:** Action to recover damages for negligence.

**FACT SUMMARY:** Ayer (P) sent a telegram through Western Union Telegraph Co. (D) offering to sell "800 M laths two ten net." The word "ten" was omitted in the transmission of the telegram.

## 🏛 RULE OF LAW
As between the sender and receiver, the party who selects the mode of communication shall bear the loss caused by the errors of that mode of communication.

**FACTS:** Ayer (P) sent a telegram through Western Union Telegraph Co. (Western Union) (D) offering to sell "800 M laths two ten net." the word "ten" was omitted in the transmission of the telegram and it read "two net" when received. The receiver immediately wired his acceptance of the offer. The mistake was discovered, but Ayer's (P) correspondent insisted he was entitled to the laths at that price, and they were shipped accordingly. Western Union (D) claims that Ayer (P) was not bound by the erroneous message and hence need not have shipped the laths at the lesser price.

**ISSUE:** As between the sender and receiver, shall the party who selects the mode of communication bear the loss caused by the errors of that mode of communication?

**HOLDING AND DECISION:** (Emery, J.) Yes. As between the sender and receiver, the party who selects the mode of communication shall bear the loss caused by the errors of that mode of communication. The first proposer can select one of many modes of communication. The receiver has no choice except as to his answer. If he cannot safely act upon the message he received through the means of communication selected by the proposer, business could be seriously hampered and delayed. However, this rule presupposes the innocence of the receiver and that there is nothing to cause him to suspect an error. Applying these principles here, Ayer (P), as the one who chose the mode of communication, was bound under the contract and must bear the loss. Accordingly, Ayer (P) is entitled to recover from Western Union (D) the difference between the two dollars and two ten as to the laths. Judgment for the plaintiff.

## ▶ ANALYSIS

There is a difference of opinion upon the question whether one who makes an offer by telegram, which is negligently altered during the transmission, is bound by the offer as it reaches the person to whom it is made. The question is often determined according to the view the court takes as to whether the telegraph company is or is not the agent of the sender. Some courts have held that in view of the character of the service rendered by a telegraph company and the fact that the sender is powerless to control the conduct of the company, the telegraph company should be considered an independent contractor rather than the sender's agent. Other courts have accepted the English rule that a telegraph company is not the agent of either party, and so a sender is not bound by an error in transmission.

---

## Quicknotes

**DAMAGES** Monetary compensation that may be awarded by the court to a party who has sustained injury or loss to his person, property or rights due to another party's unlawful act, omission or negligence.

**NEGLIGENCE** Conduct falling below the standard of care that a reasonable person would demonstrate under similar conditions.

# Laidlaw v. Organ

Tobacco seller (D) v. Tobacco buyer (P)

15 U.S. 178, 2 Wheat. 178 (1817).

**NATURE OF CASE:** Appeal from award of recovery of tobacco.

**FACT SUMMARY:** Laidlaw (D) repossessed tobacco that Organ (P) had purchased from him while remaining silent about information affecting its price.

## RULE OF LAW

A vendee is not obligated to communicate to the vendor information that might influence the price of the commodity being purchased, even if such information is exclusively within his (the vendee's) knowledge.

**FACTS:** Organ (P) desired to purchase tobacco from Laidlaw (D). Before the contract of sale was completed, though, Laidlaw (D) asked Organ (P) "if there was any news which was calculated to enhance the price or value of the tobacco." Although Organ (P) had knowledge of such information (i.e., of the peace treaty of Ghent ending the war of 1812 and the end of the British blockade of New Orleans), he remained silent and purchased the tobacco at a depressed price. Subsequently, though, Laidlaw (D) learned of the treaty and repossessed the tobacco, the value of which had risen. Thereupon, Organ (P) brought an action to recover possession of the tobacco. After a directed verdict for Organ (P), Laidlaw (D) appealed.

**ISSUE:** Is a vendee obligated to communicate to the vendor information which might influence the price of the commodity being purchased, even if such information is exclusively within his (the vendee's) knowledge?

**HOLDING AND DECISION:** (Marshall, C.J.) No. A vendee is not obligated to communicate to the vendor information which might influence the price of the commodity being purchased, even if such information is exclusively within his (the vendee's) knowledge. Of course, however, either party (vendee or vendor) may not "say" or "do" anything tending to "impose" misinformation on the other (i.e., actively imparting misinformation is fraud). Here, although Organ (P) had no duty to disclose his knowledge to Laidlaw (D), the question of whether he "imposed" misinformation on Laidlaw (D) should have been submitted to the jury (i.e., a directed verdict was improper). Reversed, new trial awarded, and remanded.

**CONCURRENCE:** (Key, J.) Here, the information which was not disclosed could have been obtained by Laidlaw (D) if he had been equally diligent or equally fortunate. In such circumstances, Organ (P) had no duty to disclose the information.

**DISSENT:** (Ingersoll, J.) "Suppression of material circumstances, within the knowledge of the vendee and not accessible to the vendor, is equivalent to fraud and vitiates the contract." That is the situation here.

## ANALYSIS

This case illustrates the fact that fraud voids a contract, but it also restricts the definition of fraud (to actively giving misinformation) in order to preserve the concept of freedom of contract. Today, though, many courts are more inclined to require disclosure of material facts. Note that there are two types of contractual fraud: (1) "fraud in executing the agreement" (i.e., one party does not know that the paper he signs is a contract), and (2) "fraud in the inducement" (i.e., misrepresentation of material facts).

## Quicknotes

**DIRECTED VERDICT** A verdict ordered by the court in a jury trial.

**DUTY TO DISCLOSE** The duty owed by a fiduciary to reveal those facts that have a material effect on the interests of the party that must be informed.

**MATERIAL FACT** A fact without the existence of which a contract would not have been entered.

**VENDEE** Purchaser.

**VENDOR** Seller.

# Marina District Development Co., LLC v. Ivey

### Casino owner (P) v. Professional gambler (D)

### 2016 WL 6138239 (D. N.J.).

**NATURE OF CASE:** Cross-motions for summary judgment in action, inter alia, for breach of contract and fraud.

**FACT SUMMARY:** When Marina District Development Co., LLC (Marina) (P), which operated the Borgata (P) casino, discovered that Ivey (D) and Sun (D) had used a secret method of shifting the odds in their favor when they played the casino game Baccarat to win over $9 million, Borgata (P) brought suit against Ivey (D) and Sun (D) for, inter alia, breach of contract and fraud. Ivey (D) and Sun (D) contended that they neither breached any contracts, nor committed fraud.

> ## 🏛 RULE OF LAW
> (1) A casino patron breaches an implied contract with the casino to abide by the state's casino regulation statute when the patron engages in conduct that violates that statute.
> (2) A casino patron does not commit fraud by failing to reveal to the casino the patron's true purposes behind his requests and actions where such non-disclosure does not violate the rules of the game being played or any statutes or regulations.

**FACTS:** Ivey (D), a professional gambler, contacted the Borgata (P) casino (owned and operated by Marina District Development Co., LLC (Marina) (P)) to arrange a visit to play high-stakes Baccarat, a casino game. Ivey (D) made five requests: (1) a private area or "pit" in which to play; (2) a casino dealer who spoke Mandarin Chinese; (3) a guest (Sun (D), who worked with Ivey (D)) to sit with him at the table while he played; (4) one 8-deck shoe of purple Gemaco Borgata (P) playing cards to be used for the entirety of each session of play; and (5) an automatic card shuffling device to be used to shuffle the cards after each shoe was dealt. Borgata (P) agreed to Ivey's (D) requests. In return, Ivey agreed to wire a "front money" deposit of $1 million to Borgata (P), and that the maximum bet would be $50,000 per hand. Under these parameters, Ivey (D) played four times, winning $9,626,000. Ivey (D) and Sun (D) were able to win this much by employing a secret "edge-sorting" method to create a deck of cards aligned in such a way as to reveal to them the face value of a card before it was turned over. Knowing the value of the card beforehand (here within a range they chose) dramatically increased the odds their resulting bets would beat the house. This edge-sorting method required all five conditions that Ivey (D) had

requested to be in place. Borgata (P) did not suspect that the accommodations would enable Ivey (D) and Sun (D) to significantly shift the odds of the games in their favor. The mechanics of "edge sorting" are as follows: The backs of casino playing cards generally contain a repeating diamond or geometrical pattern. If the cards are not cut symmetrically during the manufacturing process, the two long edges of the cards will not be identical. In other words, one edge will have more of the geometrical pattern than the other. During play, Ivey (D) and Sun (D) used the accommodations they requested from Borgata to "turn" strategically important cards so that they could be distinguished from all other cards in the deck. The dealer would first lift the card so that Sun (D) could see its value before it was flipped over all the way and placed on the table. If Sun (D) told the dealer "Hao" (pronounced "how"), which translates to English as "good card," he was instructed to continue to flip the card over so that the orientation of the long edges of the card would stay on the same side when flipped. If Sun (D) told the dealer "Buhao" (pronounced "boohow"), which translates into English as "bad card," he was instructed to flip the card side to side, so that the long edges would be reversed when flipped. By telling the dealer "good card" or "bad card" in Mandarin, the dealer would place the cards on the table so that when the cards were cleared and put in the used card holder, the leading edges of the strategically important cards could be distinguished from the leading edges of the other cards in the deck. Ivey (D) and Sun (D) "turned" the cards with the highest values so that they could be distinguished from all other cards in the deck. Ivey (D) and Sun (D) knew that if an automatic card shuffler was used, the edges of the cards would remain facing in the same direction after they were shuffled. Keeping the edges of the cards facing the same direction is the reason Ivey (D) requested the use of an automatic card shuffler. Ivey (D) also knew that if the same cards were not reused for each shoe, there would be no benefit to "edge sorting." That is why Ivey (D) requested that the same cards be reused for each shoe. The leading edge of the first card in the shoe is visible before the cards are dealt. Once the "edge sorting" was completed, Ivey (D) and Sun (D) were able to see the leading edge of the first card in the shoe before it was dealt, giving them "first card knowledge." This "first card knowledge" changed the overall odds of the game from an approximate 1.06 percent house advantage to an approximately 6.765 percent advantage for Ivey (D). When Borgata (P) learned that Ivey (D) and Sun (D) had used edge-sorting to obtain their

*Continued on next page.*

winnings, it brought suit, inter alia, for breach of contract and fraud. Borgata's (P) breach of contract claim rested on the theory that when Ivey (D) and Sun (D) played Baccarat at Borgata (P), Borgata (P) agreed to fulfill its obligations to provide a gaming experience in compliance with the state's Casino Control Act (CCA), and Ivey (D) and Sun (D) agreed to play the game in compliance with the CCA. Because Borgata (P) complied with the CCA, while allegedly Ivey (D) and Sun (D) did not, it argued that Ivey (D) and Sun (D) breached their agreement with Borgata (P). Specifically, Borgata (P) contended that the turning of the cards was "marking cards," the request to use the automatic shuffling machine constitutes a "cheating device," and that the edge sorting technique is "cheating and swindling"—all in violation of the CCA. However, there was no dispute that Ivey (D) and Sun (D) did not physically touch any of the cards at any time, and they did not have access to the card decks prior to their playing sessions. Accordingly, Ivey (D) and Sun (D) argued that they did not mark any cards or knowingly use or possess any marked cards in violations of the CCA, and they moved for summary judgment on this claim. Borgata (P) also alleged fraud and related claims, arguing that Ivey (D) and Sun (D) misrepresented that they intended to abide by the rules of honest play established and required by the CCA, and that they intentionally misrepresented their true reasons, motivation and purpose for the playing accommodations they sought. Ivey (D) and Sun (D) moved for summary judgement as to these claims as well, and Borgata (P) cross-moved for summary judgment as to all its claims.

## ISSUES:

(1) Does a casino patron breach an implied contract with the casino to abide by the state's casino regulation statute when the patron engages in conduct that violates that statute?

(2) Does a casino patron commit fraud by failing to reveal to the casino the patron's true purposes behind his requests and actions where such non-disclosure does not violate the rules of the game being played or any statutes or regulations?

## HOLDING AND DECISION: (Hillman, J.)

(1) Yes. A casino patron breaches an implied contract with the casino to abide by the state's casino regulation statute when the patron engages in conduct that violates that statute. The only way gambling at a casino is lawful is if the patrons and the casino follow the strictures of the state's casino regulation statute—here, the CCA. Contractual agreements, whether express or implied, involving casino gambling in the state must therefore include a provision that both parties agree to abide by the CCA. Although Ivey (D) and Sun (D) did not physically handle the cards, they nevertheless "marked" the cards in violation of the CCA. To "mark" a card is to surreptitiously identify the value of the card to a

player—and that player alone. The physical acts of a card being drawn on, daubed, or crimped are several ways to inform a player of its value. Nonetheless, as demonstrated by Ivey (D) and Sun's (D) edge sorting technique, a physical act is not necessary to alert a player surreptitiously of a card's value. Asking a card dealer to turn a card a particular way so that the pattern on the edge of the card will distinguish it from other cards such that it will inform the player of that card's value also constitutes "marking" within the meaning and intent of the regulatory ban. Moreover, it is not the act of "marking" a card that violates the CCA, but rather it is the "use" or "possession" of a marked card. That is because using or possessing a marked card that reveals the value of that card leads to an artificial adjustment of the set odds in the player's favor. By using cards they caused to be maneuvered in order to identify their value only to them, Ivey (D) and Sun (D) adjusted the odds of Baccarat in their favor. This was in complete contravention of the fundamental purpose of legalized gambling, as set forth by the CCA. Therefore, Ivey (D) and Sun's (D) violation of the card marking provision in the CCA constituted a breach of their mutual obligation with Borgata (P) to play by the rules of the CCA. Summary judgment is thus entered in Borgata's (P) favor, and against Ivey (D) and Sun (D), on Borgata's (P) contract-based claims. Judgment for Borgata (P)/Marina (P) as to this issue.

(2) No. A casino patron does not commit fraud by failing to reveal to the casino the patron's true purposes behind his requests and actions where such non-disclosure does not violate the rules of the game being played or any statutes or regulations. To state a claim of fraud under the common law, a plaintiff must allege facts that, if proven, would establish: (1) a material misrepresentation of a presently existing or past fact; (2) knowledge or belief by the defendant of its falsity; (3) an intention that the other person rely on it; (4) reasonable reliance thereon by the other person; and (5) resulting damages. Here, none of the actual rules of Baccarat were broken, and nothing except for Ivey (D) and Sun's (D) motivation for certain requests was hidden from Borgata (P). The rules of Baccarat do not prohibit a player from manipulating the cards, and, in some Baccarat games, the patrons are allowed to squeeze, crease, bend, or tear the cards. Baccarat is a casino game well known for unique and superstitious rituals, including asking dealers to let the players "peek" at cards before they are placed on the gaming table. Thus, Sun (D) telling the dealer to turn a card in a certain way did not raise any red flags for Borgata (P). Even though Ivey (D) and Sun (D)

*Continued on next page.*

manufactured an explanation for their instruction to the dealer to turn the cards, the rules of Baccarat do not require an explanation to permit a player to manipulate the cards. Ivey (D) and Sun's five (D) specific requests to Borgata (P), and their instruction to the dealer to turn the cards a certain way, did not violate any rules, regulations, or statutes. Ivey (D) and Sun (D) did not need to claim superstition to make their requests and card turning instructions permissible—they already were. If they had simply made their requests without explanation, Borgata (P) was still empowered to grant or deny those requests. That Borgata (P) chose to believe that Ivey (D) and Sun (D) were superstitions did not amount to detrimental reliance, when no explanation at all could have resulted in the same course of events. Even though Ivey (D) and Sun (D) did not reveal to Borgata (P) the true purpose behind their requests and actions, they were not required to provide a reason. This does not amount to legal fraud. Moreover, Borgata's (P) casting itself as an innocent victim that trusted Ivey (D) is misplaced in the context of casino gambling, where each party's goal is to profit at the expense of the other. For these reasons, summary judgment is granted to Ivey (D) and (Sun) on of Borgata's (P) fraud-based claims against them. Judgment for Ivey (D) and Sun (D) as to this issue.

## ▶ *ANALYSIS*

Ivey (D) and Sun (D) argued that the edge sorting technique is just like card counting, which has not been held to be a violation of the CCA or any casino games. A card counter is a highly skilled player who analyzes the statistical probabilities associated with blackjack and, based upon those probabilities, develops playing strategies that may afford him an advantage over the casino. Here, the court rejected Ivey (D) and Sun's (D) argument, observing that the difference between card counting and edge sorting is that a card counter uses memory and statistics, not a manipulation of the cards, to create an advantage for oneself. Thus, had Ivey (D) and Sun (D) engaged only in card counting, there would have been no breach of contract, since no game or casino rules, regulations or statutes would have been violated.

■▬■

## Quicknotes

**BREACH OF CONTRACT** Unlawful failure by a party to perform its obligations pursuant to contract.

**DETRIMENTAL RELIANCE** Action by one party, resulting in loss, which is based on the conduct or promises of another.

**FRAUD** A false representation of facts with the intent that another will rely on the misrepresentation to his detriment.

**IMPLIED CONTRACT** An agreement between parties that may be inferred from their general course of conduct.

# Vokes v. Arthur Murray, Inc.

Dance student (P) v. Dance school company (D)

Fla. Dist. Ct. App., 212 So. 2d 906 (1968).

**NATURE OF CASE:** Appeal from dismissal of action for cancellation of contracts.

**FACT SUMMARY:** Vokes (P) was continually cajoled into purchasing thousands of hours of dancing lessons at Arthur Murray, Inc. (D).

## RULE OF LAW
A party to a contract may reasonably rely on opinions as assertions of fact when given by the other party of superior knowledge on the subject, so that if the opinions fraudulently induce the contract, the contract may be cancelled.

**FACTS:** Vokes (P), at age 51, decided she wished to become an accomplished dancer. Over a period of years, by flattery, cajolery, awards, etc., Vokes (P) was convinced to sign up under a number of contracts for $31,000 worth of dancing lessons from Arthur Murray, Inc. (D). Vokes (P) was repeatedly informed that she was a promising student who was quickly becoming sufficiently skilled to pursue a career as a professional dancer. Vokes (P) subsequently brought an action to cancel the unused portion of approximately 2,302 hours of lessons to which she had subscribed. Vokes (P) alleged that she had attained little or no skill as a dancer and obviously had no such aptitude. Vokes (P) alleged that Arthur Murray (D) employees had purposefully misrepresented her skills and had taken unconscionable advantage of her. Vokes (P) alleged that she had relied on Arthur Murray (D) employees' superior knowledge as to her ability and the skills necessary to become a professional dancer. The trial court dismissed the action for failure to state a claim, and the state's intermediate appellate court granted review.

**ISSUE:** May a party to a contract reasonably rely on opinions as assertions of fact when given by the other party of superior knowledge on the subject, so that if the opinions fraudulently induce the contract, the contract may be cancelled?

**HOLDING AND DECISION:** (Pierce, J.) Yes. A party to a contract may reasonably rely on opinions as assertions of fact when given by the other party of superior knowledge on the subject, so that if the opinions fraudulently induce the contract, the contract may be cancelled. Normally, the party to a contract has no reasonable right to rely on opinions expressed by the other party to the contract. Misrepresentations of opinion are normally not actionable. However, a statement made by a party having superior knowledge may be regarded as a statement of fact even though it would be regarded as opinion if the parties were dealing on the basis of equal knowledge. Where a party undertakes to make representations based on its superior knowledge, it is under a duty to act honestly and to disclose the entire truth. Vokes (P) has stated a valid cause of action. Reversed.

## ANALYSIS

Basically, *Vokes* is concerned with reliance and credibility. One has a right to rely on opinions of attorneys, doctors, etc. *Vokes* extends such reasonable reliance to experts or those highly knowledgeable in a field in which plaintiff is generally unfamiliar. *Ramel v. Chasebrook Construction Company*, 135 So. 2d 876 (1961). To be actionable, the misrepresentation must be material, and there must be some overreaching in cases such as *Vokes*.

## Quicknotes

**MISREPRESENTATION** A statement or conduct by one party to another that constitutes a false representation of fact.

# Hill v. Jones

Real estate buyer (P) v. Real estate seller (D)

Ariz. Ct. App., 151 Ariz. 81, 725 P.2d 1115 (1986).

**NATURE OF CASE:** Appeal from summary dismissal of action for rescission of real estate purchase contract.

**FACT SUMMARY:** Before buying Jones's (D) home, Hill (P) asked whether it had been infested with termites, and Jones (D) denied that there had been previous infestations, despite firsthand knowledge of them.

## RULE OF LAW

Where the seller of a home knows of facts materially affecting the value of the property that are not readily observable and are not known to the buyer, the seller is under a duty to disclose them.

**FACTS:** During escrow for the purchase of Jones's (D) home, Hill (P) expressed concern about a "ripple" in a parquet floor. Jones (D) claimed that the problem was due to flooding from a broken water heater, when in fact it demonstrated a termite infestation. Hill (P) asked that a termite inspection report be placed in escrow. An exterminator inspected Jones's (D) home but failed to find instances of prior infestation due to strategic placement of boxes and plants. When the results of the termite report were revealed to Hill (P) by his realtor, Hill (P) closed escrow with Jones (D). After moving in, Hill (P) found termites and discovered that the previous seller of the home had paid for termite guarantees and semiannual inspections when he sold the house to Jones (D). Despite previous infestations which had been treated during Jones's (D) ownership and occupancy of the house, Jones (D) had said nothing about termites to either Hill (P) or the exterminator. Hill (P) sued to rescind the purchase contract on grounds of intentional nondisclosure of the termite damage. The trial court dismissed the action on summary judgment for failure to state a claim, and Hill (P) appealed.

**ISSUE:** Where the seller of a home knows of facts materially affecting the value of the property that are not readily observable and are not known to the buyer, is the seller under a duty to disclose them?

**HOLDING AND DECISION:** (Meyerson, J.) Yes. Where the seller of a home knows of facts materially affecting the value of the property that are not readily observable and are not known to the buyer, the seller is under a duty to disclose them to the buyer. Such a disclosure is necessary to correct mistakes of the purchaser as to a basic assumption on which he is making the contract and to protect him from misplaced trust in the vendor. The existence of termite damage in a residential dwelling is the type of material fact which gives rise to the duty to disclose because it is a matter to which a reasonable person would attach importance in deciding whether or not to purchase such a dwelling. Here, Jones (D) failed to reveal the home's prior history of termite infestation, despite knowledge of such infestation and previous attempts to treat it. Allegations to this effect raise triable issues of material fact that must be determined by the trier of fact. Whether Hill (P) was put on reasonable notice of the termite problem despite Jones's (D) nondisclosure or whether he exercised reasonable diligence in informing himself about the termite problem should also be left to the trier of fact. Reversed and remanded.

## ANALYSIS

This case is somewhat exceptional in that the court recognized a duty of disclosure between parties in an ordinary arm's-length, commercial transaction. More typically, courts will recognize a "duty to speak up" only in the presence of a confidential or fiduciary relationship. See, e.g., *Vai v. Bank of America Trust & Savings Association,* 15 Cal. Rptr. 71, 364 P.2d 247 (1961) (community property settlement set aside on grounds that husband had failed to disclose value of property involved to his wife). Beyond the existence of a confidential or fiduciary relationship, courts traditionally have imposed a duty of disclosure between businessmen only when necessary to correct a previous misstatement or mistaken impression.

## Quicknotes

**ESCROW** A written contract held by a third party until the conditions therein are satisfied, at which time it is delivered to the obligee.

**MATERIAL FACT** A fact without the existence of which a contract would not have been entered.

**RESCISSION** The canceling of an agreement and the return of the parties to their positions prior to the formation of the contract.

**SUMMARY JUDGMENT** Judgment rendered by a court in response to a motion made by one of the parties, claiming that the lack of a question of material fact in respect to an issue warrants disposition of the issue without consideration by the jury.

# Rubenstein v. Rubenstein

## Husband (P) v. Wife (D)

N.J. Sup. Ct., 20 N.J. 359, 120 A.2d 11 (1956).

**NATURE OF CASE:** Appeal from the dismissal of a complaint to set aside a property conveyance on grounds of duress.

**FACT SUMMARY:** A husband (P) argued that he signed a property conveyance to his wife (D) under psychological duress because she threatened to kill him if he did not sign it.

> ## RULE OF LAW
> Psychological pressure may constitute duress if, thereby, the subject of the pressure is overborne and deprived of the existence of his or her free will.

**FACTS:** A husband (P) brought suit against his wife (D) to set aside a deed of property conveyance to her on the grounds that he signed it only because the wife (D) had put him "in fear of his safety and under duress" to sign by a series of specific death threats during a period when her father had in fact been convicted of murders. The lower courts dismissed his complaint, and he appealed.

**ISSUE:** May psychological pressure constitute duress if, thereby, the subject of the pressure is overborne and deprived of the existence of his or her free will?

**HOLDING AND DECISION:** (Heher, J.) Yes. Psychological pressure may constitute duress if, thereby, the subject of the pressure is overborne and deprived of the existence of his or her free will. The question is whether consent was coerced; that is, was the person complaining induced by the duress or undue influence to give his or her consent and would not have done so otherwise. The age, sex, capacity, relation of the parties and all the attendant circumstances must be considered. Furthermore, the pressure must be wrongful. Here, the husband (P) produced evidence that his wife (D) had threatened gangster violence, arsenic poisoning, and a course of action designed to overcome his will, culminating in his arrest for desertion and nonsupport. The arsenic threat, he said, had a background that filled him with an overpowering sense of foreboding and dread. His wife's (D) father was then serving a life sentence for murder committed while he was identified with an "arsenic ring" engaged in killings to defraud life insurers. Such evidence suggests psychological factors bearing on the subjective standard of free will. Here, there was a prima facie showing of a compulsive yielding to the wife's (D) demand for the conveyance, rather than the volitional act of a free mind. Reversed and remanded.

## ANALYSIS

To constitute psychological pressure that rises to the level of duress, the act or conduct complained of need not necessarily be "unlawful" in the technical sense of the term; (although it clearly was in the *Rubenstein* case). It usually suffices if it is wrongful simply in the sense that it is so oppressive under given circumstances as to constrain a person to do what their free will would refuse.

## Quicknotes

**DURESS** Unlawful threats or other coercive behavior by one person that causes another to commit acts that he would not otherwise do.

**PRIMA FACIE CASE** An action where the plaintiff introduces sufficient evidence to submit the issue to the judge or jury for determination.

# Austin Instrument, Inc. v. Loral Corp.

Parts subcontractor (P) v. Government contractor (D)

N.Y. Ct. App., 29 N.Y.2d 124, 272 N.E.2d 533 (1971).

**NATURE OF CASE:** Appeal from affirmance of damages award in consolidated breach of contract action.

**FACT SUMMARY:** Austin Instrument, Inc. (P) threatened to withhold delivery of precision parts unavailable anywhere else unless Loral Corp. (D) would raise the contract price.

## 🏛 RULE OF LAW
A contract modification acceded to by one party under circumstances amounting to economic duress is not enforceable against that party.

**FACTS:** Loral Corp. (D) was under contract to produce radar sets for the government. The contract contained a liquidated damage clause for late delivery and a cancellation clause in case of default by Loral (D). Loral (D), who did a substantial portion of its business with the government, awarded Austin Instrument, Inc. (Austin) (P) a subcontract to supply some of the precision parts. Subsequently, Austin (P) threatened to cease delivery of the parts unless Loral (D) consented to substantial increases in the subcontract price. After contacting 10 manufacturers of precision gears and finding none who could produce the parts in time to meet its commitment to the government, Loral (D) acceded to Austin's (P) demand, but then refused to pay the amount of the price increase. Austin (P) sued to recover the amount still owing, and Loral (D) brought suit for damages on the ground of economic duress. The actions were consolidated, and the trial court awarded damages to Austin (P), which was affirmed by the state's intermediate appellate court. The state's highest court granted review.

**ISSUE:** Is a contract modification acceded to by one party under circumstances amounting to economic duress enforceable against that party?

**HOLDING AND DECISION:** (Fuld, C.J.) No. A contract modification acceded to by one party under circumstances amounting to economic duress is not enforceable against that party. A contract modification "is voidable on the ground of duress when it is established that the party making the claim was forced to agree to it by means of a wrongful threat precluding the exercise of his free will." Loral (D) has made out a classic case of economic duress in that: (1) Austin (P) threatened to withhold delivery of "needful goods" unless Loral (D) agreed, (2) Loral (D) could not obtain the goods from another source of supply, and (3) the ordinary remedy of an action for breach of the original subcontract would not be adequate [since so much was riding on Loral's (D) own general

contract with the government]. Thus it is "manifest" that Austin's (P) threat deprived Loral (D) of his free will. "Loral (D) actually had no choice." Modified, and as modified, affirmed.

**DISSENT:** (Bergan, J.) Here, the fact question as to economic duress was resolved by both the trial and lower appellate courts. It should not be open for different resolution here.

## ▶ ANALYSIS

Although it has generally been held that a threat to breach a contract does not constitute economic duress, courts have recently begun to hold that various kinds of unethical business compulsion do constitute duress. The present case is an example of this trend. Note that even under the Uniform Commercial Code (which recognizes modification without consideration— § 2-209) the requirement of good faith is ever-present.

---

## Quicknotes

**BREACH OF CONTRACT** Unlawful failure by a party to perform its obligations pursuant to contract.

**DAMAGES** Monetary compensation that may be awarded by the court to a party who has sustained injury or loss to his person, property or rights due to another party's unlawful act, omission or negligence.

**ECONOMIC DURESS** A defense to an action that a party was unlawfully coerced into the performance of an action by another due to fear of imminent economic loss and was not acting in accordance with his own free volition in performing the action.

**GOOD FAITH** An honest intention to abstain from taking advantage of another.

# Machinery Hauling, Inc. v. Steel of West Virginia

## Steel transporter (P) v. Steel company (D)

W. Va. Sup. Ct. App., 181 W. Va. 694, 384 S.E.2d 139 (1989).

**NATURE OF CASE:** Question certified for appeal in action for economic loss due to business compulsion.

**FACT SUMMARY:** After Steel of West Virginia (Steel) (D) hired Machinery Hauling, Inc. (P) to transport steel to a third party, the third party rejected the delivered goods as unmerchantable, and Steel (D) demanded that Machinery Hauling (P) pay it the value of the rejected goods or else lose its business.

## RULE OF LAW

Where a party is forced into a transaction as a result of unlawful threats or wrongful, oppressive, or unconscionable conduct by the other party that leaves him no reasonable alternative but to acquiesce, he may void the transaction and recover any consequent economic loss.

**FACTS:** Steel of West Virginia (Steel) (D) hired Machinery Hauling, Inc. (P) to transport steel product to a third party. The third party rejected the goods as unmerchantable. Steel (D) demanded that Machinery Hauling (P) pay the price of the undelivered loads "or else [it] would cease to do business with" it. Machinery Hauling (P) refused to pay and sued Steel (D) for the loss of business that resulted from this severance of business relations, which amounted to over $1 million per year. The lower court concluded that although under the proper facts a claim could be stated for threats against business interests, Machinery Hauling (P) had not alleged facts which would support its claim for "extortionate demands." Machinery Hauling (P) appealed; and the lower court certified the question whether threats made by one party for the purpose of inducing contract concessions from the other are actionable.

**ISSUE:** Where a party is forced into a transaction as a result of unlawful threats or wrongful, oppressive, or unconscionable conduct by the other party that leaves him no reasonable alternative but to acquiesce, may he void the transaction and recover any consequent economic loss?

**HOLDING AND DECISION:** (Miller, J.) Yes. Where a party is forced into a transaction as a result of unlawful threats or wrongful, oppressive, or unconscionable conduct by the other party that leaves him no reasonable alternative but to acquiesce, he may void the transaction and recover any consequent economic loss. This concept is known as business compulsion or economic duress and often consists of a threat that deprives the victim of his unfettered will. Between Machinery Hauling (P) and Steel (D), however, there was no such duress. They

did not have a continuing contract between them; Steel's (D) demand that Machinery Hauling (P) pay it the value of the undelivered goods was not coupled with a threat to terminate an existing contract. Further, Machinery Hauling's (P) mere prospect of doing future business with Steel (D) amounted only to expectancy, which is not a legal right upon which Machinery Hauling (P) can premise a claim of economic duress. Certified questions answered and this case dismissed from the docket.

## ANALYSIS

This case is unusual in that it appears to recognize duress as an independent tort, whereas typically duress is pled as an affirmative defense so that the transaction in question may be voided and restitution made. Further, a distinction should be made between duress by physical compulsion, which renders a contract void at its formation, and duress by threats, which merely makes a contract voidable at the election of the "threatened" party. See Restatement (Second) of Contracts § 174. Duress often takes the form of threats of criminal prosecution or civil process; in the former case, the threat is almost always considered improper and a basis for avoiding the contract, but in the latter, it is considered improper only if made in bad faith. See Restatement (Second) § 176, comments c and d.

## Quicknotes

**ACQUIESCENCE** Passive or implied consent.

**ECONOMIC DURESS** A defense to an action that a party was unlawfully coerced into the performance of an action by another due to fear of imminent economic loss and was not acting in accordance with his own free volition in performing the action.

**EXPECTANCY** The expectation or contingency of obtaining possession of a right or interest in the future.

# Williams v. Walker-Thomas Furniture Co.

Unsophisticated consumer (D) v. Retailer (P)

D.C. Ct. App., 198 A.2d 914 (1964).

**NATURE OF CASE:** Appeal from decision upholding a contract in replevin action.

**FACT SUMMARY:** After Williams (D) purchased items from the Walker-Thomas Furniture Co. (P) under installment contracts providing that payments, after the first purchase, would be prorated on all outstanding purchases, she defaulted in payments.

## 🏛 RULE OF LAW
One who signs a contract has a duty to read it or, if it is written in a language which he cannot read, to have someone read it to him before he signs it, so that if he refrains from reading a contract and in ignorance of its terms voluntarily assents thereto he will not be relieved from his bad bargain and will be bound by the terms of the contract.

**FACTS:** Williams (D), a woman with little education, was separated from her husband and maintained herself and her seven children, on $218 a month from welfare. During the period from 1957 to 1962, she purchased several household items on an installment plan from the Walker-Thomas Furniture Co. (P). In all, Williams (D) signed 14 contracts for these purchases, with each containing a long paragraph in "extremely fine print" providing that all payments, after the first purchase, were to be prorated on all purchases then outstanding. This clause had the effect of keeping a balance due on all items until the time balance was completely eliminated (i.e., the Furniture Co. (P) retained title to the first purchase until all 14 purchases were completely paid for). After she purchased the 14th item, Williams (D) defaulted on her time payments, and the Furniture Co. (P) filed a complaint in replevin for possession of all 14 items. After the Furniture Co. (P) obtained, through this writ, a bed, chest of drawers, washing machine, and stereo set purchased by Williams (D), Williams (D) brought this appeal, claiming that she had not read the contract before she signed it and, therefore, did not understand its terms.

**ISSUE:** Does one who signs a contract have a duty to read it or, if it is written in a language which he cannot read, to have someone read it to him before he signs it, so that if he refrains from reading a contract and in ignorance of its terms voluntarily assents thereto he will not be relieved from his bad bargain and will be bound by the terms of the contract?

**HOLDING AND DECISION:** (Quinn, J.) Yes. One who signs a contract has a duty to read it or, if it is written in a language which he cannot read, to have some-

one read it to him before he signs it, so that if he refrains from reading a contract and in ignorance of its terms voluntarily assents thereto he will not be relieved from his bad bargain and will be bound by the terms of the contract. Of course, if a person is induced to sign a contract through fraud or misrepresentation, he is relieved from any obligations under that contract. Here, though, there was no fraud or misrepresentation, and Williams (D) cannot be relieved of her obligations under the contract merely because she did not read its terms. Furthermore, even though the actions of the Furniture Co. (P) (i.e., selling expensive items while knowing about Williams's (D) limited income) should be condemned, there is no ground for declaring the contract void as contrary to public policy. Affirmed.

## ▶ ANALYSIS

This case was later remanded by the United States Court of Appeals and the result reversed on the basis that the contract involved was "unconscionable." *Williams v. Walker-Thomas Furniture Co.*, 350 F.2d 445 (D.C. Cir. 1965). Section 2-302 of the Uniform Commercial Code (U.C.C.) provides that "if a court finds a contract or any clause of a contract to have been unconscionable at the time it was made, the court may refuse to enforce it." However, the U.C.C. does not define unconscionability, and many factors have been used in considering whether a contract is unconscionable. Unequal bargaining power has been recognized as an important element, but it has not in itself usually been held to render a contract unconscionable. Some courts, though, have held that where a stronger party has control of negotiations over a weaker, more ignorant, unsophisticated party, there is a presumption that any unreasonable, contested terms are unconscionable.

■■■■

## Quicknotes

**REPLEVIN** An action to recover personal property wrongfully taken.

■■■■

# Jones v. Star Credit Corp.

Unsophisticated consumer (P) v. Finance company (D)

N.Y. Sup. Ct., 59 Misc. 2d 189, 298 N.Y.S.2d 264 (1969).

**NATURE OF CASE:** Action to reform a contract on grounds of unconscionability.

**FACT SUMMARY:** Jones (P) purchased a freezer from Star Credit Corp. (D) for $900 plus credit charges, but the actual retail value of the freezer was only $300.

## 🏛 RULE OF LAW
A court may reform a contract for the sale of goods on the ground that an excessive price term renders the contract unconscionable.

**FACTS:** Jones (P), a welfare recipient, purchased a freezer from Star Credit Corp. (D) for $900 ($1,439.69, including credit charges and $18 sales tax). Jones (P) had already paid $619.88 toward the purchase, but the freezer had a maximum retail value of only $300.

**ISSUE:** May a court reform a contract for the sale of goods on the ground that an excessive price term renders the contract unconscionable?

**HOLDING AND DECISION:** (Wachtler, J.) Yes. A court may reform a contract for the sale of goods on the ground that an excessive price term renders the contract unconscionable. Uniform Commercial Code (U.C.C.) § 2302 allows a court to refuse enforcement of a contract containing an unconscionable price term. The sale of a freezer having a retail value of $300 for $900 ($1,439.69, including credit charges and $18 sales tax) is unconscionable as a matter of law. But U.C.C. § 2-302 is not simply a mathematical ratio formula. Other factors in the balance include: (1) financial resources of the buyer known to the seller at the time of sale; (2) "knowing advantage" taken of the buyer; and (3) a gross inequality of bargaining power. Accordingly, the contract should be reformed by changing the payments called for therein to equal the amount already paid by Jones (P). Judgment submitted on notice.

## ▶ ANALYSIS

It is not convincing for the court simply to assert, as it does: "There is no reason to doubt ... that U.C.C. § 2-302 is intended to encompass the price term of an agreement." The court's paternalistic recognition of a kind of so-called substantive unconscionability, in which the court's valuation of the goods is substituted for that of the parties, needs further justification than it receives in this case. [See also *Williams v. Walker-Thomas Furniture Co.,* 350 F.2d 445 (D.C. Cir., 1965).] Most courts have stopped short of taking this step and have required some sort of procedural unconscionability ("bargaining nastiness") before refusing to enforce a contract. Further, the court's remedy of reformation of the contract to the amount already paid seems most suspect. How does this amount reflect anything other than pure fortuity?

■ ■ ■

## Quicknotes

**REFORMATION** A correction of a written instrument ordered by a court to cause it to reflect the true intentions of the parties.

**SUBSTANTIVE UNCONSCIONABILITY** Rule of law whereby a court may excuse performance of a contract, or of a particular contract term, if it determines that such terms are unduly oppressive or unfair to one party to the contract and violate the subordinate party's reasonable expectations.

■ ■ ■

# In re Fleet v. United States Consumer Council

Unsophisticated consumer (P) v. Private service provider (D)

95 B.R. 319 (Bankr. E.D. Pa., 1989).

**NATURE OF CASE:** Action for violation of deceptive trade practices legislation.

**FACT SUMMARY:** Fleet (P) sued United States Consumer Council, Inc. (D) for charging an unconscionable fee for its services.

## 🏛 RULE OF LAW
A fee charged by a service provider may constitute an "unconscionable commercial practice" under deceptive trade practices legislation where it is charged to unsophisticated consumers in return for a referral that they could obtain for free.

**FACTS:** Fleet (P) brought suit against United States Consumer Council, Inc. (USCC) (D), a private company holding itself out as providing financial counseling, arguing that the latter's fee of $195 to $260 simply for referring its clients to an attorney, was an unconscionable trade practice under deceptive trade practices legislation.

**ISSUE:** May a fee charged by a service provider constitute an "unconscionable commercial practice" under deceptive trade practices legislation where it is charged to unsophisticated consumers in return for a referral that they could obtain for free?

**HOLDING AND DECISION:** (Fullam, C.J.) Yes. A fee charged by a service provider may constitute an "unconscionable commercial practice" under deceptive trade practices legislation where it is charged to unsophisticated consumers in return for a referral that they could obtain for free. While the term "unconscionability" is not specifically defined in deceptive trade practices legislation or the Uniform Commercial Code, it has been characterized as "an amorphous concept obviously designed to establish a broad business ethic." Legislatures expect the courts to interpret the concept of unconscionability liberally so as to effectuate the public purpose and to pour content into it on a case-by-case basis. Here, the consumers, like Fleet (P), who turned to USCC (D) for financial counsel were financially troubled and distraught. Some were unemployed or disabled. Many were facing the loss of their homes through foreclosure. USCC (D), through its marketing scheme, represented that it could provide help to these consumers, help which USCC (D) could not and did not provide. USCC (D) then charged Fleet (P) and other consumers $195 to $260 simply for referring them to an attorney. Such a referral could be obtained for free through a bar association lawyer referral service. In light of these circumstances, the fee charged by USCC (D) constituted an unconscionable price for its services and a fraud in violation of the deceptive trade practices legislation. Judgment for Fleet (P).

## ▶ ANALYSIS

As *Fleet* makes clear, the concept of unconscionability establishes a standard of conduct contemplating good faith, honesty in fact, and observance of fair dealings. The need for application of the standard is most acute when the professional seller is seeking the trade of those most subject to exploitation—the uneducated, the inexperienced, and people of low income.

---

## Quicknotes

**DUTY OF GOOD FAITH OF FAIR DEALINGS** An implied duty in a contract that the parties will deal honestly in the satisfaction of their obligations and without an intent to defraud.

**UNCONSCIONABILITY** A situation in which a contract, or a particular contract term, is unenforceable if the court determines that such terms are unduly oppressive or unfair to one party to the contract.

---

# Ferguson v. Countrywide Credit Industries, Inc.

Employee (P) v. Employer (D)

298 F.3d 778 (9th Cir. 2002).

**NATURE OF CASE:** Appeal of the denial of a motion to compel arbitration.

**FACT SUMMARY:** When Misty Ferguson (P) sued her employer, Countrywide Credit Industries, Inc. (D), the latter argued that Ferguson (P) was bound by the arbitration provision of her employment contract.

## RULE OF LAW

An arbitration agreement is unconscionable, thus unenforceable, if there is both a procedural and a substantive element of unconscionability.

**FACTS:** Misty Ferguson (P) sued her employer, Countrywide Credit Industries, Inc. (Countrywide) (D), under state and federal law, for sexual harassment, retaliation, and hostile work environment. Countrywide (D) moved to compel arbitration. The federal district court denied the motion on grounds that the arbitration provision was void because unconscionable. Countrywide (D) appealed.

**ISSUE:** Is an arbitration agreement unconscionable, thus unenforceable, if there is both a procedural and a substantive element of unconscionability?

**HOLDING AND DECISION:** (Pregerson, J.) Yes. An arbitration agreement is unconscionable, thus unenforceable, if there is both a procedural and a substantive element of unconscionability. These two elements, however, need not both be present in the same degree. Thus, for example, the more substantively oppressive the contract term, the less evidence of procedural unconscionability is required to come to the conclusion that the term is unenforceable. Procedural unconscionability concerns the manner in which the contract was negotiated and the circumstances of the parties at that time. Here, the arbitration agreement was imposed as a condition of employment and was non-negotiable. Ferguson (P) was in a position of unequal bargaining power and was presented with the offending clause without the opportunity for meaningful negotiation, hence procedural unconscionability was present. Substantive unconscionability focuses on the terms of the agreement and whether those terms are so one-sided as to shock the conscience. Here, the arbitration agreement was unfairly one-sided because it compels arbitration of precisely those types of claims which employees are most likely to bring against Countryside (D). Furthermore, the discovery provisions of the agreement are one-sided in favor of Countryside (D), hence unconscionable. The offending provisions cannot be severed or limited. Affirmed.

## ▶ ANALYSIS

As made clear by the *Ferguson* decision, although the Federal Arbitration Act (FAA) compels the judicial enforcement of a wide range of written arbitration agreements, generally applicable defenses, such as unconscionability, may be applied to invalidate arbitration agreements without contravening the FAA.

---

## *Quicknotes*

**ARBITRATION** An alternative resolution process where a dispute is heard and decided by a neutral third party, rather than through legal proceedings.

**RETALIATION** The infliction of injury or penalty upon another in return for an injury or harm caused by that party.

**SEXUAL HARASSMENT** The practice of subjecting persons to oppressive conduct on account of their gender.

# Zapatha v. Dairy Mart, Inc.

Franchisee (P) v. Franchisor (D)

Mass. Sup. Jud. Ct., 381 Mass. 284, 408 N.E.2d 1370 (1980).

**NATURE OF CASE:** Appeal from judgment for plaintiff in action to enjoin termination of an agreement.

**FACT SUMMARY:** Dairy Mart, Inc. (D) appealed a judgment that the termination provision in its contract with the Zapathas (P) was unconscionable and that its conduct in terminating the agreement had amounted to an unfair and deceptive act or practice.

**RULE OF LAW**
Under the Uniform Commercial Code, a contract provision that permits termination of the contract without cause is not unconscionable where it is not unduly one-sided, does not have an element of surprise, and is not oppressive.

**FACTS:** The Zapathas (P) signed a franchise agreement with Dairy Mart, Inc. (D), which operated a chain of franchise "convenience" stores. It provided that Dairy Mart (D) would furnish the store and equipment, pay the rent, utility bills, and other costs of doing business, and receive a percentage of the store's gross sales as a franchise fee. The Zapathas (P) were responsible for paying for a starting inventory, maintaining a minimum inventory thereafter, paying employees and taxes, and operating the store on a daily basis. There was a termination provision permitting Dairy Mart (D) to terminate without cause on 90 days' written notice after 12 months. Termination thereunder and without cause later occurred, because the Zapathas (P) refused to sign a new agreement that had less favorable terms for them, and the Zapathas (P) sought an injunction. The trial court held that the termination provision was unconscionable and that termination had been an unfair and deceptive act or practice. Dairy Mart (D) appealed.

**ISSUE:** Under the Uniform Commercial Code, is a contract provision that permits termination of the contract without cause unconscionable where it is not unduly one-sided, does not have an element of surprise, and is not oppressive?

**HOLDING AND DECISION:** (Wilkins, J.) No. Under the Uniform Commercial Code, a contract provision that permits termination of the contract without cause is not unconscionable where it is not unduly one-sided, does not have an element of surprise, and is not oppressive. Even the Uniform Commercial Code implies that a contract provision allowing termination without cause is not per se unconscionable. Since there is no clear, all-purpose definition of "unconscionable," unconscionability is something that must be determined on a case-by-case basis. In

each instance, the focus should be on whether, at the time of the execution of the agreement, the contract provision could result in unfair surprise and was oppressive to the allegedly disadvantaged party. There was no potential for unfair surprise to the Zapathas (P), nor was there any oppression in its inclusion in the agreement. Oppression is direct to the substantive fairness to the parties of permitting the termination provision to operate as written. Under the circumstances, there was no unfairness in permitting it to operate. Furthermore, there was no violation of the general duty of good faith and fair dealing. Reversed.

**ANALYSIS**

It is clear that a party can meet the obligation to deal in "good faith" in entering into a contract that contains an unconscionable provision. Section 208 of Restatement (Second) provides that a court can refuse to enforce the entire contract if one term thereof is unconscionable or enforce the remainder of the contract without the unconscionable term or "so limit the application" of the unconscionable term "as to avoid any unconscionable result."

---

**Quicknotes**

**ENJOIN** The ordering of a party to cease the conduct of a specific activity.

**IMPLIED COVENANT OF GOOD FAITH AND FAIR DEALING** An implied warranty that the parties will deal honestly in the satisfaction of their obligations and without an intent to defraud.

**INJUNCTION** A court order requiring a person to do, or prohibiting that person from doing, a specific act.

**PER SE** An activity that is so inherently obvious that it is unnecessary to examine its underlying validity.

---

# Coursey v. Caterpillar, Inc.

Purchaser of goods (P) v. Seller of goods (D)

1995 WL 492923, 64 F.3d 662 (6th Cir. 1995).

**NATURE OF CASE:** Appeal of summary judgment in suit for breach of warranty.

**FACT SUMMARY:** Coursey (P) argued that Caterpillar, Inc.'s (D) limitation of liability for consequential damages in its contract of sale was unconscionable.

## RULE OF LAW
Under the Uniform Commercial Code, a provision in a contract that excludes the seller's liability for consequential damages is not unconscionable where it is commercially reasonable, conspicuous, unambiguous, and not unexpected or unusual.

**FACTS:** Coursey (P) purchased goods from Caterpillar, Inc. (D) which he claimed were defective and sued for consequential damages. The federal district court granted Caterpillar's (D) motion for summary judgment on the grounds that Caterpillar's (D) express limitation of liability for consequential damages in its sales contract was not unconscionable. Coursey (P) appealed.

**ISSUE:** Under the Uniform Commercial Code, is a provision in a contract that excludes the seller's liability for consequential damages unconscionable where it is commercially reasonable, conspicuous, unambiguous, and not unexpected or unusual?

**HOLDING AND DECISION:** (Per curiam) No. Under the Uniform Commercial Code, a provision in a contract that excludes the seller's liability for consequential damages is not unconscionable where it is commercially reasonable, conspicuous, unambiguous, and not unexpected or unusual. A commercial contract that excludes the seller's liability for consequential damages is not necessarily unconscionable. Here, implied warranties had been properly disclaimed by the seller, Caterpillar (D), under the Uniform Commercial Code. Caterpillar (D) did make an express warranty that the goods sold were free from defects in material and workmanship, but the contract provided that repair and replacement for breach of that warranty was the exclusive remedy. Except in cases in which consumer goods cause personal injuries, the buyer carries the burden of proving the unconscionability of a limitation-of-remedy clause. Unconscionability is rarely found to exist in a commercial setting. Here, Coursey (P) failed to come forward with any evidence that the disclaimer of consequential damages was either procedurally or substantively unconscionable since it did provide for parts replacement and

labor in the event of failure; hence there was no showing that the liability limitation was unconscionable. Affirmed.

## ANALYSIS

In *Coursey*, the court noted that a limitation of liability was not unusual or unexpected in this type of a commercial setting.

---

## Quicknotes

**BREACH OF WARRANTY** The breach of a promise made by one party to a contract on which the other party may rely, relieving that party from the obligation of determining whether the fact is true and indemnifying the other party from liability if that fact is shown to be false.

**CONSEQUENTIAL DAMAGES** Monetary compensation that may be recovered in order to compensate for injuries or losses sustained as a result of damages that are not the direct or foreseeable result of the act of a party, but that nevertheless are the consequence of such act and which must be specifically pled and demonstrated.

**DISCLAIMER** Renunciation of a right or interest.

**SUMMARY JUDGMENT** Judgment rendered by a court in response to a motion made by one of the parties, claiming that the lack of a question of material fact in respect to an issue warrants disposition of the issue without consideration by the jury.

# Sinnar v. Le Roy

Grocery store owner (P) v. Friend (D)

Wash. Sup. Ct., 44 Wash. 2d 728, 270 P.2d 800 (1954).

**NATURE OF CASE:** Appeal from judgment for plaintiff in action to recover money obtained by fraud.

**FACT SUMMARY:** Sinnar (P) attempted to obtain a beer license for his grocery store by giving money to Le Roy (D), who indicated he could get the license from Lewis, even though the only legitimate way to obtain the license was through a state agency.

## RULE OF LAW
A court will not enforce an illegal contract, even if the defense of illegality has been waived.

**FACTS:** Sinnar (P) applied for a liquor license from the state in order to sell beer in his store. He was denied the permit. Le Roy (D), Sinnar's (P) friend, suggested that a Mr. Lewis might help him obtain a permit. Sinnar (P) paid Lewis $450 to help him obtain a $60 license. Lewis kept the money but never delivered the license. Sinnar (P) sued Le Roy (D) for the $450. The trial court found for Sinnar (P). Le Roy (D) appealed on the basis that the contract was illegal. Sinnar (P) claimed that since this was never raised at trial, the defense of illegality had been waived.

**ISSUE:** Will a court enforce an illegal contract, even if the defense of illegality has been waived?

**HOLDING AND DECISION:** (Weaver, J.) No. A court will not enforce an illegal contract, even if the defense of illegality has been waived. Serious illegality renders the contract void and unenforceable. To prevent the formation of such contracts, the courts will refuse to enforce them, leaving the parties as the court found them. Here, a license could be obtained only from the state. To prevent bribery, which is illegal, violative of public policy, and immoral, such contracts will not be enforced. Sinnar (P) must have realized that $450 for a $60 permit involved some form of illegality. Such serious illegality need not be pleaded. If it appears on the record, the court itself should deny recovery. The defense cannot be waived. The court, if it suspects illegality, should examine witnesses in order to determine the true nature of the contract. A finding of such serious illegality acts as a bar to plaintiff's recovery. The evidence adduced here sustains such a finding. The judgment is reversed.

## ANALYSIS

Bribery of corporate officers, while not a crime, is violative of public policy. Therefore, recovery will be denied even though the contract is not illegal. When a legal contract subsequently becomes illegal (e.g., a trade embargo passed after the contract was entered into), it becomes void and unenforceable. However, either party may maintain an action for restitution.

## Quicknotes

**BRIBERY** The offering, giving, receiving, or soliciting of something of value for the purpose of influencing the action of an official in the discharge of his public or legal duties.

**FRAUD** A false representation of facts with the intent that another will rely on the misrepresentation to his detriment.

**RESTITUTION** The return or restoration to rightful owner to prevent unjust enrichment.

# Homami v. Iranzadi

Lender (P) v. Borrower (D)

Cal. Ct. App., 211 Cal. App. 3d 1104 (1989).

**NATURE OF CASE:** Appeal from award of damages for breach of contract.

**FACT SUMMARY:** Homami (P) made a loan to Iranzadi (D), and they agreed not to report any interest.

 **RULE OF LAW**
A contract that has an illegal purpose is contrary to public policy and void.

**FACTS:** Homami (P) loaned $250,000 to his brother-in-law Iranzadi (D) for a real estate transaction. The loan was evidenced by two identical promissory notes dated March 22, 1984, in the amount of $125,000 each. Each note recited that all monies were due and payable in two years, and that they would bear no interest. Each note was secured by real property belonging to Iranzadi (D). A later modification agreement between the parties provided for the commencement of interest payments. When Iranzadi (D) stopped making the agreed-upon payments, Homami (P) commenced foreclosure proceedings on the properties that Iranzadi (D) had put up for collateral. On October 15, 1986, Homami (P) sued for all unpaid monies, and Iranzadi (D) claimed a credit for almost $40,000 that he had paid. At trial, Homami (P) testified that the parties had orally agreed that interest would be paid on the loan, and that the income received by Homami (P) would not be reported. The trial court awarded $39,324.68 to Homami (P), finding that this amount, which Iranzadi (D) had paid, represented interest only, and no principal reduction. Iranzadi (D) appealed.

**ISSUE:** Is a contract that has an illegal purpose contrary to public policy and void?

**HOLDING AND DECISION:** (Brauer, J.) Yes. A contract that has an illegal purpose is contrary to public policy and void. The contract must have a lawful object. The general principle is well established that a contract founded on an illegal consideration, or which is made for the purpose of furthering any matter or thing prohibited by statute, is void. This rule applies to every contract which is founded on a transaction malum in se, or which is prohibited by a statute on the ground of public policy. In order to state his claim to the funds from the property used as collateral, Homami (P) was obliged to testify and did testify that he collected interest secretly in order to circumvent tax laws. Homami (P) was not entitled to the $39,624.86 he collected as unreported interest. Reversed and remanded.

**▶ ANALYSIS**

A common situation involves the unlicensed contractor, or other unlicensed professional, who seeks to collect money for services rendered. Courts have routinely refused to grant relief in such cases on the grounds that the failure to comply with licensing requirements violates a law designed to protect and benefit the public. Therefore a party who has violated the law and entered into an agreement while unlicensed cannot obtain the aid of courts to enforce the agreement. Other types of cases in which courts refuse to grant relief on contracts against public policy include actions for monies arising from illegal gambling activities and cases, such as above, where parties have attempted to circumvent tax laws.

---

## Quicknotes

**BREACH OF CONTRACT** Unlawful failure by a party to perform its obligations pursuant to contract.

**DAMAGES** Monetary compensation that may be awarded by the court to a party who has sustained injury or loss to his person, property or rights due to another party's unlawful act, omission or negligence.

**MALUM IN SE** An act that is wrong in accordance with natural law, without respect to whether it is prohibited by statute.

# Broadley v. Mashpee Neck Marina, Inc.

Injured boat owner (P) v. Marina (D)

471 F.3d 272 (1st Cir. 2006).

**NATURE OF CASE:** Appeal from summary judgment for defendant in personal injury action.

**FACT SUMMARY:** Broadley (P), a boat owner, contended that an exculpatory clause in Mashpee Neck Marina, Inc.'s (Marina's) (D) seasonal mooring contract that purported to immunize Marina (D) from claims for personal injury was overbroad and unenforceable, because, he asserted, under admiralty law a party may not completely absolve itself of liability for ordinary negligence.

## RULE OF LAW

An overbroad boilerplate exculpatory clause that is not limited to barring liability for ordinary negligence is not valid where it has not been bargained for and where it does not expressly exempt the party seeking exculpation from negligence.

**FACTS:** Broadley (P), a boat owner, was permanently injured when his foot was caught in a gap between the main dock and a floating dock where his boat was moored at the Mashpee Neck Marina, Inc. (Marina) (D). The seasonal mooring contract between the parties provided that boat owners would not make any claims against Marina (D) "arising out of any damage, loss, personal injury or death" suffered by them. Broadley (P) brought suit notwithstanding this exculpatory clause, which Marina (D) asserted precluded his claim. Broadley (P) argued that under admiralty law, which governed the contract, a party may limit but may not completely absolve itself from liability for ordinary negligence, and that the clause was overbroad and unenforceable to the extent it absolved Marina (D) for gross negligence. However, he conceded that Marina's (D) conduct did not rise to gross negligence. The district court granted summary judgment for Marina (D), reforming the clause to limit it to ordinary negligence, which, by doing so, barred Broadley's (P) claim. The court of appeals granted review.

**ISSUE:** Is an overbroad boilerplate exculpatory clause that is not limited to barring liability for ordinary negligence valid where it has not been bargained for and where it does not expressly exempt the party seeking exculpation from negligence?

**HOLDING AND DECISION:** (Boudin, C.J.) No. An overbroad boilerplate exculpatory clause that is not limited to barring liability for ordinary negligence is not valid where it has not been bargained for and where it does not expressly exempt the party seeking exculpation from negligence. The United States Supreme Court case that Broadley (P) relies on, *Bisso v. Inland Waterways Corp.*, 349 U.S. 85 (1955), does not necessarily, as he argues, lay down a flat rule forbidding exculpation for ordinary negligence in all cases. It can also be read as being limited to cases where the parties are of unequal bargaining power. This is consistent with the common law, where agreements to waive claims for mere negligence are generally enforceable, except in limited circumstances where there is unconscionability or contracts of adhesion are involved and there is unequal bargaining power, inadequate disclosure, or similar factors. The courts of appeals are split on this issue. In this circuit, prior case law has held that exculpatory clauses for mere negligence will be upheld provided they are expressed clearly and are the product of equal bargaining power. Here, Broadley (P) does not claim unequal bargaining power. Nonetheless, the clause is overbroad and against public policy insofar as it purports to absolve Marina (D) for gross negligence, recklessness and intentional wrongdoing. Thus, the question remains whether a court should be willing to narrow the clause and apply it only to the extent that it excludes liability for mere negligence. Reformation is inappropriate here, and the district court erred in applying it, because it is ordinarily used where contract language does not express the parties' actual intention. If any modification is appropriate, it would be severance of the offending clause or part thereof. However, such a remedy presupposes that the parties bargained over the provision in good faith, which did not happen here since the provision was a boilerplate provision that was not bargained for. Here, too, the clause is not an explicit disclaimer of liability for negligence, so may not effectively warn a renter that such liability is being disclaimed. Because of these concerns, the agreement's severability clause does not save the exculpatory clause. Thus, because of the exculpatory clause's great overbreadth, the lack of bargaining, and the lack of an express reference to negligence—as well as the fact that the agreement contains an attorneys' fee provision in the event a renter brings a claim—it would be unjust to hold that it is valid. Even though some of these arguments were not made by Broadley (P), the court has discretion to avoid forfeiture of the claim in the interest of justice. Reversed and remanded.

*Continued on next page.*

## ▶ *ANALYSIS*

The Restatement (Second) of Contracts § 184 provides that "A court may treat only part of a term as unenforceable . . . if the party who seeks to enforce the term obtained it in good faith and in accordance with reasonable standards of fair dealing." One of the illustrations to this section makes it clear that where the parties actually negotiated an over-broad exculpatory clause that clearly encompasses negligence, a good case can be made for narrowing it to apply only to negligence, § 184 illus. 4; but another comment, says that "[t]he fact that the [overbroad] term is contained in a standard form supplied by the dominant party argues against aiding him in this request." Id. § 184 cmt. b. The court in this case found the latter more pertinent, and applied the Restatement approach in determining to not enforce the exculpatory clause at issue.

◼▤◼

## *Quicknotes*

**EXCULPATORY CLAUSE** A clause in a contract relieving one party from liability for certain unlawful conduct.

**GROSS NEGLIGENCE** The intentional failure to perform a duty with reckless disregard of the consequences.

**NEGLIGENCE** Conduct falling below the standard of care that a reasonable person would demonstrate under similar conditions.

**PERSONAL INJURY** Harm to an individual's person or body.

**REFORMATION** A correction of a written instrument ordered by a court to cause it to reflect the true intentions of the parties.

**SUMMARY JUDGMENT** Judgment rendered by a court in response to a motion made by one of the parties, claiming that the lack of a question of material fact in respect to an issue warrants disposition of the issue without consideration by the jury.

◼▤◼

# Data Management, Inc. v. Greene

## Employer (P) v. Employee (D)

Alaska Sup. Ct., 757 P.2d 62 (1988).

**NATURE OF CASE:** Appeal from summary denial of order enjoining competition.

**FACT SUMMARY:** Greene's (D) employment contract with Data Management, Inc. (P) contained a covenant not to compete in the state of Alaska for five years following termination.

## 🏛 RULE OF LAW
An overbroad non-compete covenant will be reasonably modified to render it enforceable unless the employer did not draft the covenant in good faith.

**FACTS:** Greene (D) signed an employment contract drafted by Data Management, Inc. (P) which provided that Greene (D) would not compete with Data Management (P) anywhere in the state of Alaska for five years following termination. Greene (D) was terminated. Shortly thereafter, Data Management (P) sued to enjoin Greene (D) from providing computer services to various individuals in Alaska. Although a preliminary injunction was granted, Greene (D) eventually won a summary judgment after the trial court found that the anticompetition clause was not severable from the employment contract and therefore was wholly unenforceable. Data Management (P) appealed.

**ISSUE:** Will an overbroad non-compete covenant be reasonably modified to render it enforceable unless the employer did not draft the covenant in good faith?

**HOLDING AND DECISION:** (Matthews, C.J.) Yes. An overbroad non-compete covenant will be reasonably modified to render it enforceable unless the employer did not draft the covenant in good faith. In adopting this rule, this court rejects older rules adopted in other jurisdictions, such as the strict view implemented by the lower court here (i.e., all overbroad covenants are unconscionable and will not be enforced) and the "blue-pencil" rule (i.e., offending words may be deleted from the covenant to render it enforceable). However, the burden remains on the employer to prove the covenant was drafted in good faith. This "rule of reasonableness" test permits courts to determine, on the basis of evidence demonstrating the intent of the parties at the time of contracting, what would be reasonable between the parties. Factors courts will consider in determining reasonableness include: whether the employee has sole customer contact or possession of confidential information or trade secrets; whether the covenant stifles the inherent skill and experience of the employee or bars the employee's sole means of support; whether the forbidden employment is merely incidental to the main employment; and whether the employee's talent was developed during the period of employment. Here, because Data Management's (P) covenant was stricken in its entirety, there was no evidence received as to its good faith and the intent of the parties at the time the covenant was signed. Remanded for receipt of this evidence and determination of whether the covenant can be reasonably altered.

## ▶ ANALYSIS

The position taken by this court is consistent with the Restatement (Second) of Contracts § 184(2) and with the law of most states. It also accords with the Uniform Commercial Code § 2-302. Courts are more likely to uphold covenants not to compete which are ancillary to the sale of a business because in such cases the covenants protect the goodwill of the business being sold. And courts are not likely to uphold covenants which prohibit the employee from using general skills or knowledge obtained during the employment as opposed to trade secrets, confidential information, or customer lists. Compare *Field v. Alexander & Alexander of Indiana, Inc.*, 503 N.E.2d 627 (Ind. App. 1987) (covenant of insurance salesman not to solicit customers acquired during previous employment upheld) with *American Shippers Supply Co. v. Campbell*, 456 N.E.2d 1040 (Ind. App. 1983) (covenant could not prohibit the contacting of customers whose identity could be ascertained from trade publications or telephone directories).

## Quicknotes

**ENJOIN** The ordering of a party to cease the conduct of a specific activity.

**PRELIMINARY INJUNCTION** A judicial mandate issued to require or restrain a party from certain conduct; used to preserve a trial's subject matter or to prevent threatened injury.

**SUMMARY JUDGMENT** Judgment rendered by a court in response to a motion made by one of the parties, claiming that the lack of a question of material fact in respect to an issue warrants disposition of the issue without consideration by the jury.

# Watts v. Watts

Unmarried cohabitant (P) v. Unmarried cohabitant (D)

Wis. Sup. Ct., 137 Wis. 2d 506, 405 N.W.2d 303 (1987).

**NATURE OF CASE:** Appeal from dismissal of action for account and property division.

**FACT SUMMARY:** Sue Ann (P) sued James (D) for accounting and division of property after their 12-year nonmarital cohabitation ended.

## RULE OF LAW

An unmarried cohabitant may assert contract and property claims against the other party to the cohabitation.

**FACTS:** Sue Ann (P) and James (D) Watts had been living together, holding themselves out to the public as husband and wife. Sue Ann (P) assumed James's (D) surname as her own, and she gave birth to two children who bore the same surname. The parties filed joint income tax returns, maintained joint bank accounts, and purchased real and personal property as husband and wife. James (D) insured Sue Ann (P) as his wife on his medical insurance policy and named her as beneficiary on his life insurance policy. In short, Sue Ann (P) contributed to the relationship as a married wife would, and when the relationship ended after 12 years, she sued James (D) for breach of an express or implied-in-fact contract to share the property that the couple had accumulated during their relationship. Sue Ann (P) claimed that James (D) was unjustly enriched by his breach. At trial, Sue Ann's (P) complaint was dismissed for not pleading facts necessary to state a cause of action. This appeal followed.

**ISSUE:** May an unmarried cohabitant assert contract and property claims against the other party to the cohabitation?

**HOLDING AND DECISION:** (Abrahamson, J.) Yes. An unmarried cohabitant may assert contract and property claims against the other party to the cohabitation. Sue Ann (P) alleged that James (D) accepted and retained the benefit of services she provided knowing that she expected to share equally in the wealth accumulated during their relationship. She argued that it was unfair for James (D) to retain all the assets they accumulated under these circumstances and that a constructive trust should be imposed on the property as a result of his unjust enrichment. Unlike claims for breach of an express or implied-in-fact contract, a claim of unjust enrichment does not arise out of an agreement entered into by the parties. Rather, an action for recovery based upon unjust enrichment is grounded on the moral principle that one who has received a benefit has a duty to make restitution where retaining such a benefit would be unjust. In this case, Sue Ann (P) alleged that she

contributed both property and services to the parties' relationship. She claimed that because of these contributions the parties' assets increased, but she was never compensated for her contributions. She further alleged it would be unfair for James (D) to retain everything, knowing the Sue Ann (P) expected to share in the property accumulated. Sue Ann's (P) pleaded allegations were sufficient to state a claim for damages resulting from James's (D) breach of an express or an implied-in-fact contract to share with her the property accumulated by the efforts of both parties during their relationship. Complaint reinstated.

## ANALYSIS

The court did not judge the merits of Sue Ann's (P) claim but merely held that she should be given the chance to litigate her claim. In this type of case, the defendant often tries to show that the applicable family code law does not purport to offer relief to unmarried cohabitants on grounds that such a living arrangement is illegal and against the public policy which promotes marriage. However, the logical interpretation of such statutes is that they promote family life instead of the specific practice of marriage. The courts, aware of society's changing values, are recognizing that many couples live together as family units; hence this argument of illegality will not be allowed to unjustly enrich one party.

---

## Quicknotes

**BREACH OF CONTRACT** Unlawful failure by a party to perform its obligations pursuant to contract.

**EXPRESS CONTRACT** A contract the terms of which are specifically stated; may be oral or written.

**IMPLIED-IN-FACT CONTRACT** Refers to conditions which arise by physical or moral inference: (a) prerequisites or circumstances which a reasonable person would assume necessary to render or receive performance; and (b) the good-faith cooperation of the promisee in receiving the performance of the promisor.

**RESTITUTION** The return or restoration to rightful owner to prevent unjust enrichment.

**UNJUST ENRICHMENT** Principle that one should not be unjustly enriched at the expense of another.

# Kass v. Kass

Former wife (P) v. Former husband (D)

N.Y. Ct. App., 91 N.Y.2d 554 (1998).

**NATURE OF CASE:** Appeal from order enforcing an agreement controlling the disposition of frozen preembryos. [The complete procedural posture of the case is not presented in the casebook extract.]

**FACT SUMMARY:** In an attempt to conceive a child during their marriage, Maureen Kass (P) and Steven Kass (D) participated in *in vitro* fertilization (IVF) procedures and had five preembryos frozen. At the time, Maureen (P) and Steven (D) entered into a consent agreement that in the event they could not agree regarding the disposition of the preembryos, the preembryos would be donated to the IVF program. Shortly thereafter, Maureen (P) initiated divorce proceedings and sought custody of the preembryos; Steven (D) objected and sought specific performance of the consent agreement.

## RULE OF LAW

An agreement between progenitors, or gamete donors, regarding disposition of their pre-zygotes generally is presumed valid and binding, and to be enforced in any dispute between them.

**FACTS:** In an attempt to conceive a child during their marriage, Maureen Kass (P) and Steven Kass (D) participated in *in vitro* fertilization (IVF) procedures for around five years. They failed to conceive. As part of the final procedure, they had five preembryos (also known as "prezygotes") frozen. At the time, Maureen (P) and Steven (D) entered into a consent agreement that in the event they could not agree regarding the disposition of the preembryos, the preembryos would be donated to the IVF program for scientific research. Barely three weeks after signing the consent, and knowing that divorce was imminent, Maureen (P) and Steven (D) drew up and signed an "uncontested divorce" agreement that provided that the preembryos would be disposed of in the manner specified in the consent, and that neither Maureen (P) nor Steven (D) or anyone else would lay claim to custody of the prezygotes. Contrary to this agreement, three weeks later Maureen (P) informed the IVF program of her opposition to destruction or release of the preembryos. A month after that, she commenced a matrimonial action, requesting sole custody of the preembryos so she could undergo another implantation procedure. She argued that implantation of the preembryos was her only chance for genetic motherhood. Steven (D) opposed Maureen's (P) further attempts to become pregnant with the pre-zygotes, and he counterclaimed for specific performance of the parties' consent agreement. He objected to the burdens of unwanted fatherhood. The state's intermediate appellate court ordered

enforcement of the consent agreement, and the state's highest court granted review. [The complete procedural posture of the case is not presented in the casebook extract.]

**ISSUE:** Is an agreement between progenitors, or gamete donors, regarding disposition of their pre-zygotes generally presumed valid and binding, and to be enforced in any dispute between them?

**HOLDING AND DECISION:** (Kaye, C.J.) Yes. An agreement between progenitors, or gamete donors, regarding disposition of their pre-zygotes generally is presumed valid and binding, and to be enforced in any dispute between them. Currently, the state does not have statutes touching on the disposition of stored embryos. There are also not many cases in the country dealing with the issue presented by this case. One jurisdiction has ruled that in the absence of a written agreement between the parties—which should be presumed valid and implemented—courts should balance the parties' competing interests. Because the disposition of pre-zygotes does not implicate a woman's right of privacy or bodily integrity in the area of reproductive choice, and because pre-zygotes are not recognized as "persons" for constitutional purposes, the issue comes down to who had dispositional authority over them. Here, the parties have answered that question. Agreements between progenitors, or gamete donors, regarding disposition of their pre-zygotes should generally be presumed valid and binding, and enforced in any dispute between them. Indeed, such agreements should be encouraged, as advance directives in this area or reproductive choice can avoid costly litigation, both in hard costs as well as intangible costs. Written agreements also provide the certainty needed for effective operation of IVF programs. Especially given that the freezing of preembryos provides time for minds and circumstances to change, it is particularly important that courts honor the parties' expressions of choice made before disputes arise. Advance agreements as to disposition would have little purpose if they were enforceable only in the event the parties continued to agree. Thus, to the extent possible, it should be the progenitors—not the State and not the courts—who by their prior directive make this deeply personal life choice. Here, the consent signed by Maureen (P) and Steven (D) make clear their intent regarding disposition of the preembryos; they unambiguously directed that in the present circumstances, the pre-zygotes be donated for research to the IVF program. It is also clear that they intended that the disposition of the

*Continued on next page.*

preembryos would be their joint decision. Accordingly, the law will give effect to their intention. Affirmed.

## ▶ ANALYSIS

Although the subject of the dispute in this case was novel, the court applied common-law principles governing contract interpretation to reach its holding. One of the principles the court applied is that whether an agreement is ambiguous is a question of law for the courts and ambiguity is determined by looking within the four corners of the document, not to outside sources. Here, the court, after thoroughly examining the consent agreement, determined that the contract was not ambiguous, and that the parties' intent was clear from the consent itself. Moreover, had the court found parts of the contract to be ambiguous, it could have looked to the parties' "uncontested divorce" agreement, executed just a weeks after the consent agreement was executed, to resolve any ambiguities. While extrinsic evidence cannot be used to create an ambiguity in an agreement, it can be used to resolve any ambiguity. Here, the uncontested divorce agreement would have reaffirmed the earlier understanding that neither party would alone lay claim to possession of the pre-zygotes. Other possible approaches to cases such as the one presented here have been suggested. One approach would regard the progenitors as holding a "bundle of rights" in relation to the preembryos that can be exercised through joint disposition agreements. Another approach would hold that no embryo should be implanted, destroyed or used in research over the objection of an individual with decision-making authority.

## Quicknotes

**IN VITRO FERTILIZATION** The fertilization of a human egg using donor sperm in a controlled environment outside the womb.

# A.Z. v. B.Z.
### Former husband (P) v. Former wife (D)

Mass. Sup. Jud. Ct., 725 N.E.2d 1051 (2000).

**NATURE OF CASE:** Appeal from grant of permanent injunction prohibiting the use of frozen preembryos.

**FACT SUMMARY:** B.Z. (D), the former wife of A.Z. (P), contended that pursuant to a consent from between the couple and an *in vitro* fertilization (IVF) clinic, she should be allowed to use a vial of frozen preembryos for possible conception. A.Z. (P) opposed such use on the grounds that if conception were successful, he would be forced to become a parent over his present objection.

> ## RULE OF LAW
> An agreement permitting the use of frozen preembryos for possible conception is not enforceable against a party to the agreement where that party no longer wishes to become a parent.

**FACTS:** When A.Z. (P) and B.Z. (D) were married, they underwent *in vitro* fertilization (IVF) treatments over a period of several years that involved the freezing of preembryos. At each treatment, both A.Z. (P) and B.Z. (D) signed consent forms as to the ultimate disposition of the preembryos. A.Z. (P) signed in blank, and B.Z. filled in the disposition and other information, and then signed. B.Z. (D) indicated that if the couple was to separate, the preembryos should be returned to her for implantation. As a result of one of the treatments, B.Z. (D), the wife, conceived and gave birth to twins. During that treatment, more preembryos were formed than were necessary for immediate implantation, and two vials of preembryos were frozen for possible future implantation. Four years later, without A.Z.'s (P) knowledge, B.Z. (D) used one of the vials to attempt conception. Relations between A.Z. (P) and B.Z. (D) deteriorated around this time. B.Z. (D) sought a protective order against A.Z. (P), and they eventually separated and divorced. At the time of divorce, one vial of preembryos remained at the clinic. A.Z. (P) filed a motion for a permanent injunction to prohibit B.Z. (D) from using this vial for attempted conception. B.Z. (D) contended that the consent form governing the vial should be given effect. The trial court determined that the best solution was to balance B.Z.'s (D) interest in procreation against A.Z.'s (P) interest in avoiding procreation. The court ultimately determined that A.Z.'s (P) interest in avoiding procreation outweighed B.Z.'s (D) interest in having additional children and granted the permanent injunction in favor of A.Z. (P). The state's highest court transferred the case to itself on its own motion.

**ISSUE:** Is an agreement permitting the use of frozen preembryos for possible conception enforceable against a party to the agreement where that party no longer wishes to become a parent?

**HOLDING AND DECISION:** (Cowin, J.) No. An agreement permitting the use of frozen preembryos for possible conception is not enforceable against a party to the agreement where that party no longer wishes to become a parent. First, it is doubtful that the consent form represented the intent of the husband and the wife regarding the disposition of the preembryos in the case of a dispute between them. The form itself did not indicate that it was intended to be a binding agreement between the spouses should they later disagree as to the preembryos' disposition. Instead, it appeared that the form was intended only to define the donors' relationship as a unit with the clinic. Second, the form did not contain a duration provision. Therefore, it cannot be assumed that the donors intended the form to govern the disposition of the preembryos four years after it was executed, especially in light of their changed circumstances (i.e., divorce). Third, the form used the language "should we become separated." This language is ambiguous, and does not indicated definitively whether separation was intended to encompass divorce. Fourth, the parties' conduct in connection with the execution of the forms also creates doubt as to whether the forms represented their clear intentions. Because the husband signed the form at issue in blank, it cannot be concluded that the form represented his true intention regarding the preembryos' disposition. Finally, the consent form is not a separation agreement that is binding on the couple in a divorce proceeding. In any event, there are independent policy reasons the form should not be enforced in circumstances such as those presented by this case. Even if the agreement had been unambiguous about the disposition of the preembryos, such an agreement would not be enforceable to compel one of the donors to become a parent against his or her will. It is well-established that courts will not enforce contracts that violate public policy, and, as a matter of public policy, forced procreation is not an area amenable to judicial enforcement. In a case such as the one at bar, freedom of contract is outweighed by public policy against compelling an individual to become a parent over his or her contemporaneous objection. This policy is derived from other manifestations by the state legislature, as well as judicial precedent, that individuals shall not be compelled to enter into intimate family relationships, and

*Continued on next page.*

that the law shall not be used as a mechanism for forcing such relationships when they are not desired. This policy is grounded in the notion that respect for liberty and privacy requires that individuals be accorded the freedom to decide whether to enter into a family relationship. Here, enforcing the consent form against A.Z. (P) would compel him to become a parent against his present wishes. Public policy prohibits enforcement of the consent form. Affirmed.

## ▶ *ANALYSIS*

Few courts have addressed the issue presented by this case, and not all that have follow the reasoning of the court in this case. Some of those courts have held that agreements between donors regarding the disposition of preembryos should be presumed valid and should be enforced, on the grounds that such agreements minimize misunderstanding, maximize procreative liberty, and provide needed certainty to IVF programs. See, e.g., *Kass v. Kass,* 91 N.Y.2d 554 (N.Y. 1998).

## *Quicknotes*

**IN VITRO FERTILIZATION** The fertilization of a human egg using donor sperm in a controlled environment outside the womb.

**PERMANENT INJUNCTION** A remedy imposed by the court ordering a party to cease the conduct of a specific activity until the final disposition of the cause of action.

# Wallis v. Smith

Consensual sex partner (P) v. Consensual sex partner (D)

N.M. Ct. App., 130 N.M. 214, 22 P.3d 682, *cert. denied*, 23 P.3d 929 (2001).

**NATURE OF CASE:** Appeal of the dismissal of a damages suit.

**FACT SUMMARY:** Peter Wallis (P) sought monetary damages against Kellie Smith (D), a consensual sex partner, for bearing his child after she misrepresented to him that she was practicing birth control.

## RULE OF LAW
A party may not seek compensatory damages for the "economic injury" of paying statutory child support.

**FACTS:** Peter Wallis (P) and Kellie Smith (D) were partners in a consensual sexual relationship. Smith (D) misrepresented that she was practicing birth control when she was not, and Wallis (P) therefore unknowingly fathered her child. Wallis (P) sued Smith (D) for money damages for the costs of raising the child (child support). His suit was based on fraud, breach of contract, conversion, and tort. The trial court dismissed the suit for failure to state a claim upon which relief may be granted, and Wallis (P) appealed.

**ISSUE:** May a party seek compensatory damages for the "economic injury" of paying statutory child support?

**HOLDING AND DECISION:** (Bosson, J.) No. A party may not seek compensatory damages for the "economic injury" of paying statutory child support. Here, it is self-evident that Wallis (P) seeks to recover for the very financial loss caused him by the statutory obligation to pay child support. Making each parent financially responsible for the conception and birth of children illuminates a strong public policy that makes paramount the interests of the child. The state properly exercises *parens patriae* authority to protect the best interests of all children by ensuring that the parents provide an adequate standard of support. Placing a duty of support on each parent has the added benefit of insulating the state from the possibility of bearing the financial burden for a child. This court cannot harmonize the legislative concern for the child, reflected in the immutable duty of parental support, with Wallis's (P) effort to shift financial responsibility for his child to the mother. Affirmed.

**CONCURRENCE:** (Alarid, J.) In the absence of a clear balance favoring the imposition of legal duties of disclosure in reproductive relations between competent adult sex partners, candor in reproductive matters should be left to the ethics of the participants.

## ANALYSIS

In *Wallis* the court noted that Wallis's (P) contract analogy fails because children, the persons for whose benefit child support guidelines are enacted, have the same needs regardless of whether their conception violated a promise between the parents.

## Quicknotes

**COMPENSATORY DAMAGES** Measure of damages necessary to compensate victim for actual injuries suffered.

**MONETARY DAMAGES** Monetary compensation sought by, or awarded to, a party who incurred loss as a result of a breach of contract or tortious conduct on behalf of another party.

**PARENS PATRIAE** Maxim that the government as sovereign is conferred with the duty to act as guardian on behalf of those citizens under legal disability.

# Performance

## Quick Reference Rules of Law

# Mitchill v. Lath

Property purchaser (P) v. Property seller (D)

N.Y. Ct. App., 247 N.Y. 377, 160 N.E. 646 (1928).

**NATURE OF CASE:** Appeal from action for specific performance.

**FACT SUMMARY:** Mitchill (P) bought some property from Lath (D) pursuant to a full and complete written sales contract. She sought to compel Lath (D) to perform on his parol agreement to remove an icehouse on neighboring property.

## RULE OF LAW

An oral agreement is permitted to vary a written contract only if it is collateral in form, does not contradict express or implied conditions of the written contract, and consists of terms which the parties could not reasonably have been expected to include in the written contract.

**FACTS:** Mitchill (P), through a contract executed by her husband, bought some property from Lath (D). The written contract of sale was completely integrated. Lath (D) then made an oral agreement with Mitchill (P) that in consideration of her purchase of the property, he would remove an icehouse that he maintained on neighboring property and that Mitchill (P) found objectionable. The trial court ruled for Mitchill (P) and the state's intermediate appellate court affirmed. The state's highest court granted review.

**ISSUE:** Is an oral agreement permitted to vary a written contract only if it is collateral in form, does not contradict express or implied conditions of the written contract, and consists of terms which the parties could not reasonably have been expected to include in the written contract?

**HOLDING AND DECISION:** (Andrews, J.) Yes. An oral agreement is permitted to vary a written contract only if it is collateral in form, does not contradict express or implied conditions of the written contract, and consists of terms which the parties could not reasonably have been expected to include in the written contract. Here, the parol agreement does not meet these requirements since it is closely related to the subject of the written contract. It could also be said to contradict the conditions of the written contract. The fact that the written contract was made with her husband while the oral agreement was made with Mitchill (P) herself is not determinative since the deed was given to her, and it is evident that she, and not her husband, was the principal in the transaction. Reversed and complaint dismissed.

**DISSENT:** (Lehman, J.) Although the general rule formulated by the majority is correct, the majority errs in its application to these facts because all of the elements necessary to permit an oral agreement to vary a written one are present in this case. There is no question that the first condition was met, i.e., that the subject of the oral agreement is collateral to the written agreement. As to the second element, all the elements of the written contract were satisfied and the removal of the icehouse is not inconsistent with, and does not contradict, those terms. The dispute really boils down to whether the third element is satisfied. Here, the subject matter of the written contract was the conveyance of land. The question is whether the parties would have been expected to embody the agreement to remove the icehouse in the written contract. Proof of the oral agreement may be excluded only if it is shown that the written contract was intended to cover it. Here, on its face, the written contract was complete, and the parol agreement to remove the icehouse was not connected to the contract's subject. The only connection between the two agreements is that one would have not been made absent the other, but the overwhelming evidence establishes the oral agreement, which must be given effect.

## ▶ ANALYSIS

Uniform Commercial Code § 2-202 provides, "Terms with respect to which the writings of the parties agree or which are set forth in a writing intended by the parties as a final expression of their agreement may not be contradicted by evidence of any prior agreement or of a contemporaneous oral agreement but may be explained or supplemented by course of dealing or usage of trade, or by course of performance, and by evidence of consistent additional terms unless the court finds the writing to have been intended as a complete and exclusive statement of the terms of the agreement." The section, according to the official commentator, conclusively rejects any assumption that, because writing is final in some respects, it is to be interpreted as including all matters agreed upon by the parties.

▬▬▬

## Quicknotes

**EXPRESS CONDITION** A condition that is expressly stated in the terms of a written instrument.

**IMPLIED CONDITION** A condition that is not expressly stated in the terms of an agreement, but which is inferred from the parties' conduct or the type of dealings involved.

*Continued on next page.*

**PAROL AGREEMENT** Evidence of prior or contemporaneous agreements, which are not contained within the text of a document or contract, usually offered for the purpose of repudiating or altering the terms of a written contract.

**SPECIFIC PERFORMANCE** An equitable remedy whereby the court requires the parties to perform their obligations pursuant to a contract.

# Masterson v. Sine

Grantor of real property (P) v. Grantee of real property (D)

Cal. Sup. Ct., 68 Cal. 2d 222, 436 P.2d 561 (1968).

**NATURE OF CASE:** Appeal from judgment for plaintiffs in action for declaratory relief to establish a right to enforce an option.

**FACT SUMMARY:** Dallas Masterson and his wife, Rebecca Masterson (P), owned a ranch as tenants in common and conveyed it to Medora and Lu Sine (D) by grant deed, reserving an option to purchase the ranch back within 10 years for the same consideration as was paid for the ranch plus the depreciation value of any improvements the Sines (D) might have added. When Dallas went bankrupt, Rebecca (P) and the bankruptcy trustee (P) sought to establish their right to enforce the option.

## RULE OF LAW
Evidence of oral collateral agreements should be excluded only when the fact finder is likely to be misled.

**FACTS:** Dallas Masterson and his wife, Rebecca Masterson (P), owned a ranch as tenants in common. They conveyed by grant deed the ranch to his sister and her husband, Medora and Lu Sine (D), reserving an option to repurchase the ranch within 10 years from the date of conveyance for the consideration paid by the Sines (D) plus depreciation value of any improvements as allowed under U.S. income tax regulations. Dallas Masterson went bankrupt. Rebecca Masterson (P) and Dallas's trustee in bankruptcy (P) sought to establish their right to enforce the option. The trial court admitted extrinsic evidence to clarify the meaning of the option, but denied the Sines' (D) parol evidence that the parties wanted to retain the property in the Masterson family, thus making the option personal to the grantors and therefore not exercisable by the bankruptcy trustee. The trial court rendered judgment for Rebecca Masterson (P) and the bankruptcy trustee (P), declaring that they had the right to exercise the option. The state's highest court granted review.

**ISSUE:** Should evidence of oral collateral agreements be excluded only when the fact finder is likely to be misled?

**HOLDING AND DECISION:** (Traynor, C.J.) Yes. Evidence of oral collateral agreements should be excluded only when the fact finder is likely to be misled. Parol evidence was necessary to clarify the terms of the option, which expressly stated an intention to reserve an option. However, it was error of the trial court to exclude extrinsic evidence that the option was personal to the grantors and therefore nonassignable. When a written

contract is a complete and full embodiment of the agreement's terms, parol evidence cannot be used to add to or vary the terms. When only part of the agreement is complete, the same rule applies to that part, but parol evidence can be shown to prove elements as to the remainder not reduced to writing. It must be determined whether the parties intended the written agreement to be the complete and full embodiment of the terms. However, this rule has not been applied consistently. A parol evidence rule must take into consideration the problems of human memory being less accurate than a writing and the possibility of fraud. Accordingly, evidence of oral collateral agreements should be excluded only when the fact finder is likely to be misled. Under Restatement (First) § 240(1)(b), parol evidence of a collateral agreement is permitted if such an agreement is shown as might naturally be made as a separate agreement by parties situated as were parties to the written contract, or from an opposite standpoint which is even more liberal, if the additional terms are such that, if agreed upon, they would certainly have been included, then parol evidence is not admissible, Uniform Commercial Code § 2-202. Here, the option clause did not explicitly provide that it contained the complete agreement. The deed does not speak to assignability. Nothing showed that the parties had any warnings as to the disadvantages of failing to put the whole agreement in the deed. Therefore, it appeared that collateral agreements might naturally be made as a separate agreement. The judgment must be reversed to permit parol evidence on the issue of assignability of the option.

**DISSENT:** (Burke, J.) The majority opinion undermines the parol evidence rule; renders as suspect instruments of conveyance absolute on their face; materially lessens the reliance which might be placed upon written instruments affecting title to real estate; and opens the door, albeit unintentionally, to a new technique for the defrauding of creditors.

## ANALYSIS

In this case, California opts for the more liberal approach to the parol evidence rule as supported by Professor Corbin. Here, the California court under Chief Justice Traynor found that when any rule of law is riddled with exceptions and decisions about it are difficult to reconcile, litigation is stimulated rather than reduced. The tendency toward liberalizing the admission of parol evidence is based upon the

*Continued on next page.*

trial court judge's having control over the testimony and his determining when it would appear that proferred testimony is perjured. The more liberal rule is supposed to remove the problems found in the restrictive rule favored by Williston, which finds the intent of the parties in their writing only. In the extreme, this would disallow oral testimony as to intent whenever writing exists, thereby possibly defeating the true intent of the parties.

## Quicknotes

**BANKRUPTCY** A legal proceeding whereby a debtor, who is unable to pay his debts as they become due, is relieved of his obligation to pay his creditors either by liquidation and distribution of his remaining assets or through reorganization and payment from future income.

**EXTRINSIC EVIDENCE** Evidence that is not contained within the text of a document or contract, but which is derived from the parties' statements or the circumstances under which the agreement was made.

**PAROL EVIDENCE** Evidence given verbally; extraneous evidence.

# Alaska Northern Development, Inc. v. Alyeska Pipeline Service Co.

Equipment purchaser (P) v. Equipment seller (D)

Alaska Sup. Ct., 666 P.2d 33 (1983).

**NATURE OF CASE:** Appeal from summary judgment denying damages for breach of contract.

**FACT SUMMARY:** Alaska Northern Development, Inc. (P) contended that subject-to-approval language in its contract with Alyeska Pipeline Service Co. (D) limited the basis for approval or rejection to price matters only.

## 🏛 RULE OF LAW
Evidence that contradicts an integrated contract term is not admissible to aid in the interpretation of that term.

**FACTS:** Negotiations between Alaska Northern Development, Inc. (Alaska Northern) (P) and Alyeska Pipeline Service Co. (Alyeska) (D) resulted in a letter of intent in which Alaska Northern (P) proposed to buy Alyeska's (D) inventory of Caterpillar parts. The price term was left blank, and the letter included language that the agreement was subject to the final approval of Alyeska's (D) owner committee. Alyeska's (D) manager filled in the price and sent the letter on for approval. When Alyeska's (D) owner committee rejected the proposal, Alaska Northern (P) sued for breach of contract, contending that the subject-to-approval language meant that Alyeska's (D) owner committee was authorized only to determine whether the price was fair and reasonable. The trial court granted Alyeska's (D) motion for summary judgment, and Alaska Northern (P) appealed.

**ISSUE:** Is evidence that contradicts an integrated contract term admissible to aid in the interpretation of that term?

**HOLDING AND DECISION:** (Compton, J.) No. Evidence that contradicts an integrated contract term is not admissible to aid in the interpretation of that term. Even if the evidence is consistent, it may nevertheless be excluded if the court concludes that the consistent term would necessarily have been included in the writing by the parties, if they intended it to be part of their agreement. Limiting the owner committee to determining price only is inconsistent, and as such, cannot be included in the agreement by parol evidence. It was conceded that review by the owners, on whatever standard, would occur prior to any formal contract being negotiated and executed. Affirmed.

## ▶ ANALYSIS

In order to exclude parol evidence of interpretation, the court must determine whether the writing is integrated, i.e., intended by the parties to be their complete and final expression of their agreement with respect to some or all of the writing's terms. The court must determine whether evidence of a prior or contemporaneous agreement contradicts the integrated portion. If the evidence is inconsistent or contradicts, it is inadmissible. This case can easily be used to show how parties try to have their own interpretation of a contract term enforced. Alaska Northern (P) contended that the owner approval term meant that price was all that the committee could review. A party may have his interpretation of a contract term enforced only if the contract language is reasonably susceptible to that meaning. Here, the language used could not have been said to have limited the owner committee's review to price only.

■=■

## Quicknotes

**BREACH OF CONTRACT** Unlawful failure by a party to perform its obligations pursuant to contract.

**DAMAGES** Monetary compensation that may be awarded by the court to a party who has sustained injury or loss to his person, property or rights due to another party's unlawful act, omission or negligence.

**PAROL EVIDENCE** Evidence given verbally; extraneous evidence.

**SUMMARY JUDGMENT** Judgment rendered by a court in response to a motion made by one of the parties, claiming that the lack of a question of material fact in respect to an issue warrants disposition of the issue without consideration by the jury.

■=■

# Pacific Gas & Electric Co. v. G.W. Thomas Drayage & Rigging Co.

## Public utility (P) v. Contractor (D)

### Cal. Sup. Ct., 69 Cal. 2d 33, 442 P.2d 641 (1968).

**NATURE OF CASE:** Appeal from judgment for plaintiff in action for damages for breach of a contract.

**FACT SUMMARY:** G.W. Thomas Drayage & Rigging Co. (Thomas) (D) contracted to repair Pacific Gas & Electric Co.'s (Pacific's) (P) steam turbine and to perform work at its own risk and expense and to indemnify Pacific (P) against all loss and damage. Thomas (D) also agreed not to procure less than $50,000 insurance to cover liability for injury to property. But when the turbine rotor was damaged, Pacific (P) claimed it was covered under that policy, while Thomas (D) said it was only to cover injury to third persons.

---

**RULE OF LAW**
The test of admissibility of extrinsic evidence to explain the meaning of a written instrument is not whether the writing appears to the court to be plain and unambiguous on its face but whether the offered evidence is relevant to prove a meaning to which the language of the instrument is reasonably susceptible.

---

**FACTS:** G.W. Thomas Drayage & Rigging Co. (Thomas) (D) contracted to replace the upper metal cover on Pacific Gas & Electric Co.'s (Pacific's) (P) steam turbine and agreed to perform all work "at [its] own risk and expense" and to "indemnify" Pacific (P) against all loss, damage, expense, and liability resulting from injury to property arising out of or in any way connected with performance of the contract. Thomas (D) agreed to obtain not less than $50,000 insurance to cover liability for injury to property. Pacific (P) was to be an additional named insured, but the policy was to contain a cross-liability clause extending the coverage of Pacific's (P) property. During the work, the cover fell, damaging the exposed rotor in the amount of $25,144.51. Thomas (D) during trial offered to prove through its conduct and under similar contracts entered into by Pacific (P) that the indemnity clause was meant to cover injury to third person's property only, not to Pacific's (P). The trial court, however, finding that the agreement was unambiguous, and that its plain language required Thomas (D) to indemnify Pacific (P), refused to admit the extrinsic evidence and ruled for Pacific (P). Thomas (D) appealed, and the state's highest court granted review.

**ISSUE:** Is the test of admissibility of extrinsic evidence to explain the meaning of a written instrument not whether the writing appears to the court to be plain and unambiguous on its face but whether the offered evidence is relevant to prove a meaning to which the language of the instrument is reasonably susceptible?

**HOLDING AND DECISION:** (Traynor, C.J.) Yes. The test of admissibility of extrinsic evidence to explain the meaning of a written instrument is not whether the writing appears to the court to be plain and unambiguous on its face but whether the offered evidence is relevant to prove a meaning to which the language of the instrument is reasonably susceptible. While the trial court admitted that the contract was "the classic language for a third-party indemnity provision," it held that the plain language of the contract would give a meaning covering Pacific's (P) damage. However, this admission by the court clearly shows the ambiguous nature of the agreement and the need for extrinsic evidence in order to clarify the intentions of the parties. Extrinsic evidence for the purpose of showing the intent of the parties could be excluded only when it is feasible to determine the meaning of the words from the instrument alone. Rational interpretation requires at least an initial consideration of all credible evidence to prove the intention of the parties. Reversed.

---

**ANALYSIS**

This case strongly disapproves of the "plain meaning rule," which states that if writing appears clear and unambiguous on its face, the meaning must be determined from "the four corners" of the writing without considering any extrinsic evidence at all. The trial court applied this rule. However, the rule, while generally accepted but widely condemned, would exclude evidence of trade usage, prior dealings of the parties, and even circumstances surrounding the creation of the agreement. Uniform Commercial Code § 2-202 expressly throws out the plain meaning rule. Instead, it allows use of evidence of a course of performance or dealing to explain the writing "unless carefully negated." Here, Judge Traynor greatly expanded the admission of extrinsic evidence to show intent. When he says it should not be admitted only when it is feasible "to determine the meaning the parties gave to the words from the instrument alone," he is saying in all practicality that extrinsic evidence to show intent should be admissible in just about any case, that rarely will the instrument be so exact as to clearly show intent.

*Continued on next page.*

## *Quicknotes*

**BREACH OF CONTRACT** Unlawful failure by a party to perform its obligations pursuant to contract.

**DAMAGES** Monetary compensation that may be awarded by the court to a party who has sustained injury or loss to his person, property or rights due to another party's unlawful act, omission or negligence.

**EXTRINSIC EVIDENCE** Evidence that is not contained within the text of a document or contract, but which is derived from the parties' statements or the circumstances under which the agreement was made.

**INDEMNIFY** Securing against potential injury; compensation for injury suffered.

# Frigaliment Importing Co. v. B.N.S. International Sales Corp.

Chicken purchaser (P) v. Chicken seller (D)

190 F. Supp. 116 (S.D.N.Y. 1960).

**NATURE OF CASE:** Action for breach of warranty of a contract for the sale of goods.

**FACT SUMMARY:** Frigaliment Importing Co. (Frigaliment) (P) ordered a large quantity of "chicken" from B.N.S. International Sales Corp. (B.N.S.) (D), intending to buy young chicken suitable for broiling and frying, but B.N.S. (D) believed, in considering the weights ordered at the prices fixed by the parties, that the order could be filled with older chicken, suitable for stewing only and termed "fowl" by Frigaliment (P).

## RULE OF LAW

To prevail on a breach of contract claim, the party who seeks to interpret a contract term in a sense narrower than its everyday use bears the burden of persuasion to show that such a narrower meaning was intended by the parties.

**FACTS:** Frigaliment Importing Co. (Frigaliment) (P), a Swiss corporation, and B.N.S. International Sales Corp. (B.N.S.) (D), a New York corporation, made two almost identical contracts for the sale of chicken by the latter to the former as follows: U.S. fresh frozen chicken, Grade A, government inspected, eviscerated, all wrapped and boxed suitably for export, 75,000 lbs. 2½–3 lbs. at $33 per 100 lbs., and 25,000 lbs. 1½–2 lbs. at $36.50 per 100 lbs. The second contract was the same except for 25,000 lbs. less of the heavier chicken and a price of $37 per 100 lbs. for the lighter birds. B.N.S. (D), which was new to the poultry business, believed any kind of chicken could be used to fill the order, including stewing chickens. Most of the order for heavier birds was filled with stewers, as that was the only way B.N.S. (D) could make a profit on the contract. Frigaliment (P) sued in district court for breach of the warranty that the goods sold would correspond to the contract description.

**ISSUE:** To prevail on a breach of contract claim, does the party who seeks to interpret a contract term in a sense narrower than its everyday use bear the burden of persuasion to show that such a narrower meaning was intended by the parties?

**HOLDING AND DECISION:** (Friendly, J.) Yes. To prevail on a breach of contract claim, the party who seeks to interpret a contract term in a sense narrower than its everyday use bears the burden of persuasion to show that such a narrower meaning was intended by the parties. Frigaliment (P) failed to support its burden. While cables leading up to negotiations were predominantly in German, the use of the English word "chicken" as meaning "young chicken" rather than the German word "huhn" meaning broilers and stewers lost its force when B.N.S. (D) asked if any kind of chickens were wanted, to which an affirmative answer meaning "huhn" was given. B.N.S. (D) being new to the chicken trade, the other party must show the other's acceptance of the trade use of a term. Frigaliment (P) failed to offer such proof. There was conflicting evidence anyway as to the trade use of the word "chicken." B.N.S.'s (D) price of $33 per 100 lbs. for the larger birds was $2 to $4 less than for broilers. Frigaliment (P) could not say that the price appeared reasonable because it was closer to the $35 broiler price than the $30 stewer price. B.N.S. (D) could be expected not to sell at a loss. While the evidence is generally conflicting, overall it appeared that B.N.S. (D) believed it could comply by supplying stewing chicken. This did conform with one dictionary meaning, with the definition in the department of animal regulations to which at least there was a contractual reference, and with some trade usages. This evidence must be relied upon, as the contract language itself could not settle the question here. Complaint dismissed.

## ANALYSIS

In determining the intent of the parties, the court will turn first to the language of the contract to see whether the meaning of the ambiguous term can be raised. If this is unsuccessful, the court must look to other evidence. Under Restatement (First) § 2235 certain guidelines aid in determining meaning. First, the ordinary meaning of language throughout the country is given to words unless circumstances show that a different meaning is applicable. Also, all circumstances surrounding the transaction may be taken into consideration. Also, if after consideration of all factors, it is still uncertain what meaning should be given, a reasonable, lawful, and effective meaning to all manifestations of intention is preferred to an interpretation which leaves a part of such unreasonable, unlawful, or ineffective, Restatement (First) § 236(a). Even so, the principal apparent purpose of the parties should be given greater weight in determining the meaning to be given.

---

## Quicknotes

**BREACH OF CONTRACT** Unlawful failure by a party to perform its obligations pursuant to contract.

**BREACH OF WARRANTY** The breach of a promise made by one party to a contract on which the other party may rely,

*Continued on next page.*

relieving that party from the obligation of determining whether the fact is true and indemnifying the other party from liability if that fact is shown to be false.

**BURDEN OF PERSUASION** The duty of a party to introduce evidence to support a fact that is in dispute in an action.

# In re Katrina Canal Breaches Litigation

[Parties not identified.]

495 F.3d 191 (5th Cir. 2007).

**NATURE OF CASE:** Cross-appeals from orders dismissing, and from orders denying dismissal of, claims for insurance coverage.

**FACT SUMMARY:** In the wake of the devastation wrought by Hurricane Katrina, numerous property owners (P) brought multiple actions to obtain insurance coverage from multiple insurers (D) under insurance policies that purported to exclude coverage for damage arising from "flood," contending that the term "flood" as used in the policies was ambiguous and did not cover water damage that was the result of negligent design, construction, and maintenance of levees.

## RULE OF LAW

A contract term is not ambiguous where it fits squarely within its prevailing meaning and where giving it another meaning would lead to absurd results.

**FACTS:** As a result of Hurricane Katrina, and the rupturing of several canal levees, 80 percent of New Orleans was submerged under water. Property owners (P) who had homeowners, renters, or commercial-property all-risk insurance policies sought coverage under those policies from various insurers (D). Some of the policies excluded coverage for water damage arising from "flood, surface water, waves, tidal water, overflow of a body of water, or spray from any of these." Policies issued by State Farm (D) said that "We do not insure under any coverage for any loss which would not have occurred in the absence of one or more of the following . . ." including water damage, which was defined as in the other policies. This policy made clear that any such damage, regardless of the source or combination of sources, was excluded. The property owners (P) claimed that their losses were covered by the policies on the ground the massive inundation of water into New Orleans had been caused by the negligent design, construction, and maintenance of the levees, and the policies were ambiguous to the extent they did not exclude coverage for inundation of water induced by negligence. The insurers (D) declined coverage, and the property owners (P) brought separate state actions, which were consolidated and removed to federal district court. With respect to the non-State Farm policies, the district court ruled that the policies' flood exclusions were ambiguous and could be read to exclude only floods from natural causes, or could be read to cover floods resulting from both natural causes and negligent or intentional acts. Accordingly, as to these policies, the court denied the insurers' (D) motion for judgment on the pleadings, and held that the policies covered the property

owners' (P) losses to the extent the property owners (P) could prove the flooding resulted from levee breaches induced by negligence. With respect to the State Farm policies, however, the court found that the flood exclusion's lead-in clause removed any ambiguity and clearly excluded coverage for any kind of flood, regardless of whether its cause was natural or the result of negligent or intentional conduct. Accordingly, the court dismissed the actions against State Farm (D). The property owners (P) as well as the insurers (D) cross-appealed, and the court of appeals granted review.

**ISSUE:** Is a contract term ambiguous where it fits squarely within its prevailing meaning and where giving it another meaning would lead to absurd results?

**HOLDING AND DECISION:** (King, J.) No. A contract term is not ambiguous where it fits squarely within its prevailing meaning and where giving it another meaning would lead to absurd results. An insurance policy is a contract and must be construed using general contract interpretation rules. Words of a contract/insurance policy must be given their prevailing meanings, and if doing so does not lead to absurd results, the words are considered unambiguous, and no further inquiry is necessary. Only where the words are ambiguous must there be further inquiry into how the words fit into the context of the entire policy, or through an analysis of a reasonable insured's expectations. If, after conducting such analyses and applying other rules of contract interpretation, ambiguity remains, meaning that two or more reasonable interpretations of the ambiguous terms remain, the policy is construed against the drafter, i.e., the insurer. Here, the policies were all-risk policies, meaning that unless a risk was expressly excluded, it was covered. The issue is whether the policies unambiguously excluded flood damage. Just because the term "flood" is not defined in the policies does not by itself render that term ambiguous, nor does the fact that the exclusion's scope could have been expanded to expressly cover flooding caused by negligence. Thus, the flood exclusions are not ambiguous in light of more specific flood exclusion language used in other policies. Even where the scope of an exclusion is not readily apparent, however, its terms will be given their prevailing meaning, as determined from dictionaries, treatises, and jurisprudence. Even though these sources may provide more than one meaning for the term, that fact alone is insufficient to render the term ambiguous; instead, the prevailing meaning is used. Here, these sources provide

*Continued on next page.*

more than one meaning for the term "flood." However, the prevailing meaning that can be gleaned from these sources is an inundation of water. In light of the definitions provided by these sources, the flood exclusions are unambiguous in the context of this case, and what occurred here fits squarely within the generally prevailing meaning of the term "flood." When a body of water overflows its normal boundaries and inundates an area of land that is normally dry, the event is a flood, and that is precisely what happened in New Orleans in the aftermath of Hurricane Katrina. Even if the flooding occurs because of a levee's breach, regardless of why, that does not change the nature of the water escaping through it—the waters are still floodwaters, and the result is still a "flood." The property owners (P) claim ambiguity by asserting that a reasonable interpretation of "flood" is that it refers only to inundations of water with "natural" causes, not those with a "non-natural" cause. First, it is doubtful that the damage here occurred only as a result of non-natural causes, given the sizeable natural component of the disaster and the excess water associated with it. The non-natural component is simply that in certain areas, man's efforts to mitigate the effect of the natural disaster failed. However, if man's failure to adequately prepare for a natural disaster could alone transform the disaster into a non-natural event outside the scope of a policy's exclusion, an insurer would never be able to exclude the resulting loss since any natural event could be recharacterized as non-natural either because man's preventative measures were inadequate or because man failed to take preventative measures at all. Even assuming, arguendo, that the flood here was non-natural, the term "flood" is nevertheless not limited to only natural events. The property owners' (P) reliance on cases involving water main breaks to support their argument that the term "flood" is limited to natural events is inapposite because water mains do not involve a body of water or watercourse, whereas a "flood" does; the amount of water involved is not comparable between water main breaks and the rupture of levees; and unlike water mains, levees are flood-control devices, which by definition means they interact with a body of water, i.e., floodwaters. Dictionaries, encyclopedias, and treatises also do not support this argument. In fact, a respected treatise on insurance law opines that a distinction based on a body-of-water delineation is more useful than one based on natural/non-natural distinction. More importantly, using such a distinction would lead to absurd results, because any time a flooded watercourse encounters a man-made levee, a non-natural component is injected into the flood, but that does not cause the floodwaters to cease being floodwaters. Therefore, the result of using this natural/non-natural distinction would be that flood exclusions in insurance policies would be effectively eviscerated. The canons of contract construction are likewise not of assistance to the property owners (P). Under the canon of *noscitur a sociis*, a term is interpreted by considering the meaning of the terms associated with it. Under the canon of *ejusdem generis*, "where general words follow the enumeration of particular classes of persons or things, the general words will be construed as applicable only to persons or things of the same general nature or class as those enumerated." First, the other terms in the exclusion do not all necessarily refer only to natural events. Some of the terms surrounding "flood" in the exclusion also relate to non-natural events. Therefore, the canon of *noscitur a sociis* does not support the property owners' (P) position. Also, the canon of *ejusdem generis* is completely inapplicable because it is used to interpret general terms following a list of specific terms, but "flood" is not a general term, but is one of the specific terms in the list defining "water damage." Finally, because the term "flood" as used here is clear and unambiguous, a reasonable insured's expectations may not be used—since that is reserved for cases of ambiguity. Therefore, the district court's interpretation was erroneous. Reversed.

## ▶ *ANALYSIS*

The district court in this case reached its conclusion based on several sources. First, the court discussed dictionary definitions of the term "flood" and opined that the definitions contemplated a natural event caused by rain or tide. Second, the court looked to cases interpreting "water damage" exclusions in the context of ruptured water mains, as well as "earth movement" exclusions, wherein courts have applied a distinction between naturally and non-naturally occurring events. Finally, the court considered but rejected cases that interpreted flood exclusions as extending to inundations of water caused by the rupture of a dam or dike. Because the district's order denied the insurers' (D) motion to dismiss for failure to state a claim, the court of appeals' review was de novo, as a matter of law, and, as the case demonstrates, the court of appeals disagreed with the district court as to each of its findings. Such divergence of opinion, however, illustrates just how difficult contract interpretation can be, given that even esteemed judicial bodies can come to such disparate conclusions.

■=■=■

## *Quicknotes*

***EJUSDEM GENERIS*** Belonging to the same class or type; rule of construction applied when general words follow a specified class of persons or items, then the words are not to be applied in their broad meaning but are to apply only to those persons or items listed.

**MOTION TO DISMISS** Motion to terminate an action based on the adequacy of the pleadings, improper service or venue, etc.

**NEGLIGENCE** Conduct falling below the standard of care that a reasonable person would demonstrate under similar conditions.

■=■=■

# Centronics Corporation v. Genicom Corporation

Business seller (P) v. Business purchaser (D)

N.H. Sup. Ct., 132 N.H. 133, 562 A.2d 187 (1989).

**NATURE OF CASE:** Appeal from summary judgment denying damages for breach of implied obligation of good faith and fair dealing.

**FACT SUMMARY:** Centronics Corporation (P) agreed to sell its business assets to Genicom Corporation (D) for an amount to be determined in arbitration once a portion of the estimated price had been placed in escrow; Centronics (P), however, demanded that Genicom (D) release part of the escrow funds before arbitration had been concluded, a demand Genicom (D) rejected.

## 🏛 RULE OF LAW
A party to a contract is not bound by the implied obligation of good faith and fair dealing to do something not expressly required by the contract.

**FACTS:** Centronics Corporation (P) agreed to sell its business assets to Genicom Corporation (D) for an amount to be determined in arbitration according to the consolidated closing net book value of the assets (CCNBV). The agreement between Centronics (P) and Genicom (D) required Genicom (D) to deposit in escrow a portion of the price claimed by Centronics (P) pending this final valuation. Genicom (D) made such a deposit. However, as it became apparent that arbitration would drag on given the parties' disputes over CCNBV, Centronics (P) demanded that a portion of the amount deposited in escrow, which it claimed was "free from dispute," should be paid to it immediately. This demand was made despite the fact that the agreement required that the funds be retained in escrow until the conclusion of arbitration. Genicom (D) refused to release any funds, and Centronics (P) sued Genicom (D) for breach of the implied covenant of good faith and fair dealing in refusing to release any moneys. Genicom's (D) motion for summary judgment was granted, and Centronics (P) appealed.

**ISSUE:** Is a party to a contract bound by the implied covenant of good faith and fair dealing to do something not expressly required by the contract?

**HOLDING AND DECISION:** (Souter, J.) No. A party to a contract is not bound by the implied covenant of good faith and fair dealing to do something not expressly required by the contract. Where an agreement invests one party with discretion, which, if wrongfully exercised, could effectively deprive the other of the practical benefits of the agreement, the party invested with the discretion has an implied obligation to observe reasonable limits in exercising it consistent with the parties' purposes in contracting. Here, however, Genicom (D) had no discretion under its

contract with Centronics (P) to release funds from escrow prior to the conclusion of arbitration, even if they were, as alleged by Centronics (P), "free from dispute." Centronics (P) cannot now rewrite a contract that did not provide for a partial disbursal of funds from escrow; if it had been concerned about receiving a portion of the purchase price by a certain date, it should have demanded a mechanism for partial payments if the arbitration process lagged. However, the court will not renegotiate the contract for the parties to obtain such a result. Because Genicom (D) was not invested with discretion to release payments early, it is not necessary to decide whether a hypothetical release would have exceeded the limits of reasonableness. Accordingly, Genicom (D) did not breach the implied covenant of good faith and fair dealing in refusing to do something the contract did not require it to do. Affirmed.

## ▶ ANALYSIS

The covenant of good faith and fair dealing is also implied in two other principal categories of cases: ones concerned with contract formation and those concerned with termination of at-will employment contracts. The standard of conduct required in contract formation cases amounts to the traditional duty of cure to refrain from misrepresentation and to correct known misperceptions of the other party to the contract that concern material matters relating to the contract. In at-will employment cases, the implied covenant limits the power of an employer to terminate a wage contract by discharging the employee out of malice or bad faith in retaliation for action taken or refused by the employee in consonance with public policy. Seminal cases of these types are collected and addressed in Summers, "The General Duty of Good Faith—Its Recognition and Conceptualization," 67 *Cornell L. Rev.* 810 (1982).

▬▬▬

## Quicknotes

**ARBITRATION** An alternative resolution process where a dispute is heard and decided by a neutral third party, rather than through legal proceedings.

**DAMAGES** Monetary compensation that may be awarded by the court to a party who has sustained injury or loss to his person, property or rights due to another party's unlawful act, omission or negligence.

**ESCROW** A written contract held by a third party until the conditions therein are satisfied, at which time it is delivered to the obligee.

*Continued on next page.*

**IMPLIED COVENANT OF GOOD FAITH AND FAIR DEALING** An implied warranty that the parties will deal honestly in the satisfaction of their obligations and without an intent to defraud.

**MOTION FOR SUMMARY JUDGMENT** Judgment rendered by a court in response to a motion by one of the parties, claiming that the lack of a question of material fact in respect to an issue warrants disposition of the issue without consideration by the jury.

**SUMMARY JUDGMENT** Judgment rendered by a court in response to a motion made by one of the parties, claiming that the lack of a question of material fact in respect to an issue warrants disposition of the issue without consideration by the jury.

# Patterson v. Meyerhofer

Future property owner/seller (P) v. Property purchaser (D)

N.Y. Ct. App., 204 N.Y. 96, 97 N.E. 472 (1912).

**NATURE OF CASE:** Action for damages and to have a lien declared on property allegedly held in constructive trust.

**FACT SUMMARY:** After Meyerhofer (D) had agreed to purchase from Patterson (P) four houses he did not then own but would acquire at a foreclosure sale, Meyerhofer (D) renounced the contract and outbid Patterson (P) at the sale. Patterson (P) sued for damages and constructive trust.

## RULE OF LAW
In every contract there is an implied promise on the part of each party that he will not intentionally and purposely do anything to prevent the other party from carrying out the agreement on his part, so that a party who causes or sanctions the breach of an agreement may not interpose the other party's nonperformance as a defense to an action on the contract.

**FACTS:** Meyerhofer (D) agreed to buy from Patterson (P) four parcels of land that Patterson (P) did not then own but planned to purchase at a foreclosure sale. Before the foreclosure occurred, Meyerhofer (D) renounced the contract. At the sale, Meyerhofer (D) outbid Patterson (P) and acquired the four parcels in her own name. As a result, Meyerhofer (D) acquired the parcels for $620 less than she had obligated herself to pay under the contract with Patterson (P). Patterson (P) filed an action to recover damages equal to the difference between the contract price and the auction price for the parcels and to establish a lien on the parcels on a trust theory. The trial court held for Meyerhofer (D), finding that there was nothing in the contract's express terms that made one party the trustee of the other or otherwise precluded each party from acting in his or her best interest. The state's intermediate appellate court affirmed, and the state's highest court granted review.

**ISSUE:** In every contract is there an implied promise on the part of each party that he will not intentionally and purposely do anything to prevent the other party from carrying out the agreement on his part, so that a party who causes or sanctions the breach of an agreement may not interpose the other party's nonperformance as a defense to an action on the contract?

**HOLDING AND DECISION:** (Bartlett, J.) Yes. In every contract there is an implied promise on the part of each party that he will not intentionally and purposely do anything to prevent the other party from carrying out the agreement on his part, so that a party who causes or sanctions the breach of an agreement may not interpose the

other party's nonperformance as a defense to an action on the contract. In every contract there is an implied promise on the part of each party to refrain from hindering the performance of the other. Here, although no relation of trust can be found, Patterson (P) is not precluded from recovering his anticipated profits on the contract merely because he has also asked for too much equitable relief. Patterson (P) is excused from his nonperformance, and Meyerhofer (D) is liable in damages for breaching her implied promise. The damages may fairly be measured as Patterson's (P) lost anticipated profits. Reversed and new trial granted.

## ANALYSIS

Where one party has breached all implied promise of cooperation, the other party will be excused from any nonperformance on the theory that performance on his part, although a condition precedent to the other's obligation, has been actively prevented. The aggrieved party, nonetheless, must still be ready to show that but for the hindrance he would have been ready, willing, and able to honor his side of the contract.

## Quicknotes

**BREACH** The violation of an obligation imposed pursuant to contract or law, by acting or failing to act.

**CONSTRUCTIVE TRUST** A trust that arises by operation of law whereby the court imposes a trust upon property lawfully held by one party for the benefit of another, as a result of some wrongdoing by the party in possession so as to avoid unjust enrichment.

**DAMAGES** Monetary compensation that may be awarded by the court to a party who has sustained injury or loss to his person, property or rights due to another party's unlawful act, omission or negligence.

**IMPLIED PROMISE** A promise inferred by law from a document as a whole and the circumstances surrounding its implementation.

**LIEN** A claim against the property of another in order to secure the payment of a debt.

**SANCTIONS** A penalty imposed in order to ensure compliance with a statute or regulation.

# Market Street Associates Limited Partnership v. Frey

Lessee's assignee (P) v. Lessor (D)

941 F.2d 588 (7th Cir. 1991).

**NATURE OF CASE:** Appeal from summary judgment dismissing action seeking specific performance.

**FACT SUMMARY:** A principal of Market Street Associates Limited Partnership (P) allegedly deliberately failed to notify General Electric Pension Trust (General Electric) (D) of a particular paragraph in a contract that could result in forfeiture of General Electric's (D) property.

🏛 **RULE OF LAW**
A party to a contract may not intentionally exploit the other party's oversight of an important fact.

**FACTS:** J.C. Penney entered into a sale-leaseback arrangement with General Electric Pension Trust (General Electric) (D) on a property. Paragraph 34 in the lease provided if General Electric (D) failed to negotiate with the lessee regarding future financing, the property could be purchased at less than market value. Years later, Market Street Associates Limited Partnership (Market Street) (P), J.C. Penney's assignee, attempted to negotiate financing with General Electric (D). General Electric (D), no longer being aware of the clause, refused to negotiate. Market Street (P) then sought to exercise its option and sued for specific performance. At his deposition, the principal of Market Street (P) primarily responsible for the property testified his counterpart at General Electric (D) might not be aware of the clause and that he had realized it during negotiations. Based on this, the district court entered summary judgment dismissing the action, holding Market Street (P) to have acted in bad faith. Market Street (P) appealed.

**ISSUE:** May a party to a contract intentionally exploit the other party's oversight of an important fact?

**HOLDING AND DECISION:** (Posner, J.) No. A party to a contract may not intentionally exploit the other party's oversight of an important fact. That parties to a contract must act in good faith does not mean, as some courts seem to believe, that the parties must act in an altruistic or fiduciary manner toward each other; they need not do so. Furthermore, it is quite legitimate for a party to use his superior knowledge to drive an advantageous bargain. However, it is one thing to have superior knowledge, but it is quite another to know that the other party is unaware of a crucial fact and take advantage of this ignorance. This constitutes sharp practice, which departs from good faith. Here, the district court held that Market Street's (P) principal had engaged in such conduct. This

may be true, but it is a factual issue, addressable only at trial, not at the summary judgment level. Reversed and remanded.

▶ **ANALYSIS**

A mutual mistake is grounds for nullifying a contract or a term thereof. Unilateral mistake may or may not be. As the court stated here, unilateral mistake combined with an opponent's overreaching may be grounds for rescission.

━━━

## Quicknotes

**GOOD FAITH** An honest intention to abstain from taking advantage of another.

**MUTUAL MISTAKE** A mistake by both parties to a contract, who are in agreement as to what the contract terms should be, but the agreement as written fails to reflect that common intent; such contracts are voidable or subject to reformation.

**RESCISSION** The canceling of an agreement and the return of the parties to their positions prior to the formation of the contract.

**SPECIFIC PERFORMANCE** An equitable remedy whereby the court requires the parties to perform their obligations pursuant to a contract.

**SUMMARY JUDGMENT** Judgment rendered by a court in response to a motion made by one of the parties, claiming that the lack of a question of material fact in respect to an issue warrants disposition of the issue without consideration by the jury.

━━━

# Billman v. Hensel

### Real estate purchaser (D) v. Real estate seller (P)

Ind. Ct. App., 181 Ind. App. 272, 391 N.E.2d 671 (1979).

**NATURE OF CASE:** Appeal from recovery of earnest money deposit.

**FACT SUMMARY:** The Hensels (P) sought to recover a $1,000 earnest money deposit pursuant to a contract to sell their home that was not fulfilled by the Billmans (D) after they were unable to secure financing.

## RULE OF LAW

A clause in a real estate sales contract that makes the buyer's obtaining financing a condition precedent to his duty to perform imposes on the buyer an implied duty to make reasonable good-faith efforts to satisfy the condition.

**FACTS:** The Billmans (D) contracted to purchase the Hensels' (P) house and gave the Hensels (P) a check for a $1,000 earnest money/liquidated damage deposit, as required by the contract. The contract provided that it was conditioned by the Billmans' (D) ability to secure a $35,000 mortgage within 30 days. Following execution of the contract, Billman (D) met with an agent of a bank and was told he had to have the balance of the purchase price to secure the mortgage. Billman (D) was $6,500 short, and he told Hensel (P) he could not obtain the mortgage without a $5,000 loan, which he had been denied. Hensel (P) offered to reduce the sale price by $5,000, but Billman (D) then said he needed another $1,500 and stopped payment on the earnest money check. The Hensels (P) sued to recover the earnest money, and judgment was entered in their favor. The Billmans (D) appealed on the basis that they were not liable because the condition precedent to their duty to perform was never fulfilled, and the state's intermediate appellate court granted review.

**ISSUE:** Does a clause in a real estate sales contract that makes the buyer's obtaining financing a condition precedent to his duty to perform impose on the buyer an implied duty to make reasonable good-faith efforts to satisfy the condition?

**HOLDING AND DECISION:** (Garrard, J.) Yes. A clause in a real estate sales contract that makes the buyer's obtaining financing a condition precedent to his duty to perform imposes on the buyer an implied duty to make reasonable good-faith efforts to satisfy the condition. In this case, the Billmans (D) contacted only one financial institution and applied for a mortgage of $35,000 although they in fact required more. They then turned down the Hensels' (P) offer to reduce the sales price. These facts show the Billmans (D) breached their implied duty to make a good-faith effort to obtain financing, and therefore,

the Hensels (P) are entitled to the earnest money deposit. Affirmed.

## ANALYSIS

This case illustrates the general rule applied to so-called "subject to financing" clauses in contracts. The rationale for the rule seems to be that it promotes the reasonable expectations of the parties. Some commentators argue it is an extension of the basic rule of contract law that a promisor cannot rely upon the existence of a condition precedent to excuse his performance of the condition.

## Quicknotes

**BREACH** The violation of an obligation imposed pursuant to contract or law, by acting or failing to act.

**EARNEST MONEY** A payment made by a buyer to a seller to evidence the intent to fulfill the obligations of a contract to purchase property.

**GOOD FAITH** An honest intention to abstain from taking advantage of another.

**IMPLIED DUTY** An obligation owed by one individual to another that arises from the particular relationship or circumstances.

**LIQUIDATED DAMAGES** An amount of money specified in a contract representing the damages owed in the event of breach.

# Austrian Airlines Oesterreichische Luftverkehrs AG v. UT Finance Corporation

Airline (P) v. Finance company (D)

567 F. Supp. 2d 579 (S.D.N.Y. 2008).

**NATURE OF CASE:** Motion to dismiss action for breach of contract.

**FACT SUMMARY:** Austrian Airlines Oesterreichische Luftverkehrs AG (Austrian) (P) contended that, under the Uniform Commercial Code, UT Finance Corporation (UTF) (D) breached the parties' Aircraft Purchase Agreement (APA) by rejecting in bad faith a used aircraft tendered by Austrian (P) on the basis of allegedly minor nonconformities in the fuel tanks, because UTF's (D) rejection in fact was motivated by the desire to avoid a bad bargain. UTF (D) countered that its rejection was not made in bad faith, and that it did not breach the APA.

> ## RULE OF LAW
> (1) The good faith requirement in Article 2 of the Uniform Commercial Code for transactions between merchants, which requires adherence to industry custom, does not apply where merchants have expressly abrogated such adherence in their contract.
> (2) Under Article 2 of the Uniform Commercial Code, a buyer does not act in bad faith and breach its contract with the seller when it rejects a nonconforming tender because the market for the resale of the goods has declined.

**FACTS:** Austrian Airlines Oesterreichische Luftverkehrs AG (Austrian) (P) and UT Finance Corporation (UTF) (D) had entered into an Aircraft Purchase Agreement (APA), whereby UTF (D) would purchase a used aircraft from Austrian (P), provided all delivery conditions were met. Section 2.2A of the APA provided UTF (D) could reject the aircraft if Austrian (P) failed to satisfy the delivery conditions in any way, no matter how insignificant. The aircraft that Austrian (P) tendered had two unapproved auxiliary center fuel tanks (ACTs) that were nonconforming and that affected the aircraft's airworthiness, because the aircraft could not have received an FAA certificate of airworthiness until the ACTs were approved. Had UTF (D) accepted the aircraft, it would have been obligated to pay Austrian (P) $32 million for it, but at the time of tender, as a result of a steep decline in the market for used aircraft, the aircraft was worth only $12 million. UTF (D) rejected the aircraft on the basis of nonconformity. Austrian (P) brought suit for breach of contract on the grounds that UTF (D) acted in bad faith under Article 2 of the Uniform Commercial Code (UCC) when it rejected the aircraft on what Austrian (P) characterized as "minor"

nonconformity in the fuel tanks, and alleged that UTF (D) used the deficiencies in the fuel tanks as a pretext to avoid what had become a disadvantageous bargain. When merchants are involved in a transaction, Article 2 requires the merchants to act in good faith, which "means honesty in fact and the observance of reasonable commercial standards of fair dealing in the trade." Invoking this definition of good faith, Austrian (P) contended that one of the reasonable commercial standards of fair dealing in the aircraft trade is adherence to a custom and practice of accepting aircraft "with minor nonconformities" along with financial compensation for those shortcomings, and it argued that that UTF (D) ignored this custom, and, therefore, acted in bad faith. UTF (D) moved for dismissal.

**ISSUE:**
(1) Does the good faith requirement in Article 2 of the Uniform Commercial Code for transactions between merchants, which requires adherence to industry custom, apply where merchants have expressly abrogated such adherence in their contract?
(2) Under Article 2 of the Uniform Commercial Code, does a buyer act in bad faith and breach its contract with the seller when it rejects a nonconforming tender because the market for the resale of the goods has declined?

**HOLDING AND DECISION:** (Kaplan, J.)
(1) No. The good faith requirement in Article 2 of the Uniform Commercial Code for transactions between merchants, which requires adherence to industry custom, does not apply where merchants have expressly abrogated such adherence in their contract. Industry custom does not apply where the express terms of a contract mandate something different. Here, Section 2.2A of the APA explicitly abrogated the alleged industry custom by providing that Austrian (P) was obligated to deliver the aircraft in accordance with all of the delivery conditions contained in the APA, and that UTF (D) had no obligation whatsoever to purchase the aircraft in the event such delivery conditions were not met. Where, as here, the parties contracted in terms that gave the buyer the right to walk away from the deal in the event of a nonconforming tender, there is no reason not to give the buyer the benefit of its bargain. Judgment for UTF (D) as to this issue.
(2) No. Under Article 2 of the Uniform Commercial Code, a buyer does not act in bad faith and breach its contract with the seller when it rejects a nonconforming tender

*Continued on next page.*

because the market for the resale of the goods has declined. First, setting aside the APA, and assuming, arguendo, that UTF (D) was required to adhere to industry custom, it is clear that, even under the industry custom as delineated by Austrian (P), the ACTs affected the aircraft's airworthiness, so that these deviations from conformity were not "minor." Second, even if UTF (D) was primarily motivated by avoiding what had turned into a bad bargain, it did not act in bad faith by rejecting the aircraft on the grounds of nonconformity. To the contrary, it is assumed that UTF (D) was motivated by the decline in market value to insist upon getting everything it bargained for and, if Austrian (P) was unable to deliver in conformity with the contract, to walk away. It is common sense to recognize, for example, that the aircraft would have been less valuable to UTF (D) if, as was the case, it were ineligible to receive an FAA certificate of airworthiness than if it had conformed to the contract for the simple reason that the universe of potential purchasers or lessors would have been considerably smaller. Thus, insistence upon the benefit of its bargain was entirely reasonable behavior. However, even if UTF (D) was actively seeking to take advantage of Austrian's (P) failure to tender in conformity with the APA for the dominant purpose of getting out of the deal in light of the change in the market, such conduct does not constitute bad faith. Austrian's (P) reliance on precedent, involving a seller that had reasonable grounds to believe that a substitute tender for nonconforming goods would be acceptable, is misplaced. In that case, the court held that the seller had right to cure, that it had done so properly, and that the buyer's rejection in those circumstances placed it in breach. Here, the APA made abundantly clear that UTF (D) would have no obligation to accept a non-conforming tender. Thus, Austrian (P) contracted away any right it otherwise might have had to cure its failure to perform, so that any consideration of whether UTF (D) would have accepted a nonconforming tender at a lower price is irrelevant. Moreover, the rule for which Austrian (P) advocates does not make commercial sense. Where a buyer pursuant to a contract calling for future delivery is presented with non-conforming goods, price movements intervening between the agreement and the time for delivery often are taken into consideration in determining whether to reject. It makes sense to consider them because nonconformities often go not to the ultimate utility of the goods, but to their value, especially resale value. Where the parties, as they did here, contract in terms that give the buyer the right to walk away from the deal in the event of a nonconforming tender, there is no reason not to give the buyer the benefit of its bargain. That is especially so in a case like this, which involves highly sophisticated and well advised commercial entities. Judgment for UTF (D) as to this issue. [UTF's (D) motion for judgment of dismissal is granted.]

## ▶ ANALYSIS

In the case that Austrian (P) relied on, *Joc Oil USA, Inc. v. Consolidated Edison Co. of New York,* 107 Misc.2d 376, 434 N.Y.S.2d 623 (Sup. Ct. N.Y. Co. 1980), *aff'd sub nom. T.W. Oil, Inc. v. Consol. Edison Co. of New York,* 84 A.D.2d 970, 447 N.Y.S.2d 572 (1st Dept.1981) (table), *aff'd* 57 N.Y.2d 574, 457 N.Y.S.2d 458, 443 N.E.2d 932 (1982), the seller tendered nonconforming goods, but promptly offered to cure the defect by substituting a conforming cargo due to arrive one week later. The buyer rejected that offer, indicating that it would purchase that substitute cargo only at the then-prevailing market price. The court in *Joc Oil* began its analysis with UCC § 2–508(2), which provides that "[w]here the buyer rejects a non-conforming tender which the seller had reasonable grounds to believe would be acceptable with or without money allowance the seller may if he seasonably notifies the buyer have a further reasonable time to substitute a conforming tender." In the course of discussing the question whether the seller had reason to believe that a substitute tender would be acceptable, the court focused on a variety of circumstances including the buyer's indication that it would purchase the substitute cargo, but only at the then-prevailing market price. It concluded from that fact that the dispute centered more on price than on the nonconforming nature of the tendered goods, so that the buyer's failure to accept the offered cure constituted bad faith. The issue to which the court's comments were addressed was whether the seller had reasonable ground to believe that the buyer would accept a nonconforming tender and thus fall within § 2–508(2) and its policy of protecting sellers against surprise rejections. Evidence that a buyer would have accepted a non-conforming tender at a lower price was relevant to that question, but that was not the issue here, since Austrian (P) had contracted away any right it otherwise might have had to cure its failure to perform.

■━■

## *Quicknotes*

**BAD FAITH** Conduct that is intentionally misleading or deceptive.

**CONFORMING TENDER** Goods tendered pursuant to a contract for sale that conform with the contract's requirements.

**FAIR DEALING** An implied warranty that the parties will deal honestly in the satisfaction of their obligations and without an intent to defraud.

**GOOD FAITH REQUIREMENT** An implied warranty that the parties will deal honestly in the satisfaction of their obligations and without an intent to defraud.

■━■

# Feld v. Henry S. Levy & Sons, Inc.

Bread crumb purchaser (P) v. Bread crumb supplier (D)

N.Y. Ct. App., 37 N.Y.2d 466, 335 N.E.2d 320 (1975).

**NATURE OF CASE:** Appeal from affirmance of denial of summary judgment in suit alleging breach of an output contract.

**FACT SUMMARY:** Feld (P) contracted to purchase all bread crumbs produced by Henry S. Levy & Sons, Inc. (Levy) (D) during a certain period. Levy (D) then dismantled its crumb-making machinery because the operation proved to be "uneconomical."

---

🏛 **RULE OF LAW**
Implicit in every output contract is the understanding that the supplier will act in good faith in determining the quantity of goods he will produce.

---

**FACTS:** Feld (P) entered into a written contract to purchase all bread crumbs produced by Henry S. Levy & Sons, Inc. (Levy) (D) between June 19, 1968, and June 18, 1969. The contract included an automatic renewal provision but also gave each party the right to terminate the agreement upon six months' written notice. At the outset of the contract, Feld (P) delivered a performance bond and later presented a bond continuation certificate. Levy (D) sold bread crumbs to Feld (P) for nearly a year, but then stopped producing the crumbs, explaining that the operation was "very uneconomical." Levy (D) finally dismantled its crumb-producing machinery, although offering to resume production if Feld (P) would agree to a price increase. Feld (P) instead filed suit, claiming that the output contract between the parties obligated Levy (D) to continue producing bread crumbs. Levy (D) argued that the contract required Levy (D) to sell its entire output, if any, of bread crumbs to Feld (P) but imposed no duty upon Levy (D) to produce any bread crumbs at all. The trial court denied motions for summary judgment by both parties, and the state's intermediate appellate court affirmed. Both Feld (P) and Levy (D) then appealed, and the state's highest court granted review.

**ISSUE:** Is implicit in every output contract the understanding that the supplier will act in good faith in determining the quantity of goods he will produce?

**HOLDING AND DECISION:** (Cooke, J.) Yes. Implicit in every output contract is the understanding that the supplier will act in good faith in determining the quantity of goods he will produce. The Uniform Commercial Code clearly states that output contracts are not invalid for want of mutuality or because of indefiniteness. But, the Code does impose a requirement that both parties to such a contract act in good faith. In the context of this case, the good-faith rule obligates Levy (D) to continue producing

bread crumbs unless that conduct would threaten the viability of Levy's (D) entire operation, including the related food-producing activities in which the company (D) is engaged. A showing that Levy's (D) profits from the contract were less than had been anticipated is not sufficient to relieve Levy (D) of the obligation to perform the contract. Since the extent to which Levy (D) has acted in good faith must be determined by the trial court, the motions for summary judgment were properly denied. Affirmed.

---

▶ **ANALYSIS**

The validity of output and requirement contracts was once very much in doubt. Today, the Uniform Commercial Code has foreclosed virtually all arguments against the validity of such contracts. The good-faith requirement imposed by the Code has also reduced the hazards such contracts once entailed. No longer can the buyer demand, pursuant to a requirement contract, more goods than the seller can reasonably produce. Nor, as the *Feld* case illustrates, can the seller under an output contract produce an unreasonably small (or large) amount of merchandise.

---

## Quicknotes

**BREACH OF CONTRACT** Unlawful failure by a party to perform its obligations pursuant to contract.

**GOOD FAITH** An honest intention to abstain from taking advantage of another.

**SUMMARY JUDGMENT** Judgment rendered by a court in response to a motion made by one of the parties, claiming that the lack of a question of material fact in respect to an issue warrants disposition of the issue without consideration by the jury.

---

# Roth Steel Products v. Sharon Steel Corp.

Steel purchaser (P) v. Steel supplier (D)

705 F.2d 134 (6th Cir. 1983).

**NATURE OF CASE:** Appeal from award of damages in breach of contract action.

**FACT SUMMARY:** Sharon Steel Corp. (Sharon) (D) contended it was excused from performing under a contract with Roth Steel Products (Roth) (P) because of a modification that Roth (P) agreed to under Sharon's (D) threat to discontinue supplying steel completely.

## RULE OF LAW

A court must, in determining whether a particular modification was obtained in good faith, determine whether: (1) a party's conduct was consistent with reasonable commercial standards of fair dealing in the trade; and (2) the parties were in fact motivated to seek modification by an honest desire to compensate for commercial exigencies.

**FACTS:** In 1972, during a slump in the steel industry, Roth Steel Products (Roth) (P) contracted to purchase 200 tons of hot rolled steel per month from Sharon Steel Corp. (Sharon) (D) for $148 per ton. Subsequently, the industry experienced an increased demand, and all producers were soon operating at full capacity. Sharon (D) notified Roth (P) that it would discontinue all price concessions given in 1972. The parties renegotiated the contract, and Roth (P) agreed to a price modification primarily because it could not obtain steel elsewhere. Sharon (D) had experienced several cost increases on raw materials and was unable to get a sufficient supply of steel slab at an affordable price to allow it to operate profitably without the modification. Subsequently, Sharon (D) was unable to meet Roth's (P) steel needs, and Roth (P) sued for breach when it discovered Sharon (D) had been allocating steel to a subsidiary for sale at premium prices. Sharon (D) defended on the ground that the modification was valid and allowed it to raise prices, and Roth's (P) refusal to pay excused Sharon's (D) performance. The district court found the modification unenforceable as not sought in good faith, and Sharon (D) appealed. The court of appeals granted review.

**ISSUE:** Must a court, in determining whether a particular modification was obtained in good faith, determine whether: (1) a party's conduct was consistent with reasonable commercial standards of fair dealing in the trade; and (2) the parties were in fact motivated to seek the modification by an honest desire to compensate for commercial exigencies?

**HOLDING AND DECISION:** (Celebrezze, J.) Yes. A court must, in determining whether a particular modification was obtained in good faith, determine wheth-

er: (1) a party's conduct was consistent with reasonable commercial standards of fair dealing in the trade; and (2) the parties were in fact motivated to seek modification by an honest desire to compensate for commercial exigencies. In this case, continued performance under the original contract would cause Sharon (D) to incur a loss. Therefore, it acted consistently with reasonable commercial standards in seeking a modification. However, under the second requirement, Sharon (D) had to demonstrate its honesty in fact. Sharon (D) failed to assert its alleged right to raise prices until the trial on this matter. Its failure to give this as a justification for its failure to supply Roth (P) indicates a lack of honesty in fact in seeking the modification. As a result, the modification was not made in good faith and was invalid. Therefore, Sharon's (D) failure to ship under the original contract was a breach. Affirmed.

## ANALYSIS

Some jurisdictions ignore questions of good or bad faith is assessing the validity of a contract modification. In *Austin Instrument, Inc. v. Loral Corp.,* 272 N.E.2d 533 (1971), a New York court held that the question turns entirely upon concepts of economic duress. Such economic duress is shown where the threatened party is forced into a modification because he cannot obtain the goods elsewhere.

---

## Quicknotes

**BREACH OF CONTRACT** Unlawful failure by a party to perform its obligations pursuant to contract.

**DAMAGES** Monetary compensation that may be awarded by the court to a party who has sustained injury or loss to his person, property or rights due to another party's unlawful act, omission or negligence.

**DUTY OF GOOD FAITH OF FAIR DEALINGS** An implied duty in a contract that the parties will deal honestly in the satisfaction of their obligations and without an intent to defraud.

**ECONOMIC DURESS** A defense to an action that a party was unlawfully coerced into the performance of an action by another due to fear of imminent economic loss and was not acting in accordance with his own free volition in performing the action.

# Zapatha v. Dairy Mart, Inc.

Franchisee (P) v. Franchisor (D)

Mass. Sup. Jud. Ct., 381 Mass. 284, 408 N.E.2d 1370 (1980).

**NATURE OF CASE:** Appeal from judgment for plaintiff in action to enjoin termination of an agreement.

**FACT SUMMARY:** Dairy Mart, Inc. (D) appealed a judgment that its termination of a franchise contract with Zapatha (P) had been made in bad faith.

## ▥ RULE OF LAW
Under the Uniform Commercial Code, termination of a contract that permits termination of the contract without cause is not made in bad faith where termination is made with honesty in fact and in observance of reasonable commercial standards of fair dealing in the trade.

**FACTS:** The Zapathas (P) signed a franchise agreement with Dairy Mart, Inc. (D), which operated a chain of franchise "convenience" stores. It provided that Dairy Mart (D) would furnish the store and equipment, pay the rent, utility bills, and other costs of doing business, and receive a percentage of the store's gross sales as a franchise fee. The Zapathas (P) were responsible for paying for a starting inventory, maintaining a minimum inventory thereafter, paying employees and taxes, and operating the store on a daily basis. There was a termination provision permitting Dairy Mart (D) to terminate without cause on 90-days' written notice after 12 months. Termination thereunder and without cause later occurred, because the Zapathas (P) refused to sign a new agreement that had less favorable terms for them, and the Zapathas (P) sought an injunction. The trial court held that the termination provision was unconscionable and that termination had been an unfair and deceptive act or practice and made in bad faith. Dairy Mart (D) appealed.

**ISSUE:** Under the Uniform Commercial Code, is termination of a contract that permits termination of the contract without cause made in bad faith where termination is made with honesty in fact and in observance of reasonable commercial standards of fair dealing in the trade?

**HOLDING AND DECISION:** (Wilkins, J.) No. Under the Uniform Commercial Code (U.C.C.), termination of a contract that permits termination of the contract without cause is not made in bad faith where termination is made with honesty in fact and in observance of reasonable commercial standards of fair dealing in the trade. Here there was no evidence that Dairy Mart (D) acted dishonestly or failed to observe reasonable commercial standards of fair dealing in the trade when it terminated the contract. The key to whether a party is "honest in fact" is whether

the party was honest. Even though Dairy Mart's (D) conduct might be said to be arbitrary, it cannot be said to be dishonest. Moreover, even going beyond the U.C.C., there is no general principle of law or legislation that would render Dairy Mart's (D) conduct deceptive or rendered in bad faith. Even if the introductory circular given to Zapatha (P) by Dairy Mart (D) may have contained misleading information, there was nothing deceptive or unfair about the circular that would affect Dairy Mart's (D) right to terminate under the contract. Reversed.

## ▶ ANALYSIS

While some courts have declined to impose a duty of good faith in the termination of franchise contracts, federal and state laws have increasingly regulated the right to terminate such agreements where the franchisee has relatively less bargaining power than the franchisor, or where the franchisee enjoys a special status (e.g., service station operators). In such cases, common-law rules requiring good cause for termination may be applied despite clear contract language that permits termination without cause.

## Quicknotes

**BAD FAITH** Conduct that is intentionally misleading or deceptive.

**DUTY OF GOOD FAITH OF FAIR DEALINGS** An implied duty in a contract that the parties will deal honestly in the satisfaction of their obligations and without an intent to defraud.

**ENJOIN** The ordering of a party to cease the conduct of a specific activity.

**INJUNCTION** A court order requiring a person to do, or prohibiting that person from doing, a specific act.

# Hillesland v. Federal Land Bank Association of Grand Forks

Terminated employee (P) v. Employer (D)

N.D. Sup. Ct., 407 N.W.2d 206 (1987).

**NATURE OF CASE:** Appeal from the summary judgment dismissing a wrongful discharge suit.

**FACT SUMMARY:** When Hillesland (P) was discharged by his employer, Federal Land Bank Association of Grand Forks ("the Bank") (D), he argued that the Bank (D) had violated an implied covenant of good faith and fair dealing existing in all employment contracts.

> ## RULE OF LAW
> North Dakota rejects the implication of a covenant of good faith and fair dealing in employment contracts.

**FACTS:** Elmer Hillesland (P), an employee of Federal Land Bank Association of Grand Forks ("the Bank") (D), was discharged from employment for contacting a client of his employer and ultimately arranging for a sale of the client's property to Hillesland's (P) two sons. The rationale for the discharge was that Hillesland (P) had violated written standards of conduct, had damaged the image and reputation of the Bank (D), and had exercised poor business judgment. Hillesland (P) sued the Bank (D), alleging, among other things, that the Bank (D) had violated an implied covenant of good faith and fair dealing which exists in all employment contracts. The trial court granted summary judgment on this issue, and Hillesland (P) appealed.

**ISSUE:** Does North Dakota reject the implication of a covenant of good faith and fair dealing in employment contracts?

**HOLDING AND DECISION:** (Erickstad, C.J.) Yes. North Dakota rejects the implication of a covenant of good faith and fair dealing in employment contracts. Judicially created exceptions to, or modifications of, the at-will rule, have indeed emerged to ameliorate the sometimes harsh consequences of strict adherence to the rule. However, the at-will rule is statutory in North Dakota. Even in California and those other jurisdictions that have found an implied-in-law covenant of good faith and fair dealing in employment contracts, the application of the rule has been far from uniform. Given the somewhat erratic development of this doctrine in the courts, this court will decline to follow either the California formulation or any of the variant theories developed in other jurisdictions. An employer's interest in running his business as he sees fit must be balanced against the interest of the employee in maintaining his or her employment, and this exception does not strike the proper balance. To imply into each employment contract a duty to terminate in good faith would subject each discharge to judicial incursions into the amorphous concept of bad faith. Affirmed.

**DISSENT IN PART:** (Pederson, J.) Here, the termination was not "without cause," but for the exercise of poor judgment. Nevertheless, in all relationships between civilized persons, there is an obligation to not act in bad faith. Under circumstances that are appropriate, where there is an aggravated breach, or unconscionable conduct, the court should provide a remedy.

## ▌ ANALYSIS

The court in *Hillesland* expressed the viewpoint of a majority of American jurisdictions that, while an employer may agree to restrict or limit its right to discharge an employee, to imply such a restriction on that right from the existence of a contractual right, which, by its terms has no restrictions, is internally inconsistent. Such an intrusion into the employment relationship, say these courts, is merely a judicial substitute for collective bargaining which is more appropriately left to the legislative process.

---

## Quicknotes

**COLLECTIVE BARGAINING** Negotiations between an employer and employee that are mediated by a specified third party.

**IMPLIED COVENANT OF GOOD FAITH AND FAIR DEALING** An implied warranty that the parties will deal honestly in the satisfaction of their obligations and without an intent to defraud.

**SUMMARY JUDGMENT** Judgment rendered by a court in response to a motion made by one of the parties, claiming that the lack of a question of material fact in respect to an issue warrants disposition of the issue without consideration by the jury.

**WRONGFUL DISCHARGE** Unlawful termination of an individual's employment.

# Rogath v. Siebenmann

Painting buyer (P) v. Painting seller (D)

129 F.3d 261 (2d Cir. 1997).

**NATURE OF CASE:** Appeal from grant of partial summary judgment on claim for breach of warranty, and cross-appeal from denial, inter alia, of claims for breach of contract and fraud.

**FACT SUMMARY:** Siebenmann (D), who sold to Rogath (P) a painting, contended that there were factual issues as to what Rogath (P) knew about the painting's authenticity when Rogath (P) purchased the painting, so that a grant of summary judgment to Rogath (P) on the issue of Siebenmann's (D) breach of warranties under Article 2 of the Uniform Commercial Code was inappropriate.

## 🏛 RULE OF LAW
Under Article 2 of the Uniform Commercial Code, where there are fact issues regarding whether a seller, prior to the closing of a sale, disclosed to the buyer doubts regarding a good's qualities that the seller nevertheless expressly warranted in the contract of sale, summary judgment for the buyer on claims for breach of those warranties is precluded.

**FACTS:** Siebenmann (D) sold a painting allegedly painted by the well-known painter, Francis Bacon, to Rogath (P) for $570,000. In the bill of sale, Siebenmann (D) described the provenance of the painting and warranted that he was its sole owner, that it was authentic, and that he was not aware of any challenge to its authenticity. Three months later, when Rogath (P) sold the painting to Acquavella Contemporary Art (Acquavella), for $950,000, Acquavella learned of a challenge to the painting's authenticity and requested that Rogath (P) refund the $950,000 and take back the painting, which Rogath (P) did. Rogath (P) then sued Siebenmann (D) in federal district court for breach of contract, breach of warranty and fraud. Rogath (P) moved for partial summary judgment on the breach of warranty claims, and the district court granted his motion, concluding that (1) Siebenmann (D) was unsure of the painting's provenance when he sold it to Rogath (P); (2) he was not the sole owner of the painting; and (3) when he sold the painting to Rogath (P) he already knew of a challenge to the painting's authenticity by the Marlborough Fine Art Gallery in London. The court awarded Rogath (P) $950,000 in damages, and, in light of its breach of warranty holding, dismissed Rogath's (P) remaining claims for fraud and breach of contract. Siebenmann (D) appealed the grant of partial summary judgment, conceding that he knew of the cloud that hung over the painting's authenticity before he sold it to Rogath (P), but asserting that Rogath (P) also knew when he

bought the painting that questions of the painting's authenticity and provenance had already been raised. Siebenmann (D) maintained that Rogath (P) therefore could not rest claims for breach of warranty under Article 2 of the Uniform Commercial Code on the representations made in the bill of sale. Rogath (P) cross-appealed the denial of his breach of contract and fraud claims.

**ISSUE:** Under Article 2 of the Uniform Commercial Code, where there are fact issues regarding whether a seller, prior to the closing of a sale, disclosed to the buyer doubts regarding a good's qualities that the seller nevertheless expressly warranted in the contract of sale, is summary judgment for the buyer on claims for breach of those warranties precluded?

**HOLDING AND DECISION:** (McLaughlin, J.) Yes. Under Article 2 of the Uniform Commercial Code (U.C.C.), where there are fact issues regarding whether a seller, prior to the closing of a sale, disclosed to the buyer doubts regarding a good's qualities that the seller nevertheless expressly warranted in the contract of sale, summary judgment for the buyer on claims for breach of those warranties is precluded. Because the bill of sale was a contract for the sale of goods, Rogath's (P) breach of warranty claims are governed by U.C.C. Article 2. Uniform Commercial Code § 2–313 provides that any description of the goods that is made part of the basis of the bargain creates an express warranty that the goods shall conform to the description. Under the state law to be applied in this case, a court must evaluate both the extent and the source of the buyer's knowledge about the truth of what the seller is warranting. Where a buyer closes on a contract in the full knowledge and acceptance of facts disclosed by the seller that would constitute a breach of warranty under the terms of the contract, the buyer is foreclosed from later asserting the breach, and, unless the buyer has expressly preserved his rights under the warranties, the buyer has waived the breach. The buyer may preserve his rights by expressly stating that disputes regarding the accuracy of the seller's warranties are unresolved, and that by signing the agreement the buyer does not waive any rights to enforce the terms of the agreement. However, if the seller is not the source of the buyer's knowledge, e.g., if it is merely "common knowledge" that the facts warranted are false, or the buyer has been informed of the falsity of the facts by some third party, the buyer may prevail in his claim for breach of warranty. Accordingly, what the buyer knew and, most importantly, whether he got that knowledge from the seller

*Continued on next page.*

are the critical questions. Here, the bill of sale stated that the warranties induced Rogath (P) to buy the painting, but Rogath (P) did not "expressly preserve his rights," so that exactly what Siebenmann (D) told Rogath (P) is crucial. On the other hand, what a third party may have told Rogath (P) about the authenticity and provenance of the painting is immaterial. Only if Siebenmann (D) himself informed Rogath (P) of doubts about the provenance or challenges to authenticity will Rogath (P) be deemed to have waived any claims for breach of warranty arising from the written representations appearing in the bill of sale. Although Siebenmann (D) nowhere specifically alleged that he informed Rogath (P) of his doubts about the authenticity and provenance of the painting, but merely alluded to the "controversy" or "problems" with the Marlborough Gallery, this testimony, however ambiguous, may justify the inference that Rogath (P) knew more than he now claims to have known when he entered into the bill of sale. At the very least, there is indisputable ambiguity in the affidavits about the pivotal exchange between Rogath (P) and Siebenmann (D), so that genuine issues of fact persist. In this posture, all reasonable inferences must be drawn in Siebenmann's (D) favor. Therefore, summary judgment on Rogath's (P) claims for breach of warranties is inappropriate, and the award to Rogath (P) is now vacated and the case is remanded. On remand, the district court must reinstate Rogath's (P) breach of contract and fraud claims. Vacated and remanded.

## ▶ ANALYSIS

Under UCC § 2-313, different courts have taken different approaches to the questions of whether the "basis of the bargain" requirement implies that the buyer must rely on the seller's statements to recover and what the nature of that reliance requirement is. Some courts have reasoned that the buyer must have relied upon the accuracy of the seller's affirmations or promises in order to recover. Other courts have paid lip service to a "reliance" requirement, but have found that the requirement has been met if the buyer relied on the seller's promise as part of "the basis of the bargain" in entering into the contract. Under that interpretation, the buyer need not show that he relied on the truthfulness of the warranties. Still, other courts have reasoned that there is a "reliance" requirement only when there is a dispute as to whether a warranty was in fact given by the seller. These courts have concluded that no reliance of any kind is required where the existence of an express warranty in a contract is conceded by both parties, so that the buyer need establish only a breach of the warranty. The view of "reliance" applied in this case, which requires no more than reliance on the express warranty as being a part of the bargain between the parties, reflects the prevailing perception of an action for breach of express warranty as one that is grounded in contract, rather than in tort. Thus, the critical question is not whether the buyer believed in the truth of the warranted information, but whether he believed he was purchasing the seller's promise as to its truth.

■—■

## Quicknotes

**BASIS OF THE BARGAIN**  The promise made by the offeror that induces the return promise or performance on the part of the offeree and the promise or performance on the part of the offeree that induces the promise made by the offeror.

**BREACH OF WARRANTY**  The breach of a promise made by one party to a contract on which the other party may rely, relieving that party from the obligation of determining whether the fact is true and indemnifying the other party from liability if that fact is shown to be false.

**EXPRESS WARRANTY**  A promise made by one party to a contract that the other party may rely on a fact, relieving that party from the obligation of determining whether the fact is true and indemnifying the other party from liability if that fact is shown to be false.

**RELIANCE**  Dependence on a fact that causes a party to act or refrain from acting.

■—■

# V.S.H. Realty, Inc. v. Texaco, Inc.

Purchaser of bulk storage petroleum facility (P) v. Seller of bulk storage petroleum facility (D)

757 F.2d 411 (1st Cir. 1985).

**NATURE OF CASE:** Appeal from dismissal of claims for breach of contract, misrepresentation, and violation of a state statute prohibiting unfair and deceptive practices in business dealings.

**FACT SUMMARY:** V.S.H. Realty, Inc. (V.S.H.) (P), which sought the return of a down payment it had given to Texaco, Inc. (D) for the purchase of a bulk storage petroleum facility, contended that Texaco (D) breached the parties' contract, committed common-law misrepresentation, and violated a state statute prohibiting unfair and deceptive practices in business dealings by making only partial disclosures as to oil leaks and government inspections of the property, notwithstanding that V.H.S. (P) had averred that it accepted the property "as is."

## 🏛 RULE OF LAW
(1) One party to a business transaction states a claim for common-law misrepresentation where it alleges that it repeatedly asked the other party about a material point of information, that the other party knowingly made only partial, fragmentary, or incomplete disclosures, or failed entirely to disclose material facts, in response, that the other party's response induced it to enter into a contract with the other party, and that it consequently suffered damages.

(2) A buyer of real property states a claim for violation of a statute that prohibits unfair or deceptive acts or practices in business where the buyer alleges that the seller made partial or incomplete disclosures regarding a material point of information, or entirely failed to disclose material facts, notwithstanding that the parties' agreement contains an agreement by the buyer to purchase the property "as is".

**FACTS:** V.S.H. Realty, Inc. (V.S.H.) (P) offered to purchase from Texaco, Inc. (D) a used bulk storage petroleum facility, and gave $280,000 to Texaco (D) as a down payment. V.S.H.'s (P) offer required Texaco (D) to convey the property "free and clear of all liens, encumbrances, tenancies and restrictions", except for those set forth in the offer. Attached to the offer to purchase was an acknowledgement signed by Texaco (D) stating that, to the best of the company's knowledge and belief, it had not received "any notice, demand, or communication from any local county, state or federal department or agency regarding modifications or improvements to the facility or any part thereof."

The offer also included a disclosure by Texaco (D) that fuel oils had seeped into one of the facility's buildings. V.S.H. (P), for its part, expressly stated in the offer that it had inspected the property, and accepted it "as is" without any representation on the part of Texaco (D) as to its condition. On visits to the property, V.S.H. (P) representatives observed additional oil seepages that Texaco (D) had not previously disclosed. V.S.H. (P) informed Texaco (D) it would not go through with the transaction unless Texaco (D) either fixed the problems or reduced the purchase price. When Texaco (D) refused, V.S.H. (P) demanded return of its down payment. Texaco (D) again refused, and V.S.H. (P) filed suit in federal district court for breach of contract, misrepresentation, and violation of a state statute (chapter 93A) prohibiting unfair and deceptive practices in business dealings. V.S.H. (P) subsequently learned that Texaco (D) had failed to disclose a U.S. Coast Guard inspection of the property. As to its contract claim, V.S.H.'s (P) theory was that the seepages effectively constituted "encumbrances," so that Texaco (D) was unable to convey the property "free and clear" as required by the contract. Its misrepresentation claim rested on Texaco's (D) failure to disclose the oil seepage problems and Coast Guard investigation in the face of repeated inquiries by V.S.H. (P) about the subject, and its chapter 93A claim was based on similar allegations. Texaco (D) moved to dismiss the action in its entirety, and the district court granted Texaco's (D) motion, and dismissed all the claims. It dismissed the common-law misrepresentation claim, stating that V.S.H. (P) had failed to allege the required affirmative misrepresentation or implicit misrepresentation by partial and ambiguous statements. It dismissed the chapter 93A claim on two grounds. First, it found that an Attorney General's regulation upon which V.S.H. (P) relied was not intended to apply in a transaction between two sophisticated business entities, when one party agreed to take the property "as is," and, second, it determined that Texaco (D) had no duty to disclose the oil seepages to V.S.H. (P), so its failure to do so could not have violated chapter 93A. The Attorney General regulation, § 3.16(2), stated that an act or practice violated chapter 93A if: "Any person or other legal entity subject to this act fails to disclose to a buyer or prospective buyer any fact, the disclosure of which may have influenced the buyer or prospective buyer not to enter into the transaction." The district court dismissed the breach of contract claim without explanation. V.S.H. (P) appealed, and the court of

*Continued on next page.*

appeals granted review. [The court of appeals affirmed the dismissal of V.S.H.'s (P) breach of contract claim.]

## ISSUE:

(1) Does one party to a business transaction state a claim for common law misrepresentation where it alleges that it repeatedly asked the other party about a material point of information, that the other party knowingly made only partial, fragmentary, or incomplete disclosures, or failed entirely to disclose material facts, in response, that the other party's response induced it to enter into a contract with the other party, and that it consequently suffered damages?

(2) Does a buyer of real property state a claim for violation of a statute that prohibits unfair or deceptive acts or practices in business where the buyer alleges that the seller made partial or incomplete disclosures regarding a material point of information, or entirely failed to disclose material facts, notwithstanding that the parties' agreement contains an agreement by the buyer to purchase the property "as is"?

## HOLDING AND DECISION: (Coffin, J.)

(1) Yes. One party to a business transaction states a claim for common law misrepresentation where it alleges that it repeatedly asked the other party about a material point of information, that the other party knowingly made only partial, fragmentary, or incomplete disclosures, or failed entirely to disclose material facts, in response, that the other party's response induced it to enter into a contract with the other party, and that it consequently suffered damages. Here, V.S.H.'s (P) claim for misrepresentation is based on Texaco's (D) partial disclosure of oil seepages, the deliberate concealment of other leaks and the failure to acknowledge the U.S. Coast Guard investigation of the spills. Its damages were the down payment, which it otherwise would not have made. Under state law, a party who discloses partial information that may be misleading has a duty to reveal all the material facts he knows to avoid deceiving the other party. Although there may be no duty imposed upon one party to a transaction to speak for the information of the other, if he does speak with reference to a given point of information, voluntarily or at the other's request, he is bound to speak honestly and to divulge all the material facts bearing upon the point that lie within his knowledge. Fragmentary information may be as misleading as active misrepresentation, and half-truths may be as actionable as whole lies. The combination of Texaco's (D) affirmative disclosure of one leak, its failure to disclose the others, and its failure to acknowledge alleged Coast Guard investigation of the seepages, at a minimum, states a claim for misrepresentation, and, therefore, the district court erred in dismissing this claim at this early stage in the proceedings. Reversed as to this issue.

(2) Yes. A buyer of real property states a claim for violation of a statute that prohibits unfair or deceptive acts or practices in business where the buyer alleges that the seller made partial or incomplete disclosures regarding a material point of information, or entirely failed to disclose material facts, notwithstanding that the parties' agreement contains an agreement by the buyer to purchase the property "as is". Chapter 93A was intended to have a broad impact and, among other things, to provide for proper disclosure of information. The Attorney General regulation, § 3.16(2), which interprets chapter 93A, provides that failure to disclose a material fact is a failure to disclose a fact that may have influenced the buyer not to enter into the transaction. The district court concluded that this regulation was incomplete because unless a defendant has a duty to speak, his nondisclosure of a defect does not constitute a violation of chapter 93A even if the information may have influenced the buyer not to enter into the contract. The district court then went on to hold that Texaco (D) did not have a duty to disclose the oil leaks to V.S.H (P). The district court erred for two reasons. First, even assuming, arguendo, that nondisclosure is a violation of chapter 93A only when there is a duty to disclose, V.S.H. (P) met its burden of establishing a duty by alleging that Texaco (D) made partial or incomplete statements regarding the oil leaks on the property. Second, state case law makes clear that chapter 93A goes beyond the limitations of a common-law fraud claim, and allows a cause of action even in the absence of a duty to disclose. The district court also based its dismissal of V.S.H.'s (P) claim on its reading of chapter 93A as precluding liability where a sophisticated buyer, such as V.S.H. (P), has an opportunity to inspect the property and agrees to purchase it "as is". The district court noted that such a contractual arrangement is expressly permitted under UCC § 2–316 in non-consumer sales of goods, so that it would be anomalous to hold that "as is" contracts are permissible in sales of goods cases but not in commercial sales of land cases. The district court's view on this point is incorrect. UCC § 2–316 refers specifically to disclaimers of implied warranties, suggesting that it was intended only to permit a seller to limit or modify the contractual bases of liability that the UCC would otherwise impose on the transaction; it does not appear to preclude claims based on fraud or other deceptive conduct. State statutory law supports this interpretation of § 2–316, as it provides that obligations of good faith may not be disclaimed by agreement, and state case law also supports this view, as it provides that even if a disclaimer on its face is not unconscionable, it is subject to challenge if a plaintiff, as

*Continued on next page.*

in this case, properly raises allegations of deceit and violation of chapter 93A. Moreover, state case law unequivocally rejects assertion of an "as is" clause as an automatic defense against allegations of fraud. Although V.S.H.'s (P) experience in the real estate business, along with the presence of an "as is" clause, is relevant to the ultimate disposition of the chapter 93A claim, neither factor makes V.S.H.'s (P) claim insufficient as a matter of law. Sophistication of the parties is not mentioned in chapter 93A, nor is the statute's protection limited to small, unsophisticated businesses. For these reasons, the district court erred in dismissing the chapter 93A claim. Reversed as to this issue. [Reversed and remanded as to the misrepresentation count, and the ch. 93A count.]

**CONCURRENCE AND DISSENT:** (Breyer, J.) Although the common-law misrepresentation issue is a close one, V.S.H (P) has made sufficient allegations to avoid dismissal of the complaint. However, the majority is wrong in concluding that chapter 93A would allow a finding of liability for pure nondisclosure in a case involving sophisticated business parties and an "as is" contract. First, the majority virtually reads "as is" contracts out of state law, since, if a seller knows he will be liable for failing to disclose any material fact about which he "should have known," he will have to check the merchandise or property, and list every defect that he finds. Failure to do so certainly risks (if it does not assure) liability. Yet, it is the very purpose of an "as is" contract to shift the burden of inspection and the costs of hidden defects to the buyer. The UCC expressly authorizes "as is" contracts, so it is anomalous to read ch. 93A in a way that renders § 2–316 virtually meaningless. Second, applying ch. 93A in situations such as the one at bar may hurt consumers. By forcing knowledgeable business sellers to disclose all material facts that they "should have" known, prevents buyers and sellers from allocating costs and risks as they see fit in both the presumably rare situation involving deceptive conduct by the seller and the more typical nondeceptive situation. Such a prohibition could raise the price of the underlying goods or services by preventing the allocation of risks to the party willing to bear them most cheaply, and these increased costs could be passed on to consumers. Third, refusing to enforce an "as is" clause might be warranted where the contract is ambiguous in some way that casts doubt on whether the buyer truly intended to waive his remedies against the seller. In such a case one might hesitate to find a waiver regardless of the knowledge or sophistication of the buyers. However, that is not the case here: the "as is" clause in the Texaco (D)-V.S.H. (P) contract is clear and unambiguous. The Attorney General regulation relied on by the majority literally applies to all transactions, but to apply it to all situations does not make sense, since doing so would eviscerate § 2–316. Instead, as the district court held, that regulation was not meant to override state policy permitting "as is" contracts, at least where the contract

language is clear, the contract is made by knowledgeable business parties, and the contract is untainted by any affirmative misrepresentation, fraud, or otherwise unlawful conduct.

## ▶ *ANALYSIS*

In this case, the court concluded that even if a disclaimer on its face is not unconscionable, it is subject to challenge if a plaintiff properly raises allegations of deceit. This conclusion was supported by the public policy that in general sanctions the avoidance of a promise obtained by deceit, and precludes all attempts to circumvent the policy by means of contractual devices. Under this interpretation, it is entirely possible for a party knowingly to agree that no representations have been made to him, while at the same time believing and relying upon representations that in fact have been made and in fact are false but for which he would not have made the agreement. In other words, under this policy, only in the absence of fraud may a person make a valid contract exempting oneself from any liability to another which he may in the future incur as a result of his negligence.

## *Quicknotes*

**BREACH OF CONTRACT** Unlawful failure by a party to perform its obligations pursuant to contract.

**FRAUD** A false representation of facts with the intent that another will rely on the misrepresentation to his detriment.

**GOOD FAITH** An honest intention to abstain from taking advantage of another.

**IMPLIED WARRANTY** An implied promise made by one party to a contract that the other party may rely on a fact, relieving that party from the obligation of determining whether the fact is true and indemnifying the other party from liability if that fact is shown to be false.

**MATERIAL FACT** A fact without the existence of which a contract would not have been entered.

**MISREPRESENTATION** A statement or conduct by one party to another that constitutes a false representation of fact.

# All-Tech Telecom, Inc. v. Amway Corporation

Distributor (P) v. Marketer (D)

174 F.3d 862 (7th Cir. 1999).

**NATURE OF CASE:** Appeal from summary judgment for defendant in breach of contract suit.

**FACT SUMMARY:** Telecom, Inc. (P), brought claims of intentional and negligent misrepresentation as well as promissory estoppel against Amway Corporation (D).

## 🏛 RULE OF LAW
(1) The "economic loss" doctrine may be applied to warranties that are for both products and services to prevent a suit for negligent misrepresentation.
(2) Promissory estoppel may not be used to bring contract claims where there is an express contract and consideration for that contract is not lacking.

**FACTS:** Telecom, Inc. (All-Tech) (P), brought claims of intentional and negligent misrepresentation against Amway Corporation (Amway) (D). The district court granted summary judgment to Amway (D), finding no actionable misrepresentation on the basis of the common law doctrine of "economic loss." Alternatively, All-Tech (P) claimed promissory estoppel on the basis of Amway's (D) representations that it had thoroughly researched a certain program before offering it to distributors, and had warranted to pay for the consequences if the research that went into the program's development had not been sufficiently thorough. The district court also rejected this claim on summary judgment. The court of appeals granted review.

**ISSUE:**
(1) May the "economic loss" doctrine be applied to warranties that are for both products and services to prevent a suit for negligent misrepresentation?
(2) May promissory estoppel be used to bring contract claims where there is an express contract and consideration for that contract is not lacking?

**HOLDING AND DECISION:** (Posner, C.J.)
(1) Yes. The "economic loss" doctrine may be applied to warranties that are for both products and services to prevent a suit for negligent misrepresentation. The common law "economic loss" doctrine was designed to limit the party that could bring a tort action to only the injured party, and not those with commercial ties to that party. This was extended to the contract arena to preclude those who experienced commercial losses as a result of the injured party's losses from seeking tort remedies not otherwise provided for by contract. Thus, where there are well-developed contract remedies for torts such as fraud and misrepresentation, there is no need for tort remedies. This has been further expanded to forbid commercial contracting parties to escalate their contract dispute into a charge of tortious misrepresentation. It was on this basis that the district court dismissed All-Tech's (P) action. While this doctrine may apply to "hybrid" warranties for both products and services, it is doubtful that the doctrine would apply to intentional misrepresentations. Here, however, there were no actionable misrepresentations of any kind, so the district court correctly dismissed on this basis. Affirmed as to this issue.

(2) No. Promissory estoppel may not be used to bring contract claims where there is an express contract and consideration for that contract is not lacking. The doctrine of promissory estoppel provides an alternative basis to consideration for treating a promise as a contractual undertaking under certain circumstances. When a promise is definite enough to induce a reasonable person to rely upon it, the doctrine makes the promise enforceable. Here, the promise stressed by All-Tech (P), that Amway (D) had thoroughly researched a certain program before offering it to distributors, was not of that character. It warranted a past or existing condition rather than committing to some future action, and what is at issue is thus more precisely described as a warranty than as a promise. However, since a warranty can induce reasonable reliance, its breach can be the basis for a claim of promissory estoppel, but only in limited circumstances. A promisee cannot be permitted to use the doctrine to do "an end run" around the rule that mere puffing is not actionable as misrepresentation, or around the parol evidence rule. Here the parties had a contract covering the relationship in the course and within the scope of which the alleged warranty of thorough research was made. This either was one of the warranties of the contract, or it was not. If it was not, promissory estoppel cannot be used to bring it. Promissory estoppel is not designed to give a party "a second bite at the apple" in the event that the party fails to prove a breach of contract. Affirmed as to this issue. Affirmed.

*Continued on next page.*

## ▶ ANALYSIS

The economic-loss doctrine serves to protect contract doctrines and to prevent the piling on of duplicative remedies.

## Quicknotes

**BREACH OF CONTRACT** Unlawful failure by a party to perform its obligations pursuant to contract.

**CONSIDERATION** Value given by one party in exchange for performance, or a promise to perform, by another party.

**EXPRESS CONTRACT** A contract the terms of which are specifically stated; may be oral or written.

**NEGLIGENT MISREPRESENTATION** A misrepresentation that is made pursuant to a business relationship, in violation of an obligation owed, upon which the plaintiff relies to his detriment.

**PROMISSORY ESTOPPEL** A promise that is enforceable if the promisor should reasonably expect that it will induce action or forbearance on the part of the promisee, and does in fact cause such action or forbearance, and it is the only means of avoiding injustice.

**SUMMARY JUDGMENT** Judgment rendered by a court in response to a motion made by one of the parties, claiming that the lack of a question of material fact in respect to an issue warrants disposition of the issue without consideration by the jury.

**TORT** A legal wrong resulting in a breach of duty by the wrongdoer, causing damages as a result of the breach.

# Dove v. Rose Acre Farms, Inc.

### Employee (P) v. Employer (D)

Ind. Ct. App., 434 N.E.2d 931 (1982).

**NATURE OF CASE:** Appeal from denial of recovery of a contractual bonus.

**FACT SUMMARY:** Dove (P) contended that although he did not perform exactly as prescribed under the contact with Rose Acre Farms, Inc. (D), his employer, he substantially performed and was entitled to payment of a bonus under the contract.

## 🏛 RULE OF LAW
A party is bound to perform all conditions knowingly accepted under a contract, and unless such conditions are met, performance by the other party is not required.

**FACTS:** Rose Acre Farms, Inc. (D) was in the business of producing eggs and was run by Rust, its president. Rust instituted many bonus programs for the employees, always insisting upon strict compliance with the conditions of the bonus and always refusing payment for the slightest breach. Of these conditions, tardiness and absenteeism were of primary importance to Rust. In 1979, Rust approached Dove (P), a construction crew leader, and offered him a $5,000 bonus if certain construction work could be completed in 12 weeks. The terms of the bonus included that Dove (P) complete the work and work at least five days a week for 10 weeks. Dove (P) knew of the requirements of strict compliance and accepted the offer. Subsequently, on Thursday of the tenth week, Dove (P) contracted strep throat and told Rust he was unable to work. Rust told him he could come in to work and sleep through the remaining days or make up his absence on the weekend and still qualify for the bonus. Dove (P) refused and sought medical attention. Thereafter, Rust refused to pay the bonus because of Dove's (P) failure to fulfill the conditions. Dove (P) sued, contending he had substantially performed and was entitled to payment. The trial court found for Rose Acre Farms (D), and Dove (P) appealed.

**ISSUE:** Is a party bound to perform all conditions knowingly accepted under a contract, and unless such conditions are met, is performance by the other party not required?

**HOLDING AND DECISION:** (Neal, J.) Yes. A party is bound to perform all conditions knowingly accepted under a contract, and unless such conditions are met, performance by the other party is not required. A party is held to perform all conditions knowingly accepted under a contract, as prerequisite to recovery under the contract. In this case, completion of the project was not the exclusive theme of the bonus offer. Absenteeism was also a central theme, and such was known by Dove (P) prior to entering into the agreement. Even though the conditions were harsh, Dove (P) knowingly accepted them, and his failure to fulfill them precludes his recovery. Affirmed.

## ▶ ANALYSIS

There are two types of contractual conditions: conditions precedent and conditions subsequent. A party must fulfill a condition precedent before reciprocal performance by the other party becomes due. Condition subsequent acts to extinguish a duty to perform under the contract. The condition of attending work in the present case was a condition precedent to Dove's (P) right to payment. The failure of an insured to file a timely suit could release the insurer from its contractual indemnification obligation as a condition subsequent. The distinction between conditions precedent and subsequent is important from a procedural point of view. A party to whom a duty is owed bears the burden of proving satisfaction of a condition precedent, while a party attempting to avoid performance of a contractual duty must prove the occurrence of a condition subsequent that discharged such performance.

■■—■■

## Quicknotes

**CONDITION PRECEDENT** The happening of an uncertain occurrence which is necessary before a particular right or interest may be obtained or an action performed.

**CONDITION SUBSEQUENT** Potential future occurrence that extinguishes a party's obligation to perform pursuant to the contract.

**CONTRACTUAL CONDITIONS** Requirements of a contract; potential future occurrence upon which the existence of a legal obligation is dependent.

■■—■■

# In re Carter's Claim

[Parties not identified.]

Pa. Sup. Ct., 390 Pa. 365, 134 A.2d 908 (1957).

**NATURE OF CASE:** Appeal from judgment entered upon an arbitrator's award.

**FACT SUMMARY:** Kardon (P) sought to purchase the Edwin J. Schoettle Co. Kardon (P) alleged a breach of a warranty provision, but the seller (D) stated that the provision was a condition precedent and that Kardon's (P) only remedy was to refuse consummation of the sale.

## RULE OF LAW
An express condition precedent to a party's performance of a sales contract may not be treated as a warranty.

**FACTS:** Kardon (P) agreed to purchase the Edwin J. Schoettle Co. and its subsidiaries in which a certain amount of the purchase price was put in an escrow fund to indemnify Kardon (P) against the seller (D) for breach of the agreement to purchase. The agreement provided, among other things, under paragraph 5, the seller (D) represented, as a "warranty," that there had been no changes in the financial condition of the company other than in the ordinary course of business that were materially adverse. Also, under paragraph 9, the seller (D) stated that as a "condition precedent" to the buyer's obligation, the financial condition of the company should not be less favorable than what had been represented to Kardon (P) in an earlier statement. Kardon (P) sought to claim against the escrow fund, alleging that the financial condition on the date of purchase was less favorable than what had been represented earlier. The seller (D) contended that such fell under paragraph 9 as a "condition precedent" and not a warranty, and because Kardon (P) did not refuse consummation of the sale, he elected to waive the condition. The parties submitted to arbitration pursuant to their agreement, and the arbitrator awarded Kardon (P) around $3,000—significantly less than the approximately $70,000 he sought. Judgment for the arbitrator's award was entered, and appealed. The state's highest court granted review.

**ISSUE:** May an express condition precedent to a party's performance of a sales contract be treated as a warranty?

**HOLDING AND DECISION:** (Jones, J.) No. An express condition precedent to a party's performance of a sales contract may not be treated as a warranty. Here, the agreement distinguished between "warranties" and "conditions." The conditions-precedent in the agreement were to take place prior to the closing, and the buyer's obligation to perform was subject to their fulfillment. The argument that the financial condition of the company being less favorable than represented earlier constituted a breach of warranty is directly in conflict with the terms of the agreement in that it falls under the paragraph providing for "warranties." The paragraph on warranties provided for an entirely different situation where the financial condition of the company changed to be materially adverse other than in the ordinary course of business. Because Kardon (P) elected to accept the contract, the provisions of paragraph 9 on "conditions precedent" cease to be operative, and he is left with no right to recover damages. Affirmed.

## ANALYSIS

A warranty is an undertaking that a certain fact in relation to the subject of a contract is or shall be as it is stated or promised to be. Where a condition precedent is not fulfilled, the contract does not become effective as between the parties, but where there is a breach of warranty, the contract remains binding, but damages are recoverable for its breach. A condition precedent may be waived by a party whose obligations under the contract are dependent upon fulfillment of the condition. As such, once waived, the condition becomes extinguished, and neither party can assert it as a defense to his obligations or as a warranty for damages.

---

## Quicknotes

**ARBITRATION** An alternative resolution process where a dispute is heard and decided by a neutral third party, rather than through legal proceedings.

**BREACH OF WARRANTY** The breach of a promise made by one party to a contract on which the other party may rely, relieving that party from the obligation of determining whether the fact is true and indemnifying the other party from liability if that fact is shown to be false.

**CONDITION PRECEDENT** The happening of an uncertain occurrence which is necessary before a particular right or interest may be obtained or an action performed.

**ESCROW** A written contract held by a third party until the conditions therein are satisfied, at which time it is delivered to the obligee.

**EXPRESS CONDITION** A condition that is expressly stated in the terms of a written instrument.

**WARRANTY** An assurance by one party that another may rely on a certain representation of fact.

# Clark v. West

## Author (P) v. Publisher (D)

N.Y. Ct. App., 193 N.Y. 349 (1908).

**NATURE OF CASE:** Appeal from affirmance of demurrer in action for breach of contract and an accounting.

**FACT SUMMARY:** West (D) paid Clark (P) only $2 per page for writing a legal treatise, and Clark (P) demanded the $6 per page he had been promised if he quit drinking, alleging that West (D) had not objected when he continued to drink.

## RULE OF LAW

Waiver of a contract condition is not implied by mere acceptance of the proffered performance.

**FACTS:** West (D) entered into a contract with Clark (P) whereby Clark (P) was to write a multivolume treatise on corporations for West (D). The contract price was $6 per page if Clark (P) totally abstained from liquor during the contract or $2 per page if he drank. West (D) became aware that Clark (P) was drinking moderately during the term of the contract but made no objection. West (D) accepted Clark's (P) work and paid him $2 per page. Clark (P) sued for the difference, claiming that he was owed $6 per page. West (D) demurred, and both the trial court and the court of appeals sustained the demurrer. Clark (P) appealed, claiming that West (D) had waived the abstinence requirement and that the waiver was effective since abstinence was a mere condition precedent to West's (D) obligation to pay $6 per page.

**ISSUE:** Is waiver of a contract condition implied by mere acceptance of the proffered performance?

**HOLDING AND DECISION:** (Werner, J.) No. Waiver of a contract condition is not implied by mere acceptance of the proffered performance. A condition to a contract may be waived, but mere acceptance of performance does not constitute a waiver. While it is West's (D) contention that Clark's (P) abstinence was the consideration for the payment of $6 rather than $2, a careful analysis of the contract shows that it was the writing of the treatise, rather than abstinence, which was the bargained-for consideration. Since abstinence was not the consideration for the contract, it was a condition that could be waived without a new agreement based upon a good consideration. No formal agreement or additional consideration is required to waive a condition precedent to performance. West (D) received and accepted the bargained-for consideration, i.e., the treatise. If the condition was waived, then West (D) is liable for the $6 contract price, but mere silence and acceptance of performance will not be deemed a waiver of the condition. However, since

Clark (P) alleges an express waiver of the condition, he should be allowed to prove this at trial. The demurrer is therefore overruled and the case remanded for trial.

## ▶ ANALYSIS

Frequently, as in *Clark v. West,* it is difficult to determine whether one is dealing with a promise or a condition. Modification of a promise typically requires a new consideration, while the waiver of a condition does not. A condition may be described as qualifying a contractual duty by providing either that performance is not called for unless a stated event occurs or fails to occur or that performance may be suspended or terminated if a stated event occurs or fails to occur. Stated more simply, the condition is outside of and modifies the promised performance called for under the contract.

■■■

## Quicknotes

**BREACH OF CONTRACT** Unlawful failure by a party to perform its obligations pursuant to contract.

**DEMURRER** The assertion that the opposing party's pleadings are insufficient and that the demurring party should not be made to answer.

■■■

# Dynamic Machine Works, Inc. v. Machine & Electrical Consultants, Inc.

## Manufacturer (P) v. Distributor (D)

Mass. Sup. Jud. Ct., 444 Mass. 768, 831 N.E.2d 875 (2005).

**NATURE OF CASE:** Certified question from federal court in declaratory judgment action.

**FACT SUMMARY:** Dynamic Machine Works, Inc. (Dynamic) (P) ordered a machine from Machine & Electrical Consultants, Inc. (Machine) (D) to be delivered on a set date. The parties mutually extended the delivery date once and then Dynamic (P) extended the delivery date in writing a final time. Days after the final extension, Dynamic (P) unilaterally revoked the extension.

---

### 🏛 RULE OF LAW

(1) Under the Uniform Commercial Code, a buyer may not unilaterally retract a written extension that provides more time for the seller to cure defects in a delivered product absent reliance on the extension by the seller where the extension constitutes a modification of the agreement to purchase the product.

(2) Under the Uniform Commercial Code, a buyer may unilaterally retract a written extension that provides more time for the seller to cure defects in a delivered product where the extension constitutes a waiver of an executory portion of the agreement to purchase the product, the buyer provides reasonable notification that strict performance will be required, and the retraction would not be unjust in view of a material change of position in reliance on the waiver.

---

**FACTS:** Dynamic Machine Works, Inc. (Dynamic) (P) manufactures precision components for multiple industries. Machine & Electrical Consultants, Inc. (Machine) (D) distributes machinery. In January 2003, Dynamic (P) agreed to purchase a lathe from Machine (D). The lathe would be manufactured in Taiwan and Dynamic (P) agreed to make a down payment, partial payment upon delivery, and final payment upon acceptance. The lathe was to arrive in May 2003. Prior to June 2003, the parties agreed that the lathe was delayed due to the SARS epidemic in Taiwan. They executed extensions of the delivery date to September 19, 2003 with Machine (D) paying a $500 daily penalty for delays beyond that date. Machine (D) delivered the lathe on October 9, 2003 and spent November installing it. Dynamic (P), through its president, issued a letter to Machine's (D) president on December 9, 2003, extending the date to December 19, 2003. On December 10, 2003, Dynamic's (P) president learned the lathe would not meet

required specifications, so Dynamic (P) informed Machine (D) it would retract its latest extension. Dynamic (P) revoked acceptance of the lathe, requested the return of its down payment, demanded payment of penalty fees from Machine (D), and asked about removal of the lathe. Machine (D) had not materially relied on the latest extension. Dynamic (P) filed a declaratory judgment action based on breach of contract in state court, which was removed to federal district court. The district court certified the following question to the state's highest court: "Under the . . . Uniform Commercial Code, does a buyer have a right to retract a written extension allowing more time for the seller to cure defects in a delivered product absent reliance on the extension by the seller?"

**ISSUE:**

(1) Under the Uniform Commercial Code, may a buyer unilaterally retract a written extension that provides more time for the seller to cure defects in a delivered product absent reliance on the extension by the seller where the extension constitutes a modification of the agreement to purchase the product?

(2) Under the Uniform Commercial Code, may a buyer unilaterally retract a written extension that provides more time for the seller to cure defects in a delivered product where the extension constitutes a waiver of an executory portion of the agreement to purchase the product, the buyer provides reasonable notification that strict performance will be required, and the retraction would not be unjust in view of a material change of position in reliance on the waiver?

**HOLDING AND DECISION:** (Cordy, J.)

(1) No. Under the Uniform Commercial Code, a buyer may not unilaterally retract a written extension that provides more time for the seller to cure defects in a delivered product absent reliance on the extension by the seller where the extension constitutes a modification of the agreement to purchase the product.

(2) Yes. Under the Uniform Commercial Code (U.C.C.), a buyer may unilaterally retract a written extension that provides more time for the seller to cure defects in a delivered product where the extension constitutes a waiver of an executory portion of the agreement to purchase the product, the buyer provides reasonable notification that strict performance will be required, and the retraction would not be unjust in view of a material change of position in reliance on the waiver. The U.C.C. governs this contract for the sale of goods,

*Continued on next page.*

namely the lathe. The pertinent section of U.C.C. § 2-209 provides that a modification of the original agreement must be in writing if the modified agreement must satisfy the Statute of Frauds or if the original agreement requires such a writing, the modification must then be signed by both parties and needs no consideration. The section continues that retraction of a waiver of an executory portion of the agreement is allowed if reasonable notification is given to the other party and the other party had not materially relied on the waiver. "Waiver" and "modification" are undefined terms. State law defines waiver as intentionally relinquishing a known right. Modification requires action and agreement from both parties. Dynamic (P) argues that the December 9 extension letter is a waiver of the delivery time and not a modification of the contract terms. It points to language in the letter, such as "grant" rather than "agree," to demonstrate its unilateral action. This is primarily a fact question. The extension could be a waiver, because while a waiver can be inferred from action, it can also be in writing. The extension could be a modification because no consideration existed. This court's duty is only to answer the certified question, and does not need to decide whether the extension constituted a modification or a waiver.

## ▶ *ANALYSIS*

Parties must be wary when seeking to modify a contract governed by the Uniform Commercial Code (or a state's version of it). If the modification is ineffective, the action may constitute a waiver of the contract's nonessential terms.

▬■▬

## Quicknotes

**CERTIFIED QUESTION** A question that is taken from federal court to the state supreme court so that the court may rule on the issue or that is taken from a federal court of appeals to the United States Supreme Court.

**DECLARATORY JUDGMENT** A judgment of the court establishing the rights of the parties.

**EXECUTORY CONTRACT** A contract in which performance of an obligation has yet to be rendered.

**MODIFICATION** A change to the terms of a contract without altering its general purpose.

**WAIVER** The intentional or voluntary forfeiture of a recognized right.

▬■▬

# Ferguson v. Phoenix Assurance Company of New York

Insured (P) v. Insurer (D)

Kan. Sup. Ct., 189 Kan. 459, 370 P.2d 379 (1962).

**NATURE OF CASE:** Appeal from a plaintiff's verdict in a suit for breach of an insurance contract.

**FACT SUMMARY:** When Forrest Ferguson (P) made a claim to his insurer, Phoenix Assurance Company of New York (D), under a safe burglary provision of his storekeeper's policy, the latter denied the claim on the grounds that the evidence of entry was by visible marks on only one of the safe's doors.

## 🏛 RULE OF LAW
A rule of evidence imposed by an insurance policy provision, beyond the reasonable requirements necessary to prevent fraudulent claims, contravenes public policy.

**FACTS:** Forrest Ferguson (P) procured a "Storekeepers Burglary and Robbery Policy" from Phoenix Assurance Company of New York (Phoenix Assurance) (D) which contained a provision for recovery for burglary from a safe. The policy contained a provision permitting recovery only if there was evidence of violent entry by "visible marks" on the exterior of the safe. A burglary occurred. However, the evidence of violent entry was evidenced by visible marks on the exterior of the inner door of the safe, not on the exterior of the outer door of the safe. Phoenix Assurance (D) denied recovery under the policy. Ferguson (P) sued for breach of the insurance contract. The trial court granted recovery for Ferguson (P). Phoenix Assurance (D) appealed.

**ISSUE:** Does a rule of evidence imposed by an insurance policy provision, beyond the reasonable requirements necessary to prevent fraudulent claims, contravene public policy?

**HOLDING AND DECISION:** (Schroeder, J.) Yes. A rule of evidence imposed by an insurance policy provision, beyond the reasonable requirements necessary to prevent fraudulent claims, contravenes public policy. It is well established that insurance carriers can and must be able to select the risks they insure. However, a provision intended to determine the character of evidence necessary to show liability is another matter. Such a provision contravenes public policy when, as here, the statement of the rule in the policy itself, or its assertion by the insurance carrier, is designed to prevent recovery of an obviously justified claim. Here, money was taken from Ferguson's (P) safe by an admitted entry into the safe by actual force and violence, which was evidenced by visible marks upon the inner door of the safe. Under these circumstances, the assertion by his insurer, Phoenix Assurance (D), of the evidentiary requirement, that there be visible marks of force and violence upon the exterior of the outer door, is obviously designed to defeat recovery on a just claim under the policy which insured the felonious abstraction of money from within the safe, by a person making felonious entry into such safe by actual force and violence, where both doors of the safe were duly closed and locked. Had the insurance carrier desired to exclude loss by safe burglary where the combination of the outer door is worked by manipulation, such provision should have been incorporated under the "Exclusions" in the policy. Affirmed.

**DISSENT:** (Price, J.) concededly, this policy of insurance contains a restrictive "safe burglary" clause just as many other types of policies contain restrictions. The clause in question is plain, clear, and unambiguous, and, such being the case, should be enforced according to its terms in harmony with the universal rule pertaining to insurance contracts. This court has no business making another contract for the parties; its function is to enforce the contract as made.

## ▶ ANALYSIS

The court in *Ferguson* noted that there was in fact no provision in the insurance policy that force and violence were in fact necessary to gain entry through each of the doors of the safe.

---

## Quicknotes

**BREACH OF CONTRACT** Unlawful failure by a party to perform its obligations pursuant to contract.

# Palmer v. Fox

Real property seller (P) v. Real property buyer (D)

Mich. Sup. Ct., 274 Mich. 252, 264 N.W. 361 (1936).

**NATURE OF CASE:** Appeal from judgment for plaintiff in action to recover the balance due on a land sale contract.

**FACT SUMMARY:** Fox (D) refused to continue making payments on the land sale contract until Palmer (P) cinderized his street as he had covenanted in the contract.

## RULE OF LAW
Where conditions are concurrent and dependent, the failure of one party to perform excuses the other party's counterperformance.

**FACTS:** Palmer (P) sold Fox (D) an unimproved lot as an investment. Palmer (P) promised to make certain improvements in the subdivision. The land sale contract was to run for five years, after which Fox (D) would have paid for the land. Palmer (P) made all of the promised improvements except for cinderizing or graveling the street in front of Fox's (D) lot. Fox (D) stopped paying on the lot. Palmer (P) brought suit for the balance due under the contract. Fox (D) claimed that Palmer (P) had breached the contract by not paving the street, since, he argued, this was a dependent concurrent condition, and its breach excused Fox's (D) performance. Palmer (P) argued that the covenant was independent of Fox's (D) duty to pay and that it was an immaterial breach. The court found for Palmer (P).

**ISSUE:** Where conditions are concurrent and dependent, does the failure of one party to perform excuse the other party's counterperformance?

**HOLDING AND DECISION:** (Toy, J.) Yes. Where conditions are concurrent and dependent, the failure of one party to perform excuses the other party's counterperformance. First, the performance was concurrent. Both Fox's (D) payments and Palmer's (P) performance were to be tendered within five years. Next, Fox (D) was to surrender the contract at the end of five years for the deed. The parties must have contemplated that all covenants would have been completed by that time. Second, the conditions were dependent. There was no showing that the contract specified that they were independent or that the parties had otherwise contemplated that they be deemed independent. Since the acts are concurrent and the parties have not expressly or impliedly made them independent, they will be considered dependent. Third, this is a material breach. The promised improvements were a major consideration in inducing Fox (D) to purchase the property. Fox (D) was purchasing the property for invest-

ment purposes, and it seems unlikely that he would have purchased the lot if it were to remain unimproved. Where a party fails to perform a material dependent concurrent condition, the other party's counterperformance is excused. Therefore, Fox (D) was not in breach of the contract. Judgment reversed.

## ANALYSIS

An immaterial breach does not excuse performance. The only action available is for damages. Therefore, the fact that the bathrooms in a 40-story office building were painted the wrong color would not excuse the buyer's duty to pay for the building. Careful drafting of contracts eliminates most of these problems. Normally, the contract makes the duty of the buyer to pay independent of any breaches of covenant by the seller. Therefore, the buyer's only remedy for a breach is an action for damages.

## Quicknotes

**BREACH OF CONTRACT** Unlawful failure by a party to perform its obligations pursuant to contract.

**DAMAGES** Monetary compensation that may be awarded by the court to a party who has sustained injury or loss to his person, property or rights due to another party's unlawful act, omission or negligence.

**MATERIAL BREACH** Breach of a contract's terms by one party that is so substantial as to relieve the other party from its obligations pursuant thereto.

# Jacob & Youngs, Inc. v. Kent

Contractor (P) v. Property owner (D)

N.Y. Ct. App., 230 N.Y. 239, 129 N.E. 889 (1921).

**NATURE OF CASE:** Appeal from reversal of directed verdict for defendant in action for damages for breach of a construction contract.

**FACT SUMMARY:** Jacob & Youngs, Inc. (P) was hired to build a $77,000 country home for Kent (D). When the dwelling was completed, it was discovered that through an oversight, pipe not of Reading manufacture (though of comparable quality and price), which had been specified in the contract, was used. Kent (D) refused to make final payment of $3,483.46 upon learning of this.

🏛 **RULE OF LAW**
For damages in construction contracts, the owner is entitled merely to the difference between the value of the structure if built to specifications and the value it has as constructed.

**FACTS:** Jacob & Youngs, Inc. (Jacob) (P) built a country home for $77,000 for Kent (D) and sued for $3,483.46, which remained unpaid. Almost a year after completion, Kent (D) discovered that not all pipe in the home was of Reading manufacture, as specified in the contract. Kent (D) ordered the plumbing replaced, but as it was encased in the walls, except in those spots where it necessarily remained exposed, Jacob (P) refused to replace the pipe, stating that the pipe used was of comparable price and quality. The omission was neither fraudulent nor willful and was due to oversight of a subcontractor. Kent (D) refused to pay the balance of the construction cost still due, and Jacob (P) sued for payment. The trial court entered a directed verdict for Kent (D), but the state's intermediate appellate court reversed. The state's highest court granted review.

**ISSUE:** For damages in construction contracts, is the owner entitled merely to the difference in value of the structure built to specifications and the value it has as constructed?

**HOLDING AND DECISION:** (Cardozo, J.) Yes. For damages in construction contracts, the owner is entitled merely to the difference between the value of the structure if built to specifications and the value it has as constructed. Where the significance of the default or omission is grievously out of proportion to the oppression of the forfeiture, the breach is considered to be trivial and innocent. A change will not be tolerated if it is so dominant and pervasive as to frustrate the purpose of the contract. The contractor cannot install anything he believes to be just as good. It is a matter of degree judged by the purpose to be served, the desire to be gratified, the excuse for deviation from the letter, and the cruelty of enforced adherence.

Under the circumstances, the measure of damages should not be the cost of replacing the pipe, which would be great. Instead, the difference in value between the dwelling as specified and the dwelling as constructed should be the measure even though it may be nominal or nothing. Usually, the owner is entitled to the cost of completion but not where it is grossly unfair and out of proportion to the good to be obtained. This simply is a rule to promote justice when there is substantial performance with trivial deviation. Affirmed, with judgment absolute directed for the plaintiff.

**DISSENT:** (McLaughlin, J.) Jacob (P) failed to perform as specified. It makes no difference why Kent (D) wanted a particular kind of pipe. Failure to use the kind of pipe specified was either intentional or due to gross neglect, which amounted to the same thing. Therefore, the majority's reliance on the rule of substantial performance, with damages for unsubstantial omissions, is inapplicable under the facts of the case.

▶ **ANALYSIS**

Substantial performance cannot occur where the breach is intentional, as it is the antithesis of material breach. The part unperformed must not destroy the purpose or value of the contract. Because here there is a dissatisfied landowner who stands to retain the defective structure built on his land, there arises the problem of unjust enrichment. Usually, it would appear that the owner would pocket the damages he collected rather than remedying the defect by tearing out the wrong pipe and replacing it with the specified pipe. The owner would have a home substantially in compliance and a sum of money greatly in excess of the harm suffered by him. Note that under the doctrine of de minimis, not curat lex, that is, that the law is not concerned with trifles, trivial defects, even if willful, will be ignored. The party who claims substantial performance has still breached the contract and is liable for damages but in a lesser amount than for a willful breach.

■■■

**Quicknotes**

**BREACH OF CONTRACT** Unlawful failure by a party to perform its obligations pursuant to contract.

**DAMAGES** Monetary compensation that may be awarded by the court to a party who has sustained injury or loss to

*Continued on next page.*

his person, property or rights due to another party's unlawful act, omission or negligence.

**DIRECTED VERDICT**  A verdict ordered by the court in a jury trial.

**SUBSTANTIAL PERFORMANCE**  Performance of all the essential obligations pursuant to an agreement.

**UNJUST ENRICHMENT**  Principle that one should not be unjustly enriched at the expense of another.

# United States v. Wegematic Corp.
Federal government (P) v. Government contractor (D)

360 F.2d 674 (2d Cir. 1966).

**NATURE OF CASE:** Appeal from damages award in action for breach of a contract for the sale of goods.

**FACT SUMMARY:** In response to an invitation from the Federal Reserve Board of the United States (United States) (P), Wegematic Corp. (D) submitted a bid to supply an ALWAC 800 computer. Delivery, which was offered nine months from the date of the contract, was received, but it appeared that the ALWAC 800 was beyond the technology of the day and would not be able to be built. United States (P) obtained another computer and sued for the extra cost.

## 🏛 RULE OF LAW
Practical impossibility is not a defense to a breach of contract claim based on nondelivery of a new technology where the technology provider has assumed the risk of the technological breakthrough.

**FACTS:** In June 1956, the Federal Reserve Board of the United States (United States) (P) invited five companies to submit bids on a digital computing system, stressing the importance of early delivery. Wegematic Corp. (D), a relative newcomer in the field, proposed the sale or lease of an ALWAC 800, billed as a revolutionary concept and a great step beyond its ALWAC III-E, with which it had enjoyed great success. Delivery was promised within nine months of receipt of contract or purchase order. United States (P) ordered an ALWAC 800 for $231,800 in September 1956 for delivery in June 1957, with liquidated damages of $100 per day for delay. If Wegematic (D) failed in any provision, the Government (P) could contract elsewhere and charge the extra cost to Wegematic (D). In March 1957, Wegematic (D) requested a delay in delivery for redesign and in April suggested delivery in October with waiver of damages. After other requests for delay, Wegematic (D) stated that development of the computer was beyond technological capacities. United States (P), on October 6, 1958, obtained an IBM 650 serving relatively the same purpose as the ALWAC 800 at a rental of $102,000 with an option to purchase for $410,450, and sued for damages. The district court awarded damages to the United States (P), and the court of appeals granted review.

**ISSUE:** Is practical impossibility a defense to a breach of contract claim based on nondelivery of a new technology where the technology provider has assumed the risk of the technological breakthrough?

**HOLDING AND DECISION:** (Friendly, J.) No. Practical impossibility is not a defense to a breach of contract claim based on nondelivery of a new technology

where the technology provider has assumed the risk of the technological breakthrough. While under Uniform Commercial Code § 2-615 a delay in delivery or nondelivery is not a breach under a sales contract if performance has been made impracticable by the occurrence of a contingency, the nonoccurrence of which was a basic assumption on which the contract was made, the risk of the technological breakthrough did not fall on the purchaser. This was because it was reasonable to suppose that it already had occurred or, at least, that Wegematic (D) had assured the Government (P) that it would be found in order to permit delivery. The purchaser otherwise would be forced to accept whatever the contractor develops while he had selected the contractor on a different basis. If the contractor's technological gamble failed, the purchaser would still have to accept it. This does not appear to be the understanding particularly where Wegematic (D) agreed to liquidated damages for delay and to allowing the Government (P) to find another source in case delivery could not be made. Affirmed.

## ▶ ANALYSIS
Cases involving manufacture of new products or the use of new manufacturing processes mostly involve government contract cases, and, generally, where compliance has proved impossible under technology of the day, the contractor has been held to have assumed the risk that production was possible. If the Government has provided detailed specifications for manufacturing (as opposed to the specifications which the end product must meet), the Government has warranted that the specifications will meet the desired result. If the Government has merely suggested the manufacturing process, it has been held not to have warranted the process. Of course, when as to a material fact there is mutual mistake, the risk of which was not assumed, reallocation is justified if it appears that the Government would have assented to it at the outset if it had known the truth.

■■■

## Quicknotes
**BREACH OF CONTRACT** Unlawful failure by a party to perform its obligations pursuant to contract.

**IMPOSSIBILITY** A doctrine relieving the parties to a contract from liability for nonperformance of their duties thereunder, if the subject matter of the contract ceases to exist, a person essential to the performance of the

*Continued on next page.*

contract is deceased, or the service or goods contracted for has become illegal.

**LIQUIDATED DAMAGES** An amount of money specified in a contract representing the damages owed in the event of breach.

**MATERIAL FACT** A fact without the existence of which a contract would not have been entered.

**MUTUAL MISTAKE** A mistake by both parties to a contract, who are in agreement as to what the contract terms should be, but the agreement as written fails to reflect that common intent; such contracts are voidable or subject to reformation.

# Taylor v. Caldwell

## Concert promoter (P) v. Music hall owner (D)

K.B., 3 B. & S. 826, 122 Eng. Rep. 309 (1863).

**NATURE OF CASE:** Action for damages for breach of a contract for letting of premises.

**FACT SUMMARY:** Taylor (P) contracted to let Caldwell's (D) hall and gardens for four fetes and concerts, for four days, for £100 per day. Taylor (P) expended money in preparation and for advertising, but Caldwell (D) could not perform when the hall burned down without his fault.

### 🏛 RULE OF LAW
In contracts in which the performance depends on the continued existence of a given person or thing, a condition is implied that the impossibility of performance arising from the perishing of the person or thing shall excuse the performance.

**FACTS:** By written agreement, Caldwell (D) agreed to let the Surrey Gardens and Musical Hall at Newington, Surrey for four days for giving four "Grand Concerts" and "Day and Night Fetes." Taylor (P) was to pay £100 at the end of each day. Before any concerts were held, the hall was completely destroyed by fire without any fault of either of the parties. Taylor (P) alleged that the fire and destruction of the hall was a breach and that it resulted in his losing large sums in preparation and advertising for the concerts and fetes.

**ISSUE:** In contracts in which the performance depends on the continued existence of a given person or thing, is a condition implied that the impossibility of performance arising from the perishing of the person or thing shall excuse the performance?

**HOLDING AND DECISION:** (Lord Blackburn, J.) Yes. In contracts in which the performance depends on the continued existence of a given person or thing, a condition is implied that the impossibility of performance arising from the perishing of the person or thing shall excuse the performance. Caldwell (D) was excused from performance. First, the agreement was not a lease but a contract to "let." The entertainments that were planned could not be made without the existence of the hall. Ordinarily, when there is a positive contract to do something that is not unlawful, the contractor must perform or pay damages for not doing it even if an unforeseen accident makes performance unduly burdensome or even impossible. This is so when the contract is absolute and positive and not subject to either express or implied conditions and that it appears that the parties must have known from the beginning that the contract could not be fulfilled unless a particular, specified thing continued to exist; and when

there is no express or implied warranty that the thing shall exist, the contract is not positive and absolute. It is subject to the implied condition that the parties shall be excused in case, before breach, performance becomes impossible from the perishing of the thing without fault of the contractor. This appears to be within the intent of the parties when they enter into a contract. The excuse from the contract's performance is implied in law because from the nature of the contract it is apparent it was made on the basis of the continued existence of the particular, specified thing. Judgment for the defendants.

### ▶ ANALYSIS

It was important for Judge Blackburn not to find the agreement to be a lease; otherwise, the decision would come within direct conflict of *Paradine v. Jane*, K.B., 82 Eng. Rep. 897 (1647), which held that a lease must be performed to the letter despite unforeseen hardship or good fortune. Next, performance is excused only if the destruction of the specified thing is without fault. Had Caldwell (D) been shown to be guilty of arson in the destruction of the hall, he would not have been excused. If there is impossibility of performance due to no one's fault, the one seeking to enforce performance takes the risk. It might be said that the court was actually apportioning the loss if the contract was, in effect, a joint venture with Taylor (P) paying Caldwell (D) £100 out of each day's admission fees to the concerts [Caldwell (D) was supplying the band]. The view of this case is found in Uniform Commercial Code § 2-613, where for total destruction of the specified thing, the contract is avoided, or, if the specified thing is goods that have so deteriorated as to no longer conform, the contract can be avoided or the goods can be accepted with an allowance for their lesser value. Note that there is not a satisfactory distinction between a contract to let and a lease.

◼◼◼

### Quicknotes

**BREACH OF CONTRACT** Unlawful failure by a party to perform its obligations pursuant to contract.

**DAMAGES** Monetary compensation that may be awarded by the court to a party who has sustained injury or loss to his person, property or rights due to another party's unlawful act, omission or negligence.

**IMPOSSIBILITY** A doctrine relieving the parties to a contract from liability for nonperformance of their duties

*Continued on next page.*

thereunder, if the subject matter of the contract ceases to exist, a person essential to the performance of the contract is deceased, or the service or goods contracted for has become illegal.

---

Molasses purchaser (P) v. ...

**RULE OF LAW**
If the promisor is in some respects responsible for the event that makes performance of his promise impossible, and later no steps to alleviate the impossibility, the duty of performance is not excused.

**ISSUE:** If the promisor is in some respects responsible for the event that makes performance of his promise impossible, and takes no steps to alleviate the impossibility, is his duty of performance excused?

**HOLDING AND DECISION:** (Cardozo, C.J.) No. If the promisor is in some respect responsible for the event that makes performance of his promise impossible, and takes no steps to alleviate the impossibility, his duty of performance is not excused. Performance here was not impossibly conditioned by the refinery's producing enough molasses to fill Alcohol Co.'s (P) order, the contract made no reference to the fact of the refinery's ... did not keep ...

# Canadian Industrial Alcohol Co. v. Dunbar Molasses Co.

Molasses purchaser (P) v. Molasses seller (D)

N.Y. Ct. App., 258 N.Y. 194, 179 N.E. 383 (1932).

**NATURE OF CASE:** Appeal from judgment for plaintiff in action for damages for breach of a contract for the sale of goods.

**FACT SUMMARY:** Canadian Industrial Alcohol Co. (P) contracted to buy Dunbar Molasses Co.'s (Dunbar) (D) usual allotment of refined blackstrap molasses, about 1,500,000 wine gallons, Dunbar (D) received from a sugar refinery. That year, Dunbar (D) received much less than the amount contracted, less than 500,000 gallons in all, and could not fulfill its contracted quantity.

> ## ⚖ RULE OF LAW
> If the promisor is in some respects responsible for the event that makes performance of his promise impossible, and takes no steps to alleviate the impossibility, his duty of performance is not excused.

**FACTS:** At the end of 1927, Canadian Industrial Alcohol Co. (Alcohol Co.) (P) contracted to buy from Dunbar Molasses Co. (Dunbar) (D) about 1,500,000 wine gallons of refined blackstrap molasses, about 60 percent sugar, of the usual run from the National Sugar Refinery, Yonkers, New York. Delivery was to begin April 1, 1928, "to be spread out during the warm weather." The refinery that year produced far less than its capacity, less than a half-million gallons. Dunbar (D), which had no contract with the refinery, shipped its entire allotment, 344,083 gallons, to Alcohol Co. (P). Dunbar (D) did not attempt to enter into a contract that would have assured it would get a sufficient supply of molasses, nor did it inform Alcohol Co. (P) that it did not have such a contract. Alcohol Co. (P) sued for damages, but Dunbar (D) contended that its duty was conditioned by an implied term: the refinery's producing enough molasses to fill Alcohol Co.'s (P) order. Judgment was rendered for Alcohol Co (P), and the state's highest court granted review.

**ISSUE:** If the promisor is in some respects responsible for the event that makes performance of his promise impossible, and takes no steps to alleviate the impossibility, is his duty of performance excused?

**HOLDING AND DECISION:** (Cardozo, C.J.) No. If the promisor is in some respects responsible for the event that makes performance of his promise impossible, and takes no steps to alleviate the impossibility, his duty of performance is not excused. Performance here was not implicitly conditioned by the refinery's producing enough molasses to fill Alcohol Co.'s (P) order. The contract as read in the light of circumstances did not keep

Dunbar's (D) duty within such narrow boundaries. Dunbar (D) never even attempted to get a contract with the refinery between the time of acceptance and the start of shipments. Accordingly, contributory fault is implied to Dunbar (D), which put its faith in the mere chance that the refinery's output would remain as in past years. Dunbar's (D) customer did not take that chance; only Dunbar (D) did. Affirmed.

## ▶ ANALYSIS

There is no one rule for allowing the unforeseen risk, but the basis of all existing rules is the attempt to place the risk where the parties would have if they had foreseen it. If it is reasonably foreseeable, the promisor will have been deemed to have accepted it. Excuse of performance on grounds of impossibility involves, in the interests of justice, the creation of a condition. If the promisor is in some respects responsible for the event making performance impossible, that is, if he is guilty of contributory fault, performance will not be excused. Had the refinery in this case been destroyed without the fault of Dunbar (D), Dunbar (D) would have been excused from performance. The destruction of the refinery would not have been a risk assumed by the promisor, Dunbar (D). Even had Dunbar (D) made a contract with the refinery, it would still appear that Alcohol Co. (P) would have a cause of action and that Dunbar (D) would still not be excused, as Dunbar (D) would have a cause of action against the refinery. The refinery would then have been liable for Dunbar's (D) loss.

---

## Quicknotes

**BREACH OF CONTRACT** Unlawful failure by a party to perform its obligations pursuant to contract.

**DAMAGES** Monetary compensation that may be awarded by the court to a party who has sustained injury or loss to his person, property or rights due to another party's unlawful act, omission or negligence.

**IMPOSSIBILITY** A doctrine relieving the parties to a contract from liability for nonperformance of their duties thereunder, if the subject matter of the contract ceases to exist, a person essential to the performance of the contract is deceased, or the service or goods contracted for has become illegal.

# Dills v. Town of Enfield

Developer (P) v. Municipality (D)

Conn. Sup. Ct., 210 Conn. 705, 557 A.2d 517 (1989).

**NATURE OF CASE:** Appeal from judgment for defendant in action for damages for breach of a contract for the sale of land.

**FACT SUMMARY:** Town of Enfield (D) sold land to Dills (P) to be developed into an industrial park, but when Dills (P) later terminated the contract after he could not obtain financing, Enfield (D) refused to return his deposit, and Dills (P) filed suit for breach of contract.

> 🏛 **RULE OF LAW**
> The occurrence of a foreseeable event that was contemplated by the parties does not render the obligor's performance impractical and thereby excused.

**FACTS:** Town of Enfield (D) agreed to convey to Dills (P) property to be developed into an industrial park. The agreement required Dills (P) to submit acceptable construction plans and proof of financial capacity. The contract allowed Dills (P) to withdraw and reclaim his $100,000 deposit if, after approval of the plans, he failed to get financing. The contract also allowed Enfield (D) to terminate the contract and withhold the deposit if Dills (P) failed to submit an acceptable construction plan. Dills (P) failed to submit an acceptable construction plan when he could not obtain the financing. Enfield (D) voted to terminate the contract, but three days later Dills (P) withdrew from the contract himself. Enfield (D) refused to return the deposit, and Dills (P) filed suit. The case was decided by a referee who held for Dills (P). The trial court rejected the decision and held for Enfield (D). Dills (P) appealed.

**ISSUE:** Does the occurrence of a foreseeable event that was contemplated by the parties render the obligor's performance impractical and thereby excused?

**HOLDING AND DECISION:** (Peters, C.J.) No. The occurrence of a foreseeable event that was contemplated by the parties does not render the obligor's performance impractical and thereby excused. A party who wants his performance to be excused has to show that the nonoccurrence of the event was a basic assumption of the contract. Here, the parties expressly contemplated the financial difficulties that Dills (P) might encounter. Thus, Dills's (P) failure to obtain financing was foreseeable and contemplated at the time of the contract and cannot excuse his performance, regardless of how costly that will be to Dills (P). Affirmed.

> ▶ **ANALYSIS**

It is necessary to learn which party assumed the risk of the occurrence of an event in order to determine whether its

nonoccurrence was a basic presumption of the contract. The case above was one dealing with the sale of land and thus outside the Uniform Commercial Code The doctrine of impracticability, embodied in Uniform Commercial Code § 2-615, concerning the sale of goods, should be referred to for the approach to be taken to the events which may or may not excuse performance of commercial sales contracts for items other than real property.

---

## Quicknotes

**BREACH OF CONTRACT** Unlawful failure by a party to perform its obligations pursuant to contract.

**DAMAGES** Monetary compensation that may be awarded by the court to a party who has sustained injury or loss to his person, property or rights due to another party's unlawful act, omission or negligence.

# Centex Corporation v. Dalton

Investor (D) v. Finder (P)

Tex. Sup. Ct., 840 S.W.2d 952 (1992).

**NATURE OF CASE:** Appeal from affirmance of summary judgment for plaintiff in action for breach of contract and liquidated damages.

**FACT SUMMARY:** Centex Corporation (D) contended that its contract with Dalton (P), under which it was to pay Dalton (P) a $750,000 finder's fee, was rendered invalid and unenforceable by a governmental regulation that made the payment of the fee illegal.

## RULE OF LAW
Government regulations that make performance of a contract illegal render the contract impracticable, and, therefore, unenforceable.

**FACTS:** Centex Corporation (D) sought to acquire thrift institutions, and sought Dalton's (P) assistance in doing so, promising in a letter agreement to pay him a $750,000 finder's fee if his assistance resulted in the acquisition by Centex (D) of certain thrifts. The Federal Home Loan Bank Board (Bank Board) initially told Centex (D) that its payment to Dalton (P) would be acceptable, but five days after Centex (D) and Dalton (P) entered their agreement, Centex (D) learned that the Bank Board would not permit the payment of the fees. Centex (D), without informing Dalton (P) of this change, went ahead with the acquisition of the thrifts that Dalton (P) had found for it. Subsequently, the Bank Board adopted regulations prohibiting the payment of finder's fees. Even though Dalton (P) had performed, Centex (D) refused to pay him, on the ground that the Bank Board's regulations prohibited it from doing so and invalidated the contract. Dalton (P) brought suit, and the trial court entered summary judgment for him, which the state's intermediate appellate court affirmed. The state's highest court granted review.

**ISSUE:** Do government regulations that make performance of a contract illegal, render the contract impracticable, and, therefore, unenforceable?

**HOLDING AND DECISION:** (Gammage, J.) Yes. Government regulations that make performance of a contract illegal render the contract impracticable, and, therefore, unenforceable. The rule of impracticability is that where a party's performance is made impracticable by the occurrence of an event the non-occurrence of which was a basic assumption, on which the contract was made, his duty to render that performance is discharged. The Bank Board's regulation here is such an event, and Centex's (D) performance is excused by the doctrine of impossibility. Here, the impossibility is due to illegality, and the performance of the contract is excused by the

supervening impossibility caused by the change in the law. The application of a foreseeability test to determine how to allocate the burden of risk and which party must pay for the unanticipated occurrence is inapposite, since regardless of foreseeability of the Bank Board's regulation, Centex (D) cannot be required to pay. As a procedural matter, because Dalton (P) failed to plead quantum meruit as an alternative ground for recovery in the trial court, although he had the opportunity to do so, he is barred from doing so now. Also, Dalton's (P) being paid was conditioned on the Bank Board's approval of the acquisition by Centex (D) of the thrifts, so it cannot be said that Centex's (D) duty to pay him arose before the Bank Board rendered its prohibition. Dalton's (P) right to enforce the contract never accrued because the condition precedent of the Bank Board's approval was accompanied by its prohibition of the payment. Reversed.

**DISSENT:** (Mauzy, J.) The majority, which notes the injustice brought about by its decision, nonetheless fails to provide an equitable remedy for the injustice, and Centex (D) reaps a windfall. Here, Centex (D) proceeded with its acquisition without informing Dalton (P) of the Bank Board's changed position. If it had, Dalton (P) might have had the opportunity to appeal the Bank Board's decision. Also, although it does not seem that Centex (D) sought the prohibition, it also did not attempt to challenge it. Centex (D) could have chosen not to proceed with the acquisition on the new terms set by the Bank Board, but because it decided to proceed on the new terms, its resulting inconsistent obligations should be its burden, not Dalton's (P). The consequence of the majority's decision is that those who are in a position to influence regulatory policymaking may reap windfalls by escaping their obligations through changed regulations. The case should be remanded so Dalton (P) can make a case for an equitable remedy.

## ANALYSIS

The risk allocation test that the court in this case bypasses is expressed in Restatement (Second) of Contracts § 264, which says: "If the performance of a duty is made impracticable by having to comply with a domestic or foreign governmental regulation or order, that regulation or order is an event the non-occurrence of which was a basic assumption on which the contract was made." This gives the party seeking relief a presumption that both parties assumed that the law would not change, and, consequently,

*Continued on next page.*

the other party has the burden of rebutting this presumption. Of course, if the party seeking relief acted in bad faith, or seeks the change in the law [as the dissent hints Centex (D) may have done], relief will be denied.

---

## Quicknotes

**BAD FAITH** Conduct that is intentionally misleading or deceptive.

**BREACH OF CONTRACT** Unlawful failure by a party to perform its obligations pursuant to contract.

**IMPOSSIBILITY** A doctrine relieving the parties to a contract from liability for nonperformance of their duties thereunder, if the subject matter of the contract ceases to exist, a person essential to the performance of the contract is deceased, or the service or goods contracted for has become illegal.

**IMPRACTICABILITY** A doctrine relieving the parties to a contract from liability for nonperformance of their duties thereunder, if the subject matter of the contract ceases to exist.

**LIQUIDATED DAMAGES** An amount of money specified in a contract representing the damages owed in the event of breach.

**QUANTUM MERUIT** Equitable doctrine allowing recovery for labor and materials provided by one party, even though no contract was entered into, in order to avoid unjust enrichment by the benefited party.

**SUMMARY JUDGMENT** Judgment rendered by a court in response to a motion made by one of the parties, claiming that the lack of a question of material fact in respect to an issue warrants disposition of the issue without consideration by the jury.

**WINDFALL** Sudden gain.

# Kaiser-Francis Oil Co. v. Producer's Gas Co.

Gas well owner (P) v. Gas company (D)

870 F.2d 563 (10th Cir. 1989).

**NATURE OF THE CASE:** Appeal from partial summary judgment denying liability for breach of contract.

**FACT SUMMARY:** Producer's Gas Co. (D) agreed to take or pay for certain quantities of gas that were partially owned by Kaiser-Francis Oil Co. (P), but breached the contract when it refused to take or pay for the gas due to a decrease in market demand.

---

**RULE OF LAW**
Fluctuations in market demand or price of goods are not unexpected events excusing an obligor's promised performance.

---

**FACTS:** Producer's Gas Co. (PGC) (D) entered into two contracts with Kaiser-Francis Oil Co. (P), a partial owner of the gas wells, to take or pay for certain quantity of gas to be pumped from the wells. Provisions in both contracts stated that neither party would be liable for breach if their performance was affected by an unexpected event. PGC (D), relying on these provisions, did not take or pay for the agreed-upon quantity when the gas market price decreased. Kaiser-Francis (P) filed suit and moved for summary judgment, arguing that market demand is not an unexpected event excusing PGC's (D) performance. Partial summary judgment was granted on liability, and PGC (D) appealed.

**ISSUE:** Are fluctuations in market demand or price of goods unexpected events excusing an obligor's promised performance?

**HOLDING AND DECISION:** (Baldock, J.) No. Fluctuations in market demand or price of goods are not unexpected events excusing an obligor's promised performance. The state's highest court, in interpreting contractual force majeure provisions, similar to the ones in the instant case, has held that a decline in the market price of goods or inability to make a profit after the sale of goods are not unexpected events. Since the seller is the one who bears the risk of production, it is the buyer who should bear the risk of market demand. Affirmed.

---

**⟩ ANALYSIS**

Force majeure provisions were not meant to create a buffer against the normal risks involved in a contractual relationship. Seller gains at the expense of the buyer when the market price has decreased, while the buyer gains at the expense of the seller when the market price has increased.

Thus, fluctuations in market price are normal risks taken by all parties to a contract.

## Quicknotes

**BREACH OF CONTRACT** Unlawful failure by a party to perform its obligations pursuant to contract.

**FORCE MAJEURE CLAUSE** Clause pursuant to an oil and gas lease, relieving the lessee from liability for breach of the lease if the party's performance is impeded as the result of a natural cause that could not have been prevented.

**PARTIAL SUMMARY JUDGMENT** Judgment rendered by a court in response to a motion by one of the parties, claiming that the lack of a question of material fact in respect to one of the issues warrants disposition of that issue without going to the jury.

# Paradine v. Jane

Lessor (P) v. Lessee (D)

K.B., Aleyn, 26, 82 Eng. Rep. 897 (1647).

**NATURE OF CASE:** Action on a lease for rent past due.

**FACT SUMMARY:** Jane (D) argued that he should not have to pay rent owing on land he leased from Paradine (P) because he had been deprived of the land's use when it was occupied by the invading army of German Prince Rupert.

## 🏛 RULE OF LAW
When a party by his own contract creates a charge or duty upon himself, he is bound to make it good notwithstanding any frustration because he might have provided against such frustration in the contract.

**FACTS:** Paradine (P) brought suit upon a lease for years declaring that Jane (D) had failed to pay rent for three years on the lands held under the lease. Jane (D) answered that the lands had been occupied by the invading army of Prince Rupert of Germany and that, as a result, Jane (D) had been unable to take the profits from the land. Jane (D) argued that he was frustrated in the performance of his duties under the lease.

**ISSUE:** When a party by his own contract creates a charge or duty upon himself, is he bound to make it good notwithstanding any frustration because he might have provided against such frustration in the contract?

**HOLDING AND DECISION:** [Judge not stated in casebook excerpt.] Yes. When a party by his own contract creates a charge or duty upon himself, he is bound to make it good notwithstanding any frustration because he might have provided against such frustration in the contract. Where a lessee has agreed to repair the premises, even if the premises are burned down by lightning or destroyed by war, the lessee nevertheless has the obligation to repair the premises "Now the rent is a duty created by the parties . . . and had there been a covenant to pay it, there had been no question but the lessee must have made it good, notwithstanding the interruption by enemies, for the law would not protect him beyond his own agreement." Just as the lessee is entitled to any "casual" profits he might incidentally receive from the lease, so too must the lessee bear the risk of "casual" losses, such as those arising from war. Judgment for Paradine (P).

## ▶ ANALYSIS

Another report of this same case said that the decision was placed principally on the ground that "[i]f the tenant for years covenants to pay rent, though the lands let him be surrounded with water, yet he is chargeable with the rent, much more here." Style 47, 82 Eng. Rep. 519 (1647). This case is cited as the leading case in support of the strict seventh century English Rule that impossibility will not be recognized as an excuse for the promisor's nonperformance of his duty. Corbin writes that Jane (D) had no covenant of quiet enjoyment. "The agreed equivalent for the defendant's promise to pay rent was the conveyance of the leasehold property interest and delivery of possession. There was merely a frustration of the tenant's purpose of enjoying the profits of use and occupation." 6 Corbin § 1322.

## Quicknotes

**COVENANT OF QUIET ENJOYMENT** A promise contained in a lease or a deed that the tenant or grantee will enjoy unimpaired use of the property.

**FRUSTRATION OF PURPOSE** A doctrine relieving the parties to a contract from liability for nonperformance of their duties thereunder when the purpose of the agreement ceases to exist due to circumstances not subject to either party's control.

**IMPOSSIBILITY** A doctrine relieving the parties to a contract from liability for nonperformance of their duties thereunder, if the subject matter of the contract ceases to exist, a person essential to the performance of the contract is deceased, or the service or goods contracted for has become illegal.

# Krell v. Henry

Licensor (P) v. Licensee (D)

K.B., Ct. App., 2 K.B. 740 (1903).

**NATURE OF CASE:** Appeal from judgment for defendant in action for damages for breach of a contract for a license for use.

**FACT SUMMARY:** Henry (D) paid a deposit of £25 to Krell (P) for the use of his apartment in Pall Mall, London, for the purpose of a viewing sight for King Edward VII's coronation procession. The King became ill, causing a delay of the coronation, upon which Henry (D) refused to pay a £50 balance, for which Krell (P) sued.

## 🏛 RULE OF LAW
Where the object of one of the parties is the basis upon which both parties contract, the duties of performance are constructively conditioned upon the attainment of that object.

**FACTS:** In two letters of June 20, 1902, Henry (D) contracted through Krell's (P) agent, Bisgood, to use Krell's (P) flat in Pall Mall, London, to view the coronation procession of King Edward VII, which had been advertised to pass along Pall Mall. The contract made no mention of this purpose. The period of use of the flat was the daytime only of June 26, 27, 1902, for £75, £25 paid in deposit, with the £50 remainder due on June 24, 1902. Henry (D) became aware of the availability of Krell's (P) flat, as an announcement to that effect had been made, which was reiterated by Krell's (P) housekeeper, who showed Henry (D) the rooms. When the king became very ill, the coronation was delayed, and Henry (D) refused to pay the £50 balance, for which Krell (P) brought suit. The trial court held for Henry (D), and Krell (P) appealed.

**ISSUE:** Where the object of one of the parties is the basis upon which both parties contract, are the duties of performance constructively conditioned upon the attainment of that object?

**HOLDING AND DECISION:** (Lord Williams, J.) Yes. Where the object of one of the parties is the basis upon which both parties contract, the duties of performance are constructively conditioned upon the attainment of that object. It can be inferred from the surrounding circumstances that the rooms were taken for the purpose of viewing the processions and that that was the foundation of the contract. It was not a lease of the rooms—they could not be used at night—but a license for use for a particular purpose. With the defeat of the purpose to the contract, the performance is excused. Appeal dismissed.

## ▶ ANALYSIS

This case is an extension of *Taylor v. Caldwell,* 3 B.&S. 826, 122 Eng. Rep. (K.B. 1863), and as in that case, it was necessary to remove the roadblock of a lease in order to avoid a conflict with *Paradine v. Jane,* K.B., 82 Eng. Rep. 897 (1647). The rule explained here is "frustration of purpose" or "commercial frustration." It has not been made clear whether this doctrine rests upon the failure of consideration or the allocation of the risks. While there is a frustration, performance is not impossible. No constructive condition of performance has failed, as Krell (P) made no promise that the condition would occur. Rather, a constructive condition based upon the attainment of the purpose or object has arisen. Note that the frustration should be total or nearly total, though that is a matter of degree.

━━■■■━━

## Quicknotes

**BREACH OF CONTRACT** Unlawful failure by a party to perform its obligations pursuant to contract.

**DAMAGES** Monetary compensation that may be awarded by the court to a party who has sustained injury or loss to his person, property or rights due to another party's unlawful act, omission or negligence.

**FRUSTRATION OF PURPOSE** A doctrine relieving the parties to a contract from liability for nonperformance of their duties thereunder when the purpose of the agreement ceases to exist due to circumstances not subject to either party's control.

━━■■■━━

# Washington State Hop Producers, Inc. v. Goschie Farms, Inc.

Hop base trust (P) v. Hop base purchaser (D)

Wash. Sup. Ct., 112 Wash. 2d 694, 773 P.2d 70 (1989).

**NATURE OF THE CASE:** Appeal from affirmance of summary judgment excusing contractual performance.

**FACT SUMMARY:** Goschie Farms, Inc. (D) contracted with Washington State Hop Producers, Inc. (P) to purchase a hop base but later refused to perform the contract after the United States Department of Agriculture's (USDA's) termination of marketing orders for hop bases resulted in a drastic reduction in hop base prices.

## 🏛 RULE OF LAW
A drastic price reduction, resulting from a supervening governmental act, frustrates the purpose of a contract thereby excusing the performance of the obligor.

**FACTS:** Washington State Hop Producers, Inc. ("the Trust") (P) was a trust set up to acquire, lease and sell federal allotments of hop, known as "hop base." The Trust (P) accepted bids for the sale of two hop base pools. Pool A was to be sold in 1985, while pool B was to be sold in 1986. Goschie Farms, Inc. (D) was one of the bidders. Five days after notice of acceptance by the Trust (P), the United States Department of Agriculture (USDA) terminated the marketing orders for all hop bases. This termination caused a drastic drop in the price of the existing hop base. As a result, Goschie Farms (D) refused to pay for the hop base claiming that the termination frustrated the purpose of the contract and, thus, excused its obligation. The Trust (P) unsuccessfully sued to recover the agreed price. Both the trial and appellate court agreed that the purpose of the contract was frustrated and rescinded the contract.

**ISSUE:** Does a drastic price reduction, resulting from a supervening governmental act, frustrate the purpose of a contract thereby excusing the performance of the obligor?

**HOLDING AND DECISION:** [Judge not stated in casebook excerpt.] Yes. A drastic price reduction, resulting from a supervening governmental act, frustrates the purpose of a contract thereby excusing the performance of the obligor. A drastic decrease in market demand or price is to be considered evidence supporting the frustration of a contractual purpose that excuses the obligor's performance. The Restatement (Second) of Contracts requires the frustrated purpose to be the principal purpose of the contract. In this case, the main purpose of the contract was the control and franchising of the hop base. A 92 percent price decrease, resulting from the USDA's termination, was not the frustrated purpose itself, but only evidence of the frustration of the contractual purpose.

Furthermore, foreseeability of the frustrating event is also a factor in deciding whether the nonoccurrence of that event was a basic assumption of the parties entering into a contract. The Trust (P) claimed that the USDA's termination was foreseeable, but failed to show any supportive facts. On the contrary, the inference drawn by the court was that the event was not foreseeable. This notion was supported by the lack of incorporating language in the contract allocating the risk of termination. Affirmed.

## ▌ ANALYSIS

Frustration differs from impossibility in that supervening events may occur that destroy one's purpose in entering into a contract, even when the actual performance of the contract is not rendered impossible. The frustration doctrine is also incorporated in Uniform Commercial Code § 2-615.

━━━

## Quicknotes

**FRUSTRATION OF PURPOSE** A doctrine relieving the parties to a contract from liability for nonperformance of their duties thereunder when the purpose of the agreement ceases to exist due to circumstances not subject to either party's control.

**IMPOSSIBILITY** A doctrine relieving the parties to a contract from liability for nonperformance of their duties thereunder, if the subject matter of the contract ceases to exist, a person essential to the performance of the contract is deceased, or the service or goods contracted for has become illegal.

**SUMMARY JUDGMENT** Judgment rendered by a court in response to a motion made by one of the parties, claiming that the lack of a question of material fact in respect to an issue warrants disposition of the issue without consideration by the jury.

━━━

# Hall Street Associates, L.L.C. v. Mattel, Inc.

Landlord (P) v. Tenant (D)

552 U.S. 576 (2008).

**NATURE OF CASE:** Appeal from reversal of judgment vacating an arbitration award in an action for indemnification under a lease.

**FACT SUMMARY:** Mattel, Inc. (Mattel) (D) contended that the Federal Arbitration Act's (FAA's) grounds for prompt vacatur and modification of awards in §§ 10 and 11 are exclusive for parties seeking expedited review under the FAA and, therefore, not subject to supplementation by contract. Accordingly, Mattel (D) contended that the terms of its arbitration agreement with Hall Street Associates, L.L.C. (P), allowing the district court to vacate, modify, or correct any arbitral award where the court found the arbitrator's conclusions of law erroneous, was unenforceable and subject exclusively to the FAA's provisions.

> 🏛 **RULE OF LAW**
> The Federal Arbitration Act's (FAA's) grounds for prompt vacatur and modification of awards in §§ 10 and 11 are exclusive for parties seeking expedited review under the FAA and, therefore, not subject to supplementation by contract.

**FACTS:** Mattel, Inc. (D) leased property from Hall Street Associates, L.L.C. (Hall Street) (P). The property was used for manufacturing. The leases between Mattel (D) and Hall Street (P) provided that the tenant (Mattel) (D) would indemnify the landlord (Hall Street) (P) for any costs resulting from the failure of the tenant or its predecessor lessees to follow environmental laws while using the premises. The property's well water showed high levels of pollutants, apparently caused by Mattel's (D) predecessor lessees. Mattel (D) signed a consent order with the states' department of environmental quality providing for cleanup of the site. After Mattel (D) gave notice of its intent to terminate the lease, Hall Street (P) filed suit in state court contesting Mattel's (D) right to vacate the premises, and claiming that Mattel (D) was required to indemnify Hall Street (P) for cleanup costs. The case was removed to federal district court. The district court held for Mattel (D) on the termination of the lease issue, and eventually the parties agreed to submit the indemnification claim to arbitration. The parties' arbitration agreement, inter alia, required the district court to vacate, modify, or correct any award if the arbitrator's conclusions of law were erroneous. The arbitrator decided for Mattel (D), but the district court vacated the award for legal error, expressly invoking the agreement's legal-error review standard and citing the court of appeals' decision in *LaPine Technology Corp. v. Kyocera Corp.*, 130 F.3d 884 (9th Cir. 1997) for the propo-

sition that the Federal Arbitration Act (FAA) allows parties to draft a contract dictating an alternative review standard. On remand, the arbitrator ruled for Hall Street (P), and the district court largely upheld the award, again applying the parties' stipulated review standard. The court of appeals reversed, holding the case was controlled by its decision in *Kyocera Corp. v. Prudential-Bache Trade Servs., Inc.*, 341 F.3d 987 (9th Cir. 2003), which had overruled *LaPine* on the ground that arbitration-agreement terms fixing the mode of judicial review are unenforceable, given the exclusive grounds for vacatur and modification provided by FAA §§ 10 and 11. After the district court again held for Hall Street (P) and the court of appeals again reversed, the United States Supreme Court granted certiorari to resolve a split among the circuits.

**ISSUE:** Are the Federal Arbitration Act's (FAA's) grounds for prompt vacatur and modification of awards in §§ 10 and 11 exclusive for parties seeking expedited review under the FAA and, therefore, not subject to supplementation by contract?

**HOLDING AND DECISION:** (Souter, J.) Yes. The Federal Arbitration Act's (FAA's) grounds for prompt vacatur and modification of awards in §§ 10 and 11 are exclusive for parties seeking expedited review under the FAA and, therefore, not subject to supplementation by contract. The FAA was intended to create a national policy favoring arbitration and placing arbitration agreements on equal footing with other contracts. The FAA also supplies mechanisms for enforcing arbitration awards through a variety of judicial orders. An application for any of these orders will get streamlined treatment as a motion, obviating the separate contract action that would usually be necessary to enforce or tinker with an arbitral award in court. Under the terms of § 9, a court must confirm an arbitration award unless it is vacated, modified, or corrected as prescribed in §§ 10 and 11. Section 10 lists grounds for vacating an award, while § 11 names those for modifying or correcting one. The circuits have hitherto been split as to the exclusiveness of these statutory grounds. Some hold that the statutory recitations are exclusive, whereas others regard them as mere threshold provisions open to expansion by agreement. The split among the circuits is resolved in favor of exclusiveness. Hall Street (P) argues that the agreement to review for legal error ought to prevail simply because arbitration is a creature of contract, and the FAA is motivated by a congressional desire to enforce such agreements. This argument comes

*Continued on next page.*

up short because, although there may be a general policy favoring arbitration, the FAA has textual features at odds with enforcing a contract to expand judicial review once the arbitration is over. Even assuming §§ 10 and 11 could be supplemented to some extent, it would stretch basic interpretive principles to expand their uniformly narrow stated grounds to the point of legal review generally. Section 9 makes evident that expanding § 10's and § 11's detailed categories at all would rub too much against the grain: § 9 carries no hint of flexibility in unequivocally telling courts that they "must" confirm an arbitral award, "unless" it is vacated or modified "as prescribed" by §§ 10 and 11. Instead of fighting the text, it makes more sense to see §§ 9-11 as the substance of a national policy favoring arbitration with just the limited review needed to maintain arbitration's essential virtue of resolving disputes straight-away. Affirmed as to this issue, but vacated and remanded on independent grounds.

## ▶ ANALYSIS

Justice Stevens, joined by Justice Kennedy, dissented, arguing that the result reached by the majority conflicted with the primary purpose of the FAA and ignored the historical context in which the FAA was passed. The dissenters also found unpersuasive the majority's grounds for its decision: (1) a supposed quid pro quo bargain between Congress and litigants that conditions expedited federal enforcement of arbitration awards on acceptance of a statutory limit on the scope of judicial review of such awards; and (2) an assumption that Congress intended to include the words "and no other" in the grounds specified in §§ 10 and 11 for the vacatur and modification of awards. The dissenters, accordingly, would have permitted enforcement of what they characterized as perfectly reasonable judicial review provisions in arbitration agreements fairly negotiated by the parties and approved by the district court.

---

## Quicknotes

**ARBITRATION AGREEMENT** A mutual understanding entered into by parties wishing to submit to the decision making authority of a neutral third party, selected by the parties and charged with rendering a decision.

**INDEMNIFICATION** Reimbursement for losses sustained or security against anticipated loss or damages.

---

**HOLDING AND DECISION:** [...]

## ▶ ANALYSIS

# Michael-Curry Cos., Inc. v. Knutson Shareholders Liquidating Trust

## Purchaser (P) v. Seller (D)

### Minn. Sup. Ct., 449 N.W.2d 139 (1989).

**NATURE OF CASE:** Appeal from reversal of judgment denying applicability of arbitration clause.

**FACT SUMMARY:** Michael-Curry Cos., Inc. (P), a purchaser, alleging fraud in the inducement by the seller, Knutson Shareholders Liquidating Trust (D), sought a trial on its claim despite a clause in the purchase and sale agreement providing for arbitration.

## 🏛 RULE OF LAW
An arbitration clause requiring arbitration of claims relating to the making of the contract encompasses claims for fraud in the inducement.

**FACTS:** Michael-Curry Cos., Inc. (P), a purchaser, alleged fraud in the inducement by the seller, Knutson Shareholders Liquidation Trust (Knutson Shareholders) (D). The parties had signed an agreement requiring arbitration of "any controversy or claim arising out of, or relating to, this Agreement, or the making . . . thereof." The trial court held the clause did not require arbitration, but the state's intermediate appellate court reversed, holding that the clause was sufficiently broad to encompass fraud in the inducement. The state's highest court granted review.

**ISSUE:** Does an arbitration clause requiring arbitration of claims relating to the making of the contract encompass claims for fraud in the inducement?

**HOLDING AND DECISION:** (Keith, J.) Yes. An arbitration clause requiring arbitration of claims relating to the making of the contract encompasses claims for fraud in the inducement. Parties may validly choose to arbitrate all controversies, including fraud in the inducement. To determine whether the parties so intended, the clause itself must mention fraud or must be sufficiently broad to comprehend that a claim of fraudulent inducement be arbitrated. Fraud is not specifically listed in the clause here, but because fraud in the inducement goes to the "making" of the contract, the language is sufficiently broad. The law favors arbitration. Further, a specific list of all possible claims in an arbitration clause would be impractical, and parties would shy from contracts in which fraud was specifically mentioned. Affirmed.

## ▶ ANALYSIS

The federal government enacted a national arbitration law in 1925 that is generally in conformity with the Uniform Arbitration Act adopted by most states. The Federal Arbitration Act applies to arbitration clauses in maritime contracts or "transactions involving commerce," and has been interpreted by the Supreme Court as controlling state laws that do not allow claims arbitral under federal law or which make it more difficult to arbitrate claims arbitral under either state or federal law.

---

## Quicknotes

**ARBITRATION CLAUSE** Provision contained in a contract pursuant to which both parties agree that any disputes arising thereunder will be resolved through arbitration.

**FRAUD IN THE INDUCEMENT** Occurs when a testator is induced to execute a testamentary instrument as a result of the misrepresentation of certain facts existing at the time of its creation that may have affected the manner in which the testator disposed of his property.

# Stolt-Nielsen, S.A. v. AnimalFeeds International Corp.

## Shipping company (P) v. Customer (D)

559 U.S. 662 (2010).

**NATURE OF CASE:** Appeal from reversal of order vacating an arbitral award determining, inter alia, that class arbitration was permitted.

**FACT SUMMARY:** Stolt-Nielsen S.A. (P), a shipping company, and other shipping companies (P), contended that because their shipping contracts with AnimalFeeds International, Corp. (AnimalFeeds) (D) and other customers (D) contained arbitration clauses that were silent as to class arbitration, class arbitration of the AnimalFeeds' (D) claims was prohibited.

### RULE OF LAW
Imposing class arbitration on parties who have not agreed to authorize class arbitration is inconsistent with the Federal Arbitration Act (FAA).

**FACTS:** Stolt-Nielsen S.A. (Stolt-Nielsen) (P), a shipping company, and other shipping companies (P) provided seagoing vessels with compartments that were separately chartered to customers, including AnimalFeeds International, Corp. (AnimalFeeds) (D), who wished to ship liquids in small quantities. AnimalFeeds (D) shipped its goods pursuant to a standard contract known in the maritime trade as a charter party. The charter party that AnimalFeeds (D) used contained an arbitration clause requiring arbitration pursuant to the FAA. The arbitration clause, however, was silent as to whether class arbitration was permitted. AnimalFeeds (D) brought a class action antitrust suit against the shipping companies (P) for price fixing, and that suit was consolidated with similar suits brought by other charterers (D), including one in which the court of appeals subsequently reversed a district court ruling that the charterers' (D) claims were not subject to arbitration. AnimalFeeds (D) then sought arbitration on behalf of a class of purchasers of parcel tanker transportation services. The parties selected an arbitration panel, designated New York City as the arbitration site, and stipulated that their arbitration clause was "silent" on the class arbitration issue. The panel determined that the arbitration clause allowed for class arbitration. The shipping companies (P) then brought suit in district court to vacate the award. The district court agreed with the shipping companies (P), concluding that the arbitrators' award was made in "manifest disregard" of the law, for had the arbitrators conducted a choice-of-law analysis, they would have applied the rule of federal maritime law requiring contracts to be interpreted in light of custom and usage. The court of appeals reversed, holding that because the shipping companies (P) had cited no authority applying a maritime rule

of custom and usage against class arbitration, the arbitrators' decision was not in manifest disregard of maritime law; and that the arbitrators had not manifestly disregarded New York law, which had not established a rule against class arbitration. The United States Supreme Court granted certiorari.

**ISSUE:** Is imposing class arbitration on parties who have not agreed to authorize class arbitration inconsistent with the FAA?

**HOLDING AND DECISION:** (Alito, J.) Yes. Imposing class arbitration on parties who have not agreed to authorize class arbitration is inconsistent with the FAA. An arbitration decision may be vacated under FAA § 10(a)(4) on the ground that the arbitrator exceeded his powers only when an arbitrator strays from interpretation and application of the agreement and effectively dispenses his own brand of industrial justice. The arbitration panel appears to have rested its decision on AnimalFeeds' (D) public policy argument for permitting class arbitration under the charter party's arbitration clause. However, because the parties agreed that their agreement was "silent" on the class arbitration issue, the arbitrators' proper task was to identify the rule of law governing in that situation. Instead, the panel based its decision on certain arbitral decisions without mentioning whether they were based on a rule derived from the FAA or on maritime or New York law. Rather than inquiring whether those bodies of law contained a "default rule" permitting an arbitration clause to allow class arbitration absent express consent, the panel proceeded as if it had a common-law court's authority to develop what it viewed as the best rule for such a situation. Finding no reason to depart from its perception of a consensus among arbitrators that class arbitration was beneficial in numerous settings, the panel simply imposed its own conception of sound policy and permitted class arbitration. The panel's few references to intent do not show that the panel did anything other than impose its own policy preference. Thus, under FAA § 10(b), this Court must either "direct a rehearing by the arbitrators" or decide the question originally referred to the panel. Because there can be only one possible outcome on the facts here, there is no need to direct a rehearing by the arbitrators. The FAA imposes rules of fundamental importance, including the basic precept that arbitration "is a matter of consent, not coercion." Whether enforcing an agreement to arbitrate or construing an arbitration clause, courts and arbitrators must give effect to the parties'

*Continued on next page.*

contractual rights and expectations. The parties' intentions control, and the parties are generally free to structure their arbitration agreements as they see fit; they may agree to limit the issues arbitrated and may agree on rules under which an arbitration will proceed. They may also specify with whom they choose to arbitrate their disputes. It follows that a party may not be compelled under the FAA to submit to class arbitration unless there is a contractual basis for concluding that the party agreed to do so. Here, the arbitration panel imposed class arbitration despite the parties' stipulation that they had reached no agreement on that issue. The panel's conclusion is fundamentally at war with the foundational FAA principle that arbitration is a matter of consent. It may be appropriate to presume that parties to an arbitration agreement implicitly authorize the arbitrator to adopt those procedures necessary to give effect to the parties' agreement. However, an implicit agreement to authorize class action arbitration is not a term that the arbitrator may infer solely from the fact of an agreement to arbitrate, because class-action arbitration changes the nature of arbitration to such a degree that it cannot be presumed the parties consented to it by simply agreeing to submit their disputes to an arbitrator. In bilateral arbitration, parties forgo the procedural rigor and appellate review of the courts in order to realize the benefits of private dispute resolution: lower costs, greater efficiency and speed, and the ability to choose expert adjudicators to resolve specialized disputes. On the other hand, complex class-action arbitration rules, procedures, and stakes are markedly different from those of simple bilateral arbitration. Those differences between simple bilateral and complex class action arbitration are too great for a presumption that the parties intended to include class action arbitration in their agreement without expressly saying so. Reversed and remanded.

**DISSENT:** (Ginsburg, J.) The issue addressed by the majority (whether arbitration may proceed on behalf of a class when the arbitration clause is silent on the question) is not ripe for judicial review, and the petition for review was, therefore, improvidently granted. Even if the merits were reached, however, the strict limitations that the FAA places on judicial review of arbitral awards should be given effect, and, accordingly, the plea for vacating the arbitrators' decision should have been rejected.

▶ **ANALYSIS**

For arbitrators to consider whether a claim should proceed on a class basis, this decision apparently demands contractual language one can read as affirmatively authorizing class arbitration. The majority ties the requirement of affirmative authorization to the basic precept that arbitration is a matter of consent, not coercion, and that parties may specify with whom they choose to arbitrate, just as they may limit the issues they choose to arbitrate. However, as the dissent points out, arbitrators, in delineating an appro-

priate class, need not, and should not, disregard such contractual constraints. In this case, for example, Animal-Feeds (D) propose to pursue, on behalf of a class, only "claims . . . arising out of any [charter party agreement] . . . that provides for arbitration." If the arbitrators certified the proposed class, they would adjudicate only the rights of persons "with whom" Stolt-Nielsen (P) and the other shipping companies (P) agreed to arbitrate, and only "issues" subject to arbitration. Further, arbitration provisions are a species of forum-selection clauses. There is little question that if the parties had designated a court, state or federal, to resolve their disputes, that court would have authority to conduct claims like AnimalFeeds' (D) on a class basis. Arguably, there is not a good distinguishing reason why the class-action prospect should vanish when the "any dispute" clause is contained in an arbitration agreement, rather than in a traditional judicial forum selection clause.

━━■■■━━

## Quicknotes

**ARBITRATION** An alternative resolution process where a dispute is heard and decided by a neutral third party, rather than through legal proceedings.

**FORUM SELECTION CLAUSE** Provision contained in a contract setting forth the particular forum in which the parties would resolve a matter if a dispute were to arise.

━━■■■━━

# AT&T Mobility LLC v. Concepcion

Cell phone service provider (D) v. Consumer (P)

563 U.S. 333 (2011).

**NATURE OF CASE:** Appeal from affirmance of denial of motion to compel arbitration in a consumer class action.

**FACT SUMMARY:** AT&T Mobility LLC (AT&T) (D) contended that the enforceability of the arbitration provision in its cell phone service agreement could not be conditioned by the states on the availability of classwide arbitration procedures, since the states were preempted by the Federal Arbitration Act (FAA) from so doing.

## RULE OF LAW

The Federal Arbitration Act (FAA) prohibits states from conditioning the enforceability of arbitration agreements on the availability of classwide arbitration procedures.

**FACTS:** The cell phone service contract between the Concepcions (P) and AT&T Mobility LLC (AT&T) (D) provided for arbitration of all disputes, but did not permit classwide arbitration. After the Concepcions (P) were charged sales tax on the retail value of phones provided free under their service contract, they sued AT&T (D) in a California federal district court. Their suit was consolidated with a class action alleging, inter alia, that AT&T (D) had engaged in false advertising and fraud by charging sales tax on "free" phones. The district court denied AT&T's (D) motion to compel arbitration under the Concepcions' (P) contract. Relying on the California Supreme Court's decision in *Discover Bank v. Superior Court,* 36 Cal. 4th 148, 30 Cal. Rptr. 3d 76, 113 P. 3d 1100 (2005), it found the arbitration provision unconscionable because it disallowed classwide proceedings and AT&T had failed to show that bilateral arbitration adequately substituted for the deterrent effects of class actions. The court of appeals agreed that the provision was unconscionable under California law and held that the Federal Arbitration Act (FAA), which in Section 2 makes arbitration agreements "valid, irrevocable, and enforceable, save upon such grounds as exist at law or in equity for the revocation of any contract," did not preempt its ruling. The United States Supreme Court granted certiorari.

**ISSUE:** Does the Federal Arbitration Act (FAA) prohibit states from conditioning the enforceability of arbitration agreements on the availability of classwide arbitration procedures?

**HOLDING AND DECISION:** (Scalia, J.) Yes. The Federal Arbitration Act (FAA) prohibits states from conditioning the enforceability of arbitration agreements on the availability of classwide arbitration procedures. The

FAA's Section 2 reflects a "liberal federal policy favoring arbitration" and the "fundamental principle that arbitration is a matter of contract." Thus, courts must place arbitration agreements on an equal footing with other contracts and enforce them according to their terms. Section 2's saving clause permits agreements to be invalidated by "generally applicable contract defenses," but not by defenses that apply only to arbitration or derive their meaning from the fact that an agreement to arbitrate is at issue. Under *Discover Bank,* class waivers in consumer arbitration agreements are unconscionable if the agreement is in an adhesion contract, disputes between the parties are likely to involve small amounts of damages, and the party with inferior bargaining power alleges a deliberate scheme to defraud. The Concepcions (P) claim that the *Discover Bank* rule is a ground that "exist[s] at law or in equity for the revocation of any contract" under FAA § 2. When state law prohibits outright the arbitration of a particular type of claim, the FAA displaces the conflicting rule. But the inquiry is more complex when a generally applicable doctrine is alleged to have been applied in a fashion that disfavors or interferes with arbitration. Although § 2's saving clause preserves generally applicable contract defenses, it does not suggest an intent to preserve state-law rules that stand as an obstacle to the accomplishment of the FAA's objectives. The FAA's overarching purpose is to ensure the enforcement of arbitration agreements according to their terms so as to facilitate informal, streamlined proceedings. Parties may agree to limit the issues subject to arbitration, to arbitrate according to specific rules, and to limit with whom they will arbitrate. Class arbitration, to the extent it is manufactured by *Discover Bank* rather than consensual, interferes with fundamental attributes of arbitration. The switch from bilateral to class arbitration sacrifices arbitration's informality and makes the process slower, more costly, and more likely to generate procedural morass than final judgment. Also, class arbitration greatly increases risks to defendants. The absence of multilayered review makes it more likely that errors will go uncorrected. That risk of error may become unacceptable when damages allegedly owed to thousands of claimants are aggregated and decided at once. Arbitration is poorly suited to these higher stakes. In litigation, a defendant may appeal a certification decision and a final judgment, but FAA § 10 limits the grounds on which courts can vacate arbitral awards. Reversed and remanded.

**CONCURRENCE:** (Thomas, J.) the FAA requires that an agreement to arbitrate be enforced unless a party

*Continued on next page.*

successfully challenges the formation of the arbitration agreement, such as by proving fraud or duress. Under such an interpretation, a court cannot follow both the FAA and the *Discover Bank* rule, which does not relate to defects in the making of an agreement. Arguably, the language of § 2's savings clause does not include all defenses applicable to any contract but rather some subset of those defenses. Since the section's exception pertains only to grounds for "revocation" of a contract, presumably Congress intended to limit those grounds to defects in the formation of the contract. *Discover Bank's* holding was premised on public policy, not on whether there were defects in contract formation. Therefore, *Discover Bank* is preempted.

**DISSENT:** (Breyer, J.) The rule enunciated by *Discover Bank* does not conflict with the FAA and is consistent with its language and primary objective. Where the circumstances articulated by that rule are met, class action waivers are unconscionable under state law. The rule thus sets forth a general principle of unconscionability that does not apply to all class action waivers in the consumer context. Because it applies equally to class action litigation waivers in contracts without arbitration agreements as it does to class arbitration waivers in contracts with such agreements, the rule falls directly within the scope of the FAA's exception permitting courts to refuse to enforce arbitration agreements on grounds that exist "for the revocation of any contract." The majority is wrong, however, in finding that the *Discover Bank* rule stands as an obstacle to achievement of the FAA's objectives, and it does not provide support for its belief that individual, rather than class, arbitration is a fundamental attribute of arbitration. Because California applies the same legal principles to address the unconscionability of class arbitration waivers as it does to address the unconscionability of any other contractual provision, the merits of class proceedings should not factor into our decision. Moreover, class proceedings have well-known countervailing advantages, such as encouraging the bringing of small claims—and the acceptance of them by attorneys. Under our federalist system, states are considered sovereigns; here, California is entitled to weigh the pros and cons of all class proceedings alike, and its law should be upheld, not preempted.

## ▶ ANALYSIS

Since almost all class actions occur between parties who are in transactional relationships with one another, such as shareholders and corporations, consumers and merchants, employees and employers, etc., it is arguable that this decision will permit the party with greater bargaining power in any particular transaction to force the weaker parties to accept class waivers with no recourse—other than not entering into the transaction at all.

---

## Quicknotes

**ARBITRATION AGREEMENT** A mutual understanding entered into by parties wishing to submit to the decision making authority of a neutral third party, selected by the parties and charged with rendering a decision.

**CLASS ACTION** A suit commenced by a representative on behalf of an ascertainable group that is too large to appear in court, who shares a commonality of interests and who will benefit from a successful result.

**UNCONSCIONABLE** A situation in which a contract, or a particular contract term, is unenforceable if the court determines that such term(s) are unduly oppressive or unfair to one party to the contract.

---

# Remedies

## Quick Reference Rules of Law

# Hochster v. De La Tour

Future employee (P) v. Future employer (D)

Q.B., 2 E. & B. 678, 118 Eng. Rep. 922 (1853).

**NATURE OF CASE:** Action to recover damages for breach of contract.

**FACT SUMMARY:** Before Hochster (P) was due to perform his contract of employment for De La Tour (D), De La Tour (D) announced his intention to repudiate the contract, whereupon Hochster (P) immediately commenced an action for breach of contract.

## 🏛 RULE OF LAW
When the time for performance has not arrived, but one party nevertheless indicates his intention not to perform, the other party does not have to wait until the performance should have occurred before bringing action for breach of contract.

**FACTS:** In April, Hochster (P) contracted to serve as De La Tour's (D) employee beginning on June 1. On May 11, De La Tour (D) wrote to Hochster (P) that he had changed his mind and declined Hochster's (P) services. On May 22, Hochster (P) brought this action for breach of contract.

**ISSUE:** When the time for performance has not arrived, but one party nevertheless indicates his intention not to perform, does the other party have to wait until the performance should have occurred before bringing action for breach of contract?

**HOLDING AND DECISION:** (Lord Campbell, C.J.) No. When the time for performance has not arrived, but one party nevertheless indicates his intention not to perform, the other party does not have to wait until the performance should have occurred before bringing action for breach of contract. "The man who wrongfully renounces a contract into which he has deliberately entered cannot justly complain if he is immediately sued for compensation in damages by the man whom he has injured; and it seems reasonable to allow an option to the injured party, either to sue immediately, or to wait till the time when the act was to be done." If Hochster (P) had to wait until June 1 to sue, he would not be able to enter any employment which would interfere with his promise to begin work at that time. But it is surely more rational that after renunciation by De La Tour (D), Hochster (P) should be at liberty to consider oneself absolved from any future performance. Thus, he would be free to seek other employment in mitigation of damages. De La Tour's (D) renunciation may be treated as a breach of contract. Judgment for the Plaintiff.

## ▶ ANALYSIS

This is the leading case on the so-called doctrine of anticipatory breach. The court's reasoning is erroneous insofar as it felt that Hochster (P) would otherwise be caught in a dilemma: to remain idle and hope for a favorable future judgment or to obtain other employment and thereby forfeit his rights against De La Tour (D). The court overlooked the rule that where a party manifests prospective unwillingness to perform, the other party may suspend his performance and change his position without surrendering his right to sue after the breach occurs. In other words, the court could have considered the repudiation as (1) a defense to an action brought by De La Tour (D) and (2) an excuse of the constructive condition that Hochster (P) is ready, willing, and able to perform on June 1.

---

## Quicknotes

**ANTICIPATORY BREACH** Breach of a contract subsequent to formation but prior to the time performance is due.

**BREACH OF CONTRACT** Unlawful failure by a party to perform its obligations pursuant to contract.

**DAMAGES** Monetary compensation that may be awarded by the court to a party who has sustained injury or loss to his person, property or rights due to another party's unlawful act, omission or negligence.

# Taylor v. Johnston

## Horse breeder (P) v. Stallion owner (D)

Cal. Sup. Ct., 15 Cal. 3d 130, 539 P.2d 425 (1975).

**NATURE OF CASE:** Appeal from award of damages for breach of contract.

**FACT SUMMARY:** Taylor (P) contracted to breed his mares with the Johnstons' (D) stallion. The Johnstons (D) later sold their stallion, and as a consequence of subsequent events, the stallion was never bred with Taylor's (P) mares. Taylor (P) sued for breach of contract and damages, and the Johnstons (D) countersued for stud fees.

## RULE OF LAW

A party is not deemed to have anticipatorily breached a contract if he has caused the other party to believe that he will not perform the agreement but has not expressly repudiated or unequivocally refused to perform the contract.

**FACTS:** Taylor (P) entered into a contract to breed two of his mares, Sunday Slippers and Sandy Fork, with a stallion owned by the Johnstons (D). The agreement provided that breeding with the stallion, Fleet Nasrullah, would take place in the following year, 1966, and contained a clause allowing a free breeding the next year for a mare which failed to produce a live foal as a result of the 1966 breeding. Late in 1965, the Johnstons (D) sold Fleet Nasrullah, and the horse was shipped to Kentucky, where various shareholders acquired the right to breed their mares with him. The Johnstons (D) notified Taylor (P) of the sale, advising Taylor (P) that they considered themselves released from their agreement with him by reason of the sale. When Taylor (P) threatened litigation, the Johnstons (D) agreed to allow Sunday Slippers and Sandy Fork to breed with Fleet Nasrullah in Kentucky. During early 1966, both mares were in foal, and Sunday Slippers gave birth on April 17 and Sandy Fork did likewise on June 5. Taylor's (P) agent tried three times to arrange for Fleet Nasrullah to breed with Sunday Slippers while the mare was in heat and tried once to arrange for the breeding of Fleet Nasrullah and Sandy Fork. No appointments could be made for Taylor's (P) horses because shareholders of Fleet Nasrullah had booked his services for the days that the Taylor (P) mares were to be in heat. Taylor (P) eventually gave up trying to book Fleet Nasrullah and, in June of 1966, bred each mare with Chateaugay, a former Kentucky Derby winner. Both mares became pregnant by Chateaugay but were subsequently aborted when it was discovered that they were carrying twins. Taylor (P) eventually sued the Johnstons (D) for breach of contract, and the Johnstons (D) counterclaimed for stud fees. The trial court, concluding that the sale of Fleet Nasrullah coupled with the

subsequent inability of the Johnstons' (D) agents to arrange for the stallion to breed with the two mares constituted repudiation and a breach of the contract, rendered judgment for Taylor (P) in the amount of more than $103,000. On appeal to the state's highest court, the Johnstons (D) claimed that they had not repudiated or breached the contract and that it had been Taylor's (P) conduct in breeding his horses with Chateaugay which had made performance of the agreement impossible.

**ISSUE:** Is a party deemed to have anticipatorily breached a contract if he has caused the other party to believe that he will not perform the agreement but has not expressly repudiated or unequivocally refused to perform the contract?

**HOLDING AND DECISION:** (Sullivan, J.) No. A party is not deemed to have anticipatorily breached a contract if he has caused the other party to believe that he will not perform the agreement but has not expressly repudiated or unequivocally refused to perform the contract. Anticipatory breach occurs only when one of the parties to a contract has expressly or impliedly repudiated the agreement. An express repudiation requires a clear, positive, unequivocal refusal to perform. And an express repudiation results when one party puts it out of his power to perform the contract. In this case, the Johnstons (D) did initially repudiate the contract by telling Taylor (P) that the sale of Fleet Nasrullah made performance impossible. But, Taylor (P) elected to treat the agreement as still in force, and the Johnstons (D) retracted their prior repudiation when they made Fleet Nasrullah available for breeding with Taylor's (P) mares in Kentucky. Once the contract had been thus reinstated, the Johnstons (D) had until the end of 1966 or, at a minimum, until the end of the 1966 breeding season to mate Fleet Nasrullah with Sunday Slippers and Sandy Fork. The Johnstons (D), for all that the evidence discloses, stood willing to perform their contractual obligation. Performance became impossible only when Taylor (P) elected to breed his mares with Chateaugay instead of with Fleet Nasrullah. It follows that the Johnstons (D) did not repudiate or commit an anticipatory breach and therefore are not liable to Taylor (P) for damages. Reversed.

## ▶ ANALYSIS

Even when it is clear that an anticipatory breach has occurred, the nonbreaching party has a choice of remedies to pursue. He may treat the contract as at an end and sue

*Continued on next page.*

for damages immediately. However, he may also wait until the time fixed for performance has arrived and may sue for damages at that time if the prescribed performance is not tendered. The latter course may be advantageous in that it allows the breaching party an additional opportunity to perform, but if that party cures the breach, the aggrieved party may not, of course, recover damages for the anticipatory breach which occurred but was condoned.

## Quicknotes

**ANTICIPATORY BREACH** Breach of a contract subsequent to formation but prior to the time performance is due.

**BREACH OF CONTRACT** Unlawful failure by a party to perform its obligations pursuant to contract.

**DAMAGES** Monetary compensation that may be awarded by the court to a party who has sustained injury or loss to his person, property or rights due to another party's unlawful act, omission or negligence.

# Alaska Pacific Trading Co. v. Eagon Forest Products, Inc.

Log seller (P) v. Log purchaser (D)

Wash. Ct. App., 85 Wash. App. 354 (1997).

**NATURE OF CASE:** Appeal from summary judgment granted to buyer on the seller's breach of contract claim.

**FACT SUMMARY:** Alaska Pacific Trading Company (ALPAC) (P) and Eagon Forest Products, Inc. (Eagon) (D) contracted to sell and buy raw logs. After months of communications between the parties, the delivery date passed with no shipment, and Eagon (D) canceled the contract. ALPAC (P) brought suit for breach of contract, contending that failure to timely deliver the goods was not a material breach and that the parties modified the delivery date. Alternately, it argued that Eagon (D) breached the contract by failing to provide adequate assurances or repudiating the contract.

## RULE OF LAW

Under Uniform Commercial Code Article II, a seller breaches its contractual duty to deliver goods and releases the buyer from its duty to accept the goods by failing to timely deliver the goods where the parties have not waived or modified the delivery date, the seller has not adequately requested reassurances that the buyer would perform, and the buyer has not anticipatorily repudiated the contract.

**FACTS:** Alaska Pacific Trading Company (ALPAC) (P) and Eagon Forest Products, Inc. (Eagon) (D) were companies that bought and sold raw logs. They contracted for ALPAC (P) to sell, and Eagon (D) to buy, logs, to be delivered by August 31, 1993. After the parties entered the contract, the market for logs began to soften, making the contract less attractive to Eagon (D). ALPAC (P) became concerned that Eagon (D) would try to cancel the contract. Kimura, ALPAC's (P) executive, and Ahn, Eagon's (D) executive, began a series of meetings and letters, apparently in an effort to assure ALPAC (P) that Eagon (D) would purchase the logs. On August 23, Eagon (D) received a fax from ALPAC (P) suggesting that the price and volume of the contract be reduced. Eagon (D) did not respond to the fax. During a business meeting soon after, Kimura asked Ahn whether he intended to accept the logs. Ahn admitted that he was having trouble getting approval. Kimura thereafter believed that Eagon (D) would not accept the shipment, and, accordingly, ALPAC (P) canceled the vessel that it had reserved for the logs. The logs were not shipped by August 31, but Ahn and Kimura continued to discuss the contract into September. On September 7, Ahn told Kimura that he would continue to try to convince headquarters to accept the delivery. Ahn also indicated that he did not want Kimura to sell the logs

to another buyer. The same day, Ahn sent a letter to Eagon's (D) head office indicating that "the situation of our supplier is extremely grave" and that Eagon (D) should consider accepting the shipment in September or October. By September 27, ALPAC (P) had not shipped the logs. It sent a final letter to Eagon (D) stating that Eagon (D) had breached the contract because it failed to take delivery of the logs. Eagon (D) responded by stating that there was no contract any longer because ALPAC's (P) breach excused Eagon's (D) performance. ALPAC (P) brought suit for breach of contract. The trial court granted summary judgment to Eagon (D) and dismissed the action. The state's intermediate appellate court granted review.

**ISSUE:** Under Uniform Commercial Code Article II, does a seller breach its contractual duty to deliver goods and release the buyer from its duty to accept the goods by failing to timely deliver the goods where the parties have not waived or modified the delivery date, the seller has not adequately requested reassurances that the buyer would perform, and the buyer has not anticipatorily repudiated the contract?

**HOLDING AND DECISION:** (Agid, J.) Yes. Under Uniform Commercial Code Article II, a seller breaches its contractual duty to deliver goods and releases the buyer from its duty to accept the goods by failing to timely deliver the goods where the parties have not waived or modified the delivery date, the seller has not adequately requested reassurances that the buyer would perform, and the buyer has not anticipatorily repudiated the contract. ALPAC (P) relies on common-law contract cases to support its position that, when the parties have not indicated that time is of the essence, late delivery is not a material breach which excuses the buyer's duty to accept the goods. However, because the contract at issue is one for the sale of goods, it is governed by Uniform Commercial Code, Article II (U.C.C. II), which replaced the common-law doctrine of material breach with the "perfect tender" rule. Under this rule, if the goods or the tender of delivery fail in any respect to conform to the contract, the buyer may reject the whole. Because the contract specified a date for shipment and the logs were not shipped by that date, under the "perfect tender" rule, ALPAC (P) breached its duty under the contract and released Eagon (D) from its duty to accept the logs. ALPAC (P) next contends that, even if failure to timely deliver is a breach, the parties modified the delivery date or Eagon (D) waived timely delivery. U.C.C. II changed the common law of contracts to eliminate the

*Continued on next page.*

need for consideration in contract modifications but did not otherwise alter the common law. Mutual assent is still required, and one party may not unilaterally modify a contract. ALPAC (P) argues that Eagon (D) agreed to modify the delivery date because it did not object to ALPAC's (P) proposed changes in the amount and delivery time. It asserts that, if Eagon (D) had not been silent during the discussions about the contract, the logs would have been shipped. Because the law requires mutual assent, Eagon's (D) mere silence is not sufficient to establish a material issue of fact about modification. ALPAC (P) also argues that Eagon (D) waived the shipping date because it failed to comment on its passage and continued to discuss the contract after the shipping date had passed. Waiver is a factual question. If both parties to a contract allow the reasonable time for delivery to pass without complaint, a court may infer that the parties have extended the time for performance. Ahn and Kimura continued to negotiate until September 7. Thus, Eagon (D) may initially have waived the original shipment date as negotiations continued. However, by the end of September, when they exchanged their final correspondence, ALPAC (P) still had not shipped the logs. Thus, even if the parties did waive the original date, ALPAC (P) still had a duty to deliver the logs within a reasonable time. Its failure to ship the logs for an additional 20 days, while the price of logs continued to drop, was unreasonable and a breach. ALPAC's (P) next contention is that summary judgment was inappropriate because a material factual issue existed about whether it requested assurances from Eagon (D), and Eagon (D) failed to respond. Although the courts in this state have not directly addressed whether a demand for assurances under U.C.C. § 2–609 must always be in writing, courts in other jurisdictions have held that the demand for assurances must be made in writing, absent a pattern of interaction that demonstrates a clear understanding between the parties that suspension of the demanding party's performance was the alternative, if its concerns were not adequately addressed by the other party. Here, while Ahn had some idea that Kimura and ALPAC (P) were concerned about the status of the contract, he did not understand that ALPAC (P) would withhold performance as a result. Here, Eagon (D) and ALPAC (P) each made assumptions about the other's performance under the contract, but neither clearly expressed a need for assurance. To hold that, in every case where a contract becomes less favorable for one party, general discussions between the parties can be considered requests for assurances, would defeat the purpose of U.C.C. § 2–609, which requires a clear demand so that all parties are aware that, absent assurances, the demanding party will withhold performance. An ambiguous communication is not sufficient. Alternatively, ALPAC (P) argues that it did provide a written request for assurances in the August 23 fax from Kimura to Eagon (D). A written demand for assurances must generally be clear and unequivocal, and a less clear statement will be considered sufficient only when the interaction between the parties is such that they understand that the demanding party will withhold performance unless assurances are tendered. Here, although both parties knew that the contract was no longer favorable to Eagon (D), there was no showing that Eagon (D) would not perform, or that ALPAC (P) expressed its belief that Eagon (D) would not perform. The fax Kimura sent to Ahn stated only that ALPAC (P) was willing to negotiate new terms for the contract, not that it believed Eagon (D) would not perform. Therefore, neither the parties' interactions nor their correspondence rose to the level of a demand for assurances. Finally, ALPAC (P) contends that Eagon (D) repudiated the contract prior to the delivery date. It argues that Eagon's (D) concern about the drop in log prices and its difficulty in getting final approval from its head office were sufficient to present a material factual issue about whether Eagon (D) intended to accept the logs. ALPAC (P) correctly argues that the question of anticipatory repudiation is one of fact. However, a court will not infer repudiation from doubtful and indefinite statements that performance may or may not take place. Rather, the anticipatory breach must be a clear and positive statement or action that expresses an intention not to perform the contract. Here, Ahn never stated that he would not accept the cargo. Rather, Kimura assumed that the problems with approval from the home office were the equivalent of an inability or unwillingness to accept the cargo. This state's courts have refused to hold that a communication between contracting parties that raises doubt as to the ability or willingness of one party to perform, but is not an outward denial, is a repudiation of the contract. Therefore, as a matter of law, neither Eagon's (D) expressed unhappiness about the drop in timber prices, nor its problems completing the contract rise to the level of repudiation. [Affirmed.]

## ▶ *ANALYSIS*

Uniform Commercial Code § 2–609 provides that: "A contract for sale imposes an obligation on each party that the other's expectation of receiving due performance will not be impaired. When reasonable grounds for insecurity arise with respect to the performance of either party the other may in writing demand adequate assurance of due performance and until he receives such assurance may if commercially reasonable suspend any performance for which he has not already received the agreed return." As this case illustrates, the section raises several issues that are factual in nature, e.g., what constitutes "reasonable grounds for insecurity," or what constitutes "adequate assurance of due performance?" As this case also illustrates, such factual issues may be resolved on summary judgment only if reasonable persons could reach only one conclusion, taking all inferences in favor of the non-moving party.

■■◼■■

*Continued on next page.*

## Quicknotes

**ANTICIPATORY REPUDIATION** Breach of a contract subsequent to formation but prior to the time performance is due.

**BREACH OF CONTRACT** Unlawful failure by a party to perform its obligations pursuant to contract.

**PERFECT TENDER** Goods tendered pursuant to a contract for sale, which conform precisely to the contract's requirements.

# Northern Indiana Public Service Co. v. Carbon County Coal Co.

## Public utility (P) v. Coal supplier (D)

799 F.2d 265 (7th Cir. 1986).

**NATURE OF CASE:** Cross-appeals from award of damages for counterclaim plaintiff and from denial of specific performance in action for declaratory relief.

**FACT SUMMARY:** Northern Indiana Public Service Co. (P), which had agreed to buy 1.5 million tons of coal every year for 20 years from Carbon County Coal Co. (D), sought to be excused from the contract when the price of electricity fell dramatically.

## 🏛 RULE OF LAW
The remedy of specific performance will be awarded only when damages at law are inadequate to compensate the injured party.

**FACTS:** Northern Indiana Public Service Co. (NIPSCO) (P) and Carbon County Coal Co. (Carbon County) (D) signed a 20-year contract that required Carbon County (D), the owner and operator of a coal mine, to sell, and NIPSCO (P) to buy, about 1.5 million tons of coal every year. The price, initially set at $24/ton, could and did go up under the contract terms, to $44/ton. But when oil prices and the cost of electricity plummeted, NIPSCO (P) had alternative sources of fuel available at much lower costs. It filed a declaratory relief action against Carbon County (D), seeking to be excused from the contract. Carbon County (D) counterclaimed for damages due to breach and won a jury verdict for $181 million, but its request for specific performance was denied. Both parties cross-appealed, and the court of appeals granted review.

**ISSUE:** Will the remedy of specific performance be awarded only when damages at law are inadequate to compensate the injured party?

**HOLDING AND DECISION:** (Posner, J.) Yes. The remedy of specific performance will be awarded only when damages at law are inadequate to compensate the injured party. An order of specific performance is not available if damages are an adequate remedy, and if it is unlikely the order would ever be implemented. Here, the damage award of $181 million was not argued to be an unreasonable estimate of the loss suffered by Carbon County (D), calculated as the difference between the contract price times quantity, and the cost of mining coal. Therefore, damages were adequate to compensate Carbon County (D) and specific enforcement was unnecessary. Specific performance would also have been undesirable because the breach by NIPSCO (P) was economically efficient, halting a production process that was no longer cost-justified. A decree of specific performance would have been unenforceable in any event because NIPSCO (P) and

Carbon County (D) would have independently negotiated a cancellation of the contract given NIPSCO's (P) interest in minimizing its losses under the contract. Finally, the miners of Carbon County (D) were not third party real parties in interest to the contract such that the consequences of denying specific performance should have been considered; they assumed the risk that the coal mine would close down if uneconomical. Affirmed.

## ▶ ANALYSIS

Posner is well known for his economist's approach to the resolution of legal issues such as this. However, his denial of specific performance on the grounds that the jury award was not shown to be unreasonable ignored the fact that the contract at issue had many years to run and that the price of coal over its course would most likely be highly volatile. In such a case, damages are speculative at best and hard to calculate, and it seems less likely that the award would accurately forecast the future.

■=■

## Quicknotes

**BREACH OF CONTRACT** Unlawful failure by a party to perform its obligations pursuant to contract.

**COUNTERCLAIM** An independent cause of action brought by a defendant to a lawsuit in order to oppose or deduct from the plaintiff's claim.

**DAMAGES** Monetary compensation that may be awarded by the court to a party who has sustained injury or loss to his person, property or rights due to another party's unlawful act, omission or negligence.

**SPECIFIC PERFORMANCE** An equitable remedy whereby the court requires the parties to perform their obligations pursuant to a contract.

■=■

# Walgreen Co. v. Sara Creek Property Co.

## Tenant (P) v. Landlord (D)

966 F.2d 273 (7th Cir. 1992).

**NATURE OF CASE:** Appeal from a grant of permanent injunctive relief in suit for breach of contract.

**FACT SUMMARY:** Walgreen Co. (P) filed suit to enforce a clause contained in its lease agreement that provided that no space in the mall would be rented to a competing pharmacy.

**RULE OF LAW**
Where the costs of injunctive relief are less than the costs of a damages remedy, injunctive relief is an appropriate remedy, even when the damages remedy is not shown to be inadequate.

**FACTS:** Walgreen Co. (P) operated a pharmacy in a mall under a lease that provided that the landlord, Sara Creek Property Co. (Sara Creek) (D), would not lease space to anyone else who wanted to operate a pharmacy or store containing a pharmacy in the mall. After losing its primary tenant, Sara Creek (D) informed Walgreen (P) that it intended to lease space to Phar-Mor, a "deep discount" chain. The Phar-Mor store would include a pharmacy. Walgreen (P) filed a diversity suit for breach of contract and asked for injunctive relief mandating compliance with the nonrental clause. Sara Creek (D) offered evidence that Walgreen's (P) damages were readily ascertainable. The injunction was granted and Sara Creek (D) appealed.

**ISSUE:** Where the costs of injunctive relief are less than the costs of a damages remedy, is injunctive relief an appropriate remedy even when the damages remedy is not shown to be inadequate?

**HOLDING AND DECISION:** (Posner, J.) Yes. Where the costs of injunctive relief are less than the costs of a damages remedy, injunctive relief is an appropriate remedy, even when the damages remedy is not shown to be inadequate. Generally, the plaintiff seeking an injunction has the burden of persuasion. In the case of a permanent injunction, it must be shown that damages are inadequate. If it is likely that the costs of the damages remedy would exceed the costs of the injunction, then for the sake of efficiency, the injunction is the proper remedy. In this case, despite testimony by Sara Creek (D) to the contrary, the damage remedy would have been difficult to compute. It would have required calculation of lost profits for at least ten years into the future. An injunction, on the other hand, removes the evidentiary issue from the court. And since supervision of the injunction would rest with Walgreen (P), the future cost to the court is likewise minimal. By imposing the injunction on Sara Creek (D), the issue becomes one of private bargaining. The parties are free to

negotiate a fee for the removal of the injunction. The trial court properly weighed the costs and benefits of injunctive relief. Affirmed.

## ANALYSIS

Certain categories of contracts will regularly win equitable remedies. Where subject matter is unique, such as with real estate, specific performance will usually be granted; the rationale is that money damages cannot adequately compensate for the loss of a unique item. This is, however, something of a fallacy since most individuals would be willing to bargain away rights to a specific item for some price. The problem, however, rests with the trier of fact, as it is next to impossible to determine the appropriate premium to pay for the loss of a unique item.

## Quicknotes

**BREACH OF CONTRACT** Unlawful failure by a party to perform its obligations pursuant to contract.

**INJUNCTION** A court order requiring a person to do, or prohibiting that person from doing, a specific act.

**INJUNCTIVE RELIEF** A court order issued as a remedy, requiring a person to do, or prohibiting that person from doing, a specific act.

# Bernstein v. Nemeyer

Partner (P) v. Partner (D)

Conn. Sup. Ct., 213 Conn. 665, 570 A.2d 164 (1990).

**NATURE OF THE CASE:** Appeal from denial of rescission and restitution.

**FACT SUMMARY:** Bernstein (P) sought to rescind his partnership agreement with Nemeyer (D) after Nemeyer (D) breached his negative cash flow guarantee, leading to the loss of their entire investment.

## 🏛 RULE OF LAW
An injured party is not entitled to restitution where the breaching party has not been enriched and cannot be put back in the position he would have been in before the contract.

**FACTS:** Nemeyer (D) induced Bernstein (P) to invest $1,050,000 for the purchase and renovation of two apartment complexes by guaranteeing a negative cash flow. Although Bernstein (P) was aware of the risks of foreclosure due to the negative cash flow, he entered into this partnership for the purpose of creating a tax shelter. Nemeyer (D) defaulted on their obligations, which resulted in foreclosure of the apartment complexes. Thus, both parties lost their investment. Bernstein (P) filed suit to rescind the contract and requesting restitution of his initial investment. The trial court denied relief, holding that Nemeyer's (D) breach of guarantee was not material. Bernstein (P) appealed.

**ISSUE:** Is an injured party entitled to restitution where the breaching party has not been enriched and cannot be put back in the position he would have been in before the contract?

**HOLDING AND DECISION:** (Peters, C.J.) No. An injured party is not entitled to restitution where the breaching party has not been enriched and cannot be put back in the position he would have been in before the contract. The objective of a restitutionary remedy is to prevent unjust enrichment of the breaching party and to put him back in the position he would have been but for the contract. The courts have the discretion to award a restitutionary remedy. First, contrary to the trial court's ruling, the breach here was material. A material breach of a contract, however, does not automatically entitle the injured party to restitution; it only discharges the injured party's duty to perform and allows recovery of damages. Thus, the plaintiff has to prove his right to a restitutionary remedy. To be entitled to restitution, the plaintiff must show that he has attempted as best as possible to put the defendant in the same situation that existed before the contract was made. Here, however, Bernstein (P) was not entitled to recover restitutionary damages because the rec-

ord was unclear as to whether he made any efforts to tender back his partnership interests to Nemeyer (D), as required for rescission and restitution. Furthermore, the facts indicated that Nemeyer (D) was not unjustly enriched but that he suffered a great loss himself. Affirmed.

## ▶ ANALYSIS

The Restatement (Second) of Contracts provides a formula to measure the restitutionary remedy available to an injured party. It allows the injured party to recover the reasonable value of his performance less any benefits he may have received.

---

## Quicknotes

**RESCISSION** The canceling of an agreement and the return of the parties to their positions prior to the formation of the contract.

**RESTITUTION** The return or restoration to rightful owner to prevent unjust enrichment.

**UNJUST ENRICHMENT** Principle that one should not be unjustly enriched at the expense of another.

# Glendale Federal Bank, FSB v. United States

Bank (P) v. Federal government (D)

378 F.3d 1308 (Fed. Cir. 2004), *cert. denied*, 544 U.S. 904 (2005).

**NATURE OF CASE:** Appeal and cross-appeal from damages award following remand in action for breach of contract and damages.

**FACT SUMMARY:** The Government (D) contended that Glendale Federal Bank, FSB (Glendale) (P) was not entitled to a damages award of $381 million for "wounded bank" reliance damages because Glendale (P) allegedly failed to prove that it would have remained in capital compliance in the absence of the Government's (D) breach. Glendale (P) contended that it was entitled to an additional $527 million for its actual out-of-pocket losses.

## RULE OF LAW

Post-breach reliance damages may be awarded for a breach of contract where they are not speculative and represent real costs that the plaintiff would not have incurred but for the defendant's breach, and where other damages theories are inapposite.

**FACTS:** During the 1980s savings and loan (S&L) crisis, the Government (D), through the Federal Home Loan Bank Board (FHLBB), induced healthy S&L banks, including Glendale Federal Bank, FSB (Glendale) (P), to acquire and operate failed S&Ls. The benefit to the Government (D) was that the liability of the Federal Savings and Loan Insurance Corporation (FSLIC) would be lessened. In return, the Government (D) promised to treat the goodwill (excess of purchase price over fair market value) as capital to meet bank reserve requirements and to amortize the capital over 40 years. Subsequently, the Government (D), through new regulations (Financial Institutions Reform, Recovery, and Enforcement Act of 1989 [FIRREA]), repudiated such favorable treatment of the good will, and instead required the acquiring banks to contribute new capital to meet their reserve requirements. Some of the acquiring banks, including Glendale (P), sued the Government (D) for breach of contract, and the United States Supreme Court held in *United States v. Winstar*, 518 U.S. 839 (1996), that the Government (D) was liable for the breach, but remanded these cases to the Federal Court of Claims for a determination of damages. In Glendale's (P) case, Glendale's (P) first damages trial resulted in a $909 million damages award, which was based on theories of restitution and "expectancy damages" based on lost profits. On appeal, the Federal Circuit vacated the judgment and remanded for a new damages trial, finding that only reliance damages actually incurred could be awarded. These amounted to $381 million, based on post-breach damages. At the second damages trial, Glendale (P) sought to rein-

state these reliance damages, which it called "wounded bank" damages. It also claimed an additional $527 million for actual out-of-pocket losses. The Government (D), on the other hand, determined that damages were zero. The trial court awarded the "wounded bank" damages, but denied the out-of-pocket damages, finding that Glendale's (P) reliance damages model failed to measure the actual losses it sustained as a result of the Government's (D) breach. The Government (D) appealed the award of "wounded bank" damages, and Glendale (P) cross-appealed the denial of the additional damages. The court of appeals granted review.

**ISSUE:** May post-breach reliance damages be awarded for a breach of contract where they are not speculative and represent real costs that the plaintiff would not have incurred but for the defendant's breach, and where other damages theories are inapposite?

**HOLDING AND DECISION:** (Plager, J.) Yes. Post-breach reliance damages may be awarded for a breach of contract where they are not speculative and represent real costs that the plaintiff would not have incurred but for the defendant's breach, and where other damages theories are inapposite. The "expectancy damages" theory is inapposite for the case at hand because damages such as lost profits are too speculative and present proof problems. While such a theory is not per se barred as a matter of law, given the proof problems and speculative nature of the damages, in this case (and the other *Winstar* cases like it) the use of this theory is a waste of time. A restitution theory of damages is also flawed because it is based on the Government's (D) theoretical gains, which in this case are also speculative and indeterminate. Such a theory, however, may have limited use where it is used to return the acquiring bank to the status quo ante when specific initial contributions to an acquired bank have been established. Reliance damages—a form of restitutionary damages that are based on recovery of expenditures by the bank in performing the contract—are supportable when they are based on actual losses that are fully proven. Here, Glendale's (P) "wounded bank" reliance damages are basically the increase in the cost of funds Glendale (P) allegedly incurred as a result of the breach, which occurred three years after the breach when Glendale (P) could no longer meet its capital reserve requirements, depositors and others became nervous about placing funds with it, the bank was required to pay more interest to attract depositors, and it was required to pay higher fees for deposit

*Continued on next page.*

insurance. The Government (D) argues, however, that Glendale (P) failed to prove that it would have remained in capital compliance absent the breach, and that its "wounded bank" damages were based on the same model it used to prove lost profits under a now-discredited expectancy damages theory. The trial court rejected this argument, and was correct in doing so, since its "wounded bank" damages were not clearly erroneous, and were supported by the record. Whether such damages properly include the higher costs to a bank of conducting its general business after FIRREA is a matter of proof, and, if such damages are too speculative, they can and should be denied. Also, if a reasonable probability of damage can be clearly established, uncertainty as to the amount will not preclude recovery, and the court's duty is to make a fair and reasonable approximation of damages. With these considerations in mind, reliance damages that are susceptible of proof should be used in all the *Winstar* cases. Here, taking these considerations into account, there was no clear showing that the trial court's decision was clearly erroneous. Affirmed.

▶ *ANALYSIS*

As this decision demonstrates, certain types of damages may be particularly suited to, or even tailored to, certain types of cases. One of the primary purposes of contract damages is to put the nonbreaching party in the position it would have been in if the breaching party had fully performed, but, as also illustrated here, it may be difficult to determine without speculation what that position would have been. Thus, damages are usually limited to those that can be reasonably ascertained and proven—in this case, reliance damages.

■▬■

*Quicknotes*

**BREACH OF CONTRACT** Unlawful failure by a party to perform its obligations pursuant to contract.

**DAMAGES** Monetary compensation that may be awarded by the court to a party who has sustained injury or loss to his person, property or rights due to another party's unlawful act, omission or negligence.

**EXPECTATION DAMAGES** Damages awarded in actions for non-performance of a contract, which are calculated by subtracting the injured party's actual dollar position as a result of the breach from that party's expected dollar position had the breach not occurred.

**RELIANCE DAMAGES** The injury suffered by a party to a breached contract as the result of that party's dependence on the agreement.

**REMAND** To send back for additional scrutiny or deliberation.

**REPUDIATION** The actions or statements of a party to a contract that evidence his intent not to perform, or to continue performance, of his duties or obligations thereunder.

**RESTITUTION** The return or restoration to rightful owner to prevent unjust enrichment.

■▬■

# Clark v. Marsiglia

Owner of paintings (D) v. Painting restorer (P)

N.Y. Sup. Ct., 1 Denio 317 (1845).

**NATURE OF CASE:** Appeal from judgment for plaintiff in an action to enforce a service contract.

**FACT SUMMARY:** Clark (D), who had contracted with Marsiglia (P) to restore some of Clark's (D) paintings, argued that once he instructed Marsiglia (P) to stop work, Clark (D) could only be liable for Marsiglia's (P) damages, rather than the price agreed on in the contract.

## RULE OF LAW
Where one party to a contract for services repudiates, the other party must cease performance where doing so would mitigate damages.

**FACTS:** Clark (D) contracted with Marsiglia (P) to restore two sets of Clark's (D) paintings. The price for restoring the first set was $75, and the price for the second was $156. After Marsiglia (P) finished work on the first set, and started on the second, Clark (D) instructed Marsiglia (P) to cease work. Marsiglia (P) ignored this instruction and completed the work. When Clark (D) refused to pay for work performed after Clark (D) made his instruction to cease, Marsiglia (P) sued for payment of the entire contract price to restore the second set of paintings. The trial court instructed the jury that Marsiglia (P) had a right to finish (and charge for) the work on the second set once he had started the work. Accordingly, the jury returned a verdict for Marsiglia (P). The state's highest court granted review.

**ISSUE:** Where one party to a contract for services repudiates, must the other party cease performance where doing so would mitigate damages?

**HOLDING AND DECISION:** (Per curiam.) Yes. Where one party to a contract for services repudiates, the other party must cease performance where doing so would mitigate damages. The trial court erred in permitting Marsiglia (P) to recover as though he had no notice of Clark's (D) repudiation. By repudiating, Clark (D) would be liable for the time spent and materials used by Marsiglia (P), as well as any legal damages for breach of contract, but Marsiglia (P) "had no right, by obstinately persisting in the work, to make the penalty upon [Clark (D)] greater than it would otherwise have been." To hold otherwise could lead to injustice for the repudiating party. In such cases, the just claims of the non-repudiating party are satisfied when he is fully compensated for his part performance and indemnified for his loss in respect to the part left unexecuted; to persist in the work in a manner that enlarges the repudiating party's damages is not consistent with good faith towards that party. Reversed.

## ANALYSIS

*Clark* is a seminal mitigation case, and has been followed almost universally. Although the principles announced by *Clark* apply mainly in the context of service contracts, they have also been applied to contracts for the sale of goods, as where a nonrepudiating party ships goods—at great expense—to the place of delivery notwithstanding that it has received notice that the repudiating party will not accept delivery.

## Quicknotes

**REPUDIATION** The actions or statements of a party to a contract that evidence his intent not to perform, or to continue performance, of his duties or obligations thereunder.

# Spang Industries, Inc., Fort Pitt Bridge Division v. Aetna Casualty & Surety Co.

Steel supplier (P) v. Steel buyer's surety (D)

512 F.2d 365 (2d Cir. 1975).

**NATURE OF CASE:** Appeal from damages award in action to recover money due on a contract.

**FACT SUMMARY:** Spang Industries, Inc., Fort Pitt Bridge Division (Fort Pitt) (P) agreed to supply steel to Torrington Construction Co., Inc. (Torrington) (D) for use on a construction project, but delays in delivery resulted in inconvenience and extra work for Torrington's (D) employees. Fort Pitt (P) contended that Torrington (D) could not offset these damages against the contract price.

> ## RULE OF LAW
> A party who breaches a contract may be held liable for all damages that could reasonably have been anticipated at the time the agreement was entered into.

**FACTS:** Spang Industries, Inc., Fort Pitt Bridge Division (Fort Pitt) (P), promised to supply Torrington Construction Co., Inc. (Torrington) (D) with steel Torrington (D) needed to erect a bridge. Their agreement was confirmed by a letter from Fort Pitt (P) which stated, "Delivery to be mutually agreed upon." Torrington (D), in November of 1969, advised Fort Pitt (P) that the steel would be needed late in June 1970, and Torrington (D) verified that date in the middle of January. On January 29, Fort Pitt (P) informed Torrington (D) that the June delivery date could probably not be met, but, pursuant to Torrington's (D) threat to cancel the contract, Fort Pitt (P) agreed to ship the steel early in August. Delivery finally commenced in late August, although not until September 16 was there enough steel on hand to begin work on the bridge. This delayed the pouring of concrete until late October, by which time threats of freezing weather made it necessary for Torrington (D) to make use of extra equipment and pay its employees overtime. This resulted in additional expenses for Torrington (D), which had already incurred unexpected expenses when it had to unload some of the steel itself because Fort Pitt (P) had failed to notify the subcontractor responsible for the unloading. Fort Pitt (P) sued the Aetna Casualty & Surety Co. (D), which had posted a general contractor's bond, to recover money due under the contract. Torrington (D) then sued in a different court to recover for damages sustained as a result of Fort Pitt's (P) delay in delivering the steel. Fort Pitt (P) counterclaimed for the amount Torrington (D) owed on the contract. The two actions were consolidated for trial, and the judge ruled that Fort Pitt's (P) tardy delivery of the steel constituted breach of the contract and entitled Tor-

rington (D) to recover more than $7,600 in damages. The judge also ruled that Fort Pitt (P) was entitled to recover the amount Torrington (D) owed on the contract, less the $7,600. Judgment was then entered against Torrington (D) and Aetna (D) in the amount of nearly $16,000. Fort Pitt (P), however, appealed, contending that Torrington (D) should not have been allowed to recover any damages because the expenses it suffered had not been reasonably within the contemplation of the parties at the time that they had entered into the contract. The court of appeals granted review.

**ISSUE:** May a party who breaches a contract be held liable for all damages that could reasonably have been anticipated at the time the agreement was entered into?

**HOLDING AND DECISION:** (Mulligan, J.) Yes. A party who breaches a contract may be held liable for all damages that could reasonably have been anticipated at the time the agreement was entered into. This is the rule that was established by the well-known case of *Hadley v. Baxendale*, 156 Eng. Rep. 145 (Ex. 1854). Fort Pitt (P) argued that it did not know at the time the contract was entered into that delivery of the steel would be expected in June 1970. However, the parties both agreed that a mutually acceptable delivery date would be arranged, and Fort Pitt (P) acquiesced on the June date. In so doing, Fort Pitt (P) must have realized that any extensive delays in shipment would, by reason of unsatisfactory weather conditions that might arise, occasion added efforts and costs on the part of Torrington (D). Since the costs incurred by Torrington (D) were entirely foreseeable, the trial court quite properly awarded damages to Torrington (D). Affirmed.

## ANALYSIS

It seems fair to require a breaching party to bear the cost of damages that are caused by his conduct. But, in order to prevent liability from being imposed in an amount totally disproportionate to the nature and extent of the breaching party's conduct, the courts have developed the rule that a party may be held liable only for anticipated damages. Some courts have modified the *Hadley v. Baxendale* rule, 9 Exch. 341, 156 Eng. Rep. 145 (Ct. of Exchequer 1854), by imposing no liability for damages which, though foreseeable, would occur only under extremely unusual circumstances. The *Hadley v. Baxendale* rule is virtually identical with the rule that holds a tortfeasor liable for the natural and probable (foreseeable) consequences of

*Continued on next page.*

his acts and is embodied, in slightly different language, in § 2-715(2) of the Uniform Commercial Code.

## Quicknotes

**BREACH OF CONTRACT**  Unlawful failure by a party to perform its obligations pursuant to contract.

**DAMAGES**  Monetary compensation that may be awarded by the court to a party who has sustained injury or loss to his person, property or rights due to another party's unlawful act, omission or negligence.

# Hydraform Products Corp. v. American Steel & Aluminum Corp.

Steel purchaser (P) v. Steel seller (D)

N.H. Sup. Ct., 127 N.H. 187, 498 A.2d 339 (1985).

**NATURE OF CASE:** Appeal in action for negligent misrepresentation and breach of contract.

**FACT SUMMARY:** American Steel & Aluminum Corp. (D), supplying steel to Hydraform Products Corp. (P), attempted to enforce a limitation of damages clause in its contract which barred consequential damages.

## 🏛 RULE OF LAW
Consequential damages must be reasonably foreseeable, ascertainable, and unavoidable.

**FACTS:** Hydraform Products Corp. (Hydraform) (P) entered into a contract with American Steel & Aluminum Corp. (American) (D) to supply steel used in the fabrication of wood stoves. The delivery receipt, signed by agents of Hydraform (P), disclaimed liability for consequential damages. Some of the steel deliveries were late. When Hydraform (P) complained, American (D) promised that if steel for 400 stoves was ordered, American (D) would stockpile steel in advance. Deliveries continued to be slow or defective. Hydraform (P) finally attempted to obtain steel elsewhere, but it was unsuccessful. Hydraform (P) sold its wood stove division for $150,000 after selling only 250 stoves. Hydraform (P) then filed suit for breach of contract, claiming $100,000 for lost profits and $220,000 for the loss on the sale. The jury at trial awarded consequential damages of $80,245.12. American (D) appealed the award of consequential damages.

**ISSUE:** Must consequential damages be reasonably foreseeable, ascertainable, and unavoidable?

**HOLDING AND DECISION:** (Souter, J.) Yes. Consequential damages must be reasonably foreseeable, ascertainable, and unavoidable. First, a seller must know of general or particular requirements and needs of the buyer to be bound by foreseeability. Second, damages sought must be reasonable consequences of the breach. Third, consequential damages may only be recovered if they could not be prevented by cover or otherwise. In this case, the contract with American (D) contemplated the sale of 400 stoves. Thus, lost profits up to 400 stoves were foreseeable and ascertainable. Hydraform (P) attempted to cover, so the lost profits were not avoidable. However, damages beyond the 400 stoves were not clearly foreseeable. And damages for subsequent years were not readily ascertainable. Furthermore, the diminution of value on the sale of the business was based upon future profits, which were not readily ascertainable. The jury should only have been entitled to consider a claim for lost profits on stoves, the difference between the 400 referenced in the contract and the 250 actually sold. Reversed.

## ▶ ANALYSIS

Proving loss of future profits is a difficult proposition. However, the history of business is one source for such proof if the business has a long track record upon which to infer lost profits. Of course, even a new business can recover lost future profits if they can be ascertained with reasonable certainty.

---

## Quicknotes

**BREACH OF CONTRACT** Unlawful failure by a party to perform its obligations pursuant to contract.

**CONSEQUENTIAL DAMAGES** Monetary compensation that may be recovered in order to compensate for injuries or losses sustained as a result of damages that are not the direct or foreseeable result of the act of a party, but that nevertheless are the consequence of such act and which must be specifically pled and demonstrated.

**NEGLIGENT MISREPRESENTATION** A misrepresentation that is made pursuant to a business relationship, in violation of an obligation owed, upon which the plaintiff relies to his detriment.

# American Mechanical Corp. v. Union Machine Co. of Lynn, Inc.

Asset seller (P) v. Asset buyer (D)

Mass. App. Ct., 21 Mass. App. Ct. 97, 485 N.E.2d 680 (1985).

**NATURE OF THE CASE:** Appeal from award of nominal damages for breach of contract action.

**FACT SUMMARY:** When Union Machine Co. of Lynn, Inc.'s (D) repudiation of its contract with American Mechanical Corp. (American) (P) to purchase its real estate and machinery led to the foreclosure of its property, American (P) filed suit for breach of contract.

## RULE OF LAW

For breach of a real estate purchase contract, an injured party is entitled to recover his actual losses when the traditional recovery formula is inadequate.

**FACTS:** American Mechanical Corp. (American) (P) agreed to sell its real property to Union Machine Co. of Lynn, Inc. (Union) (D) for $135,000. Union (D) entered into the contract knowing that American (P) was in financial difficulty and was pressed by the bank to sell the real property. One month later, Union (D) repudiated the contract. After American (P) was unable to find another purchaser, the bank foreclosed and sold the property for $55,000. The machinery was sold for $35,000. In an action brought by American (P), the trial court concluded that there was a breach of contract but awarded only nominal damages. The state's intermediate appellate court granted review.

**ISSUE:** For breach of a real estate purchase contract, is an injured party entitled to recover his actual losses when the traditional recovery formula is inadequate?

**HOLDING AND DECISION:** (Fine, J.) Yes. For breach of a real estate purchase contract, an injured party is entitled to recover his actual losses when the traditional recovery formula is inadequate. The general rule is to place the injured party in the position he would have been had the contract been performed. Thus, in case of a breach, the injured party can recover foreseeable damages that were contemplated by the parties at the time of the contract. In an action for breach of a real estate purchase contract, the damages are measured by calculating the difference between the contract price and the market price at the time of the breach. When this formula creates an inadequate remedy, as in this case, the injured party should be compensated for the actual losses he has incurred. Here, the property was sold at a foreclosure sale for below the full market value. Thus, to give an adequate remedy, the correct measure of damages should be the difference between the contract price and the foreclosure sale price. American (P) proved that it suffered a $45,000 loss after receiving only $90,000 after the foreclosure of the property and sale of his machinery. [The judgment was vacated, and American (P) was awarded $46,000 plus interest.]

## ANALYSIS

The amount of damages awarded could have been reduced to the extent that American (P) could have mitigated its damages. The breaching party has the burden of proving that certain losses could have been avoided. The court found as a matter of fact that American (P) was unable to secure another purchaser on time. It should also be noted that the formula assessing damages by the difference between the contract price and the market price has generally been applied to contracts for sale of improved property or for lease of realty.

---

## Quicknotes

**BREACH OF CONTRACT** Unlawful failure by a party to perform its obligations pursuant to contract.

**DAMAGES** Monetary compensation that may be awarded by the court to a party who has sustained injury or loss to his person, property or rights due to another party's unlawful act, omission or negligence.

**MEASURE OF DAMAGES** Monetary compensation that may be awarded by the court to a party who has sustained injury or loss to his person, property or rights due to another party's unlawful act, omission or negligence.

# Locks v. Wade

Lessor (P) v. Lessee (D)

N.J. Super. Ct., App. Div., 36 N.J. Super. 128, 114 A.2d 875 (1955).

**NATURE OF CASE:** Appeal from judgment for plaintiff in action to recover for breach of contract.

**FACT SUMMARY:** Wade (D) breached its contract to rent a jukebox from Locks (P). Locks (P) rented the jukebox to someone else. There was evidence that jukeboxes were readily available on the market but that locations were hard to get.

## 🏛 RULE OF LAW
Where a lessee defaults on an agreement to lease an article, the supply of which is not limited, the lessor is not required to reduce his damages by the amount he actually did, or reasonably could, realize on a reletting of the article.

**FACTS:** Under a contract between them, Locks (P) leased to Wade (D) a jukebox for two years. Before the machine was installed, Wade (D) repudiated the contract. After the breach, Locks (P) rented the same machine to another person. He introduced evidence that jukeboxes were readily available on the market but that locations were difficult to get. Locks (P) sued for damages and awarded the total rent less his costs and depreciation by the trial court. The state's intermediate court of appeals granted review.

**ISSUE:** Where a lessee defaults on an agreement to lease an article, the supply of which is not limited, is the lessor required to reduce his damages by the amount he actually did, or reasonably could, realize on a reletting of the article?

**HOLDING AND DECISION:** (Clapp, J.) No. Where a lessee defaults on an agreement to lease an article, the supply of which is not limited, the lessor is not required to reduce his damages by the amount he actually did, or reasonably could, realize on a reletting of the article. For if there had been no breach and another customer had appeared, the lessor could as well have secured another such article and entered into a second lease. In the case of realty, which is specific and cannot be duplicated on the market, the lessor should not recover two profits merely because of the first lessee's default since that default enabled the lessor to make the second lease. Gains made by a lessor on a lease entered into after the lessee's breach should not be deducted from his damages unless the breach enabled him to make the gains. Opinion limited to the actual situation. [Affirmed.]

## ▶ ANALYSIS

In *Locks v. Wade*, the court computed lost profit by subtracting the cost to the plaintiff of purchasing the machine from the contract price. This figure was adjusted to reflect savings to Locks (P) from being relieved of performance and depreciation on the machine. This approach, rather than a simple comparison of contract and market price, is often employed in contracts for the manufacture and sale of goods where the seller is in the middle of performance at the time of the buyer's repudiation and elects to stop work and sue for damages. This method has a built-in mitigation feature—to compute actual loss caused by the breach, the plaintiff must first deduct from the contract price any savings realized by the breach.

■■■

## Quicknotes

**BREACH OF CONTRACT** Unlawful failure by a party to perform its obligations pursuant to contract.

■■■

# Inchaustegui v. 666 5th Avenue Limited Partnership

Injured individual (P) v. Landlord (D)

N.Y. App. Div., 268 A.D.2d 121, 706 N.Y.S.2d 396 (2000), *aff'd*, 725 N.Y.S.2d 627 (2001).

**NATURE OF CASE:** Appeal from summary judgment and damages award for a defendant third-party plaintiff in a breach of contract suit.

**FACT SUMMARY:** When a landlord was sued for premises injuries and failed to have liability insurance coverage because the landlord's sub-tenant neglected to name it as an additional insured under the sub-tenant's liability insurance policy, the landlord brought a third-party action against the sub-tenant for breach of its contract to have procured liability insurance with the landlord named as an additional insured.

## 🏛 RULE OF LAW
Where a tenant fails to procure insurance as required by a lease, the landlord may recover not only the cost of substitute insurance but also out-of-pocket costs not covered by that insurance.

**FACTS:** The sub-tenant (Petrofin) of a commercial lease was contractually required to maintain comprehensive liability insurance with the sub-lessor and landlord as additional insureds. When Petrofin obtained the policy, he failed to name the landlord as an additional insured. The plaintiff suffered personal injuries on the premises and sued the landlord. The landlord, in turn, brought a third-party claim against Petrofin, alleging violation of the lease's insurance procurement provision and moved for summary judgment, contending that Petrofin's failure to name the landlord as an additional insured constituted a breach of the sublease agreement, entitling the landlord to indemnity as well as money damages, including the costs incurred in the defense of the action. The trial court granted the motion but limited damages to the cost of maintaining and securing an independent policy of insurance. The state's intermediate appellate court granted review.

**ISSUE:** Where a tenant fails to procure insurance as required by a lease, may the landlord recover not only the cost of substitute insurance but also out-of-pocket costs not covered by that insurance?

**HOLDING AND DECISION:** (Saxe, J.) Yes. Where a tenant fails to procure insurance as required by a lease, the landlord may recover not only the cost of substitute insurance but also out-of-pocket costs not covered by that insurance. When a tenant breaches a contract with the landlord, as here, with respect to the procurement of insurance to cover the risk of liability to third parties, the usual penalty is to be liable for all the resulting damages. Where the landlord has procured its own insurance, case law limits the recovery to the cost of buying the insurance, i.e., contract damages. If, as here, the tenant fails to obtain the contemplated insurance coverage on behalf of the landlord (whether because the tenant procured no coverage at all, or because it neglected to have the landlord included as a named insured) in the absence of the contemplated coverage, any ultimate liability judgment against the landlord falls within the category of consequential damages. Under such circumstances, the landlord is entitled to recoup that amount, as well as any litigation expenses, from the tenant, since the tenant's failure to procure insurance on behalf of the landlord could reasonably be expected to result in such economic injury to the landlord. Moreover, the collateral source rule, developed for tort cases, is inapplicable to the analysis here because any insurance payments to the landlord are irrelevant here. Instead, the analysis is: to what extent did the cost of the landlord's insurance policy plus any other expenses not covered by the policy exceed the cost of insurance to Petrofin. The concept of subrogation focuses on permitting the insurer to recoup its payment from the party who has caused the damage, but here, Petrofin did not cause damage—it merely breached a contract. For these reasons, the landlord may recover not only the cost of its insurance policy, but any other consequential out-of-pocket damages not covered by the policy, such as co-payments, deductibles, premium increases, etc. Affirmed as modified.

## ▶ *ANALYSIS*

The *Inchaustegui* court noted that its position did not contravene the collateral source rule since the nature of contract damages is quite distinct from that of tort damages. While tort damages are expansive, focusing on the full spectrum of the harm caused by the tortfeasor, damages for a breach of contract are restrictive, limited to the economic injury actually caused to the claimant as a consequence of the other party's breach.

---

## *Quicknotes*

**BREACH OF CONTRACT** Unlawful failure by a party to perform its obligations pursuant to contract.

**DAMAGES** Monetary compensation that may be awarded by the court to a party who has sustained injury or loss to his person, property or rights due to another party's unlawful act, omission or negligence.

**PERSONAL INJURY** Harm to an individual's person or body.

*Continued on next page.*

**SUMMARY JUDGMENT** Judgment rendered by a court in response to a motion made by one of the parties, claiming that the lack of a question of material fact in respect to an issue warrants disposition of the issue without consideration by the jury.

**TORT DAMAGES** Monetary compensation awarded by the court to a party injured as the result of the tortious act of another.

# Reliance Cooperage Corp. v. Treat

Barrel staves purchaser (P) v. Barrel staves seller (D)

195 F.2d 977 (8th Cir. 1952).

**NATURE OF CASE:** Appeal from award of damages in action for breach of a contract for the sale of goods.

**FACT SUMMARY:** Reliance Cooperage Corp. (P) contracted to buy barrel staves from Treat (D) at $450 per thousand for bourbon quality and $40 per thousand for oil grade quality. When the price rose during the four months between the contracting date and delivery date, Treat (D) did not perform.

## RULE OF LAW
Whether a seller breaches a contract by giving the buyer notice of renunciation or simply fails to perform, the damages awarded the buyer shall be measured as the difference between the contract price and the market price on the date delivery was due.

**FACTS:** Reliance Cooperage Corp. (Reliance) (P) contracted to buy barrel staves from Treat (D) at $450 per thousand for bourbon quality and $40 per thousand for oil grade quality. The contract was signed July 12, 1950, with delivery set for no later than December 31, 1950. On August 12, 1950, Treat (D) wrote Reliance (P), stating its inability to deliver staves at the contract price, as the market price had risen from $475 to $500 per thousand for bourbon quality. On October 6, 1950, after receiving notice by telephone in either August or September from Treat (D) that staves would not be delivered, Reliance (P) wrote Treat (D), stating its expectation that Treat (D) would fulfill its obligation. The market price of staves on December 31, 1950, was about $750 per thousand. Treat (D) never delivered. At trial, the jury was instructed that Reliance (P) had a duty to mitigate, and accordingly awarded Reliance (P) only $500 in damages. Reliance (P) appealed, and the court of appeals granted review.

**ISSUE:** Whether a seller breaches a contract by giving the buyer notice of renunciation or simply fails to perform, shall the damages awarded the buyer be measured as the difference between the contract price and the market price on the date delivery was due?

**HOLDING AND DECISION:** (Sanborn, J.) Yes. Whether a seller breaches a contract by giving the buyer notice of renunciation or simply fails to perform, the damages awarded the buyer shall be measured as the difference between the contract price and the market price on the date delivery was due. Treat's (D) notice of repudiation in no way affected his liability. The measure of damages remained the same as for simple nonperformance. Reliance (P) should receive the difference between the contract price and the market price on the date of delivery. This measure would have remained the same had Reliance (P) accepted the anticipatory repudiation as an actionable breach of the contract. Under Restatement (First) § 338, repudiation does not accelerate the time fixed for performance, nor does it change the measure of damages. A party has no duty to mitigate damages until there are damages to mitigate. Damages did not arise until December 31, 1950. To hold that Reliance (P) had to mitigate before December 31, 1950, while still holding itself open to accept Treat's (D) performance during the same period has no justification. To so hold would encourage repudiations as the market rose and fell. Reversed and remanded.

## ANALYSIS

The rule of this case has been changed by Uniform Commercial Code § 2-713(1). While the measure is still the difference between the market price and the contract price, it is applied to the day notice of breach was made rather than to the day of delivery because of an additional code provision. Under the new provision, the buyer may cover, that is, make a good-faith purchase or contract to purchase substitute goods without unreasonable delay. Buyer may then recover the difference between the contract price and the cover price. This helps to remove the difficulty of proving market price at trial. By measuring damages under the Uniform Commercial Code on the day notice of breach was made (or the day the buyer learned of the breach), that day is the time when buyer should cover the market for substitute goods. Note, however, that if buyer breaches, the day of measure remains the day set for delivery.

### Quicknotes

**ANTICIPATORY REPUDIATION** Breach of a contract subsequent to formation but prior to the time performance is due.

**BREACH OF CONTRACT** Unlawful failure by a party to perform its obligations pursuant to contract.

**DAMAGES** Monetary compensation that may be awarded by the court to a party who has sustained injury or loss to his person, property or rights due to another party's unlawful act, omission or negligence.

*Continued on next page.*

**MEASURE OF DAMAGES** Monetary compensation that may be awarded by the court to a party who has sustained injury or loss to his person, property or rights due to another party's unlawful act, omission or negligence.

**RENUNCIATION** The abandonment of a right or interest.

# Rivers v. Deane

### Contractor (D) v. Property owner (P)

N.Y. App. Div., 209 A.D.2d 936, 619 N.Y.S.2d 419 (1994).

**NATURE OF CASE:** Appeal of damages award calculation in an action for breach of contract.

**FACT SUMMARY:** An addition to a home was constructed in such a faulty manner as to render it unusable, and damages were awarded at trial based upon diminution of value.

## 🏛 RULE OF LAW
In the case of faulty construction, the proper measure of damages is the market value of the cost to repair the faulty construction.

**FACTS:** Deane (P) contracted with Rivers (D) to build an addition to Deane's (P) home. The addition was so faulty that the third floor of the addition was unusable. Deane (P) filed suit. At trial, the court awarded Deane (P) damages for the diminution in value of the home, the difference between market value with proper construction and market value as completed. Rivers (D) appealed the calculation method of damages.

**ISSUE:** In the case of faulty construction, is the proper measure of damages the market value of the cost to repair the faulty construction?

**HOLDING AND DECISION:** [No judge stated in casebook excerpt.] Yes. In the case of faulty construction, the proper measure of damages is the market value of the cost to repair the faulty construction. In cases where a builder's failure to perform is very trivial, the cost of repair can be greater than the diminution of value to the house on the market. Where that is the situation, diminution of value is the proper manner to calculate damages. In this case, however, the failure to perform was severe. A portion of the house was unusable. Here, the proper manner to calculate damages is the cost to correct the work, not the diminution of market value. Modified, and as modified affirmed.

## ▶ ANALYSIS

When construction is defective, contract law generally favors awarding the injured party sufficient compensation to correct the defect. However, contract law attempts to avoid needless waste by declining to award correction damages when the cost to repair a minor defect is much greater than the diminution of value. Economic efficiency is balanced against the expectations of the aggrieved party.

## Quicknotes

**BREACH OF CONTRACT** Unlawful failure by a party to perform its obligations pursuant to contract.

**DAMAGES** Monetary compensation that may be awarded by the court to a party who has sustained injury or loss to his person, property or rights due to another party's unlawful act, omission or negligence.

**MEASURE OF DAMAGES** Monetary compensation that may be awarded by the court to a party who has sustained injury or loss to his person, property or rights due to another party's unlawful act, omission or negligence.

# Peevyhouse v. Garland Coal & Mining Company

Lessor of land (P) v. Lessee (D)

Okla. Sup. Ct., 1962 OK 267, 382 P.2d 109 (1962).

**NATURE OF CASE:** Cross-appeals from award of damages for breach of contract.

**FACT SUMMARY:** Garland Coal & Mining Company (D) promised it would perform restorative and remedial work on the Peevyhouses' (P) farm at the end of a lease period, but then argued that the cost of the repair work would far exceed the total value of the farm.

## RULE OF LAW
Where a lease provision breached is merely incidental to the lease's main purpose, and where the economic benefit that would result to lessor by full performance is grossly disproportionate to the cost of performance, the damages that lessor may recover are limited to the diminution in value resulting to the premises because of the nonperformance.

**FACTS:** The Peevyhouses (P) owned a farm with coal deposits on it. This land was leased in November 1954 to Garland Coal & Mining Company (Garland) (D) for five years for coal mining purposes. Garland (D) also agreed to perform restorative and remedial work at the end of the lease period at a cost estimated at about $29,000. After Garland (D) failed to restore the land, Peevyhouse (P) sued for $25,000. Garland (D) introduced testimony at trial as to the diminution of value of the farm due to Garland's (D) failure to perform under the contract. The jury awarded Peevyhouse (P) $5,000, which was more than the total value of the farm even after the remedial work was done, but only a fraction of the cost of performance. Peevyhouse (P) appealed, arguing that damages should be the cost to obtain performance of the work not done due to Garland's (D) default. The state's highest court granted review.

**ISSUE:** Where a lease provision breached is merely incidental to the lease's main purpose, and where the economic benefit that would result to lessor by full performance is grossly disproportionate to the cost of performance, are the damages that lessor may recover limited to the diminution in value resulting to the premises because of the nonperformance?

**HOLDING AND DECISION:** (Jackson, J.) Yes. Where a lease provision breached is merely incidental to the lease's main purpose, and where the economic benefit that would result to lessor by full performance is grossly disproportionate to the cost of performance, the damages that lessor may recover are limited to the diminution in value resulting to the premises because of the nonperformance. This is an issue of first impression. Here, if the remedial work were to be performed, the increase in market value to the premises would be $300. The damages recoverable are to be a reasonable amount that is not contrary to substantial justice. No reasonable property owner would pay $29,000 to improve his property to increase its value by only $300. Weighing the expense to improve and the relative economic benefit to be gained, the Peevyhouses (P) may not recover a greater amount for breach of an obligation than would have been gained by full performance. The judgment was excessive and should be reduced to $300, the diminution in value resulting from non-performance.

**DISSENT:** (Irwin, J.) Garland (D) knew that the cost of performance would be disproportionate to the value or benefits received by Peevyhouse (P) when it entered into the contract. The function of a court is to enforce a contract as it is written. Peevyhouse (P) was entitled to specific performance, or failing that, the cost of that performance.

## ANALYSIS

The Restatement (Second) of Contracts, § 348, reflects this court's decision. Section 348(2)(a) states that "if a breach results in defective or unfinished construction and the loss in value to the injured party is not proved with sufficient certainty, he may recover damages based on the diminution in the market price of the property caused by the breach." Under § 348(2)(b), the injured party may, in the alternative, recover damages based on "the reasonable cost of completing performance or of remedying the defects if that cost is not clearly disproportionate to the probable loss of value."

## Quicknotes

**BREACH OF CONTRACT** Unlawful failure by a party to perform its obligations pursuant to contract.

**DAMAGES** Monetary compensation that may be awarded by the court to a party who has sustained injury or loss to his person, property or rights due to another party's unlawful act, omission or negligence.

**NONPERFORMANCE** Failure to perform a duty.

**SPECIFIC PERFORMANCE** An equitable remedy whereby the court requires the parties to perform their obligations pursuant to a contract.

# American Standard, Inc. v. Schectman

Property owner (P) v. Contractor (D)

N.Y. App. Div., 439 N.Y.S.2d 529 (1981).

**NATURE OF CASE:** Appeal from award of damages for breach of contract.

**FACT SUMMARY:** Schectman (D) contended that the correct measure of damages for his failure to complete grading American Standard, Inc.'s (P) land was the diminution in value of the land, rather than the cost of completion.

## RULE OF LAW
Only where the cost of completing a contract entails unreasonable economic waste is the correct measure of damages for breach of a construction contract diminution in value of the property in relation to what its value would have been if performance had been properly completed.

**FACTS:** Schectman (D) contracted to grade and to take down certain foundations to one foot below grade on American Standard Inc.'s (American's) (P) land. Schectman's (D) performance substantially deviated from the grading specifications in the contract. American (P) sued for breach and was awarded damages equal to the cost of completing the grading properly. Schectman (D) appealed, contending the trial court erred by refusing to admit evidence that American (P) sold the property for only $3,000 less than its full market value and therefore suffered no appreciable loss due to the breach. As a result, Schectman (D) argued, the correct measure of damages was this $3,000 diminution in value of the property due to the breach, rather than the cost of completion.

**ISSUE:** Only where the cost of completing a contract entails unreasonable economic waste, is the correct measure of damages for breach of a construction contract diminution in value of the property in relation to what its value would have been if performance had been properly completed?

**HOLDING AND DECISION:** (Hancock, J.) Yes. Only where the cost of completing a contract entails unreasonable economic waste is the correct measure of damages for breach of a construction contract diminution in value of the property in relation to what its value would have been if performance had been properly completed. The generally accepted measure of damages for breach of a construction contract is the cost of completing performance properly. Only where such cost of completion would entail unreasonable economic waste will the measure of damages be the diminution in the value of the property caused by the breach. Completing the job properly in this case would not require destruction of past work, only that

performance is completed. The fact that the sale price of the property was not markedly affected by the breach is irrelevant to the measure of damages determination. No unreasonable economic waste would result from awarding cost of completion damages; therefore, that measure was properly used. Affirmed.

## ANALYSIS
Some commentators criticize the result in this case as bestowing upon American (P) a windfall recovery. Not only was it able to sell the property for virtually its fair market value, $183,000, it also received a judgment against Schectman (D) for $90,000. Other commentators justify cost of completion awards as protecting the plaintiff's subjective value ascribed to the property.

### Quicknotes
**BREACH OF CONTRACT** Unlawful failure by a party to perform its obligations pursuant to contract.

**DAMAGES** Monetary compensation that may be awarded by the court to a party who has sustained injury or loss to his person, property or rights due to another party's unlawful act, omission or negligence.

**MEASURE OF DAMAGES** Monetary compensation that may be awarded by the court to a party who has sustained injury or loss to his person, property or rights due to another party's unlawful act, omission or negligence.

# Lowy v. United Pacific Insurance Co.

Contractor (D) v. Property owner (P)

Cal. Sup. Ct., 67 Cal. 2d 87, 429 P.2d 577 (1967).

**NATURE OF CASE:** Appeal from award of damages in a breach of contract action.

**FACT SUMMARY:** United Pacific Insurance Co. (P) refused to pay Lowy (D) the contract price for grading work he performed on a development because the work was not completed by Lowy (D).

> ⚖ **RULE OF LAW**
> A contractor may recover for work actually performed under a construction contract if he has substantially performed his contractual duty in good faith.

**FACTS:** United Pacific Insurance Co. (United Pacific) (P) entered into a contract whereby Lowy (D), a contractor, would perform certain excavation and grading work on lots and streets. The contract also required Lowy (D) to perform street improvement work, including paving and installing curbs and gutters. Payment for the grading work and for street improvements was to be made separately and was calculated on different scales. A separate surety bond was to be posted by Lowy (D) for each phase of the work. Lowy (D) completed 98 percent of the grading work before refusing to continue due to a dispute with United Pacific (P). United Pacific (P) hired another contractor to finish the grading and sued Lowy (D) for breach of contract. Lowy (D) cross-complained for breach, contending he could recover for his substantial performance of the grading portion of the contract. The trial court granted recovery to Lowy (D), holding the contract was severable and that United Pacific's (P) failure to pay Lowy (D) for his substantial performance of the grading work excused Lowy's (D) further performance of the contract. United Pacific (P) appealed.

**ISSUE:** May a contractor recover for work actually performed under a construction contract if he has substantially performed his contractual duty in good faith?

**HOLDING AND DECISION:** (McComb, J.) Yes. A contractor may recover for work actually performed under a construction contract if he has substantially performed his contractual duties in good faith. In this case, Lowy (D) ceased work due to a good-faith dispute over his responsibility for work not covered by the contract. At the time he stopped work, only two percent of the grading remained incomplete. Clearly, he had substantially performed the grading portion of the contract. Because the consideration under the contract was apportioned, the contract was severable. Therefore, even though no work was performed on the street improvement portion, this does not defeat recovery for the grading work. As a result, Lowy (D) was entitled to recover under the contract. Affirmed.

▶ **ANALYSIS**

The Restatement (Second) of Contracts, in § 240, states that the determination whether a contract is severable or not rests on whether the "performances to be exchanged under an exchange of promises can be apportioned into corresponding pairs of part performances so that the parts of each pair are properly regarded as agreed equivalents." Another approach to severability, used in the present case, looks to the apportionability of the consideration. The parties' intent to create a severable contract is implied where consideration is easily apportionable.

---

## Quicknotes

**BREACH OF CONTRACT** Unlawful failure by a party to perform its obligations pursuant to contract.

**DAMAGES** Monetary compensation that may be awarded by the court to a party who has sustained injury or loss to his person, property or rights due to another party's unlawful act, omission or negligence.

**DUTY OF GOOD FAITH OF FAIR DEALINGS** An implied duty in a contract that the parties will deal honestly in the satisfaction of their obligations and without an intent to defraud.

**IMPLIED CONTRACT** An agreement between parties that may be inferred from their general course of conduct.

**SUBSTANTIAL PERFORMANCE** Performance of all the essential obligations pursuant to an agreement.

# New Era Homes Corp. v. Forster

Contractor (P) v. Property owner (D)

N.Y. Ct. App., 299 N.Y. 303, 86 N.E.2d 757 (1949).

**NATURE OF CASE:** Appeal from affirmance of verdict for plaintiff in action to recover payment due under a contract.

**FACT SUMMARY:** Under its contract to remodel Forster's (D) home, New Era Homes Corp. (P) was to be paid certain amounts at certain stages. When Forster (D) refused to make the third payment, New Era Homes (P) brought suit to recover the amount of the payment.

## RULE OF LAW
The inclusion of a provision in a construction contract for partial payments to be made as the work progresses does not render the contract divisible where it is not clear from the contract terms that each progress payment is intended to be so apportioned to the corresponding portion of the work as to be the full consideration for that portion of work.

**FACTS:** New Era Homes Corp.'s (New Era's) (P) construction contract with Forster (D) fixed a total price for the work, but payments were to be paid upon the signing of the contract, upon New Era's (P) starting work, upon its completion of the rough carpentry, and upon completion of the whole job. When the rough carpentry was done, Forster (D) refused to make the third payment, and New Era (P) brought suit to recover the amount of the payment. New Era (P) offered no other proof of damages, and Forster (D) contended that New Era (P) could only recover the actual loss if sustained due to Forster's (D) breach. A jury returned a verdict for New Era (P), and the state's intermediate appellate court affirmed. The state's highest court granted review.

**ISSUE:** Does the inclusion of a provision in a construction contract for partial payments to be made as the work progresses render the contract divisible where it is not clear from the contract terms that each progress payment is intended to be so apportioned to the corresponding portion of the work as to be the full consideration for that portion of work?

**HOLDING AND DECISION:** (Desmond, J.) No. The inclusion of a provision in a construction contract for partial payments to be made as the work progresses does not render the contract divisible where it is not clear from the contract terms that each progress payment is intended to be so apportioned to the corresponding portion of the work as to be the full consideration for that portion of work. The parties to a construction contract may make it divisible and stipulate the value of each divisible part, but there is no sign here that New Era (P) and Forster (D) so

intended. Hence, New Era (P) can recover either in quantum meruit for what had been finished or in contract for the value of what New Era (P) had lost—the contract price, less payments made and less the cost of completion—but it cannot simply recover the amount of the payment. Reversed and new trial granted.

**DISSENT:** (Lewis, J.) The parties evidenced their intent to make the contract divisible by making payments due upon completion of discrete parts of the project. Therefore, the contract was divisible. Hence, New Era (P) should be able to recover the amount of the third payment.

## ANALYSIS

The tendency of many cases is to view provisions for progress payments in construction contracts as being designed for the convenience of the contractor, by providing him with funds as the work progresses or for the mutual convenience of both parties rather than as being intended to apportion the consideration into parts equivalent to corresponding parts of the work. Hence, such contracts have been held to be entire rather than divisible. There are, however, several cases that agree with the dissent in *New Era*.

## Quicknotes

**QUANTUM MERUIT** Equitable doctrine allowing recovery for labor and materials provided by one party, even though no contract was entered into, in order to avoid unjust enrichment by the benefited party.

# Britton v. Turner

## Laborer (P) v. Employer (D)

N.H. Sup. Ct., 6 N.H. 481 (1834).

**NATURE OF CASE:** Appeal from judgment for plaintiff in action to recover in quantum meruit for work done.

**FACT SUMMARY:** Britton (P) contracted to work for Turner (D) for an entire year but left without cause before the year was up.

🏛 **RULE OF LAW**
A defaulting party, although unable to recover on a contract, may recover under a quasi-contractual theory the reasonable value of his services less any damages to the other party arising out of the default.

**FACTS:** Britton (P) was under contract to labor for Turner (D) for one year and to be paid $120 for the work. Britton (P), without cause, left Turner's (D) employ after nine and one-half months and sought to recover the reasonable value of his labor. A jury awarded Britton (P) a verdict for $95.

**ISSUE:** May a defaulting party, although unable to recover on a contract, recover under a quasi-contractual theory the reasonable value of his services less any damages to the other party arising out of the default?

**HOLDING AND DECISION:** (Parker, J.) Yes. A defaulting party, although unable to recover on a contract, may recover under a quasi-contractual theory the reasonable value of his services less any damages to the other party arising out of the default. Although it is clear that one who has labored for only a portion of the contract term may not recover on the contract, he may recover in quantum meruit the reasonable value of his services to the extent that the other party has received a benefit in excess of damages arising from the breach. A contrary result would be unjust and unequal in its operation. By that result, "the party who attempts performance may be placed in a much worse situation than he who wholly disregards his contract, and the other party may receive much more, by the breach of the contract, than the injury, which he sustained by such breach, and more than he could be entitled to if he was seeking to recover damages by an action." In the present case, Turner (D) has been receiving benefit from day to day which he cannot now reject, and the circumstance is not distinguishable from those circumstances surrounding contracts to build houses where quantum meruit recoveries have been allowed despite deviations from the building contracts. Since Turner (D) has alleged no damages arising from Britton's (P) breach, the jury's verdict should be affirmed.

▶ *ANALYSIS*

The court here acknowledges the contrary rule that will not allow a breaching party any recovery after only part performance (subject to the doctrine of substantial performance). Even today the present case still represents the minority view, although the trend is in its direction. The Court emphasizes the injustice of the prevailing role that one who attempts performance is in a worse position than one who totally ignores the contract. Although there is a temptation to respond, "So what?" courts following Britton's lead have pointed to the arbitrary forfeitures which breachers would suffer and the pure windfalls to the breachees. Further, the current trend in contract law is not to treat a "breach" as an inherently evil thing; the effect of allowing an unabashed forfeiture would be to sanction a kind of punitive damage.

▬▬■▬

## Quicknotes

**BREACH OF CONTRACT** Unlawful failure by a party to perform its obligations pursuant to contract.

**DEFAULT** Failure to carry out a legal obligation.

**PUNITIVE DAMAGES** Damages exceeding the actual injury suffered for the purposes of punishment of the defendant, deterrence of the wrongful behavior or comfort to the plaintiff.

**QUANTUM MERUIT** Equitable doctrine allowing recovery for labor and materials provided by one party, even though no contract was entered into, in order to avoid unjust enrichment by the benefited party.

▬▬■▬

# Kaplan v. Mayo Clinic

## Patient (P) v. Health care company (D)

947 F. Supp. 2d 1001 (D. Minn. 2013).

**NATURE OF CASE:** Motion in limine, in remanded case, to disallow evidence of pain and suffering and emotional distress in support of breach of contract damages.

**FACT SUMMARY:** Kaplan (P), who had been misdiagnosed with pancreatic cancer, sought damages for pain and suffering and emotional distress in his breach of contract action against the Mayo Clinic (Mayo) (D), which had performed a surgical procedure to remove his non-existent cancer, but had failed to perform an intraoperative biopsy to confirm the cancer, which it allegedly had promised to do.

---

### 🏛 RULE OF LAW
Pain and suffering and emotional distress damages are not recoverable for breach of a contract between a physician and his patient.

---

**FACTS:** Kaplan (P) was misdiagnosed with pancreatic cancer. Dr. Nagorney, of Mayo Clinic (Mayo) (D), performed a surgical procedure to rid Kaplan (P) of the cancer, which, unbeknownst to Dr. Nagorney, was in fact nonexistent. Allegedly, Dr. Nagorney had promised to perform an intraoperative biopsy to determine if Kaplan (P) had cancer, but Dr. Nagorney failed to perform the biopsy. After the surgery, it was discovered that Kaplan (P) never had cancer. Kaplan (P) sued the diagnosing doctor, Dr. Burgart, Dr. Nagorney, and Mayo (D) in federal district court on claims for breach of contract and negligent failure to diagnose. The district court granted judgment as a matter of law against Kaplan (P) on the breach of contract claim, and the jury returned a verdict against Kaplan (P) on the claim for negligent failure to diagnose. The court of appeals reversed as to the breach of contract claim, concluding that a reasonable jury could find that Dr. Nagorney, on behalf of Mayo (D), formed a contract with Kaplan (P) when Nagorney told Kaplan (P) that he would perform the intraoperative biopsy to confirm the cancer diagnosis before proceeding with the surgery. The court of appeals found that Nagorney breached this contract when he failed to perform the promised biopsy, and it remanded for further proceedings on the breach of contract claim. On remand, Mayo (D) moved in limine to exclude evidence of pain and suffering and emotional distress.

**ISSUE:** Are pain and suffering and emotional distress damages recoverable for breach of a contract between a physician and his patient?

**HOLDING AND DECISION:** (Tunheim, J.) No. Pain and suffering and emotional distress damages are not recoverable for breach of a contract between a physician and his patient. A damage award in a breach of contract action is intended to place the nonbreaching party in the position in which he would be if the contract were performed. Thus, as a general matter, a plaintiff may recover those damages sustained by reason of the breach that have arisen naturally from the breach or could reasonably be supposed to have been contemplated by the parties when making the contract as the probable result of the breach. Extra-contractual damages, on the other hand, are those that do not flow naturally from the breach and are not reasonably anticipated by the parties to the contract. In this state, extra-contractual damages are not recoverable for breach of contract except in exceptional cases where the breach is accompanied by an independent tort. Here, a jury rejected Kaplan's (P) tort claims and the court of appeals affirmed the verdict, so there is no independent tort in the present case and Kaplan (P) cannot recover any extra-contractual damages. The difficulty, however, is determining whether pain and suffering and emotional distress damages constitute extra-contractual damages in the context of the alleged contract between Mayo (D) and Kaplan (P), especially since such damages might seem to be the natural proximate cause of a breach in certain types of contracts, such as the one at bar. The courts in this state, however, have expanded the prohibition on recovering such damages in a breach of contract action, even where those damages could be reasonably within the contemplation of the parties based on the nature of the contract. Instead of examining solely the foreseeability of certain damages to determine whether such damages may be extra-contractual, state law appears to restrict recoverable contractual damages more generally to those that are pecuniary in nature. Thus, under this state's approach, damages that are incapable of definite calculation and must necessarily rest in the discretion of the jury are considered to be extra-contractual and are recoverable only in tort actions. The legal issue presented has not been squarely decided by the state's highest court, so it is necessary for this court to predict how it would resolve the issue. Some courts that have considered the issue have held that where liability is predicated on the failure to perform an agreed undertaking rather than upon negligence, the damages are restricted to the payments made, the expenditure for nurses and medicines, or other damages that flow naturally from the breach of the contract between patient and physician, and do not include the patient's pain and suffering as in malpractice actions. Other courts, however, have applied the

*Continued on next page.*

general rule of contract law that a plaintiff may recover damages that were within the contemplation of the contracting parties. Based upon the state's general law governing contractual damages, it is likely the state's highest court would likely preclude Kaplan (P) from recovering pain and suffering and emotional distress damages based upon the breach of any contract formed with Mayo (D). Although it is possible that pain and suffering and emotional distress could have reasonably been within the contemplation of the parties based upon the nature of the contract at issue, the state's highest court has expressly rejected the approach of examining the underlying nature of the contract to determine whether damages such as those for mental anguish and pain and suffering are recoverable. Instead state law limits damages in a contract action to those capable of measurement by some definite rule or standard of compensation, and to the actual pecuniary loss naturally and necessarily flowing from the breach. Kaplan's (P) pain and suffering as well as any emotional distress he may have suffered are damages that, although recoverable in tort, do not appear to be recoverable in a breach of contract action under state law. Therefore, Mayo's (D) motion will be granted and Kaplan (P) will be precluded from presenting evidence of pain and suffering or emotional distress at trial to support his breach of contract action. This conclusion is supported by the court of appeals' determination that Kaplan (P) provided sufficient evidence of economic damages resulting from the surgery to meet the final requirement for making out the contract claim. The court of appeals noted that its conclusion was in keeping with the purpose of limiting extra-contractual damages, i.e., to preserve the boundary between contract and tort law. Kaplan (P) cannot use the breach of contract claim to attempt to recover all of the damages that may have been recoverable in the tort claims that were rejected by the jury. Although allegedly based on some of the same conduct, Kaplan's (P) breach of contract action is distinct as to theory, proof and damages from his tort claims; therefore he may not recover damages for pain and suffering and emotional distress. Motion granted.

## ▶ ANALYSIS

The rule disallowing extra-contractual damages in breach of contract actions is designed to insure that contract law is not swallowed by tort law, and, as in this case, courts limiting recoverable damages for breach of a contract by a physician have done so in part to maintain a clear distinction between tort and contract claims. Such courts emphasize that although actions of malpractice and breach of contract may arise out of the same transaction, they are distinct as to theory, proof and damages. On the other hand, courts that allow a plaintiff to recover mental anguish and pain and suffering damages in a contract with a physician focus on the underlying subject matter of the parties' agreement, reasoning that such contracts are concerned not with trade and commerce but with life and

death, a breach of which would inevitably and necessarily result in mental anguish, pain and suffering. These courts hold that in such cases the parties may reasonably be said to have contracted with reference to the payment of damages for mental anguish and pain and suffering in the event of breach.

■══■

## Quicknotes

**CONTRACT DAMAGES** Monetary compensation awarded by the court to a party as the result of a breach of contract by another party.

**MOTION IN LIMINE** Motion by one party brought prior to trial to exclude the potential introduction of prejudicial evidence.

**PAIN AND SUFFERING** Refers to a type of recovery in tort for both physical and mental injuries.

■══■

# Plotnik v. Meihaus et al.

## Neighbor (P) v. Neighbor (D)

Cal. Ct. App., 208 Cal. App. 4th 1590 (2012).

**NATURE OF CASE:** Appeal from verdicts finding breach of contract and awarding emotional distress damages in action for breach of a settlement agreement.

**FACT SUMMARY:** The Plotniks (P) and Meihaus (D), adjacent neighbors, had entered a settlement agreement to resolve significant problems they had had with each other, and had agreed to restrain their conduct so similar problems would not arise in the future. The Plotniks (P) brought suit, claiming that Meihaus (D) had violated the settlement agreement, and a jury returned verdicts in the Plotniks (P) favor, and awarded them damages, including emotional distress damages. Meihaus (D) contended that insufficient evidence supported the finding that he had breached the contract; that the damages awards were excessive; and that Joyce Plotnik's (P) breach of the agreement precluded her recovery on the contract.

## RULE OF LAW

(1) A jury verdict finding a breach of contract will be upheld where the finding is supported by sufficient evidence.

(2) Where one of the express objects of a contract is the well-being of one of the contracting parties, a breach of the contract may give rise to damages for mental suffering or emotional distress.

(3) Where one party to a contract materially breaches the contract, such a material breach excuses performance by the other party.

**FACTS:** Joyce Plotnik (P) and David Plotnik (P) (collectively, "the Plotniks (P)") and their children started having problems with their adjacent neighbors, the Meihaus (D) family, shortly after moving into their home. After the Plotniks (P) built a six-foot-high fence along the parcels' common boundary, the Meihauses (D) sued the Plotniks (P) and that lawsuit was resolved by a written settlement. The agreement contained a mutual restraint provision, whereby the parties agreed not to harass, vex or annoy each other either personally or by employing or encouraging others to do so. The parties also agreed to not disparage or slander each other. The settlement provided for an award of attorneys' fees to the prevailing party in a suit related to or arising out of a breach of the settlement agreement. Apparently, after entering the settlement agreement, the Meihauses (D) engaged in repeated conduct that served to annoy, harass, or vex the Plotniks (P), and they even injured the Plotniks' (P) dog, Romeo. The Plotniks (P) brought suit against the Meihauses (D)

for breach of the settlement agreement, and sought damages for emotional distress. The Plotniks (P) testified that shortly after entering into the settlement, they began to find yard clippings and debris on their property along the rear fence. The clippings were similar to the foliage in the Meihauses' (D) yard. This conduct continued for about a year and a half. In addition, Meihaus (D) repeatedly made a vulgar gesture when they and their children passed him on the street. Meihaus (D) also intentionally staring at Joyce (P) for an extended time at the community pool. Meihaus (D) filed a cross-complaint against the Plotniks (P) for breach of the agreement, alleging that Joyce (P) had told her friends about the lawsuit and that Meihaus (D) had hit Romeo with a baseball bat. A jury found that Meihaus (D) had breached the settlement agreement, and it awarded emotional distress damages: $35,000 to David (P) and $70,000 to Joyce (P). Meihaus (D) appealed, contending that insufficient evidence supported the finding that he had breached the contract; that the damages awards were excessive; and that Joyce's (P) breach of the agreement precluded her recovery on the contract. The state's intermediate appellate court granted review.

**ISSUE:**

(1) Will a jury verdict finding a breach of contract be upheld where the finding is supported by sufficient evidence?

(2) Where one of the express objects of a contract is the well-being of one of the contracting parties, may a breach of the contract give rise to damages for mental suffering or emotional distress?

(3) Where one party to a contract materially breaches the contract, does such a material breach excuse performance by the other party?

**HOLDING AND DECISION:** (Rylaarsdam, J.)

(1) Yes. A jury verdict finding a breach of contract will be upheld where the finding is supported by sufficient evidence. Some of the evidence the Plotniks (P) presented about the parties' encounters would not support recovery of damages for annoying or harassing behavior. Public interaction with people, even unfriendly neighbors, is a part of everyday life in an urban environment. Thus, testimony by Joyce (P) and her friends about passing Meihaus (D) family members on public streets or seeing them driving through the neighborhood was irrelevant. The same is true for Meihaus's (D) one-time comment to Joyce (P) to curb her dog's urination on neighbors' lawns. However, the other evidence adduced by the Plotniks (P), i.e., regarding the Meihauses' (D)

*Continued on next page.*

yard clippings, Meihaus's (D) vulgar gestures, and Meihaus's (D) extensive staring at Joyce (P) at the community pool, supported the jury's breach of contract verdicts and its conclusion that Meihaus (D) breached the settlement agreement. Affirmed as to this issue.

(2) Yes. Where one of the express objects of a contract is the well-being of one of the contracting parties, a breach of the contract may give rise to damages for mental suffering or emotional distress. Although damages for mental suffering and emotional distress generally are not compensable in contract actions, there are exceptions to this general rule. One such exception occurs where the breach is of such a kind that serious emotional disturbance is a particularly likely result, as where the express object of the contract is the mental and emotional well-being of one of the contracting parties. This is such a case. Although such damages are appropriate, the amount of damages must be reasonable. There is no fixed or absolute standard by which to compute the monetary value of emotional distress, and a jury is entrusted with vast discretion in determining the amount of damages to be awarded. Here, given the repeated and continuous nature of Meihaus's (D) harassing, vexing, and annoying actions, it cannot be said that the jury's contractual damage awards are excessive as a matter of law. Affirmed as to this issue.

(3) Yes. Where one party to a contract materially breaches the contract, such a material breach excuses performance by the other party. Meihaus (D) argues the contract damages awarded to Joyce (P) must be reversed because the jury found she also breached the settlement agreement's mutual restraint clause. It is elementary a plaintiff suing for breach of contract must prove it has performed all conditions on its part or that it was excused from performance. Thus, one who himself breaches a contract cannot recover for a subsequent breach by the other party. However, a material breach excuses further performance by the innocent party. Ordinarily, the question of whether a breach of an obligation is a material breach, so as to excuse performance by the other party, is a question of fact. Here, viewing the evidence in the light most favorable to plaintiffs, Meihaus's (D) repeated acts of harassment supported a finding he materially breached the settlement agreement, thereby excusing Joyce's (P) noncompliance with the mutual restraint clause's prohibition by making disparaging statements about him to others. Affirmed as to this issue.

## ▶ ANALYSIS

The Restatement (Second) of Contracts § 353 supports the recovery of damages for emotional distress in situations such as the one in *Plotkin*, where the contract at issue is of such a nature that its breach will likely result in serious emotional distress. That section provides that: "Recovery for emotional disturbance will be excluded unless the breach also caused bodily harm or the contract or the breach is of such a kind that serious emotional disturbance was a particularly likely result." Categories of contracts that have traditionally supported recovery for emotional distress include contracts of carriers and innkeepers with passengers and guests, contracts for the carriage or proper disposition of dead bodies, and contracts for the delivery of messages concerning death.

━━■■■━━

## *Quicknotes*

**EMOTIONAL DISTRESS** Extreme personal suffering that results from another's conduct and for which damages may be sought.

**SETTLEMENT AGREEMENT** An agreement entered into by the parties to a civil lawsuit agreeing upon the determination of rights and issues between them, thus disposing of the need for judicial determination.

━━■■■━━

# Acquista v. New York Life Insurance Company

## Insured (P) v. Insurer (D)

### N.Y. App. Div., 730 N.Y.S.2d 272 (2001).

**NATURE OF CASE:** Appeal from dismissal of claims for, inter alia, breach of contract and bad faith arising from insurer's denial of claims under insurance policies.

**FACT SUMMARY:** Acquista (P) contended that New York Life Ins. Co. (NY Life) (D) breached its contract and engaged in bad faith when it denied his claims under disability insurance policies and undertook a conscious campaign calculated to delay and avoid payment on his claims, while having determined at the outset that it would deny coverage.

---

### RULE OF LAW

(1) An insured's claims against an insurer under a disability insurance policy cannot be decided, as a matter of law, on a motion to dismiss where there is a factual dispute as to whether the insured's illness has left him unable to perform the "substantial and material duties" of his regular job within the meaning of the policy.

(2) Where an insured alleges that an insurer has acted in bad faith by undertaking a conscious campaign calculated to delay and avoid payment on his claims under a disability insurance policy, after having determined at the outset that it would deny coverage, the insured states a claim for consequential damages beyond the limits of the policy for the insurer's alleged breach of contract.

---

**FACTS:** Acquista (P), a physician with specialties in internal and pulmonary medicine, became ill and was largely unable to practice medicine, though he could still see a limited number of patients who could come to his office. He had three disability insurance policies with New York Life Ins. Co. (NY Life) (D), and submitted claims for full disability benefits thereunder. NY Life (D) rejected his claims on the ground that he could still perform some of "the substantial and material duties" of his regular job or jobs and therefore was not "totally disabled." Acquista (P) sued NY Life (D), asserting claims for, inter alia, breach of contract and bad faith. He claimed that NY Life (D) undertook a conscious campaign calculated to delay and avoid payment on his claims, while having determined at the outset that it would deny coverage. He alleged that NY Life (D) engaged in an ongoing pattern of avoiding the claim, by which it would make multiple requests for additional documentation, upon receipt of which further documents would be demanded, after which his claims

file would then be transferred to a new examiner, who in turn would make more requests. Acquista (P) pointed out that NY Life (D) waited more than two years to request or schedule an independent medical examination. He sought damages for emotional distress as well as economic and non-economic injuries. NY Life (D) moved to dismiss, and the trial court granted the motion, except as regarding policy provisions for residual and partial disability benefits. In doing so, the trial court concluded that, as a matter of law, Acquista (P) could still perform some of "the substantial and material duties" of his regular job. The state's intermediate appellate court granted review.

**ISSUE:**
(1) Can an insured's claims against an insurer under a disability insurance policy be decided, as a matter of law, on a motion to dismiss where there is a factual dispute as to whether the insured's illness has left him unable to perform the "substantial and material duties" of his regular job within the meaning of the policy?

(2) Where an insured alleges that an insurer has acted in bad faith by undertaking a conscious campaign calculated to delay and avoid payment on his claims under a disability insurance policy, after having determined at the outset that it would deny coverage, does the insured state a claim for consequential damages beyond the limits of the policy for the insurer's alleged breach of contract?

**HOLDING AND DECISION:** (Saxe, J.)
(1) No. An insured's claims against an insurer under a disability insurance policy cannot be decided, as a matter of law, on a motion to dismiss where there is a factual dispute as to whether the insured's illness has left him unable to perform the "substantial and material duties" of his regular job within the meaning of the policy. The question of whether Acquista (P) can still perform some of "the substantial and material duties" of his regular job is a factual one, which the trial court should not have decided as a matter of law on a motion to dismiss. The question is whether those tasks that Acquista (P) is still demonstrably able to handle, such as seeing a limited number of patients who can make office visits, are substantial enough to amount to the ability to perform "the substantial and material duties" of his regular job or jobs as they existed prior to the onset of his illness. Because this question involves a factual determination, dismissal of Acquista's (P) breach of contract claim was precluded at this stage of the proceedings. Reversed as to this issue.

*Continued on next page.*

(2) Yes. Where an insured alleges that an insurer has acted in bad faith by undertaking a conscious campaign calculated to delay and avoid payment on his claims under a disability insurance policy, after having determined at the outset that it would deny coverage, the insured states a claim for consequential damages beyond the limits of the policy for the insurer's alleged breach of contract. NY Life (D) is correct that state law has not recognized an independent tort cause of action for an insurer's alleged failure to perform its contractual obligations under an insurance policy, and that an insurer's failure to make payments or provide benefits in accordance with a policy of insurance constitutes merely a breach of contract, which is remedied by contract damages. However, courts and commentators around the country have increasingly acknowledged that a fundamental injustice may result when such a traditional contract analysis is applied to circumstances where insurance claims were denied despite the insurers' lack of a reasonable basis to deny them. Under the traditional analysis, the damages available for an insurer's failure to pay or provide benefits have been limited to the amount of the policy plus interest. Such an award, at the conclusion of litigation, of money damages equal to what the insurer should have paid in the first place, may not actually achieve the goal of contract damages, which is to place the plaintiff in the position he would have been in had the contract been performed. There are several reasons why this traditional concept of damages may be inadequate. First, it presumes that a plaintiff has access to an alternative source of funds from which to pay that which the insurer refuses to pay. This is frequently an inaccurate assumption. Second, an insured's inability to pay that which the insurer should be covering may result in further damages to the insured. Third, limiting the potential damages to the policy amount also fails to address the potential for emotional distress or even further physical injury that may result where a plaintiff under the strain of serious medical problems is forced to also undertake the stress of extended litigation. Fourth, if statutory interest is lower than that which the insurer can earn on the sums payable, the insurer has a financial incentive to decline to cover or pay on a claim. Given these inadequacies where an insurer purposefully declines or avoids a claim without a reasonable basis for doing so, a majority of states have responded by adopting a tort cause of action applicable to circumstances where an insurer has used bad faith in handling a policyholder's claim. A minority of states has responded by expanding the scope of contract remedies to encompass more than just the policy limits. These courts have held that the contract damages available, where an insurer fails to pay benefits to which the insured was entitled, may include foreseeable money damages beyond the policy limit. Some of these states exclude compensation for mental or emotional distress unrelated to physical injury that is caused by the denial of a claim, whereas others include the possibility of consequential damages for mental distress or aggravation and inconvenience where they were a foreseeable result of a breach at the time the policy was entered into. This court now joins the minority of states. To adopt a "bad faith" tort remedy to redress an insurer's bad faith refusal of benefits under its policy, would constitute an extreme change in the law of this state. To provide an insured with an adequate remedy in this context, however, it is not enough to continue with the traditional approach. Instead, recovery must be allowed to extend past the policy limits. There is no reason to limit damages recoverable for breach of a duty to investigate, bargain, and settle claims in good faith to the amount specified in the insurance policy. Nothing inherent in the contract law approach mandates this narrow definition of recoverable damages. Although the policy limits define the amount for which the insurer may be held responsible in performing the contract, they do not define the amount for which it may be liable upon a breach. Accordingly, Acquista's (P) allegations may be employed to interpose a claim for consequential damages beyond the limits of the policy for the claimed breach of contract. As to the dissent's suggestion that the claim of bad faith is undermined by the finding that an issue of fact exists as to whether Acquista (P) is entitled to coverage at all, the dissent seems to forget that the ruling is made in the context of a motion to dismiss. Just as it may ultimately be found that Acquista (P) was entitled to coverage, it may also be found, as he alleges, that the insurer's delay, avoidance and ultimate rejection of the claim was based not upon a reasonable assessment of the situation but rather, solely upon its own financial self-interest. For a court to say, in the context of a dismissal motion, that the denial of benefits was reasonable as a matter of law, is to reject out of hand Acquista (P) factual assertions and to accept the facts as defendant insurer alleges them to be. Reversed as to this issue.

**DISSENT:** (Andrias, J.) Although the majority is correct that factual issues remain that preclude dismissal of Acquista's (P) breach of contract claims, it errs in permitting his claims that sound in tort to proceed. His claims of bad faith, founded on allegations of NY Life's (D) delay and dilatory tactics, and wrongful and unjustifiable denial of his policy claims, describe what "is essentially a 'private' contract dispute over policy coverage and the processing of a claim that is unique to these parties, not conduct that affects the consuming public at large" (*New York Univ. v. Continental Ins. Co.*, 87 N.Y.2d 308 (1995)). Because there are remaining issues of fact as to whether Acquista's (P) ailments qualify him for coverage under the subject policies, it would be premature to permit causes of action

*Continued on next page.*

based upon NY Life's (D) alleged bad faith in processing and denying Acquista's (P) claim to proceed at this juncture, since despite NY Life's (D) thorough investigation and evaluation of the claim there is still uncertainty as to its merits. Such encouragement of premature settlement of claims would contravene an insurer's contractual right and obligation of thorough investigation. Further, state law precedents require that a claim based on an alleged breach of the implied covenant of good faith and fair dealing should be dismissed as duplicative of a cause of action for breach of contract. Moreover, Acquista's (P) allegation that NY Life (D) undertook a conscious campaign to delay rendering a decision on his claims is insufficient to establish bad faith in this context. Instead, a bad-faith plaintiff must establish that the defendant insurer engaged in a pattern of behavior evincing a conscious or knowing indifference to the probability that an insured would be held personally accountable for a large judgment if a settlement offer within the policy limits were not accepted. To satisfy the necessary "gross disregard for the insured's rights" standard, a plaintiff would have to allege and ultimately prove that the insurer unreasonably failed to carry out an investigation, failed to evaluate the feasibility of settlement or pay the insured's claim or, failed to offer the policy limits or pay the plaintiff's claim, after the merits of the claim were clearly and fully assessed. Here, on the other hand, Acquista's (P) complaint is really the opposite: that NY Life (D) took too much time in investigating and evaluating his claim before denying it, after its merits were clearly and fully assessed.

## ▶ ANALYSIS

In fashioning a remedy in this case, the majority noted that the problem of dilatory tactics by insurance companies seeking to delay and avoid payment of proper claims had apparently become widespread enough to prompt most states to respond with some sort of remedy for aggrieved policyholders. Accordingly, the majority responded to the dissent's assertion that the claim at bar was unique to the parties in the case, and therefore not warranting a remedy beyond that traditionally available for an insurer's failure to pay on a claim, by saying that the dissent utterly ignored this ubiquitous problem.

## *Quicknotes*

**BREACH OF CONTRACT** Unlawful failure by a party to perform its obligations pursuant to contract.

**CONSEQUENTIAL DAMAGES** Monetary compensation that may be recovered in order to compensate for injuries or losses sustained as a result of damages that are not the direct or foreseeable result of the act of a party, but that nevertheless are the consequence of such act and which must be specifically pled and demonstrated.

**MOTION TO DISMISS** Motion to terminate an action based on the adequacy of the pleadings, improper service or venue, etc.

# Boise Dodge, Inc. v. Clark

Car dealer (P) v. Car purchaser (D)

Idaho Sup. Ct., 92 Idaho 902, 453 P.2d 551 (1969).

**NATURE OF CASE:** Appeal from award of punitive damages in action on claim recover monies owed and counterclaim to recover damages.

**FACT SUMMARY:** Boise Dodge, Inc. (P) sold Clark (D) what was supposedly a new car. Clark (D) later discovered that the car was used and that Boise Dodge (P) had turned back the odometer.

## RULE OF LAW
Although an award of punitive damages must be reasonably proportionate to the amount of actual damages suffered by the plaintiff, a judge or jury is entitled to exercise considerable discretion in determining the amount of punitive damages to be assessed.

**FACTS:** Clark (D) purchased a car from Boise Dodge, Inc. (P). The car's odometer registered 165 miles, and the salesman described the vehicle as "new." Clark (D) later learned that the car had been used as a demonstrator and that the odometer had registered nearly 7,000 miles before Boise Dodge (P) had turned it back. Clark (D) then stopped payment on two checks that, together with a trade-in car worth $1,100, had been given as consideration for the "new" car. Boise Dodge (P) sued on the checks, but Clark (D) counterclaimed for actual and punitive damages, alleging breach of contract and deceit. A jury awarded Clark (D) $350 in actual damages, representing the difference between the purported value of the car and its true worth, and also awarded $12,500 in punitive damages. On appeal, Boise Dodge (P) challenged the award of punitive damages.

**ISSUE:** Although an award of punitive damages must be reasonably proportionate to the amount of actual damages suffered by the plaintiff, is a judge or jury entitled to exercise considerable discretion in determining the amount of punitive damages to be assessed?

**HOLDING AND DECISION:** (McQuade, J.) Yes. Although an award of punitive damages must be reasonably proportionate to the amount of actual damages suffered by the plaintiff, a judge or jury is entitled to exercise considerable discretion in determining the amount of punitive damages to be assessed. In this case, it was proper to assess punitive damages against Boise Dodge (P) despite its corporate status. A corporation may not insulate itself from punitive damages merely by disavowing the acts of its employees, especially when, as in the present case, management personnel were apparently aware of and responsible for deceitful conduct. And it cannot be said

that the amount of punitive damages assessed against Boise Dodge (P) was unreasonable. All jury instructions relating to punitive damages were properly issued, and the jury was entitled to consider various factors in determining the appropriate amount of those damages. Boise Dodge (P) perpetrated a particularly reprehensible fraud, not only against Clark (D) but against the consuming public generally. In fixing punitive damages at $12,500, the jury was apparently motivated not by passion or prejudice but by a desire to deter similar conduct in the future. Therefore, the award of the court below must be affirmed.

## ANALYSIS

Ordinarily, punitive damages are not recoverable for breach of contract. However, such damages may be awarded for wanton and malicious breach or when a claim sounds in both tort and contract. Most courts are reluctant to articulate or employ any mechanical formula for fixing the appropriate amount of punitive damages. Since a major purpose of punitive damages is to deter a wrongdoer from repeating his unlawful conduct, the amount of punitive damages that should be awarded in a particular case may depend on the financial status of the defendant. In other words, a comparatively large punitive damage assessment may be necessary in order to deter a multimillion-dollar corporation from engaging in deceitful practices, whereas a smaller award may serve as an effective deterrent if a tiny company or an individual is involved.

## Quicknotes

**BREACH OF CONTRACT** Unlawful failure by a party to perform its obligations pursuant to contract.

**DAMAGES** Monetary compensation that may be awarded by the court to a party who has sustained injury or loss to his person, property or rights due to another party's unlawful act, omission or negligence.

**PUNITIVE DAMAGES** Damages exceeding the actual injury suffered for the purposes of punishment of the defendant, deterrence of the wrongful behavior or comfort to the plaintiff.

# White Plains Coat & Apron Co., Inc. v. Cintas Corp.

## Linen rental company (P) v. Competitor (D)

### N.Y. Ct. App., 867 N.E.2d 381 (2007).

**NATURE OF CASE:** Question certified by federal court of appeals to state's highest court.

**FACT SUMMARY:** White Plains Coat & Apron Co., Inc. (White Plains) (P) contended that its competitor, Cintas Corp. (D), tortiously interfered with White Plains' (P) existing customer contracts, and that because Cintas (D) did not have a prior economic relationship with, or an economic interest in, White Plains' (P) customers, Cintas (D) could not avail itself of the economic interest defense.

### RULE OF LAW

A generalized economic interest in soliciting business for profit does not constitute a defense to a claim of tortious interference with an existing contract for an alleged tortfeasor with no previous economic relationship with the breaching party.

**FACTS:** White Plains Coat & Apron Co., Inc. (White Plains) (P), a linen rental company, had five-year exclusive service contracts with customers. White Plains (P) alleged that its competitor, Cintas Corp. (D), induced dozens of White Plains' (P) customers to breach their contracts and enter into rental agreements with Cintas (D). After White Plains (P) sent a cease and desist letter to Cintas (D), Cintas (D) denied knowledge of any contracts and continued its solicitation. White Plains (P) then sued Cintas (D) in federal district court for tortious interference with existing customer contracts. The district court granted summary judgment to Cintas (D), ruling that Cintas' (D) legitimate interest as a competitor to solicit business and make a profit alone triggered the defense of economic justification, and that Cintas (D) did not need to have an ownership interest in a breaching customer's business to assert the economic interest defense. The court of appeals, although satisfied that the defense applies when the tortfeasor has a preexisting legal or financial relationship with the breaching party—not present in the case at bar—sought clarification as to the broader reach of the defense where the alleged tortfeasor does not have a preexisting legal or economic relationship with the breaching party. Accordingly, the court certified the question to the state's highest court.

**ISSUE:** Does a generalized economic interest in soliciting business for profit constitute a defense to a claim of tortious interference with an existing contract for an alleged tortfeasor with no previous economic relationship with the breaching party?

**HOLDING AND DECISION:** (Kaye, C.J.) No. A generalized economic interest in soliciting business for profit does not constitute a defense to a claim of tortious interference with an existing contract for an alleged tortfeasor with no previous economic relationship with the breaching party. In a contract interference case, the plaintiff must show the existence of its valid contract with a third party, defendant's knowledge of that contract, defendant's intentional and improper procuring of a breach, and damages. In response to such a claim, a defendant may raise the economic interest defense—that it acted to protect its own legal or financial stake in the breaching party's business. The defense has been applied, for example, where defendants were significant stockholders in the breaching party's business, or where the defendant was the breaching party's creditor. A defendant who is simply plaintiff's competitor and knowingly solicits its contract customers is not economically justified in procuring the breach of contract. "When the defendant is simply a competitor of the plaintiff seeking prospective customers and plaintiff has a customer under contract for a definite period, defendant's interest is not equal to that of plaintiff and would not justify defendant's inducing the customer to breach the existing contract." (PJI2d 3:56, at 507-508 (2007)) To conclude otherwise would blur the distinction between tortious interference with existing, enforceable contracts and tortious interference with prospective contractual relations, where, as a matter of policy, the balance of interests is different. However, protecting existing contractual relationships does not negate a competitor's right to solicit business, where liability is limited to improper inducement of a third party to breach its contract. Sending regular advertising and soliciting business in the normal course does not constitute inducement of breach of contract. A competitor's ultimate liability will depend on a showing that the inducement exceeded a minimum level of ethical behavior in the marketplace. The certified question is answered in the negative.

### ANALYSIS

In a contract interference action, one who intentionally and improperly interferes with the performance of a contract (except a contract to marry) between another and a third person by inducing or otherwise causing the third person not to perform the contract, is subject to liability to the other for the pecuniary loss resulting to the other from the failure of the third person to perform the contract. At bottom, as a matter of policy, this action requires courts to strike a balance between two valued interests: protection of enforceable contracts, which lends stability and

*Continued on next page.*

predictability to parties' dealings, and promotion of free and robust competition in the marketplace. Although such an action can apply to interference with both prospective and existing contracts, greater protection is accorded an interest in an existing contract (as to which respect for individual contract rights outweighs the public benefit to be derived from unfettered competition) than to the less substantive, more speculative interest in a prospective relationship (as to which liability will be imposed only on proof of more culpable conduct on the part of the interferer).

---

## Quicknotes

**INTERFERENCE WITH CONTRACTUAL RELATIONS** An intentional tort whereby a defendant intentionally elicits the breach of a valid contract resulting in damages.

**TORTIOUS INTERFERENCE WITH CONTRACTUAL RELATIONSHIP** An intentional tort whereby a defendant intentionally elicits the breach of a valid contract resulting in damages.

# Curtice Brothers Co. v. Catts

Canning company (P) v. Tomato farmer (D)

N.J. Ch. Ct., 72 N.J. Eq. 831, 66 A. 935 (1907).

**NATURE OF CASE:** Action to specifically perform a contract for the sale of services and personalty.

**FACT SUMMARY:** After Catts (D) defaulted on his contract to supply Curtice Brothers Co. (P) with tomatoes for its canning company, Curtice Brothers Co. (P) was unable to purchase any replacement tomatoes elsewhere.

## RULE OF LAW

Specific performance of a contract for personalty will be granted where damages are inadequate, the goods cannot be obtained elsewhere, and they are necessary to the plaintiff's business.

**FACTS:** Curtice Brothers Co. (Curtice) (P) contracted with Catts (D) to buy his tomato crop. Catts (D) then repudiated the contract and said he would not sell to Curtice (P). Curtice (P) attempted to buy replacement tomatoes elsewhere; however, none could be purchased. Curtice (P) brought an action in equity to specifically enforce the contract. Curtice (P) alleged that its canning operation required an adequate supply of tomatoes and that it would be severely injured by Catts's (D) refusal to perform the contract since no replacements were available. Catts (D) defended on the basis that specific performance was normally denied for contracts to convey personalty and that the contract also involved Catts's (D) personal services, which were also an inappropriate subject for specific performance. Curtice (P) alleged that damages would be an inadequate remedy.

**ISSUE:** Will specific performance of a contract for personalty be granted where damages are inadequate, the goods cannot be obtained elsewhere, and they are necessary to the plaintiff's business?

**HOLDING AND DECISION:** (Leaming, V.Chan.) Yes. Specific performance of a contract for personalty will be granted where damages are inadequate, the goods cannot be obtained elsewhere, and they are necessary to the plaintiff's business. Under these circumstances, specific performance will be granted. Here, the tomatoes are necessary for Curtice's (P) business. Curtice (P) cannot operate profitably without an adequate supply, and it could not obtain replacements elsewhere. Curtice (P) cannot honor its commitments without an adequate supply. The distinction between specific enforcement of realty and personalty has been on the decline. Where there is no adequate remedy at law, equity will grant specific performance. The fact that services are involved is immaterial to this case. An injunction may be issued forbidding Catts's

(D) selling his crop to another. Finally, if appropriate, a receiver may be appointed to harvest the crops. Specific performance is granted.

## ANALYSIS

Specific performance may also be granted in other situations involving personalty. Uniqueness of chattel (e.g., a rare painting or custom goods) and avoidance of multiple lawsuits are examples of adequate grounds for decreeing specific performance. Personal service contracts may or may not be specifically enforced, depending on the nature of the services. If the court can adequately compel or supervise performance, it may be specifically enforceable.

## Quicknotes

**REPUDIATION** The actions or statements of a party to a contract that evidence his intent not to perform, or to continue performance of, his duties or obligations thereunder.

**SPECIFIC PERFORMANCE** An equitable remedy whereby the court requires the parties to perform their obligations pursuant to a contract.

# Lumley v. Wagner

Theater owner (P) v. Singer (D)

Ct. Chan., 1 De GM and G 604, 42 Eng. Rep. 687 (1852).

**NATURE OF CASE:** Appeal from order enjoining performer from accepting other employment.

**FACT SUMMARY:** Lumley (P), who had contracted with Wagner (D) for the latter to perform at his theater, sought to enjoin her from performing at another location.

## RULE OF LAW
A court may enjoin a performer from engaging in employment when the performer is under contract with another employer.

**FACTS:** Lumley (P) hired Wagner (D), a singer, to perform at his theater. After signing the contract, Wagner (D) sought to perform elsewhere. Lumley (P) obtained an injunction against Wagner (D) performing elsewhere. Wagner (D) appealed.

**ISSUE:** May a court enjoin a performer from engaging in employment when the performer is under contract with another employer?

**HOLDING AND DECISION:** (Lord St. Leonards, C.) Yes. A court may enjoin a performer from engaging in employment when the performer is under contract with another employer. A court of equity may fashion an order in the nature of specific performance even if, in a literal sense, performance is not ordered. Where an order not to do something tends to encourage the specific performance of a contract, such an order may be made if specific performance is a proper remedy. Here, the court cannot force Wagner (D) to sing; however, by enjoining her from engaging in other performance, it properly invoked its jurisdiction to compel compliance with the contractual terms. Affirmed.

## ANALYSIS

The court here did not discuss whether specific performance was a proper remedy. It apparently assumed that it was. Generally speaking, contracts involving performers are appropriate for specific performance because of the uniqueness of each performer.

━━━

## Quicknotes

**INJUNCTION** A remedy imposed by the court ordering a party to cease the conduct of a specific activity.

**SPECIFIC PERFORMANCE** An equitable remedy whereby the court requires the parties to perform their obligations pursuant to a contract.

# Curb Records, Inc. v. McGraw

Recording company (P) v. Recording artist (D)

Tenn. Ct. App., 2012 WL 4377817 (2012).

**NATURE OF CASE:** Appeal from denial of injunctive relief in action for breach of contract.

**FACT SUMMARY:** Curb Records, Inc. (Curb) (P), which had a recording agreement with the well-known and highly successful recording artist Tim McGraw (McGraw) (D), contended that McGraw (D) breached the agreement, that Curb (P) would suffer irreparable harm if McGraw (D) provided his recording services to any entity other than Curb (P) as long as he failed to fulfill his obligations under the agreement, and that such irreparable harm supported the grant of an injunction enjoining McGraw (D) from rendering such services to other entities until his contractual obligations were met.

## RULE OF LAW

Where a contract concerns unique and extraordinary personal services, it is not an abuse of discretion to deny injunctive relief under the contract where the contract does not provide sufficiently definite terms, the injunction would amount to requiring involuntary servitude, and the contract's duration depends upon the exercise of discretion by the party seeking the injunction.

**FACTS:** Tim McGraw (McGraw) (D), a well-known and highly successful country music recording artist, entered into a recording agreement with Curb Records, Inc. (Curb) (P) in 1997. Under the agreement, McGraw (D) agreed to record exclusively with Curb (P) until he fulfilled certain recording obligations during an initial term followed by six option periods, which could be extended upon the happening of certain events. The agreement, however, had no definite termination date. The agreement provided that after providing Curb (P) with three albums during the initial term (which McGraw (D) did), he would deliver to Curb (P) sufficient materials, in the form of "Masters," to make up one album in each of the following six option periods. Each option period started at the expiration of the previous option period, and continued until McGraw (D) delivered all required Masters during such period. Curb (P) had approval power over which Masters would be recorded. Additionally, McGraw (D) was to record and deliver Masters in fulfillment of each album no earlier than 12 months, nor later than 18 months, following delivery to Curb (P) of the immediately preceding album. If Curb (P), in its sole discretion, elected to release a "Greatest Hits" album, those time frames were extended by six months in any single instance. The agreement further provided Curb (P) would be the perpetual owner of all Masters and all other recordings made by McGraw (D)

during the agreement's term. The parties abided by the terms of the agreement without dispute until October 22, 2010, when McGraw (D) gave to Curb (P) a group of masters for an album entitled *Emotional Traffic*, and Curb (P) refused to accept these masters in satisfaction of McGraw's (D) contractual obligations for the fifth option period. According to Curb (P), McGraw (D) was required to record and deliver the album for the fifth option period during the six month period ending on April 20, 2011, so that his recording and delivery of *Emotional Traffic* prior to that period constituted a breach of the recording agreement. In other words, Curb's (P) position was that McGraw (D) recorded and delivered *Emotional Traffic* too soon after the fourth option period. Curb (P) brought suit against McGraw (D) for breach of contract and for injunctive relief, seeking to enjoin McGraw (D) from providing personal services as a recording artist, or agreeing to do so, other than to Curb (P) for as long as he, among other things, failed to record and deliver to Curb (P) the fifth option period album and the sixth option period album under the recording agreement. The trial court, with the parties' consent, bifurcated the proceedings, whereby it would first rule on whether Curb (P) was entitled to prevent McGraw (D), by injunction or otherwise, from recording for entities other than Curb (P), followed by a trial on the merits. After a hearing, the trial court denied Curb's (P) request for injunctive relief. In reaching its decision, the trial court found that Curb (P) had not made a showing of irreparable harm sufficient to warrant a grant of a temporary injunction preventing McGraw (D) from continuing his recording career. Additionally, the court concluded that Curb (P) was, in part seeking specific performance in a personal services agreement against McGraw (D), and that such relief was disfavored under state law, especially where the parties had differences—as here—that would make specific performance extremely difficult. The trial court also found that Curb (P) was seeking permanent injunctive relief prohibiting McGraw (D) from continuing his recording career as a musician for any other recording company. The trial court held such relief would be heavy-handed and legally impermissible under the circumstances, given: (1) the limited nature and extent of the alleged breach of contract upon which Curb (P) had shown some likelihood of success; (2) the fact that McGraw's (D) alleged breach occurred near the end of a multiple-year contractual relationship with Curb (P); (3) McGraw (D) provided unique services as a recording artist that the public had an interest in being made

*Continued on next page.*

available while this dispute proceeded through the courts, subject to any monetary judgment the court might award after the trial on the merits; (4) McGraw's (D) conduct in recording *Emotional Traffic* and delivering it to Curb (P) afforded Curb (P) the benefit of McGraw's (D) unique and extraordinary talent; and (5) an injunction would likely have an adverse and disproportionate effect on the body of musical recording work McGraw (D) would be permitted to produce during this important period in McGraw's (D) musical career. Based on these findings and conclusions, the trial court determined that Curb (P) would not suffer irreparable harm, and that it had an adequate remedy at law. Curb (P) appealed, and the state's intermediate appellate court granted review.

**ISSUE:** Where a contract concerns unique and extraordinary personal services, is it an abuse of discretion to deny injunctive relief under the contract where the contract does not provide sufficiently definite terms, the injunction would amount to requiring involuntary servitude, and the contract's duration depends upon the exercise of discretion by the party seeking the injunction?

**HOLDING AND DECISION:** (Bennett, J.) No. Where a contract concerns unique and extraordinary personal services, it is not an abuse of discretion to deny injunctive relief under the contract where the contract does not provide sufficiently definite terms, the injunction would amount to requiring involuntary servitude, and the contract's duration depends upon the exercise of discretion by the party seeking the injunction. The trial court's decision to deny both temporary and permanent injunctive relief is reviewed for an abuse of discretion. A reviewing court will find an abuse of discretion only if the trial court applied incorrect legal standards, reached an illogical conclusion, based its decision on a clearly erroneous assessment of the evidence, or employed reasoning that causes an injustice to the complaining party. Curb (P) asserts that the factual findings made by the trial court necessitate the legal conclusion that Curb (P) suffered irreparable harm. It argues that breach of an exclusive personal services contract by a unique and exceptional performer constitutes irreparable harm. Although it is undisputed that McGraw (D) is a unique and exceptional artist, and the trial court assumed, for purposes of ruling on injunctive relief, that McGraw (D) breached the recording agreement, these two facts do not necessitate a conclusion of irreparable harm. The general rule in respect of contracts for personal services is that for breach thereof a party must avail himself of the remedy afforded at law, and that courts of equity will not exercise jurisdiction to grant a decree for specific performance of a contract for personal services except in very exceptional cases or under very exceptional circumstances. The same is true for injunctions that are being used to indirectly enforce a contract. Nonetheless, unique and extraordinary services do not make such exceptional injunctive relief appropriate in all cases, and such relief may not be appropriate where the contract

does not provide sufficiently definite terms and/or where an injunction would amount to an involuntary servitude. It may also be inappropriate where duration depends upon the exercise of discretion by the party seeking the injunction. Thus, even though McGraw (D) is undisputedly an entertainer offering unique and extraordinary services, the trial court neither erred nor abused its discretion in finding that there was no irreparable harm, or in concluding that injunctive relief was not appropriate. Here, the requested injunction would essentially place McGraw (D) in a position of choosing between the end of his recording career or the indefinite continuation of a relationship with Curb (P) that had become contentious. Therefore, it was appropriate to deny such relief. Affirmed.

## ▶ *ANALYSIS*

Typically, there are four factors to be considered by a trial court in deciding whether to issue a temporary injunction: the threat of irreparable harm, the balance between the harm to be prevented and the injury to be inflicted if the injunction issues, the probability that the applicant will succeed on the merits, and the public interest. With respect to permanent injunctive relief, the analysis differs somewhat, as in the typical situation the court has ruled in favor of the applicant on the merits and must determine whether permanent injunctive relief is an appropriate remedy. Here, however, the parties agreed to submit the issue of permanent injunctive relief for resolution prior to a trial on the merits, so the trial court essentially merged the consideration of the requested temporary injunction with consideration of the permanent injunction.

■=■=■

## *Quicknotes*

**INJUNCTION** A court order requiring a person to do, or prohibiting that person from doing, a specific act.

**INJUNCTIVE RELIEF** A court order issued as a remedy, requiring a person to do, or prohibiting that person from doing, a specific act.

**INVOLUNTARY SERVITUDE** Being in a state of forced labor for the benefit of another person.

**IRREPARABLE HARM** Such harm that because it is either too great, too small or of a continuing character that it cannot be properly compensated in damages, and the remedy for which is typically injunctive relief.

**SPECIFIC PERFORMANCE** An equitable remedy whereby the court requires the parties to perform their obligations pursuant to a contract.

■=■

# Southwest Engineering Co. v. United States

Government contractor (P) v. Federal government (D)

341 F.2d 998 (8th Cir.), *cert. denied*, 382 U.S. 819 (1965).

**NATURE OF CASE:** Appeal from summary judgment dismissing action to recover sum of money.

**FACT SUMMARY:** The Government (D) withheld from the contract price paid to Southwest Engineering Co. (P), a government contractor, liquidated damages stipulated for in the event of delay past the completion date, although the Government (D) admitted that it suffered no harm from the delay.

## RULE OF LAW
A provision included in a contract fixing the amount of damages payable on breach will be interpreted as an enforceable liquidated damages clause rather than an unenforceable penalty clause if, at the time the contract is entered, (1) the amount so fixed is a reasonable forecast of just compensation for the harm that is caused by the breach, and (2) the harm that is caused by the breach is one that is incapable or very difficult of accurate estimation.

**FACTS:** Southwest Engineering Co. (Southwest) (P) entered into four contracts with the Government (D) for the construction of three radio facilities and a high-intensity approach light lane. A liquidated damage clause in the contract provided that for each day's delay past the fixed completion date, the Government (D) would withhold either $100 or $50, depending on the project. No liquidated damages were to be assessed if, in the Government's (D) judgment, the delay was justified. Southwest (P), upon completion of the projects, was assessed for an aggregate delay of 146 days. Southwest (P) brought an action to recover the money withheld as liquidated damages. At trial, the Government (D) admitted that it suffered no actual damage on any project as a result of the delays. The district court granted summary judgment for the Government (D), dismissing the action, and the court of appeals granted review.

**ISSUE:** Will a provision included in a contract fixing the amount of damages payable on breach be interpreted as an enforceable liquidated damages clause rather than an unenforceable penalty clause if, at the time the contract is entered, (1) the amount so fixed is a reasonable forecast of just compensation for the harm that is caused by the breach, and (2) the harm that is caused by the breach is one that is incapable or very difficult of accurate estimation?

**HOLDING AND DECISION:** (Van Oosterhout, J.) Yes. A provision included in a contract fixing the amount of damages payable on breach will be interpreted

as an enforceable liquidated damages clause rather than an unenforceable penalty clause if, at the time the contract is entered, (1) the amount so fixed is a reasonable forecast of just compensation for the harm that is caused by the breach, and (2) the harm that is caused by the breach is one that is incapable or very difficult of accurate estimation. Since parties are free to contract, liquidated damages are not viewed with disfavor. Thus, the fact that the damages suffered are shown to be less than the damages contracted for is not fatal so long as, at the time the contract was executed, the liquidated damages clause was reasonable. Each party, in entering into such a contract, took a calculated risk which it is bound to accept. In the present case, since there is no proof that the liquidated damages for delay provided for are beyond damages reasonably contemplated by the parties at the time of the contract, Southwest (P) is not entitled to the return of the sum withheld. Affirmed.

## ANALYSIS

Uniform Commercial Code § 2-718(1) provides that liquidated damages may be agreed upon "but only at an amount which is reasonable in the light of the anticipated or actual harm caused by the breach, the difficulties of proof of loss, and the inconvenience or nonfeasibility of otherwise obtaining an adequate remedy." The Uniform Commercial Code has thus made one significant departure from the common-law rule: a liquidated damages provision will be found, and upheld, even if the sum provided for in the case of breach was not a reasonable forecast of probable harm so long as, judged in the light of the actual harm, it appears reasonable.

---

## Quicknotes

**BREACH** The violation of an obligation imposed pursuant to contract or law, by acting or failing to act.

**LIQUIDATED DAMAGES** An amount of money specified in a contract representing the damages owed in the event of breach.

**SUMMARY JUDGMENT** Judgment rendered by a court in response to a motion made by one of the parties, claiming that the lack of a question of material fact in respect to an issue warrants disposition of the issue without consideration by the jury.

# Cellphone Termination Fee Cases

[Parties not identified.]

Cal. Ct. App., 193 Cal. App. 4th 298 (2011).

**NATURE OF CASE:** Cross-appeals from judgment in consumer class action against a wireless telephone carrier.

**FACT SUMMARY:** Sprint Spectrum, L.P. (Sprint) (D) contended that, in a consumer class action against it, the trial court erred in holding that early termination fees (ETFs) Sprint (D) had in its contracts with consumers (P) were unlawful penalties under state law. The court's holding was based on its determinations, inter alia, that Sprint (D) failed to reasonably endeavor to determine whether the amount of the ETFs represented fair compensation for the loss Sprint (D) would sustain, and that the ETFs did not operate to give consumers (P) "alternative performance" by giving them a rational choice of either paying the ETF or completing the contract. Sprint (D) claimed these rulings were erroneous.

## RULE OF LAW

(1) A consumer contract provision providing for damages upon breach of the contract operates as an unlawful liquidated damages clause where the provision's proponent has failed to reasonably endeavor to determine that the amount of the damages represents fair compensation for the loss sustained as a result of the breach, notwithstanding that the proponent's actual damages exceed the damages provided in the contract.

(2) A contract provision does not provide an option of alternative performance of an obligation where it does not provide a party with a rational choice of performing that obligation.

**FACTS:** Consumers (P) who were subscribers of Sprint Spectrum, L.P.'s (Sprint's) (D) wireless cellular telephone service brought a class action against Sprint (D) challenging, as unlawful penalties under state law, early termination fees (ETFs) Sprint (D) had in its contracts with consumers (P) that were triggered when customers terminated service prior to expiration of defined contract periods. The consumers (P) contended that the ETFs had been implemented to reduce erosion of Sprint's (D) consumer base and were unlawful liquidated damages provisions. The trial court found the ETFs were unlawful penalties, enjoined enforcement of the ETFs, and granted restitution/damages to the consumer (P) class in the amount of ETFs collected by Sprint (D) during the class period, $73,775,975. A jury found that class members who had been charged ETFs had violated the terms of their contracts with Sprint (D), but that Sprint's (D) actual damages exceeded the ETF

charges Sprint (D) had collected. The resulting setoff negated any monetary recovery to the class. The trial court, reasoning that the jury had failed to follow its instructions on Sprint's (D) actual damages, granted the consumers' (P) motion for a partial new trial on that issue. Sprint (D) appealed the decision invalidating the ETFs and enjoining their enforcement, as well as the trial court's grant of the motion for partial new trial on damages. Specifically, Sprint (D) argued, inter alia, that the trial court had erred in determining that Sprint (D) had failed to reasonably endeavor to determine whether the amount of the ETFs represented fair compensation for the loss Sprint (D) would sustain. However, there was evidence that Sprint (D) failed to make any study or written analysis of whether the ETFs were reasonably related to losses Sprint (D) would sustain upon a customer's early termination of the contract. Instead, Sprint (D) presented evidence that its actual damages were substantially greater than the ETFs charged—the jury found these to be $225,697,433, which represented the amount of ETFs charged to class members, but which were unpaid. Sprint (D) also argued that, contrary to the trial court's holding, the ETFs operated to give consumers (P) "alternative performance" by giving them a rational choice of either paying the ETF or completing the contract. The consumers (P) cross-appealed, alleging that the trial court erred in permitting Sprint (D) to assert damage claims as setoffs to class claims for recovery of ETFs paid. The state's intermediate appellate court granted review. [The appellate court affirmed the trial court's ruling that the state laws at issue were not preempted by federal law.]

## ISSUE:

(1) Does a consumer contract provision providing for damages upon breach of the contract operate as an unlawful liquidated damages clause where the provision's proponent has failed to reasonably endeavor to determine that the amount of the damages represents fair compensation for the loss sustained as a result of the breach, notwithstanding that the proponent's actual damages exceed the damages provided in the contract?

(2) Does a contract provision provide an option of alternative performance of an obligation where it does not provide a party with a rational choice of performing that obligation?

## HOLDING AND DECISION: (Bruiniers, J.)

(1) Yes. A consumer contract provision providing for damages upon breach of the contract operates as an unlawful liquidated damages clause where the provision's

*Continued on next page.*

proponent has failed to reasonably endeavor to determine that the amount of the damages represents fair compensation for the loss sustained as a result of the breach, notwithstanding that the proponent's actual damages exceed the damages provided in the contract. Under state law, a provision in a consumer contract liquidating damages for the breach of the contract is void except that the parties to such a contract may agree therein upon an amount which shall be presumed to be the amount of damage sustained by a breach thereof, when, from the nature of the case, it would be impracticable or extremely difficult to fix the actual damage. Thus, liquidated damages clauses in consumer contracts are presumed void, and the proponent bears the burden of rebutting that presumption. To do so, the proponent must show that (1) fixing the amount of actual damages must be impracticable or extremely difficult, and (2) the amount selected must represent a reasonable endeavor to estimate fair compensation for the loss sustained. Here, it is undisputed that fixing the amount of actual damages would be impractical because it would be impractical to determine Sprint's (D) avoidable costs, and, therefore, actual damages, at the inception of the contracts. Thus, Sprint (D) has satisfied the first test. As to the second test, determining whether a reasonable endeavor was made depends upon both (1) the motivation and purpose in imposing the charges, and (2) their effect. If the charge was intended to substantially exceed the loss to create a profit, and bears no reasonable relationship to the range of actual damages that the parties could have anticipated would flow from a breach, the charge is an unlawful penalty that compels forfeiture upon a breach of contract. To establish that the proponent of the clause made the reasonable endeavor required, the proponent must show that it actually engaged in some form of analysis to determine what losses it would sustain from a breach, and that it made a genuine and non-pretextual effort to estimate a fair average compensation for the losses to be sustained. Here, the trial court found that Sprint (D) had made no such analysis, i.e., it did no analysis that considered the lost revenue from contracts, the avoidable costs, and expected lost profits from contract terminations, but its ETFs were made purely on a competitive basis to prevent customers from leaving. Sprint's (D) argument that the ETFs were not intended to exceed losses, and that Sprint officials were aware that their ETFs would recover only a fraction of the revenue lost as a result of early terminations, is unavailing. As to Sprint's (D) motive and purpose, whatever information as to costs and revenues Sprint (D) may have been "aware" of, there was no evidence this information was part of the calculus in deciding to impose ETFs, or in determining the amount of an ETF. Thus, Sprint (D) failed to meet the first prong of the reasonable endeavor test. Its focus on the "effect" prong of the test is unpersuasive. Sprint (D) argues that so long as the ETF amount is shown in

practice to be less than Sprint's actual damages, the effect is not to generate a profit, whatever Sprint's (D) motive and purpose, and nothing more is required to meet the test. That is not correct, as is Sprint's (D) assertion that any charge that does not overstate actual damages be a penalty. Sprint (D) was required to show that it actually engaged in some form of analysis to determine what losses it would sustain from breach, and that it made a genuine effort to estimate a fair average compensation for the losses to be sustained. Although Sprint (D) may be correct that in retrospect its ETFs were reasonable in amount in light of its actual loss, and that they may actually have been beneficial in practice to at least some of its customers, "institutional intuition is not a substitute for analytical evaluation, and retrospective rationalization does not excuse the objective assessment required at the inception of the contract." Affirmed as to this issue.

(2) No. A contract provision does not provide an option of alternative performance of an obligation where it does not provide a party with a rational choice of performing that obligation. To render a contract clause an unlawful liquidated damages clause, the conduct triggering the payment must in some manner breach the contract, and a provision that merely provides an option of alternative performance of an obligation does not impose damages, and, therefore, is not per se void because the alternative conduct cannot be said to breach the contract. If a provision provides an option of alternative performance, its true function and operation must be determined. If there is only one definite performance possible under the contract, with an additional charge contingent on the breach of that single performance, it cannot be said the provision has provided an option of alternative performance. Here, the ETF provisions did not give customers a rational choice of paying the ETF or completing the contract, because the language of the ETF provision permitted Sprint (D) to impose the fee on customers involuntarily. Sprint (D) declared contracts breached, terminated service, and imposed ETFs as liquidated damages resulting from the asserted breaches. Accordingly, the predominant effect of the ETFs was not to provide consumers (P) with an alternate means of performing their contracts. Affirmed as to this issue.

## ▶ ANALYSIS

Although Sprint (D) claimed its ETF provision gave customers an option of alternate performance, the court here determined that customers did not have a real choice under Sprint's (D) contract, since the fee was imposed after the contract was terminated. If, however, the contract had stated that customers could terminate term contracts early by paying a fee, as a front-end price that was part of

*Continued on next page.*

the initial deal, then the fee likely would be considered an alternative means of performance, and, therefore, not a penalty.

---

## Quicknotes

**BREACH OF CONTRACT** Unlawful failure by a party to perform its obligations pursuant to contract.

**LIQUIDATED DAMAGES** An amount of money specified in a contract representing the damages owed in the event of breach.

# Lewis Refrigeration Co. v. Sawyer Fruit, Vegetable, and Cold Storage Co.

Freezer seller (P) v. Freezer buyer (D)

709 F.2d 427 (6th Cir. 1983).

**NATURE OF CASE:** Appeal from award of consequential damages on counterclaim for breach of contract in action to recover unpaid money.

**FACT SUMMARY:** Lewis Refrigeration Co. (P) contended, among other things, the trial court erred in awarding Sawyer Fruit, Vegetable, and Cold Storage Co. (D) consequential damages for lost profits and excess costs on its counterclaim for breach in light of a clause in the contract excluding consequential damages and because the trial court erred in permitting the jury to consider whether a repair and rescission provision failed its essential purpose.

## 🏛 RULE OF LAW
(1) Where a contract provides in the case of a defective product for repair or rescission as the exclusive remedy, it is not error for a jury to reach the issue of whether such an exclusive remedy has failed to achieve its essential purpose where there is sufficient evidence for a reasonable person to conclude that the remedy in fact failed to achieve its purpose.
(2) The Uniform Commercial Code does not confine breach of warranty damages to a benefit of the bargain measure of damages.
(3) Contractual limitations on the recovery of consequential damages for breach are valid unless it is established that the limitations are unconscionable.

**FACTS:** Lewis Refrigeration Co. (Lewis) (P) sued Sawyer Fruit, Vegetable, and Cold Storage Co. (Sawyer) (D) to recover the balance of the purchase price of a freezer. Sawyer (D) counterclaimed, asserting, among other things, that Lewis (P) breached the contract. The contract provided that in the event the freezer malfunctioned, the only remedy was either that Lewis (P) would have the right to repair or replace, or rescission. The contract also contained a provision that excluded consequential damages. The district court permitted the jury to consider whether the repair and rescission limitation failed its essential purpose; did not disallow consequential damages in favor of benefit of the bargain damages; and did not consider whether the consequential damages exclusion was unconscionable. The jury awarded Sawyer (D) damages for lost profits and excess costs of operating the freezer caused by the breach. Lewis (P) appealed, contending the trial court had erred by permitting the jury to consider whether the repair and rescission limitation failed its essential purpose; by not disallowing consequential damages generally, and by failing

to hear evidence and instruct the jury on the validity of a contract clause which purported to exclude the recovery of consequential damages, which would have necessarily denied recovery for lost profits and increased costs if the clause was found not to be unconscionable. The court of appeals granted review.

**ISSUE:**
(1) Where a contract provides in the case of a defective product for repair or rescission as the exclusive remedy, is it error for a jury to reach the issue of whether such an exclusive remedy has failed to achieve its essential purpose where there is sufficient evidence for a reasonable person to conclude that the remedy in fact failed to achieve its purpose?
(2) Does the Uniform Commercial Code confine breach of warranty damages to a benefit of the bargain measure of damages?
(3) Are contractual limitations on the recovery of consequential damages for breach of contract valid unless it is established that the limitations are unconscionable?

**HOLDING AND DECISION:** (Newblatt, J.)
(1) No. Where a contract provides in the case of a defective product for repair or rescission as the exclusive remedy, it is not error for a jury to reach the issue of whether such an exclusive remedy has failed to achieve its essential purpose where there is sufficient evidence for a reasonable person to conclude that the remedy in fact failed to achieve its purpose. Had the jury not reached this issue, it would not have been able to award Sawyer (D) lost profits. It is evident and practically conceded that the repair remedy failed its essential purpose because there was sufficient evidence that Lewis (P) was unable to repair promptly to meet performance warranties. State law provides that a seller's inability to repair fully a product causes the repair and rescission remedy to fail its essential purpose. Thus, it is clear here that a jury could reasonably have concluded that the repair remedy failed its essential purpose. As for the rescission remedy although rescission could have been ordered by a court, to do so would have entailed severe financial hardship for Sawyer (D), which would have lost significant business and revenues as a result. Moreover, it seemed that Lewis (P) deliberately concealed a defect in the freezer, and state case law holds that an exclusive remedy fails its essential purpose where a conceded defect is not detectable until it is impractical to effectuate the exclusive remedy. On balance, therefore, it was not error for the district court to

*Continued on next page.*

permit the jury to consider these circumstances. Affirmed as to this issue.

(2) No. The Uniform Commercial Code (U.C.C.) does not confine breach of warranty damages to a benefit of the bargain measure of damages. Lewis's (P) contrary contention is patently wrong, since U.C.C. § 2-714(3) authorizes consequential damages in appropriate cases, as where there are losses that cannot be mitigated by cover. Here, cover is not an issue. There was enough evidence that Lewis (P) should have foreseen that its breach of warranty would cause significant consequential damages, so that it was not erroneous for the district court to not generally preclude such damages. Affirmed as to this issue.

(3) Yes. Contractual limitations on the recovery of consequential damages are valid unless it is established that the limitations are unconscionable. This rule, codified in U.C.C. § 2-719(3), is designed to protect consumers against abuse in contract formation and to allow merchants to allocate business risks. This ability to allocate the potential losses is consistent with the U.C.C.'s general purpose to promote freedom in commercial transactions. As a result, it was error for the district court to not make a determination as to whether the consequential damages exclusion clause in the contract was conscionable. Apparently the district court believed that if the jury determined that the exclusive repair and rescission remedy failed in its essential purpose, the exclusion of consequential damages provision automatically became unconscionable under the U.C.C. However, given the independent mandate in U.C.C. § 2-719(3), which is supported as a matter of statutory interpretation, in the absence of an unconscionability determination, the district court should have allowed the consequential damages exclusion to stand. Verdict vacated, and case remanded.

## ▶ ANALYSIS

Generally, clauses attempting to exclude consequential damages are used in conjunction with other clauses as a package of commercial warranties. The other items usually included are: (1) an express warranty to the purchaser of the goods that they are free of defects in workmanship and materials; (2) a disclaimer of all other express or implied warranties; (3) limits on the remedy for breach of any express warranty to replace or repair defects.

■■■

## Quicknotes

**BREACH OF CONTRACT** Unlawful failure by a party to perform its obligations pursuant to contract.

**BREACH OF EXPRESS WARRANTY** The breach of an express promise made by one party to a contract on which the other party may rely, relieving that party from the obligation of determining whether the fact is true and

indemnifying the other party from liability if that fact is shown to be false.

**BREACH OF WARRANTY** The breach of a promise made by one party to a contract on which the other party may rely, relieving that party from the obligation of determining whether the fact is true and indemnifying the other party from liability if that fact is shown to be false.

**CONSEQUENTIAL DAMAGES** Monetary compensation that may be recovered in order to compensate for injuries or losses sustained as a result of damages that are not the direct or foreseeable result of the act of a party, but that nevertheless are the consequence of such act and which must be specifically pled and demonstrated.

**COUNTERCLAIM** An independent cause of action brought by a defendant to a lawsuit in order to oppose or deduct from the plaintiff's claim.

**RESCISSION** The canceling of an agreement and the return of the parties to their positions prior to the formation of the contract.

■■■

# Ed Bertholet & Associates, Inc. v. Stefanko

Former employer (P) v. Former employee (D)

Ind. Ct. App., 690 N.E.2d 361 (1998).

**NATURE OF CASE:** Appeal from denial of preliminary injunction in action to enforce an employment agreement's non-competition covenant.

**FACT SUMMARY:** Ed Bertholet & Associates, Inc. (Bertholet) (P) contended that a provision in its employment agreement with Stefanko (D), requiring an injunction prohibiting Stefanko (D) from competing with Bertholet (P) in the event of a breach of the agreement's non-competition covenant, had to be judicially enforced.

## 🏛 RULE OF LAW
Contract provisions requiring the issuance of an injunction are not binding upon a trial court.

**FACTS:** Stefanko (D) signed an employment agreement with Ed Bertholet & Associates, Inc. (Bertholet) (P) that contained a non-competition covenant. The covenant included a provision that provided for an injunction in the event of a breach of the covenant. After Stefanko (D) breached the covenant, Bertholet (P) brought suit to enforce the covenant and sought an injunction. The trial court denied the requested injunctive relief, finding that Bertholet (P) failed to demonstrate irreparable harm—one of the elements necessary for the issuance of an injunction. Bertholet (P) appealed, claiming that the court was bound by the contract at issue, notwithstanding that Bertholet's (P) petition failed to meet the state's requirements for an injunction. The state's intermediate appellate court granted review.

**ISSUE:** Are contract provisions requiring the issuance of an injunction binding upon a trial court?

**HOLDING AND DECISION:** (Garrard, J.) No. Contract provisions requiring the issuance of an injunction are not binding upon a trial court. A trial court's determination to grant or deny a preliminary injunction rests within the court's equitable discretion; and the court's determination may be overturned only for abuse of discretion. In this state there are four requirements that must be met before a trial court may issue an injunction—one of those being a showing of irreparable harm to the petitioning party in the absence of the injunction. Contrary to Bertholet's (P) argument, the trial court is not bound by the contract Bertholet (P) had with Stefanko (D) because parties may not contractually oust the court's jurisdiction. The contract provision for an issuance of an injunction would impermissibly remove the determination of whether to grant or deny an injunction from the discretion of the trial court and oust that court's inherent jurisdiction. Accordingly, the trial court was not contractually bound to

issue the injunction. Because the record supports the trial court's determination that Bertholet (P) failed to make a showing of irreparable harm, the trial court did not abuse its discretion, and the court did not err in denying Bertholet's (P) petition for an injunction. Affirmed.

## ▶ ANALYSIS

Here, after determining that the trial court was not contractually bound to issue the requested injunction, the appellate court upheld the trial court's decision, in part because the contract at issue contained a liquidated damages provision that required Stefanko (D) to pay Bertholet (P) a certain amount of the money he made competing with Bertholet (P). From this the court found that Bertholet (P) had an adequate remedy at law, and so did not qualify for an equitable remedy. The Restatement (Second) of Contracts, § 361, however, provides that a provision for liquidated damages will not bar injunctive relief.

---

## Quicknotes

**INJUNCTION** A court order requiring a person to do, or prohibiting that person from doing, a specific act.

**IRREPARABLE HARM** Such harm that because it is either too great, too small or of a continuing character that it cannot be properly compensated in damages, and the remedy for which is typically injunctive relief.

**NONCOMPETE CLAUSE** A provision, typically contained in an employment contract or a contract for the sale of a business, pursuant to which the promisor agrees not to compete with the promisee for a specified time period and/or within a particular geographic area.

# Third-Party Interests

## Quick Reference Rules of Law

# Allhusen v. Caristo Construction Corp.

Assignee of claim (P) v. General contractor (D)

N.Y. Ct. App., 303 N.Y. 446, 103 N.E.2d 891 (1952).

**NATURE OF CASE:** Appeal from affirmance of dismissal of action by an assignee to recover damages for breach of contract.

**FACT SUMMARY:** One Kroo assigned to Allhusen (P) rights against Caristo Construction Corp. (D) under the parties' contract in spite of an antiassignment clause.

## 🏛 RULE OF LAW
A contractual provision clearly prohibiting assignment will be given effect unless it violates public policy or a principle of law.

**FACTS:** Caristo Construction Corp. (Caristo) (D), a general contractor, subcontracted with Kroo to do painting. The subcontract contained the following provision: "The assignment by the second party (Kroo) of this contract or any interests therein or of any money due or to become due by reason of the terms hereof without the written consent of the first party [Caristo (D)] shall be void." Kroo subsequently and without written consent from Caristo (D) assigned rights (including "moneys due and to become due") to a third company, which in turn assigned them to Allhusen (P). The contracts were not "assigned," and no question of improper delegation was involved. Allhusen (P) sought to recover on the assignment, but Caristo (D) contended that the contract prohibition against assignments must be given effect. The trial court dismissed the action, the state's intermediate appellate court affirmed, and the state's highest court granted review.

**ISSUE:** Will a contractual provision clearly prohibiting assignment be given effect unless it violates public policy or a principle of law?

**HOLDING AND DECISION:** (Froessel, J.) Yes. A contractual provision clearly prohibiting assignment will be given effect unless it violates public policy or a principle of law. A term of a contract with language clearly prohibiting assignment will be upheld, although in the absence of such clear language a prohibitory clause will normally be interpreted as merely a covenant not to assign (for which the obligor may have an action for breach). In the present case, it is clearly and unequivocally provided that an "assignment . . . shall be void." In such a situation, courts, while striving to uphold freedom of assignability, have recognized the greater interest in freedom of contract. "No sound reason appears why an assignee should remain unaffected by a provision in the very contract which gave life to the claim he asserts." Such a holding is not violative of public policy, and the question of free alienation of property does not deem to be involved. Affirmed, with costs.

## ▶ ANALYSIS

Although some cases have held an antiassignment clause to be an unlawful restraint on alienation (the present court to the contrary notwithstanding), most courts have refused to interfere with "freedom of contract" so explicitly. Instead, a court, while allowing an antiassignment clause in theory, will tend to find that the particular provision before it is not drafted with sufficient clarity to accomplish its purpose of prohibiting assignment. As such, the provision is held merely as a promise not to assign for breach of which the obligor has a theoretical action. ("Theoretical" because damages for such a breach will ordinarily be nominal.) In the present case, the court could not shut its eyes to the clear language and even admitted that "violence" would be done to that language by construing it as a mere promise. [See also Uniform Commercial Code (U.C.C.) § 2-210(2) and Restatement (Second) §§ 149(2)c and 154(2); and cf. U.C.C. § 9-318(4), comments to which expressly reject the present decision.]

━■━

## Quicknotes

**ASSIGNMENT** A transaction in which a party conveys his or her entire interest in property to another.

**BREACH OF CONTRACT** Unlawful failure by a party to perform its obligations pursuant to contract.

━■━

# Owen v. CNA Insurance/Continental Casualty Company

Assignor (P) v. Insurer (D)

N.J. Sup. Ct., 167 N.J. 450, 771 A.2d 1208 (2001).

**NATURE OF CASE:** Appeal of the reversal of summary judgment for plaintiff in declaratory judgment action.

**FACT SUMMARY:** When Owen (P) assigned her benefits under a structured settlement agreement she had negotiated with CNA Insurance Company (D), the latter contended that a non-assignment clause in the settlement agreement prevented her from doing so.

## RULE OF LAW

Where language in the non-assignment clause of a structured settlement agreement does not specifically restrict the power of assignment and an assignment would not materially increase the insurer's burden of risk, the non-assignment clause is unenforceable.

**FACTS:** Owen (P) signed a release in favor of parties she had sued in a personal injury action arising out of a slip-and-fall accident. In connection with the release, Owen (P) entered into a settlement agreement with CNA Insurance Company (CNA) (D) under the terms of which she was entitled to receive an initial lump sum, attorney's fees, and five deferred periodic payments. The non-assignment provision of the settlement agreement stated in part that the claimant had the right to change the payee at any time by filing a written notice with the insurer, such change to be effective when accepted by the company in writing. Owen (P) subsequently sold her rights and benefits under the structured settlement agreement. Accordingly, Owen (P) sent CNA (D) a notarized letter directing it to send all future payments to a new address. CNA (D) responded by arguing that the deferred payments were not subject to assignment. Owen (P) brought suit against CNA (D) for a declaratory judgment that the non-assignment clause was unenforceable. The trial court granted summary judgment in favor of Owen (P), but the intermediate appellate court reversed. Owen (P) appealed, and the state's highest court granted review.

**ISSUE:** Where language in the non-assignment clause of a structured settlement agreement does not specifically restrict the power of assignment and an assignment would not materially increase the insurer's burden of risk, is the non-assignment clause unenforceable?

**HOLDING AND DECISION:** (Stein, J.) Yes. Where language in the non-assignment clause of a structured settlement agreement does not specifically restrict the power of assignment and an assignment would not materially increase the insurer's burden of risk, the non-

assignment clause is unenforceable. Because Article 9 of the Uniform Commercial Code (U.C.C.) regulates commercial transactions, a threshold question is whether the validity of the non-assignment provision is governed by the U.C.C. Although Article 9 generally prohibits non-assignment provisions, it does not apply to assignments of claims arising out of tort. At issue here is the assignment of proceeds of a tort claim. Arguably, therefore, Article 9 is inapplicable. However, it is not necessary to reach Article 9's applicability here, because, irrespective of whether Article 9 applies to proceeds from tort claims, existing state law makes clear that the non-assignment clause at issue is unenforceable. The state's assignment statute provides that all judgments and decrees recoverable in any of the courts of the state are assignable. Thus, state law generally permits the assignment of settlement proceeds unless the parties have expressly agreed otherwise. Under common law, a non-assignment provision may be disregarded where it is not the main purpose of the contract. Therefore, since the main purpose of the assignment of proceeds under a life insurance contract is to provide a modest, regular income to the assignee, a clause prohibiting such assignment is not effective. Sections 322 and 317 of the Restatement (Second) of Contracts provide the best framework for determining whether a non-assignment provision may be enforced. Section 322 provides that a non-assignment provision operates only to limit the parties' right to assign the contract, but not their power to assign, unless the parties manifest with specificity an intent to the contrary. Absent such intent, the breach of the non-assignment provision merely gives rise to damages, but the assignment itself remains valid. Here, the language in the non-assignment provision in Owen's (P) structured settlement agreement did not specifically restrict Owen's (P) power of assignment, and such assignment would not materially increase the burden of risk of the insurer CNA (D). Essentially, it was a covenant not to assign, and therefore not void under Restatement § 322(2). Under Restatement § 317, an assignment is valid unless it unduly burdens the obligor. Here, there is no merit to CNA's (D) argument that the assignment of Owen's (P) rights under the settlement agreement would cause it to face tax-reporting issues it allegedly bargained to avoid. CNA (D) simply undertook itself to make the periodic payments to Owen (P), and the Internal Revenue Code does not appear to entitle CNA (D) to an offsetting deduction for periodic payments made to Owen (P). Accordingly, the assignment is valid under § 317 because the tax provisions do not appear to entitle

*Continued on next page.*

CNA (D) to an offsetting deduction that it never was entitled to in the first place. Reversed and remanded.

## ▶ *ANALYSIS*

In the *Owen* case, the court emphasized that its holding was based on the specific record before it and should not be understood to indicate that non-assignment provisions in structured settlement agreements generally are unenforceable *if* they are explicit and *if* they would materially increase the burden or risk of the insurance company.

■■◄■

## *Quicknotes*

**ASSIGNMENT** A transaction in which a party conveys his or her entire interest in property to another.

**DECLARATORY JUDGMENT** A judgment of the court establishing the rights of the parties.

**SUMMARY JUDGMENT** Judgment rendered by a court in response to a motion made by one of the parties, claiming that the lack of a question of material fact in respect to an issue warrants disposition of the issue without consideration by the jury.

■■◄■

# Continental Purchasing Co. v. Van Raalte Co.

Assignee (P) v. Assignor's employer (D)

N.Y. App. Div., 251 App. Div. 151, 295 N.Y.S. 867 (1937).

**NATURE OF CASE:** Appeal from judgment for defendant in action to recover assigned wages.

**FACT SUMMARY:** Mrs. Potter assigned all of her wages from the Van Raalte Co. (D) to the Continental Purchasing Co. (P), but the Van Raalte Co. (D), even after notification of the assignment, continued to pay all wages to Mrs. Potter.

## 🏛 RULE OF LAW
If, after notification of an assignment, an obligor continues to pay to the assignor money assigned to the assignee, he is liable to the assignee for the resulting damages.

**FACTS:** In 1934, Mrs. Potter assigned to the Continental Purchasing Co. (P) all of her wages earned or to be earned from the Van Raalte Co. (D). Thereafter, the Continental Purchasing Co. (P) gave written notice of this assignment to the Van Raalte Co. (D), which acknowledged receipt of such notice. Subsequently, however, the Van Raalte Co. (D) continued to pay Mrs. Potter's wages directly to her. In response, the Continental Purchasing Co. (P) brought an action against the Van Raalte Co. (D) to recover those wages paid to Mrs. Potter after the assignment. After a judgment for Van Raalte Co. (D), the Continental Purchasing Co. (P) appealed, and the state's intermediate appellate court granted review.

**ISSUE:** If, after notification of an assignment, an obligor continues to pay to the assignor money assigned to the assignee, is he liable to the assignee for the resulting damages?

**HOLDING AND DECISION:** (Edgcomb, J.) Yes. If, after notification of an assignment, an obligor continues to pay to the assignor money assigned to the assignee, he is liable to the assignee for the resulting damage. Of course, before such notification, an obligor has no liability to the assignee (i.e., he can continue to pay the money assigned to the assignor). Here, however, the Van Raalte Co. (D), the obligor, received notice of the assignment from Mrs. Potter, the assignor, to the Continental Purchasing Co. (P), the assignee. As such, the Van Raalte Co. (D) is liable to the Continental Purchasing Co. (P) for any wages paid to Mrs. Potter after notice of the assignment. Reversed.

## ▶ ANALYSIS

This case points up the importance of the notice requirement in the assignment and delegation areas. Note that at common law, until notice was received, the obligor was under no duty to perform to the assignee whatsoever.

Furthermore, the obligor and assignor could alter their contractual agreement at any time prior to notice of the assignment to the obligor. The Uniform Commercial Code has retained these common-law rules almost completely but has ruled that the basic contractual agreement may still be modified even after notice of the assignment.

━━━■■■━━━

## Quicknotes

**ASSIGNMENT** A transaction in which a party conveys his or her entire interest in property to another.

━━━■■■━━━

# Sally Beauty Co. v. Nexxus Products Co., Inc.

Exclusive distributor's successor (P) v. Hair care company (D)

801 F.2d 1001 (7th Cir. 1986).

**NATURE OF CASE:** Appeal from summary denial of damages for breach of contract.

**FACT SUMMARY:** Nexxus Products Co., Inc. (D) hired Best Beauty as its exclusive distributor in Texas of its hair care products, but cancelled the agreement when Best Beauty was acquired by Sally Beauty Co. (P), a subsidiary of Nexxus's (D) competitor, Alberto-Culver.

## 🏛 RULE OF LAW
An obligor may not delegate his duties under an executory contract without the consent of the obligee where the obligee has a substantial interest in having the original promisor perform or control the contractual acts.

**FACTS:** Nexxus Products Co., Inc. (D) hired Best Beauty as its exclusive distributor of its hair care products to barbers and stylists in Texas. When Best Beauty merged into Sally Beauty Co. (P), Nexxus (D) cancelled the agreement. Sally Beauty (P) was a subsidiary of Alberto-Culver, a major manufacturer of hair products and a Nexxus (D) competitor. Sally Beauty (P) sued for breach of contract. The district court held that Nexxus's (D) contract was for personal services and was therefore not assignable. The court of appeals granted review.

**ISSUE:** May an obligor delegate his duties under an executory contract without the consent of the obligee where the obligee has a substantial interest in having the original promisor perform or control the contractual acts?

**HOLDING AND DECISION:** (Cudahy, J.) No. An obligor may not delegate his duties under an executory contract without the consent of the obligee where the obligee has a substantial interest in having the original promisor perform or control the contractual acts. Uniform Commercial Code (U.C.C.) § 2-210(l) allows the delegation of performance under an executory sales contract, but only if it would be satisfactory to the obligee. The obligee may withhold its consent to the delegation if it has a substantial interest in having the original promisor control the acts required by contract. Here, Nexxus (D) contracted for Best Beauty's "best efforts" in promoting the sale of its products in Texas. Nexxus (D) should not be required to accept the "best efforts" of Sally Beauty (P) when those efforts are subject to the control of its competitor, Alberto-Culver. Sally Beauty's (P) position as a competitor's subsidiary per se, not the contract's classification as one for personal services, warrants upholding the district court's judgment. Affirmed.

**DISSENT:** (Posner, J.) If Nexxus (D) was concerned that Sally Beauty (P) would not have used its "best efforts" to promote its products, its remedy was not to cancel the contract, but under U.C.C. § 2-609 to demand assurances of due performance, or under common law to sue for breach of the implied "best efforts" clause of the distributorship agreement. The merger of Best Beauty into Sally Beauty (P) did not represent an inability to perform and an anticipatory repudiation. It is commonplace and legitimate for businesses to sell or distribute a competitor's products.

## ▶ ANALYSIS

Of course, an obligee's intention that the duties under a contract not be delegated may be expressly set forth in the contract; terms prohibiting or restraining delegation will always be enforced. Further, and as mentioned in Judge Posner's dissent, U.C.C. § 2-210 expressly provides that in a contract for the sale of goods, delegation is a reasonable ground for insecurity which can warrant a demand for assurance of performance.

---

## Quicknotes

**ANTICIPATORY REPUDIATION** Breach of a contract subsequent to formation but prior to the time performance is due.

**BREACH OF CONTRACT** Unlawful failure by a party to perform its obligations pursuant to contract.

**DAMAGES** Monetary compensation that may be awarded by the court to a party who has sustained injury or loss to his person, property or rights due to another party's unlawful act, omission or negligence.

# KMART Corp. v. Balfour Beatty, Inc.

Retailer (P) v. Shopping center developer (D)

994 F. Supp. 634 (D.V.I. 1998).

**NATURE OF CASE:** Defense motion for summary judgment in breach of contract suit.

**FACT SUMMARY:** When its shopping center store was damaged by winds, KMART Corp. (P) sued Balfour Beatty, Inc. (BBI) (D), contending that it was a third-party beneficiary of the construction contract between BBI (D) (the shopping center developer) and Tutu Park Ltd. which had constructed the store for BBI (D).

## 🏛 RULE OF LAW
A promise in a contract creates a duty in the promisor to any intended beneficiary to perform the promise, and the intended beneficiary may enforce the duty.

**FACTS:** Balfour Beatty, Inc. (BBI) (D) entered into a contract with Tutu Park Ltd. (TPL) for the design and construction of a shopping center. The shopping center's roof was subsequently damaged by winds. KMART Corp. (P) was one of the tenants of the shopping center. Contending it was a third-party beneficiary of the construction contract, KMART (P) sued BBI (D), alleging breach of contract and negligence and arguing that several provisions in the relevant documents indicated that the parties intended to convey a benefit to KMART (P). Specifically, the contract's construction specifications required compliance with KMART's (P) requirements; design phase drawings had to be submitted to KMART (P); and work warranties were to be executed in KMART's (P) favor and submitted directly to KMART (P). BBI (D) moved for summary judgment, contending that since KMART (P) was not a party to the BBI (D)-TPL construction contract, KMART (P) therefore could not claim relief under the contract.

**ISSUE:** Does a promise in a contract create a duty in the promisor to any intended beneficiary to perform the promise, and may the intended beneficiary enforce the duty?

**HOLDING AND DECISION:** (Moore, C.J.) Yes. A promise in a contract creates a duty in the promisor to any intended beneficiary to perform the promise, and the intended beneficiary may enforce the duty. One is an intended beneficiary, rather than a mere incidental beneficiary (to whom no duty is owed), when performance of the promise, as here, will satisfy an actual or supposed or asserted duty of the promisee to the beneficiary. Here, KMART (P) was a third-party beneficiary of the construction contract between BBI (D) and TPI because the

contractual duty of performance (to construct the shopping center in which KMART (P) was located) owed by BBI (D) to TPI would satisfy TPI's duty to its beneficiary [KMART (P)]. The language of the instant contract conveys intent among the contracting parties to bestow a benefit upon KMART (P). The specifications, drawings, and schedules, all were required to meet KMART's (P) requirements and approval. All of these facts support the conclusion that BBI (D) and TPL entered into the construction contract to erect a building for the benefit of KMART (P). Furthermore, even though a provision of the contract refers to warranties to the "owner," even if the paragraph could be interpreted as creating an ambiguity as to KMART (P) being an intended third-party beneficiary, such ambiguity, at this early stage of litigation, must be resolved in KMART's (P) favor. Motion for summary judgment is denied and arbitration is ordered.

## ▶ ANALYSIS

As noted in the *KMART* case, some courts have applied different standards to determine whether contracting parties intended to benefit one claiming third-party beneficiary status. Some attempt to determine if the performance of the contract runs to the putative third-party beneficiary. Others, and the increasingly more modern view, hold that it is sufficient that the promisor understood that the promisee had intent to benefit the third party. Under either formulation, the result in the *KMART* case would have been the same.

━■■■━

## Quicknotes

**BREACH OF CONTRACT** Unlawful failure by a party to perform its obligations pursuant to contract.

**INTENDED BENEFICIARY** A third party who is the recipient of the benefit of a transaction undertaken by another.

**NEGLIGENCE** Conduct falling below the standard of care that a reasonable person would demonstrate under similar conditions.

**SUMMARY JUDGMENT** Judgment rendered by a court in response to a motion made by one of the parties, claiming that the lack of a question of material fact in respect to an issue warrants disposition of the issue without consideration by the jury.

# Hale v. Groce

Intended testamentary beneficiary (P) v. Attorney (D)

Or. Sup. Ct., 304 Or. 281, 744 P.2d 1289 (1987).

**NATURE OF CASE:** Appeal from affirmance of dismissal of third-party beneficiary action for breach of attorney-client agreement.

**FACT SUMMARY:** Groce (D) failed to make a testamentary bequest to Hale (P) as requested by Groce's (D) client.

## 🏛 RULE OF LAW
A third party intended by a testator to be the beneficiary of a bequest by will or trust may sue for contract damages the lawyer who failed to include the bequest.

**FACTS:** Groce (D), an attorney, was directed by a client to prepare testamentary instruments including a bequest of a specified sum to Hale (P). After the client's death, it was discovered the gift was not included in the testator's will or a related trust instrument. Hale (P) sued Groce (D) in contract as the intended beneficiary of the testator's professional contract with Groce (D) and in tort based on Groce's (D) breach of professional duty. The trial court dismissed both claims, and the state's intermediate appellate court affirmed on the contract claim. The state's highest court granted review.

**ISSUE:** May a third party intended by a testator to be the beneficiary of a bequest by will or trust sue for contract damages the lawyer who failed to include the bequest?

**HOLDING AND DECISION:** (Linde, J.) Yes. A third party intended by a testator to be the beneficiary of a bequest by will or trust may sue for contract damages the lawyer who failed to include the bequest. Hale (P) was an "intended" third-party beneficiary of Groce's (D) promise to his client that he makes a will or trust including the gift to Hale (P). The promise here, of course, was not that Groce (D) would pay Hale (P) the amount of the bequest, and it is too late for Groce (D) to perform on the promise he made to his client, but these facts do not preclude recovery by Hale (P) of damages for the nonperformance. Hale's (P) contract claim should not have been dismissed. Reversed in part.

## ▶ ANALYSIS

Despite this holding, a majority of courts hold that the lack of privity between the attorney and the third party bars a beneficiary's recovery against attorneys. The court also refers to a "balancing test" adopted by the California courts which examines six factors to determine negligence: (1) whether the contract was intended to benefit plaintiff; (2) foreseeability of harm to plaintiff; (3) certainty of plain-

tiff's injury; (4) how closely plaintiff's injuries and defendant's conduct are connected; (5) moral blame of defendant's conduct; and (6) public policy in avoiding similar harm in the future.

---

## Quicknotes

**ATTORNEY-CLIENT PRIVILEGE** A doctrine precluding the admission into evidence of confidential communications between an attorney and his client made in the course of obtaining professional assistance.

**BEQUEST** A transfer of property that is accomplished by means of a testamentary instrument.

**CONTRACT DAMAGES** Monetary compensation awarded by the court to a party as the result of a breach of contract by another party.

# Zigas v. Superior Court

HUD housing tenants (P) v. Court (D) [Landlords are real parties in interest]

Cal. Ct. App., 120 Cal. App. 3d 827 (1981).

**NATURE OF CASE:** Petition for a writ following a demurrer to breach of contract action.

**FACT SUMMARY:** Certain owners of rental property charged rents in excess of amounts that they contracted with the Department of Housing and Urban Development that they would charge.

## RULE OF LAW
When the federal government has contracted with landlords to provide apartment financing in return for rent ceilings, tenants have standing to seek enforcement or damages.

**FACTS:** The Department of Housing and Urban Development (HUD) helped finance certain apartments. In exchange, the landlords contracted that they would adhere to certain rent schedules. The landlords did not so adhere, charging rents in excess of the schedules. Several tenants (P) brought a class-action suit seeking enforcement and damages. The trial court sustained a demurrer predicated on lack of standing, and the tenants (P) petitioned for a writ from the state's intermediate appellate court.

**ISSUE:** When the federal government has contracted with landlords to provide apartment financing in return for rent ceilings, do tenants have standing to seek enforcement or damages?

**HOLDING AND DECISION:** (Feinberg, J.) Yes. When the federal government has contracted with landlords to provide apartment financing in return for rent ceilings, tenants have standing to seek enforcement or damages. Here, the tenants (P) did not have standing under a federal statutory right of action. However, under state law, where a contract is made specifically for the benefit of a third party, that third party may enforce it any time prior to rescission. The question then becomes whether such a third-party right inheres where the government contracts with a private party, as occurred here. Case law holds that where the benefits are incidental, the third parties may not so enforce the contract between the government and private party, but where the benefits are intended the third parties may enforce the contract. The question, therefore, is whether the tenants (P) were intended to be beneficiaries. Here, there can be no doubt that this is the case, since the only possible purpose for the contract was to benefit them. The tenants (P) are entitled to maintain their third-party action against the landlords. Writ granted.

## ANALYSIS

To reach the result it did, the court here had to distinguish between two somewhat conflicting cases. *Shell v. Schmidt*, 126 Cal. App. 2d 279 (1954), would have permitted recovery here; *Martinez v. Sucoma Companies*, 11 Cal. 3d 384 (1974), would not have. The court here held that *Martinez* only involved incidental beneficiaries, as opposed to the intended beneficiary situation of *Shell*.

## Quicknotes

**BREACH OF CONTRACT** Unlawful failure by a party to perform its obligations pursuant to contract.

**CLASS ACTION** A suit commenced by a representative on behalf of an ascertainable group that is too large to appear in court, who shares a commonality of interests and who will benefit from a successful result.

**DAMAGES** Monetary compensation that may be awarded by the court to a party who has sustained injury or loss to his person, property or rights due to another party's unlawful act, omission or negligence.

**DEMURRER** The assertion that the opposing party's pleadings are insufficient and that the demurring party should not be made to answer.

# Tweeddale v. Tweeddale

## Brother (P) v. Brother (D)

Wis. Sup. Ct., 116 Wis. 517, 93 N.W. 440 (1903).

**NATURE OF CASE:** Appeal from dismissal of foreclosure action on a bond and mortgage by a third-party beneficiary.

**FACT SUMMARY:** After Daniel Tweeddale (D) gave a bond for support secured by a mortgage which provided that if the mortgaged land was sold, certain sums would be due to Edward Tweeddale (P) and others, the land was sold and the mortgage discharged before Edward Tweeddale (P) knew about the provision.

## 🏛 RULE OF LAW
A third-party beneficiary to a contract has an immediate right of action upon the contract that does not depend upon his acceptance, given that the contract may not be rescinded while he is still ignorant of it and before he assents to it.

**FACTS:** Daniel Tweeddale (D) gave a bond for support to his mother secured by a mortgage on certain land. The bond provided that in case the land was sold, certain sums would be due to Edward Tweeddale (P), Daniel's (D) brother, and others. Daniel (D) sold the land, making the obligation to Edward (P) operative. However, before Edward (P) even knew of the bond and mortgage, the mother discharged Daniel's (D) debt to her and released the mortgage. Edward (P) brought a foreclosure action against Daniel (D), arguing that the release did not bar his recovery. Edward (P) appealed a judgment for Daniel (D), and the state's highest court granted review.

**ISSUE:** Does a third-party beneficiary to a contract have an immediate right of action upon the contract that does not depend upon his acceptance, given that the contract may not be rescinded while he is still ignorant of it and before he assents to it?

**HOLDING AND DECISION:** (Marshall, J.) Yes. A third-party beneficiary to a contract has an immediate right of action upon the contract that does not depend upon his acceptance, given that the contract may not be rescinded while he is still ignorant of it and before he assents to it. The law immediately operates upon the acts of the contracting parties to establish privity between the promisor and the third-party beneficiary so that the liability is at once binding. No party can thereafter change the situation without the consent of the third-party beneficiary. As such, the satisfaction of the mortgage here was void as regards the third-party beneficiary, Edward Tweeddale (P). Reversed.

## ▶ ANALYSIS

The view here is that a third-party beneficiary has an immediate vested interest in the subject matter of the contract when made. Such is contrary to the law in most jurisdictions which prescribes that the third party must have had at least notice of his rights whether or not he changes his position in reliance thereon. Because there was no notice until after the bond and mortgage were discharged *Tweeddale* results in the anomaly of having the discharge declared void to a third-party beneficiary who never knew he was a beneficiary until the entire transaction was over.

---

## Quicknotes

**FORECLOSURE** An action to recover the amount due on a mortgage of real property where the owner has failed to meet the mortgage obligations, terminating the owner's interest in the property which must then be sold to satisfy the debt.

**VESTED INTEREST** A present right to property, although the right to the possession of such property may not be enjoyed until a future date.

---

## Common Latin Words and Phrases Encountered in the Law

**A FORTIORI:** Because one fact exists or has been proven, therefore a second fact that is related to the first fact must also exist.

**A PRIORI:** From the cause to the effect. A term of logic used to denote that when one generally accepted truth is shown to be a cause, another particular effect must necessarily follow.

**AB INITIO:** From the beginning; a condition which has existed throughout, as in a marriage which was void ab initio.

**ACTUS REUS:** The wrongful act; in criminal law, such action sufficient to trigger criminal liability.

**AD VALOREM:** According to value; an ad valorem tax is imposed upon an item located within the taxing jurisdiction calculated by the value of such item.

**AMICUS CURIAE:** Friend of the court. Its most common usage takes the form of an amicus curiae brief, filed by a person who is not a party to an action but is nonetheless allowed to offer an argument supporting his legal interests.

**ARGUENDO:** In arguing. A statement, possibly hypothetical, made for the purpose of argument, is one made arguendo.

**BILL QUIA TIMET:** A bill to quiet title (establish ownership) to real property.

**BONA FIDE:** True, honest, or genuine. May refer to a person's legal position based on good faith or lacking notice of fraud (such as a bona fide purchaser for value) or to the authenticity of a particular document (such as a bona fide last will and testament).

**CAUSA MORTIS:** With approaching death in mind. A gift causa mortis is a gift given by a party who feels certain that death is imminent.

**CAVEAT EMPTOR:** Let the buyer beware. This maxim is reflected in the rule of law that a buyer purchases at his own risk because it is his responsibility to examine, judge, test, and otherwise inspect what he is buying.

**CERTIORARI:** A writ of review. Petitions for review of a case by the United States Supreme Court are most often done by means of a writ of certiorari.

**CONTRA:** On the other hand. Opposite. Contrary to.

**CORAM NOBIS:** Before us; writs of error directed to the court that originally rendered the judgment.

**CORAM VOBIS:** Before you; writs of error directed by an appellate court to a lower court to correct a factual error.

**CORPUS DELICTI:** The body of the crime; the requisite elements of a crime amounting to objective proof that a crime has been committed.

**CUM TESTAMENTO ANNEXO, ADMINISTRATOR (ADMINISTRATOR C.T.A.):** With will annexed; an administrator c.t.a. settles an estate pursuant to a will in which he is not appointed.

**DE BONIS NON, ADMINISTRATOR (ADMINISTRATOR D.B.N.):** Of goods not administered; an administrator d.b.n. settles a partially settled estate.

**DE FACTO:** In fact; in reality; actually. Existing in fact but not officially approved or engendered.

**DE JURE:** By right; lawful. Describes a condition that is legitimate "as a matter of law," in contrast to the term "de facto," which connotes something existing in fact but not legally sanctioned or authorized. For example, de facto segregation refers to segregation brought about by housing patterns, etc., whereas de jure segregation refers to segregation created by law.

**DE MINIMIS:** Of minimal importance; insignificant; a trifle; not worth bothering about.

**DE NOVO:** Anew; a second time; afresh. A trial de novo is a new trial held at the appellate level as if the case originated there and the trial at a lower level had not taken place.

**DICTA:** Generally used as an abbreviated form of obiter dicta, a term describing those portions of a judicial opinion incidental or not necessary to resolution of the specific question before the court. Such nonessential statements and remarks are not considered to be binding precedent.

**DUCES TECUM:** Refers to a particular type of writ or subpoena requesting a party or organization to produce certain documents in their possession.

**EN BANC:** Full bench. Where a court sits with all justices present rather than the usual quorum.

**EX PARTE:** For one side or one party only. An ex parte proceeding is one undertaken for the benefit of only one party, without notice to, or an appearance by, an adverse party.

**EX POST FACTO:** After the fact. An ex post facto law is a law that retroactively changes the consequences of a prior act.

**EX REL.:** Abbreviated form of the term "ex relatione," meaning upon relation or information. When the state brings an action in which it has no interest against an individual at the instigation of one who has a private interest in the matter.

**FORUM NON CONVENIENS:** Inconvenient forum. Although a court may have jurisdiction over the case, the action should be tried in a more conveniently located court, one to which parties and witnesses may more easily travel, for example.

**GUARDIAN AD LITEM:** A guardian of an infant as to litigation, appointed to represent the infant and pursue his/her rights.

**HABEAS CORPUS:** You have the body. The modern writ of habeas corpus is a writ directing that a person (body) being detained (such as a prisoner) be brought before the court so that the legality of his detention can be judicially ascertained.

**IN CAMERA:** In private, in chambers. When a hearing is held before a judge in his chambers or when all spectators are excluded from the courtroom.

**IN FORMA PAUPERIS:** In the manner of a pauper. A party who proceeds in forma pauperis because of his poverty is one who is allowed to bring suit without liability for costs.

**INFRA:** Below, under. A word referring the reader to a later part of a book. (The opposite of supra.)

**IN LOCO PARENTIS:** In the place of a parent.

**IN PARI DELICTO:** Equally wrong; a court of equity will not grant requested relief to an applicant who is in pari delicto, or as much at fault in the transactions giving rise to the controversy as is the opponent of the applicant.

**IN PARI MATERIA:** On like subject matter or upon the same matter. Statutes relating to the same person or things are said to be in pari materia. It is a general rule of statutory construction that such statutes should be construed together, i.e., looked at as if they together constituted one law.

**IN PERSONAM:** Against the person. Jurisdiction over the person of an individual.

**IN RE:** In the matter of. Used to designate a proceeding involving an estate or other property.

**IN REM:** A term that signifies an action against the res, or thing. An action in rem is basically one that is taken directly against property, as distinguished from an action in personam, i.e., against the person.

**INTER ALIA:** Among other things. Used to show that the whole of a statement, pleading, list, statute, etc., has not been set forth in its entirety.

**INTER PARTES:** Between the parties. May refer to contracts, conveyances or other transactions having legal significance.

**INTER VIVOS:** Between the living. An inter vivos gift is a gift made by a living grantor, as distinguished from bequests contained in a will, which pass upon the death of the testator.

**IPSO FACTO:** By the mere fact itself.

**JUS:** Law or the entire body of law.

**LEX LOCI:** The law of the place; the notion that the rights of parties to a legal proceeding are governed by the law of the place where those rights arose.

**MALUM IN SE:** Evil or wrong in and of itself; inherently wrong. This term describes an act that is wrong by its very nature, as opposed to one which would not be wrong but for the fact that there is a specific legal prohibition against it (malum prohibitum).

**MALUM PROHIBITUM:** Wrong because prohibited, but not inherently evil. Used to describe something that is wrong because it is expressly forbidden by law but that is not in and of itself evil, e.g., speeding.

**MANDAMUS:** We command. A writ directing an official to take a certain action.

**MENS REA:** A guilty mind; a criminal intent. A term used to signify the mental state that accompanies a crime or other prohibited act. Some crimes require only a general mens rea (general intent to do the prohibited act), but others, like assault with intent to murder, require the existence of a specific mens rea.

**MODUS OPERANDI:** Method of operating; generally refers to the manner or style of a criminal in committing crimes, admissible in appropriate cases as evidence of the identity of a defendant.

**NEXUS:** A connection to.

**NISI PRIUS:** A court of first impression. A nisi prius court is one where issues of fact are tried before a judge or jury.

**N.O.V. (NON OBSTANTE VEREDICTO):** Notwithstanding the verdict. A judgment n.o.v. is a judgment given in favor of one party despite the fact that a verdict was returned in favor of the other party, the justification being that the verdict either had no reasonable support in fact or was contrary to law.

**NUNC PRO TUNC:** Now for then. This phrase refers to actions that may be taken and will then have full retroactive effect.

**PENDENTE LITE:** Pending the suit; pending litigation under way.

**PER CAPITA:** By head; beneficiaries of an estate, if they take in equal shares, take per capita.

**PER CURIAM:** By the court; signifies an opinion ostensibly written "by the whole court" and with no identified author.

**PER SE:** By itself, in itself; inherently.

**PER STIRPES:** By representation. Used primarily in the law of wills to describe the method of distribution where a person, generally because of death, is unable to take that which is left to him by the will of another, and therefore his heirs divide such property between them rather than take under the will individually.

**PRIMA FACIE:** On its face, at first sight. A prima facie case is one that is sufficient on its face, meaning that the evidence supporting it is adequate to establish the case until contradicted or overcome by other evidence.

**PRO TANTO:** For so much; as far as it goes. Often used in eminent domain cases when a property owner receives partial payment for his land without prejudice to his right to bring suit for the full amount he claims his land to be worth.

**QUANTUM MERUIT:** As much as he deserves. Refers to recovery based on the doctrine of unjust enrichment in those cases in which a party has rendered valuable services or furnished materials that were accepted and enjoyed by another under circumstances that would reasonably notify the recipient that the rendering party expected to be paid. In essence, the law implies a contract to pay the reasonable value of the services or materials furnished.

**QUASI:** Almost like; as if; nearly. This term is essentially used to signify that one subject or thing is almost analogous to another but that material differences between them do exist. For example, a quasi-criminal proceeding is one that is not strictly criminal but shares enough of the same characteristics to require some of the same safeguards (e.g., procedural due process must be followed in a parole hearing).

**QUID PRO QUO:** Something for something. In contract law, the consideration, something of value, passed between the parties to render the contract binding.

**RES GESTAE:** Things done; in evidence law, this principle justifies the admission of a statement that would otherwise be hearsay when it is made so closely to the event in question as to be said to be a part of it, or with such spontaneity as not to have the possibility of falsehood.

**RES IPSA LOQUITUR:** The thing speaks for itself. This doctrine gives rise to a rebuttable presumption of negligence when the instrumentality causing the injury was within the exclusive control of the defendant, and the injury was one that does not normally occur unless a person has been negligent.

**RES JUDICATA:** A matter adjudged. Doctrine which provides that once a court of competent jurisdiction has rendered a final judgment or decree on the merits, that judgment or decree is conclusive upon the parties to the case and prevents them from engaging in any other litigation on the points and issues determined therein.

**RESPONDEAT SUPERIOR:** Let the master reply. This doctrine holds the master liable for the wrongful acts of his servant (or the principal for his agent) in those cases in which the servant (or agent) was acting within the scope of his authority at the time of the injury.

**STARE DECISIS:** To stand by or adhere to that which has been decided. The common law doctrine of stare decisis attempts to give security and certainty to the law by following the policy that once a principle of law as applicable to a certain set of facts has been set forth in a decision, it forms a precedent which will subsequently be followed, even though a different decision might be made were it the first time the question had arisen. Of course, stare decisis is not an inviolable principle and is departed from in instances where there is good cause (e.g., considerations of public policy led the Supreme Court to disregard prior decisions sanctioning segregation).

**SUPRA:** Above. A word referring a reader to an earlier part of a book.

**ULTRA VIRES:** Beyond the power. This phrase is most commonly used to refer to actions taken by a corporation that are beyond the power or legal authority of the corporation.

## Addendum of French Derivatives

**IN PAIS:** Not pursuant to legal proceedings.

**CHATTEL:** Tangible personal property.

**CY PRES:** Doctrine permitting courts to apply trust funds to purposes not expressed in the trust but necessary to carry out the settlor's intent.

**PER AUTRE VIE:** For another's life; during another's life. In property law, an estate may be granted that will terminate upon the death of someone other than the grantee.

**PROFIT A PRENDRE:** A license to remove minerals or other produce from land.

**VOIR DIRE:** Process of questioning jurors as to their predispositions about the case or parties to a proceeding in order to identify those jurors displaying bias or prejudice.